INSECT ECOLOGY

ENCYCLOPAEDIA OF ENTOMOLOGY - V

INSECT ECOLOGY

By

Dr. M. Prakash

Dept. of Zoology

M.M.H. Post Graduate College

Ghaziabad

(U.P.)

DISCOVERY PUBLISHING HOUSE PVT. LTD.

NEW DELHI-110 002

Published by:

DISCOVERY PUBLISHING HOUSE PVT. LTD.
4383/4B, Ansari Road, Darya Ganj
New Delhi-110 002 (India)
Phone : +91-11-23279245; 23253475; 43596065
E-mail : discoverybooksindia@gmail.com
discoverypublishinghouse@gmail.com
namitwasan9@gmail.com
web : www.discoverypublishinggroup.com

First Published: **2008**
Reprinted: **2022**

ISBN: 978-93-5056-571-1 (Set)

ISBN: 978-81-8356-291-1

Insect Ecology

Printed at:
Infinity Imaging Systems
Delhi

Preface

Most insects are exhibitionists. They move about and engage in their daily tasks of acquiring food, courting, and reproduction undaunted by the watchful eyes of an observer. Over the span of human life on this planet people have almost certainly been fascinated and entertained by the activities of insects—what child have never stopped to admire a passing butterfly or sat and watched the coming and goings of a column of foraging ants? From such basic observations we have gained considerable insight into the biology of insects, but only recently have we begun to integrate our knowledge of behaviour, hormones, physiology and ecology into a more complete view.

The present title **Insect Ecology** has been carefully compiled and edited to meet the long felt needs of increasingly large number of those who have to deal with the different aspects of biology of insects in colleges, universities and research institutes. It provides a balanced and integrated treatment of the entire field of insect Biology. The title is intelligible to the educated layman but it deals with some complex ideas. It is an adequate text for all requirements in this area for most university students. Special efforts have been made to explain ideas in non-mathematical term. The primary aim throughout has been clarity, simplicity and the high standard. It will definitely prove to be a boon to teachers, students and research works in the field of Insect Biology.

The primary aim throughout has been clarity so as to make the text selective and meaningful. We hope also that general Entomologists and students of Agricultural Entomology will find in this book valuable and recent informations about the subject and also allied branch of the subject. The book provides a nucleus around which the teacher can plan a successful course without much bearing on complementary and supplementary readings. The theme of the book is novel and for the first time the various chapters in different volumes have been organised reviewing the available literature. All the topics have been illustrated with line diagrams, graphs and tables wherever necessary.

In the preparation of this book large number of books and research papers have been consulted. So no authenticity is claimed.

The author wishes to express his deepest appreciation to the many people who have contributed in one way or the other to the preparation of this title.

The author expresses his gratitude to Mr. Wasan and staff of M/s Discovery Publishing House for their whole hearted co-operation in the publication of this book.

The author tried hard to be accurate and upto date in statement and realises the impossibility of completely avoiding errors therefore, the author will greatly appreciate having his attention called to any questionable statement.

—Author

CONTENTS

INTRODUCTION

Insects that spend part or all of their lives in soil or water exhibit special, structural and behavioural adaptations to the physical, chemical, and biotic conditions found in each. In this chapter we shall examine some of the distinctive features of these media as habitats for erect life and discuss how these features are related to insect biology. We shall also note the important role of insects as decomposers in the renewal of these vital natural resources. The chapter concludes with a discussion of the early evolution of insects in soil and water.

SOIL INSECTS

Soil is the medium that connects all habitats of the land, from the intertidal to the alpine. It is also a distinct realm and one on which green plants and ultimately all forms of terrestrial life depend. The soil surface and overlying litter of plant debris are inhabited by at least some members of nearly all insect orders, as well as by other terrestrial arthropods. Beneath the surface the variety of species markedly declines, but millipedes, mites, spring-tails, beetles, termites, ants, and fly larvae are still represented, sometimes abundantly. Relatively few kinds of insects inhabit caves, but they are nonetheless interesting because of their unique adaptations.

Soil as a Habitat for Insects

The process of soil formation leads to horizontal layers that are readily visible in a cross section such as a road cut. On the surface is usually a duff, or litter of whole or partly decayed leaves and other plant parts. The nature of the litter varies with moisture and the covering vegetation, i.e., grasslands, coniferous forest; deciduous forest, or lichens and mosses. The soils uppermost layer, topsoil, is darkened by a complex, organic substance called *humus*. Topsoil is the place where most plant roots and soil organisms occur. The transformation of the litter into humus is accomplished in stages. Arthropods contribute significantly to the process by ingesting organic matter at the surface, mechanically breaking it down, and defecating deeper in the soil. Their excavations also mix the surface layer between litter and soil. Bacteria and fungi in the moister regions below then act on the fragments, now with greater surface area, to produce numus. The deeper subsoil, if present, is paler, being only slightly enriched from above, and grades below into the unaltered rock of the earth's crust.

Cracks, old root channels, and tiny cavities between soil particles create pore spaces in soil. The total pore space of topsoil is usually about a third of the soil volume, but in some places may exceed half the volume. At greater depths, the soil is more compact and has smaller pore spaces. Depending on the nature of the soil particles, rainfall, groundwater, and drainage, the pore spaces are filled partly by air and partly by water held by capillary forces. Soil air is usually saturated with water vapour except near the soil surface. In welldrained topsoil, oxygen in soil air is replenished by gaseous diffusion from the atmosphere. Soil water derives its oxygen from soil air. Oxygen, however, diffuses 10,000 times slower in water. The consumption of oxygen in soil water by bacterial decomposition of organic matter can create anaerobic conditions in as short a distance as 1 mm from a water-air interface. Deeper in the soil gaseous diffusion from the atmosphere decreases. Here the respiration of plants and animals reduces oxygen and increases the carbon dioxide content of soil air.

Providing the covering vegetation is not too dense, sunlight penetrates the litter, open burrows, and superficial soil crevices. Below the surface, at depths of only a few centimeters at most, is permanent darkness. In deserts, grasslands, alpine regions, and deciduous forests after the leaves have fallen, the surface is largely exposed to the sun's radiation. Thus heated by the sun, the surface temperature of soil rapidly climbs well above that of either the air or the soil at slight depths beneath. Surface temperatures above 50°C are not infrequent even in the Temperate Zone. Owing to the low thermal conductivity of soil, the heating and cooling of deeper layers lags behind the fluctuations in temperature of the air, litter, and the soil surface. Heat acquired during day penetrates into the soil quite slowly. While the surface cools in the evening, the deeper layers of soil are still rising in temperature. In the morning, the deeper layers have cooled but the surface is now being heated by the sun, creating a steep, vertical gradient in temperature. A high moisture content in soil will reduce the amplitude of these daily fluctuations in temperature. "Cover objects," such as large rocks of logs resting on the surface, shelter the soil beneath from extreme temperatures and maintain a high humidity by preventing evaporation. The spaces beneath cover objects provide insects a place to escape from predators and environmental extremes, especially in grasslands.

Litter Insects

The most numerous insects in the litter and superficial layers of top soil, in terms of both species and individuals, are colonies of Isoptera, colonies of Formicidae, all stages of Coleoptera, immature Diptera, and immature Lepidoptera, especially pupae. The most numerous arthropods of all here are the Acarina and Colembola. Each of the other insect orders is represented by at least one species, except the Ephemeroptera, Plecoptera and Phthiraptera. The insects of certain orders spend their entire lives in litter, often in association with cover objects (Archeognatha, Thysanura, Grylloblatodea, Zoraptera, and some species of Blattodea, Dermaptera, Embioptera and Orthoptera). Other orders are represented at least by the immature stages which feed as scavengers or predators or which feed on algae, fungi, or mosses (Mantodea, Thysanoptera, Psocoptera, Neuroptera, Raphidioptera, Mecoptera, and Siphonaptera). Parasitoids and parasites, including Strepsiptera, attack other litter insects. Remarkably few aquatic insects are also active in moist litter, even though the habitat would seem suitable and, in most instances, the aquatic forms probably evolved from litter inhabitants. Exceptions are the terrestrial naiads of *Megalagrion* (Odonata) in Hawaii, and the terrestrial larvae of *Enoicyla pusilla* (Trichoptera) in forest litter of Europe. Megaloptera and aquatic Coleoptera, however regularly pupate out of water in soil. The transition between aquatic and terrestrial life is often made by fly larvae. For example, crane-fly larvae (Tipulidae) readily burrow from beneath streams into moist soil.

Immobile stages of insects are commonly spent on the ground. Eggs are often deposited here: Phasmatodea drop eggs in litter, and Acrididae lay *eggs* in soil. Lepidoptera pupae and the resting "pupae" of Thysanoptera are in litter. Periods of quiescence or diapause also may be spent among dead leaves. Aggregations of diapausing adults of *Hippodamia convergence* (Coccinellidae) are found on the ground in Sierra Nevada of California from June to February.

The active stages of litter insects are greatly varied in shape: Most are somewhat dorsoventrally compressed, and often parallel-sided or anteriorly narrow, a form that facilitates movement among varied obstacles. Most are agile and possess well-developed means for locomotion on ground. Escape by jumping is often a. characteristic (Archeognatha, Collembola, Orthoptera, Schizopteridae (Hemiptera), alticine Chrysomelidae, and rhynchaenine Curculionidae). The antennae and tactile sense organs are usually well-developed. Exposed, membranous wings are apparently an encumbrance in narrow passage ways. Except for mating and dispersal, flight is an unnecessary investment of energy and structure. The Embioptera spin silken runways to move out from cover objects into the litter. The wings of male web spinners, if present, are flexible and bend freely inside the tunnels. The Collembola, Diplura, Protura, and Apterygota are, of course, wingless, and immature pterygotes have small wing pads at most. Among adult pterygotes some have protective forewings (Orthoptera, Dermaptera and Coleoptera); others fail to develop wings (some Psocoptera, Grylloblattoidea, and the sterile castes of Isoptera and Formicidae); or discard them after mating and dispersal (Zoraptera, reproductive castes of Isoptera and"Formicidae). Certain features of the body are evidently correlated with daily illumination and hazard of predation by visual hunters such as birds; the compound eyes are well-developed; circadian rhythms in behaviour are present, often with nocturnal activity; and the body is often pigmented with concealing patterns. Litter insects are generally resistant to desiccation. Respiration is by tracheae, and the spiracles are usually fitted with closing devices.

Soil Insects

Below the litter layer and soil surface the variety of arthropod taxa drops abruptly, yet some groups are found here only, Collembola and Acarina are the most numerous of the permanent residents. All species of Pauropoda, Symphyla, Diplura, and Protura are entirely confined to soils, moist litter, or crevices under cover objects. No entire order of insects is similarly restricted, but some groups in various orders spend part or all of their lives underground.

The most common are Isoptera, Hymenoptera (Formicidae and certain other aculeates), Diptera, Coleoptera, Hemiptera and

Orthoptera. Of these, the Coleoptera are the most numerous in species. All stages of the life cycle of Coleoptera can be found in soil, but generally only the immature stages of Diptera are present. Termites and ants make their nests in soil. Their excavations and the plant matter brought into the nest contribute to soil development. Galleries of *Atta* ants may be enormous and reach 3 to 6 m in depth. Many species of bees and predatory wasps excavate simple burrows in earth that are stocked with provisions for their young. Roots are the food of nymphal Cicadidae and certain other subterranean Hemiptera. Mole crickets feed on roots but also take insect larvae. These orthopterans and omnivorous Stenopeimatinae (Gryllacrididae) are true in habitants of the soil.

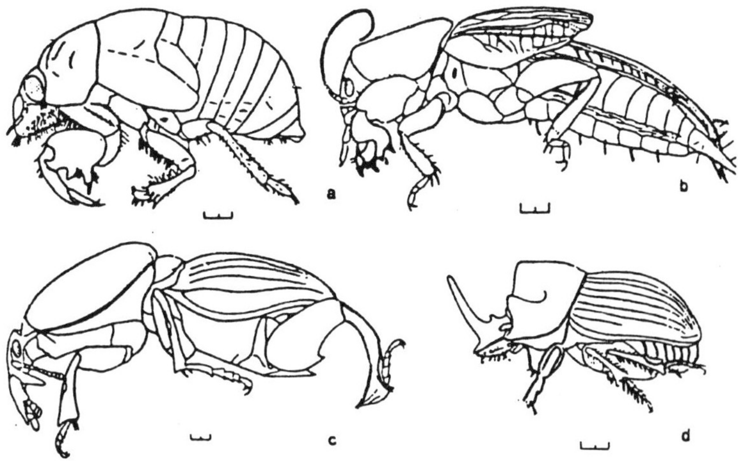

Fig. 1.1. Examples of soil insects: a, cicada nymph, Okanagana sp. (Cicadidae); b, mole cricket Gryllotalpa sp. (Gryllotalpidae); c, unusual soil- dwelling cerambycid beetle from Brzil, Hypocephaluc annals; d, dung beetle, Copris lugubris (Scarabaeidae).

The high humidity of soil air, films of soil water, and moderate emperature of soil create conditions approaching an aquatic environment. Many invertebrate phyla are represented in soil by minute aquatic forms that are found elsewhere in freshwater. Protozoia, for example, are the most numerous soil animals. In the soil air'of pore spaces live the smaller Collembola, Acarina, Pauropoda, Symphyla, Diplura and Protura. When the number and size of organisms are compared to the surface area of the walls of pore spaces, it is evident that the cavities are greatly underpopulated.

An important factor limiting insects in soil is the obvious difficulty in moving about. Unlike the small arthropods listed above, insects are generally not small enough to negotiate interconnecting pore spaces for any distance. They must either tunnel by pushing aside particles and squeezing through, or excavate the soil in front and deposit it behind. The physical resistance of the soil, therefore, raises the energetic cost of locomotion and reduces the distance to which an individual can hunt for mates or food. Sight and wind-borne odours are also eliminated as aids in the search. For this reason, mating of insects is usually accomplished above ground. Except for the roots of green plants, insects must find their food in the form of other soil organisms, dead or alive. Active excavators such as ants, termites, silphid beetles, larval cicindelids, wasps, and bees obtain their food from richer sources above ground.

Reduction in wings is a characteristic of soil insects as well as of litter insects. Soil insects are generally round in cross section but are greatly varied in shape otherwise. "Tunnelers" have reduced or no legs and are of two kinds. Larval Elateridae and Therevidae are smooth, stiff bodied, and slender. By sinuous movements of the trunk, they force their hard, tapered heads forward through the substrate. Larval Tipulidae and Bibionidae are soft-bodied and use peristaltic movements to penetrate soil. "Excavators" may be fairly thick-bodied and often exhibit conspicuous molelike modifications of the head and forelegs for digging. Such fossorial adaptations are seen in Gryllotalpidae, Cydnidae, nymphal Cicadidae, and Scarabaeidae (*Copris, Geotrupes*), to list only a few. Worker ants and termites are not so clearly equipped for digging, but they effectively use their mandibles to remove and carry away particles. In the absence of light, soil insects and the other hexapodous arthropods tend to have reduced or no compound eyes; antennae variably developed, even absent (Protura); well-developed tactile sense organs; and pale pigmentation of the integument without patterns. They are usually repelled by light and higher temperatures. The upper limits of tolerance to temperature are relatively low, but some soil insects can remain active a few degrees above 0°C. Rhythmic behaviour has been poorly, studied. Vertical migration in response to daily temperature fluctuations may occur if the soil is exposed to solar radiation. Resistance to desiccation is low, probably because the epicuticle becomes abraded by soil particles or is naturally permeable to water. Some respire cutaneously. Those that normally inhabit the deeper subsoil are tolerant of higher levels of carbon dioxide, at least for several days (some Collembola, larval Elateridae, Scarabaeidae).

Many insects that inhabit deserts are frequently dependent on the sandy substrate for protection against extreme temperatures and desiccation. Those running on the surface during the day may have long legs that lift the body well above the hot surface (Mutillidae, Tenebrionidae). During the host season many forage openly only at night, spending the day in burrows or simply immersed in sand. Edney as shown that surface temperatures up to 72°C and humidity of 10 per cent are avoided by the desert cockroach *Arenivaga investigate.* At depths of 30 to 45 cm in sand, the roach inhabits a zone where daily temperatures are well below the upper lethal limit (about 45.5 to 48.5°C) and humidity may reach above 82 per cent, a level at which the roach can actually absorb water vapor. Like some tenebrionid beetles, the roach literally swims in sand. The body is biconvex in cross section, oval, and smooth, and has sharp lateral margins, resembling that of an aquatic beetle.

Cave Insects

Insects found in caves may be the same species that are normally found in litter or soil outside. Certain flying insects, especially flies (Culicidae, Mycetophilidae), seek shelter in caves during the day. The darkness, high humidity, even temperature, and absence of green plants are conditions similar to those of deeper soil, but without the physical restraint. Soil insects, therefore, already have many of the modifications required for continuous life in caves. The absence of plants except for their roots, however, largely limits cave-dwelling insects to scavenging, parasitism, or predation. Phytophagous insects are usually absent. New organic matter must be washed in or be deposited as waste by organisms that enter and leave. Bats attract several taxa of parasites (Polyctenidae, Streblidae, and Nycterbiidae; some Siphonaptera and Cimicidae) and the accumulated feces of bats (called guano) attracts scavengers. Animals which are adapted to continuous life in caves and which reproduce there are called *troglobites.* Insects and other hexapodous arthropods in this category are almost entirely limited to Collembola (Entomobryidae), Diplura (Campodeidae), Orthoptera, and Coleoptera (Pselaphidae; trechine Carabidae). Aquatic insects are absent, but some cave Collembola and beetles have been observed submerged and alive in bodies of water in caves.

The restriction of troglobite insects to caves has stimulated research into their origin and geographic distribution. Most troglobites inhabit caves in the Northern Hemisphere, where colder climates and glaciation occurred in the Pleistocene. Apparently, insects became adapted to cold, humid, forest litter near the edges of glaciers. At that time glaciers extended to lower latitudes and altitudes. When the glaciers receded, some cool-adapted insects found refuge in caves, while the remainder of the fauna moved to higher latitudes and altitudes or became extinct. The scarcity of food and lower temperatures of caves in the Temperate Zone place strong selection pressure on efficient use of food at a low metabolic rate. In separate, isolated cave systems, insects independently evolved economizing adaptations; reductions of eyes, wings, flight muscles, pigmentation, and, in some beetles, number of offspring. Troglobites are rare in tropical regions. Presumably this is because food entering the caves is more abundant, and less selection pressure exists for energy-economizing adpatations.

Troglobite insects and Collembola exhibit various degrees of these reductions. On the average, individuals of cave species tend to be larger than their close relatives outside. Cave crickets and trechine Carabidae have more slender bodies and longer appendages.

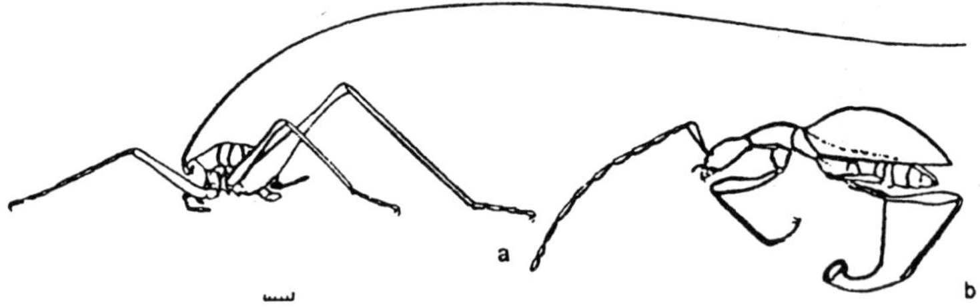

Fig. 1.2. Examples of cave insects; a, cave cricket. Tropidischia xanthostoma (Gryllacrididae, scale equals 5 mm); b, blind cave beetle. Glacicavicola bathvscioides.

Antennae are generally longer, sometimes exceeding the length of the body in Collembola. Beetles may have erect, long hairs scattered over the body that are probably tactile. Most troglobites are repelled by light. The tracheal system and spiracles of trechine carabids are rudimentary; respiration probably takes place through the membranous abdominal terga. Resistance to desiccation and higher temperature is low. Long periods without food are tolerated, and growth is slow. Rhythmic activity and rest in bathysciine beetles are independent of days but are associated with temperature fluctuations. Some bathysciine beetles that live far from the entrance where food is rare have larvae that do not feed. The female lays one egg at a time; each is large and full of yolk. Shortly after hatching the larva builds a clay capsule and remains inside 5 to 6 months, then pupates. The adult searches widely for food, in a manner not possible for a young larva. Adults live for about 3 years.

AQUATIC INSECTS

In this section we discuss insects that spend at least the immature stages of their lives floating or submerged in water. Aquatic insects are a minor fraction of all insects, probably numbering no more than 3 to 5 per cent of all species. The limited number is probably the result of the limited amount of freshwater habitat in comparison with the land surface. Yet these insects are taxonomically diverse are fascinating in structure and biology, and some of them such as mosquitoes, are of extreme importance in public health. A few insects are truly marine. Some other live in the intertidal zone, in brackish coastal waters or saline lakes. Most aquatic insects however, are restricted to freshwater, where they are among the most important organisms in the aquatic ecosystem. As herbivores, predators, scavengers, and even parasitoids, insects function in the trophic structure and, in turn, are food for fish, birds and amphibians.

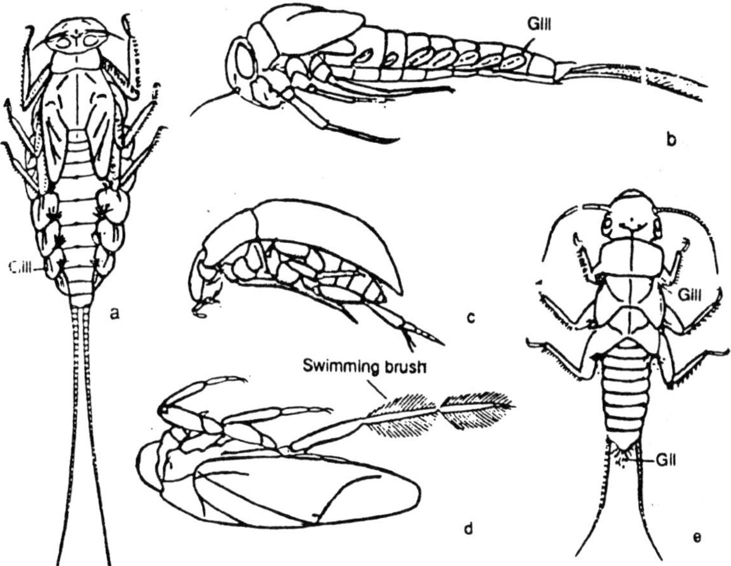

Fig. 1.3. Examples of aquatic insects; a, mayfly naiad, Epeonts *sp. (Heptagendae);* b, *mayfly naiad,* Ameletus *sp. (Siphlonuridae); c, water beetle,* Tropistemus ellipticus *(Hydrophildae),* d, *back swimmer,* Notonecta undulata *(Notonectidae),* e, *stone-fly, naiad,* Acroneuria paciftca *(Peridae).*

Aquatic insects exhibit conspicuous adaptations for respiration and locomotion within the constraints of a liquid medium. Similar adaptations, especially for respiration, can be observed among insects in semiliquid media; scavengers in decaying plant or animal bodies or animal waste; phytophagous insects that burrow in juicy fruits or other plant tissues; and endophagous parasites and parasitoids immersed in the hosts' blood.

Marine Insects

Whereas insects constitute nearly three-quarters of the earth's animal species, they are greatly reduced in number of species in the earth's largest habitat, the ocean. By no means are insects scarce as individuals on the coasts or even far out at sea. Some are exceedingly abundant. Each marine species has over- come certain physical barriers: tidal submergence (the collembolan *Anurida maritima;* insects in several orders, including the hemipteran *Aepophilus bonairei* of England and Europe); wave action [especially midges of the genus *Clunio* and the barnacle-eating larvae of the dryomyzid fly *Oedoparena glauca*]; salinity (especially salt-marsh mosquitoes, ephydrid flies, and the water boatman *Trichocorixa*); depth (the midge *Chironomus oceanitus* dredged from 20 fathoms); and life away from land (five species of the pelagic water striders, *Halobates,* that occur hundreds of miles from land).

Of these barriers perhaps the most limiting is the inability to respire for long beneath the surface. No marine insect is known to spend its entire life under water. Usinger has pointed out that insects are no more successful in colonizing deep freshwater lakes. Only certain midge larvae and perhaps the peculiar stone*fly* *Capnia* spp. can exist indefinitely in deep, still water. Added to the physical barriers is the intense biological competition from marine arthropods and other organisms, plus the threat of predatory fish. During the Paleozoic Era while insects flourished on land, the marine fauna was diversifying and occupying the habitats of the sea. The oceans now seem effectively closed to insects.

Extent of Freshwater Habitats

On a global scale the total extent of freshwater is remarkably small. Freshwater lakes and rivers constitute less than 0.01 per cent of the total volume of water in the biosphere. Even including the inland seas such as the Black and Caspian, all inland bodies of still water occupy only 1.8 per cent of the land surface. Rivers or running waters occupy about 0.001 per cent. Much freshwater is concentrated in a few large lakes in the Temperate and Subarctic regions of the Northern Hemisphere. Luke Baikal in Siberia and the Laurentian Great Lakes of North America each contain about 20 per cent of all freshwater.

Freshwater has been available to terrestrial life because of the hydrological cycle. Actual geological evidence of ancient freshwater habitats is scarce. The sediments of lakes and rivers, like other terrestrial deposits, seldom escape destruction by erosion. At any instant lakes contain about 100 times more than rivers, but rivers are continually renewed. Over a year rivers, lake, promoting the growth of free-floating algae in sunny, open water. The gradual enriclunent of water with nutrients, especially nitrogen and phosphorus, is called *cutrophication.* Continued addition leads to the production of orgànic matter in excess of decomposition. The decomposed organisms in deep water deplete the water of its oxygen, leaving the organic matter to accumulate with other sediments. Older lakes, rich in nutrients and shallow, are called *cutrophic.* When lakes receive large amounts of acid humic substances from the watershed, the water becomes stained brown and poor in variety of aquatic life. Organic matter accumulates from plants in the shallow marginal waters. Such lakes or bogs are called *dystrophic.* Ultimately both eutorphic and dystrophic lakes fill completely with organic matter, are overgrown by vegetationand disappear.

Slender fly larvae dominate the insect life of the deeper, open waters and the bottom beneath. The thin sediments of oligotrophic lakes are characterized by colourless midge larvae of *Tanytarsus* (Chironomidae). On the surface of the bottom ooze of eutrophic lakes, where oxygen is often depleted, the predominate or only insects are red, hemoglobin-containing larvae of *Chironomus.* These are able to survive the irregular oxygen supply and continue to function as important decomposers. The open waters of eutrophic lakes are inhabited by the phantom midge larvae, *Chaoborus* (Culicidae). As one of the few free-floating insects, the predatory *Chaoborus* spend the day near the bottom and swim toward the surface at night. The phantom larva is nearly transparent - hence the na - Gas sacs are visible at each end and act as organs of equilibrium. The volume of gas is controlled by the nervous system. When the sacs are compressed, the larva sinks; when they are expanded, it rises.

Adult midges emerge synchronously in enormous numbers from productive lakes throughout the world. *Chaoborus edulis* forms spectacular clouds seen at great distances over Lake Malawi in Africa. The emergence of *C, astictopus,* the Clear Lake gnat of Clear Lake, California, creates an annual nuisance to resort owners. When carried over land by winds, the masses of chironomids and *Chaoborus* remoye significant quantities of organic matter from the lake eco-system. The shallow water of lakes and ponds contains more different kinds of insects than the deeper, open waters. Certain areas approximate the physical and chemical conditions of running water. On the wave-washed, rocky shore of oligotrophic lakes we find some of the same mayflies, stone flies, and caddis flies that are in streams. Stone flies are sensitive to. low oxygen and are rare in lakes except in such places. The numbers and variety of insects in shallow water increase with eutrophication. Mayflies, caddis flies, dragonflies, and damselflies live among submerged plants or on the bottom. These insects have gills and do not rise to the surface for air. Also confined to quiet water are the many Hemiptera, Coleoptera, and Diptera that breath air, either directly or in air bubbles. On the surface are the water striders, Gerridae, Veliidae, and marsh traders, Hydrometridae. Shallow lakes may be created watch year by rain and snow melt. These last but a few weeks or months before the water is lost through evaporation or absorption into the soil. Such bodies of water formed in the spring are called *vernal lakes* or *ponds*. Insect life ordinarily teems in these temporary habitats because predatory fish are absent. Even the small volumes held in tree holes, cavities at the bases of leaves . of plants such as the tropical bromeliads, and hoofprints are sufficient for some insects to complete their life. Growth is usually quite rapid. For example, less than 2 weeks is needed for the yellow-fever mosquito, *Aedes aegypti* to complete development.

INSECT SCAVENGERS

Many, but by no means all, insects that live in soil and water are scavengers. Perhaps the word "scavenger" is poorly chosen. Does it indicate an animal that eats whatever comes along, one that eats mostly dead things, or one whose diet consists of items so small and miscellaneous that an accounting is difficult? Here we intend all these meanings when we call certain insects scavengers. The term is broad enough to convey the diversity of food that some insects are known to eat while also concealing our ignorance of the exact diets of others.

A complex terminology has developed to describe the diets of scavengers. Some may be *omnivorous,* eating plants or animals whether they are dead or alive. *Saprophagous* scavengers feed on dead organisms and have been subdivided into *xylophagous* forms boring into and feeding on sound or decaying wood; *phytosaprophagous* forms, feeding on decaying vegetable matter; *scatophagous* or *coprophagous* forms, feeding on feces or dung; and *zoosaprophagous* or *necrophagous* forms, feeding on dead animals. *Detritivores* feed on small bits of animal or vegetable trash. The food of saprophagous insects, however, is not all dead matter, because microbes such as bacteria, fungi, and yeast flourish in such places and are nutritious. Small living food is taken by *microphytic* insects that selectively eat bacteria, yeasts, fungi, algae, diatoms, lichens, spores, and loose pollen. Animal foods include Protozoa, and small invertebrates and their eggs. Fungi *vorous* insects are adapted to feeding exclusively on living and dead fungi. Thus among the insects loosely scavengers are those with specific choices of food.

Saprophagous insects have unity in an ecological sense because they function in the complex world of the decomposers. These should be counted among our most beneficial insects. Intact bodies of dead vascular plants and vertebrates, smaller dead organisms, and excrement are progressively disintegrated. The nutrients in streams and soils are derived from plant material that is decomposed initially by insects and other arthropods. Scavenging species are usually specific to either plant or animal matter. In terrestrial environments the species appear in a predictable sequence as characteristic chemicals are emitted from the decaying organism at each stage of disintegration. Tissue is ingested and partially or completely digested, often with the aid of symbionts or unusual enzymes such as cellulose, keratinous, or collagenase. The feces of scavengers are further decomposed by other scavengers or microbes, thus aiding in nutrient recycling.

EVOLUTION OF INSECTS IN SOIL AND WATER

It is generally agreed that insects evolved from some form of marine arthropod. Opinions vary, however, as to whether the intermediate steps in this evolution took place in water or on land. In other words, were the first insects originally aquatic and secondarily terrestrial or *vice versa*? The weight of evidence favours a terrestrial origin. The tracheal system of insects and their allies seems to have evolved for the transport of air in ' a terrestrial environment. The aquatic stages of insects possess the same gas-filled tracheae as terrestrial environment. The aquatic stages of insects possess the same gas-filled tracheae as terrestrial insects. Only by special modifications can the tracheal system functions under water. Even then, many insects must return frequently to the surface for air.

In most groups of aquatic insects the immature stages alone are aquatic. The adults are aerial or terrestrial, returning near the water or recentering it for oviposition. The aquatic Hemiptera and Coleoptera are the only large groups of insects that live submerged in water as adults. Neither has entirely relinquished its terrestrial adaptations; both usually retain functional wings, and most beetles pupate in soil away from the water. Furthermore, only the specialized Aphelocheiridae (Henuptera) of Europe, and possibly some *Capniq spp.* (Nemouridae, Plecoptera) are able to remain submerged throughout their lives. For these reasons, one must conclude that insects were originally terrestrial and are incompletely adapted to life under water.

During the evolutionary history of insects, aquatic forms have evolved repeatedly, perhaps hundreds of times, from terrestrial ancestors. Often, but not always, the more primitive orders of a group of orders, or the more primitive families in an order, are aquatic. Life in water offers certain advantages, especially for the imatue stages. They are sheltered from desiccation and freezing and protected from certain natural enemies such as parasitoids. The aquatic habitat was apparently colonized early during each new evolutionary radiation of insects, and the aquatic forms tended to outlast their terrestrial progenitors. Hence the more primitive forms are well represented in the aquatic environment because they survived there, not because insects originated in water.

Turning now to the early terrestrial environment, the first episode of plant evolution on land began in the late Silurian Period and ended with the close of the Devonian Period. During this relatively short span of time, a rapid succession of vascular plants appeared; the Subdivisions Psilopsida, Lycopsida, Sphenopsida, and the ferns or Pteropsida. The diversity of this early flora can be estimated by the 83 "genera" of spores that have been described. When the sporophyte plant was preserved, it was sometimes treelike. The Devonian *Pseudosporochnus* reached 2 m of more in height. All these plants were confined to wet places because the flagellated sperm of the gametophyte generation required water in which to swim to the egg cells.

The fossil record indicates that a variety of aquatic mollusks, worms, and arthropods could have served as decomposers when plants fell in the water. But on land, few animal fossils exist to reconstruct the ancient food webs of the early Paleozoic Era. The moist, decaying plant matter would have been a suitable place for arthropods to make the transition from aquatic to terrestrial life. Here was an uncontested food supply, including spores and microbial life as well as protection from desiccation. The fossils that do exist from this time support this line of reasoning. Predatory scorpions are represented in both the

Silurian and Devonian Periods. The earlier forms may have been aquatic, but the later scorpions were terrestrial. A myriapod, *Archidesmus,* is known from the Silurian and may have been a terrestrial scavenger. In the Devonian a mite, *Protacants,* and a few small arachnids have been found. The mites were probably microphytic and the arachnids predatory. Thus some evidence exists that arthropod scavengers and predators colonized the land as early as the Silurian and Devonian. Furthermore, they probably lived in litter. Certain protective characteristics of the spores of terrestrial plants and fungi that lived at this time indicate that they may have been fed upon and disperded by arthropods. Fragments of arthropods have also been found inside a fossil stem fragment and inside fossil sporangia, further supporting the idea that arthropods probably thrived in litter.

Definite insect fossils are not known from the Devonian, yet about 30 million years later an abundance of varied insects are found in strata of the Upper Carboniferous Period. It seems most probable that insects evolved as scavengers in plant litter and made their appearance at least by the close of the Devonian. The Apterygota are probably representative of the early insects, and it is not coincidental that they are scavengers in litter today. Other survivors of the same early radiation of terrestrial arthropods include the Pauropoda, Symphyla, Collembola, Diplura, Protura, Chilopoda, Diplorpoda, and the arachnids, Pseudoscorpionida, Scorpionida, Palpigrada, Podogona (Ricinulei), and the more primitive Acarina and Phalangida. These groups are also found today mostly in moist soil and litter.

Evolution of Scavenger

As the diet of Paleozoic insects became predominantly living prey, blood fungi, or green plants, scavengers became predators, parasites, fungivores, or herbivores respectively. Most evolutionary lineages in insects seem to be from scavenging to other feeding habits. Except for the mouthparts of larval and adult Diptra, the mouthparts of the scavenging taxa are of the chewing type. This versatile design is readily modified into more specialized feeding structures. In the Carboniferous Period, the amount of food for scavengers increased enormously. A rise in the carbon dioxide content off the atmosphere is thought to have created a "greenhouse effect" and produced a warm, moist climate. The increased availability of carbon dioxide plus a favourable climate resulted in an increase in photosynthetic activity and the explosive growth of land plants. The dominant lycopod,*Lepidodendron,* reached over 40 m in height. The rapid accumulation of dead plants created the great coal deposits upon which we now depend for fuel. The animal decomposers preserved as fossils were insects, mites, millipedes, and giant arthropods (now extinct) of the Class Arthropleurida. The last were shaped like millipeds and-measured up to 2 m in length. They were probably the world's largest exclusively land arthropods and a dramatic measure of the amount of food available to scavengers. Other decomposers, such as pulmonate snails and terrestrial isopods, were apparently absent.

At this time insects evolved wings and the Paleoptera made their appearance. Adult Paleoptera, with their outstretched wings, would have been prevented from returning to life among the crevices in the litter. The nymphs were probably less restricted, and those with chewing mouthparts probably continued as scavengers. The scavengers and herbivores were prey to increasing numbers of predators. These now included amphibians and the first reptiles, as well as the first spiders and other arachnids, predatory insects, and possibly chilopods. The pressure to escape terrestrial prediction may be responsible for the origins of the aquatic nymphs in the Odonata and Ephemeroptera. The latter continued their scavenging habits in their new environment. The evolution of the wing-folding mechanism permitted the entire life cycle of the early Neoptera to be completed in or near the litter. The success of this adaptation can be judged by the prevalence of scavengers among the early Neoptera that survive today. Furthermore, the first scavenging Neoptera to be fossilized were the Blattodea. They were so abundant that the period is often called the "*Age of Cockroaches*."

The Permian Period was characterized by geologic and climatic disturbances, often violent. Some areas were glaciated, some became windblown deserts and in other regions thick salt deposits were laid down from drying seas. One can imagine the stresses placed on the Carboniferous insect fauna that had become adapted to moist, warm forests over a period of 80 million years. Besides struggling to survive under new climatic regimes and amidst the competition caused by shrinking forests, they were confronted with an increasing variety of reptiles which doubtless included insectivores. During this period of changing and adverse conditions, the holometabolous life cycle was evolved. The larvae of scavengers were able to bore into decaying tissues, or into soil, thus gaining increased protection from desiccation and predators, as well as access to new food sources. Among the first scavenging endoptergotes to be preserved as fossils are Coleoptera of the Family Cupesidae. This family survives today, and the larvae bore in decaying wood.

Through the Mesozoic and into the Tertiary, the scavenging endopterygotes became specialists on larger, dead organisms and their wastes. Wood and decaying foilage of the gymnosperms and angiosperms were peneyrated. Alone among the exopterygote orders, the Isoptera were also able to penetrate sound wood. The dead bodies of reptiles and later mammals, and their excrement, were invaded by insects able to feed and respire in semilizuid media. The higher metabolic activity of mammals was accompanied by higher food intake and increased quantities of feces. Dead animals and mammalian feces as habitats are exclusively occupied by endopterygotes, especially Coleoptera and Diptera. Scavengers in the nests of birds and mammals became scavenging ectoparasites such as the Phthiraptera (Suborder Mallophaga), and some became obligate bloodsuckers. Certain dung-feeding maggots became myiasis-producing parasites. Insects feeding on seeds stored by mammals or the provisions of presocial and eusocial insects later became pests of human granaries and pantries.

2

Environmental Factors

The abiotic environment influences the life very much and it includes habitat, gases, solar radiation, temperature, moisture and unorganic and organic nutrients. The abiotic factors may exert their effects on insects either directly or indirectly (through their effects on other organisms) and in the short or long term (light, for example, may exert an immediate effect on the orientation of an insect as it searches for food, and may induce changes in an insect's physiology in anticipation of adverse conditions some months in the future). Another abiotic factor to which insects are now routinely subjected (deliberately or otherwise) are pesticides. Apart from the obvious effect of lethal doses of such chemicals, pesticides may have more subtle, indirect effects on the distribution and abundance of species, for example, alteration of predator-prey ratios and, in sublethal doses, changes in fecundity or rates of development.

The combination of environmental factors, both biotic and abiotic, determines the distribution and abundance of a species. Frequently the effect of one one factor modifies the normal response of an organism to another factor. For example, light, by inducing diapause, may make an insect unresponsive to (unaffected by) temperature fluctuations. As a result an insect is not harmed by abnormally low temperatures, but nor is it *"fooled"* into reactivity by temporary periods of warmer weather which may occur in the middle of winter.

TEMPERATURE

Effect on Developmental Rate

Insects are the poikilothermic animals, and their body temperature normally follows closely the temperature of the surroundings. Within limits, therefore, metabolic rate is proportional to ambient temperature. Consequently, the rate of development . is inversely proportional to temperature. Outside these temperature limits the rate of development no longer bears an inversely linear relationship to temperature, presumably because of the deleterious effects of extreme temperatures on the enzymes which regulate metabolism, and eventually temperatures are reached (the so-called upper and lower lethal limits) where death occurs.

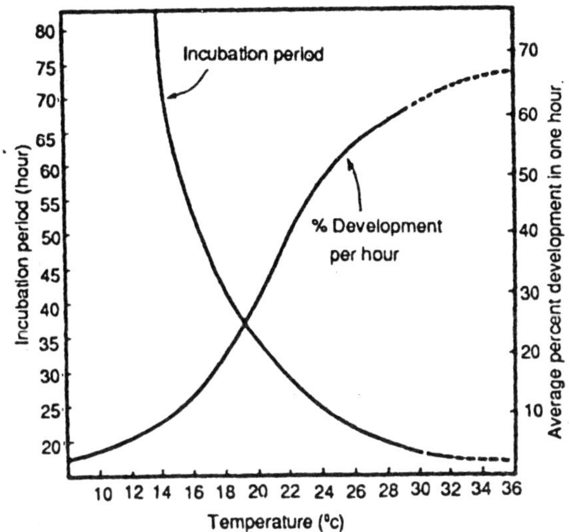

Fig. 2.1. Relationship between temperature and rate of development in eggs of Drosophila melanogaster *(Diptera).*

Within the range of linearity the product of temperature multiplied by time required for development will be constant. This constant, known as the thermal constant or heat budget, is commonly measured in units of degree-days. This relationship will hold even when the temperature fluctuates, provided that the fluctuations do not exceed the range of linearity.

The temperature limits outside which development cases and the rate of development at a given temperature vary among species, points which, though seemingly obvious, were apparently overlooked in some early attempts at biological control of insect pests. A predator which, on the basis of laboratory tests and short-term field trials, had good control potential, was found to exert little or no control of the pest under natural conditions. Further study showed this to be due to the differing effects of temperature on development, hatching, and activity between the pest and its predator.

There is a broad correlation exists between the temperature limits for development and the habitat occupied by members of a species. For example, many Arctic insects which overwinter in the egg stage complete their entire development (embryonic + postembryonic) in the temperature range 0-4°C, whereas in the Australian grasshopper, *Austroicetes cruciata,* development ceases below 16°C. This means that the distribution of a species will be limited by the range of temperature experienced in different geographic regions, as well as by other factors. However, the distribution of a species may be significantly greater than that anticipated on the basis of temperature data for the following reasons: (1) temperature adaptation may occur; that is, genetically different strains may evolve, each capable of surviving within a different temperature range; (2) the temperature limits of development may differ among developmental stages this also serves as an important developmental synchronizer in some species; and (3) the insect may have mechanisms for surviving extreme temperatures.

Because of the ameliorating effects of the water surrounding them aquatic insects are not normally exposed to the temperature extremes experienced by terrestrial species. Further, because ice is a good insulator, development may continue through the winter in some aquatic species in temperature climates, though air temperatures render development of terrestrial species impossible. Indeed, through evolution there has been a trend in some insects (for example, species of Ephemeroptera and Plecoptera) to restrict their period of growth to the winter, passing the summer as eggs in diapause. Such species, whose developmental threshold is usually only slightly above 0°C, appear to gain at least two advantages from this arrangement. First, through the winter there is an abundance of food in the form of rotting vegetation, yet relatively little competition for it. Second, they are relatively safe from predators (fish) which are sluggish and feed only occasionally at these temperatures. Such a life cycle may also allow some species to inhabit temporary or still bodies of water that dry up or become anaerobic during summer.

Effects on Migration and Dispersal

Through its effect on metabolic rate temperature clearly will affect the activity of insects. Many of the generalizations made above with regard to the influence of temperature on development have their parallel in relation to activity. Thus, there is a range of temperature within which activity is normal, though this range may vary among different strains of the same species. The temperature range for activity is correlated with a species' habitat; for example, in the Arctic, chironomid larvae are normally active in water at 0°C, and adults can *fly* at temperatures as low as 3.5°C. By affecting an insect's ability to *fly* temperature may have a marked effect on a species' dispersal and, therefore, distribution. Further, because flight is of such importance in food and/or mate location and ultimately, reproduction, temperature is of great consequence in determining the abundance of species. Insects utilize various means of raising their body temperature to that at which flight is possible even when the ambient temperature is low. For example, they may be darkly coloured so as to absorb solar radiation, or they may bask on dark surfaces, again using the sun's heat. Some moths and bumblebees beat their wings while at rest in order to increase their body temperature. A dense coat of hairs or scales covers the body of some insects, which, by its insulating effect, will retard loss of heat generated or absorbed.

In extremely cold climates, such as that of the Arctic, these physiological, behavioural, or structural features may no longer be sufficient to enable flight to occur, especially in a larger-bodies, egg-carrying female. Thus, different temperature-adaptation strategies are employed, some of which are exemplified especially well by Arctic blackflies (Simuliidae: Diptera). Typical southern species are, as adults, active insects which mate in flight and may, in the case of females, fly considerable distances in search of a blood meal necessary for egg maturation. In contrast, females of Arctic species seldom fly. Their mouthparts are reduced and eggs mature from nutrients acquired during larval life. Mating occurs on the ground as a result of chance encounters close to the site of adult emergence. In two species parthenogenesis has evolved, thereby overcoming the difficulty of being located by a mate. Temperature change, through its effect on the solubility of oxygen in water, may markedly modify the activity and, ultimately, the distribution and survival of aquatic insects. Members of many aquatic species are restricted to habitats whose oxygen content remains relatively high throughout the year. Such habitats include rivers and streams which are normally well oxygenated because of their turbulent flow and lower summer temperature, and high altitude or latitude ponds and lakes, which generally remain cool through the summer. Alternatively, as noted in previous section, the life cycle of some species is such that the warmer (oxygen-deficient) conditions are passed through in a resistant, diapausing, egg stage.

Effect on Emergence

In the majority cases the insects exhibit highly synchronized larval development (all larvae are more or less at the same developmental stage) and/or synchronized eclosion, especially those which live in habitats where the climate is suitable for growth and reproduction for a limited period each year. Synchronized eclosion increases the chances of finding a mate. It may also increase the probability of finding suitable food or oviposition sites, or of escaping potential predators. Synchronized larval development, also may be related to the availability of food, and in some situations it may be necessary in order to avoid interspecific competition for the same resource. For certain carnivorous species, such as Odonata, synchronized development may help reduce the incidence of cannibalism among larvae.

Perhaps not surprisingly in view of its effects on rate of development and activity, temperature is an important synchronizing factor in the life of insects. Its importance may be illustrated by reference to the life history of *Coenagrion angulatum,* which, along with several other species of damselflies (Odonata: Zygoptera), is found in or around shallow ponds on the Canadian prairies. For these insects the season for growth and reproduction lasts from about mid-May to mid-October. For the remaining 7 months of the year *Coenagrion angulatum* exists as more or less mature larvae, which, between about November and April, are encased in ice as the ponds freeze to the bottom. In C. *angulatum* both larval development and eclosion are synchronized by temperature. Synchronized development is achieved by means of different temperature thresholds for development in different instars; that is, younger larvae can continue to grow in the fall after the growth of older larvae has been arrested by decreasing water temperatures and by a photoperiodically induced diapause. Thus, samples collected in mid-September include larvae of the last seven instars, whereas those from early October are composed almost entirely of larvae of the last three instars. Conversely, after the ice melts the following April, younger larvae can continue their development earlier than their more mature relatives, so that by mid-May more than 90%

of the larvae are in the final instar. After their release from the ice larvae migrate into shallow water at the pond margin whose temperature parallels that of the air. Thus, larvae are able to "monitor" the air temperature and determine when it is suitable for emergence. Emergence occurs when the air temperature is 20-21°C (and the water temperature is about 12°C). It begins normally during the last week of May and reaches a peak within 10 days. Emergence of C. *angulatum* follows that of various chironomids and chaoborids (Diptera), which form the main food of the adult damselflies during the period of sexual maturation. The development and emergence of other damselfly species which inhabit the same pond are also highly synchronized but occur at different times of the growing season. This enables the species to occupy the same pond and make use of the same resources, yet avoid interspecific competition. Temperature may also have an important influence on diapause and other photoperiodically induced phenomena, and this aspect is dealt with below.

Survival at Extreme Temperatures

At several places as in many tropical areas the climatic conditions are suitable for year-round development and reproduction in insects. In other areas of the world, the year is divisible into distinct seasons, in some of which growth and/or reproduction is not possible. One reason for this arrest of growth and reproduction may be the extreme temperatures which occur at this time and are potentially lethal to an insect. In many instances shortage of food would also occur under these conditions. To avoid the detrimental effects of periods of moderately low (down to freezing) or high temperature, insects may employ a number of behavioural and physiological mechanisms. First, the life history of many species is so arranged that the period of adverse temperature is passed as the immobile, non-feeding egg or pupa. Second, prior to the advent of adverse conditions and it should be realized that an insect "anticipates" the onset of these conditions an insect may actively seek out a habitat in which the full effect of the detrimental temperature is not felt. For example, it may burrow or oviposit in soil, litter, or plant tissue, which acts as an insulator. Third, it may enter diapause where it physiological systems are largely inactive and resistant to extremes of temperature.

Effect on Low Temperature

For insects in environments which experience temperatures below 0°C, an additional problem presents itself, namely, how to avoid being damaged by freezing of the body cells. The formation of ice crystals within cells causes irreversible damage and frequently death of an organism. (1) by physical disruption of the protoplasm, and (2) by dehydration, reduction of the liquid water content which is essential for normal enzyme activity. Insects which survive freezing temperatures fall into two categories: (1) freezing-susceptible species which avoid freezing by lowering the freezing point of the body fluids and by supercooling, and (2) freezing-tolerant (= freezing-resistant = frost-resistant) species whose extracellular body fluids can freeze without damage to the insect. In both systems, one or more cryoprotectants (substances which protect against freezing) are normally involved. Cryoprotectants identified to date include the polyhydric alcohols, glycerol and sorbitol, and the disaccharide trehalose, each of which contains a number of hydroxyl groups, the significance of which is discussed below. However, in order to appre- ciate the mode of action of these cryoprotectants, it is necessary first to understand the process of freezing. When water is cooled the speed at which individual molecules move decreases, and the molecules aggregate. As cooling continues there is an increased probability that a number of aggregated molecules will become so oriented with respect to each other as to from a minute rigid latticework, that is, a crystal. Immediately this minute crystal (nucleator) is formed the rest of the water freezes rapidly as additional molecules bind to the solid frame now available to them. Freezing of a liquid does not always depend on the formation of a nucleator, but can be induced by foreign nucleating agents such as dust particles or, in the present context, particles of food in the gut or a rough surface such as that of the cuticle.

Hence, the problem for a freezing-susceptible species is to reduce as much as possible the chance that its hemolymph, and subsequently its intracellular fluid, will freeze. For many species, this includes emptying the gut of food; for others, it may be an additional reason for overwintering as a nonfeeding pupa. By selecting dry locations in which to overwintering and/or by building structures that prevent contact with moisture an insect reduces the possibility of nucleation on its body surface that eventually may cause internal freezing. The presence of an hydrophobic wax layer also reduces this possibility. The most important mechanism, however, for avoiding freezing is the production of cryo-protectants (antifreezes). These molecules not only increase the concentration of solutes in the body fluid (an effect which is achieved in some species by active excretion of water) so that the freezing point is depressed, but by their chemical nature they facilitate considerable supercooling; that is, the body fluids remain liquid at temperatures much below their normal freezing point. The known cryoprotectants, because of their hydroxyl groups, are capable of extensive hydrogen bonding with the water within the body. The binding of the water has two important effects with respect to supercooling. First, it greatly reduces the chance of the water molecules ,to aggregate and form a nucleating crystal, and second, even if an ice nucleus is formed, the rate at which freezing spreads through the body is greatly retarded because of the increased viscosity of the fluid.

A remarkable degree of supercooling can be achieved through the use of cryoprotectants. In the overwintering larva of the parasitic wasp *Bracon cephi,* for example, glycerol makes up 25% of the fresh body weight and lowers the supercooling point of the hemolymph to - 47°C. Perhaps a disadvantage to the use of supercooling as a means of overwintering is that the probability of freezing occurring increases both with duration of exposure and with the degree of supercooling so that for example, an insect might freeze in 1 minute at -19°C but survive for 1 month at -10°C. Thus, to ensure survival an insect must have the ability to remain supercooled at extreme temperatures for significant periods of time, even though the average temperatures to which it is exposed may be 10-15°C higher. In other words, it may have to produce much more antifreeze in anticipation of those extremes than would be judged necessary on the basis of the average temperature.

The alternative method, employed by freezing-tolerant species, is to permit (be able to withstand) a limited amount of freezing within the body. Freezing must be restricted to the extracellular fluid, as intracellular freezing damages cells. Ice formation in the extracellular fluid, which is accompanied by release of heat (latent heat of fusion), will therefore reduce the rate at which the body's tissues cool as the ambient temperature falls. Thus, it will be to an insect's advantage to have a large volume of hemolymph (and there is evidence that this is characteristic of pupae) and to be able to tolerate freezing of a large proportion of the water within it. The problems for an insect are twofold. First, it must be able to prevent freezing from extending to the cell surfaces (and hence into the cells), and second, it must prevent damage to cells as a result of dehydration (as water in the extracellular fluid freezes, the osmotic pressure of the remaining liquid will increase, so that water will be drawn out of the cells by osmosis). Both problems are overcome by the use of polyhydroxyl cryoprotectant molecules with their ability to bind extensively with water. Extracellular cryoprotectant will retard the rate at which freezing spreads, while intracellular cryoprotectants will hold water within cells, to counteract the outwardly pulling osmotic force. It has also been suggested that the cryoprotectants may bind with plasma membranes to reduce their permeability to water.

Of interest is the evolutionary selection of glycerol as a cryoprotectant because in high concentration this molecules is toxic at above freezing temperatures. Thus, insects which use this molecule should possess biochemical mechanisms for synthesizing it in increasing amounts as the temperature falls progressively below 0°C and, equally, for degrading it when temperature increases. Such has been shown to be the case in *Pterostichus breviccmis* an Arctic carabid beetlelike which overwinters as a freezing-tolerant adult. In P. *brevicomis* glycerol synthesis begins when an insect is exposed to a fall temperature of 0°C, and by the following December-January the concentration of this molecule may reach or exceed 30 g%, sufficient to enable an insect to withstand the –40 to –50°C temperatures to which it may be exposed at this time. Conversely, as temperatures increase toward 0°C with the advent of spring, the glycerol concentration falls and the cryoprotectant disappears from the hemolymph by about the end of April, coincident with the return of above freezing average temperatures. A comparable situation is observed in *Eurosta solidagenis,* gall-forming fly which overwinters as a freezing-tolerant third instar larva. The larva has a three phase cryoprotectant system which comprises glycerol, sorbitol and trehalose. Production of the molecules begins somewhat above 0° C but is probably triggered by declining temperatures. At temperatures below 0°C, production of glycerol and sorbitol is greatly enhanced. With the return of warm wheather in spring, the concentration of the three molecules rapidly declines.

LIGHT

All life on this planet runs on sunlight and it exerts a major influence on the ability of almost all insects to survive and multiply. A well-developed visual system enables insects to respond immediately and directly to light stimuli of various kinds in their search for food, a mate, a "home," or an oviposition site, and in avoidance of danger. But light influences the biology of many insects in another manner which stems from the earth's rotation about its axis, resulting in a regularly recurring 24-hour cycle of light and darkness, the photoperiod.' Because the earth's axis is not perpendicular to the plane of the earth's orbit around the sun, and because the orbit varies throughout the year, the relative amounts of light and darkness in the photoperiod change seasonally and from point to point over the earth's surface. Photoperiod influences organisations in two ways: it may either induce short-term (diurnal) behavioral responses which occur at specified times in the 24-hour cycle, or bring about long-term (seasonal) physiological responses which keep organisms in tune with changing environmental conditions. In both situations, however, a key feature is that the organisms which respond have the ability to measure time. In short-term responses the time interval between the onset of light or darkness and commencement of the activity is important; for seasonal responses, the absolute daylength (number of hours of light in a 24-hour period) is usually critical, though in some species it is the day-to-day increase or decrease in the light period which is measured. In other words, organisms which exhibit photoperiodic responses are said to possess a "biological clock," the nature of which is unknown, though its effects in animals are frequently manifest through changes in endocrine activity.

Various advantages may accrue to members of a species through the performance of particular activities at set times of the photoperiod. It may be advantageous for some insects to become active at down, dusk, or through the night when ambient temperatures are below the upper lethal limit, chances of predation are reduced, and the rate of water loss through the cuticle is lessened by the generally greater relative humidity which occurs at these times. For other insects, in which visual stimuli are important, activity during specific daylight hours may be advantageous; for example, food may be available for only a limited part of the day, or conversely, other detrimental factors may restrict feeding to a specific period. For many species it is clearly beneficial for its members to show synchronous activity as this will increase the chance of contact between sexes. "Activity" in this sense is not restricted to locomotion, however. For example, in many species of moths, it is by and large only the males who exhibit daily rhythms of locomotor activity. The females are sedentary, but, in their virgin condition, have daily rhythms of "calling" (secretion of male-attracting pheromones) which enable males to locate them.

Circadian Rhythms

In a few species daily rhythms of activity are triggered by environmental cues and are therefore of exogenous origin. For example, the activity of the stick insect *Carausius morosus* is directly provoked by daily changes in light intensity. However, in most species these rhythms are not simply a response to the onset of daylight or darkness; that is, dawn or dusk do not act as a trigger that switches the activity on or off. Rather, the rhythms are endogenous (originate within the organism itself) but are subject to modification (regulation) by photoperiod and other environmental factors. That the rhythm originates internally may be demonstrated by placing the organism in constant light or darkness: The organism continues to begin its activity at approximately the same time of the 24-hour cycle, as it did when subject to alternating periods of light and darkness. Because the rhythm has an approximately 24-hour cycle, it is described as a circadian rhythm. When the rhythm is not influenced by the environment, that is, when environmental conditions are kept constant, the rhythm is said to be free-running. When environmental conditions vary regularly in each 24- hour cycle, and the beginning of the activity occurs at

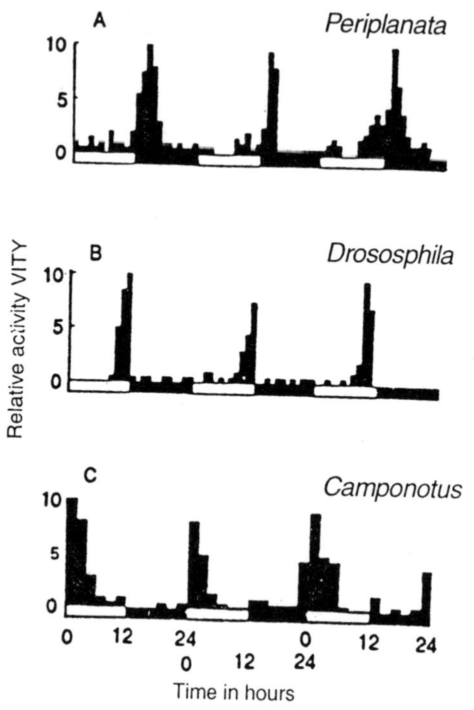

Fig. 2.2. Locomotor activity rhythms in insects, illustrating photoperiodic entrainment.

precisely the same time in the cycle, the rhythm is said to be entrained. For example, if a cockroach begins its locomotor activity 2 hours after darkness, this activity is described as being photoperiodically entrained. The role of photoperiod is therefore to adjust (phase set) the endogenous rhythm so that the activity occurs each day at the same time in relation to the onset of daylight or darkness. Though photoperiod is probably the most important regulator of circadian rhythms in insects. Other environmental factors such as temperature, humidity, and light intensity as well as physiological variables such as age, reproductive state, and degree of desiccation or starvation may modify behaviour patterns. Photoperiodically entrained daily rhythms are known to occur in relation to locomotor activity, feeding; mating behaviour (including swarming), oviposition, and eclosion, examples of which are given below.

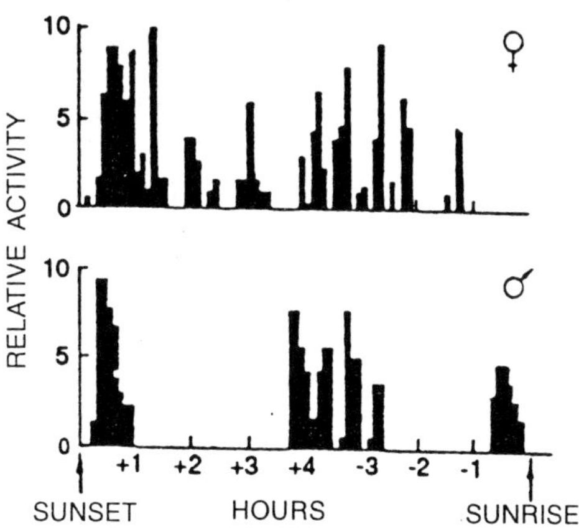

Fig. 2.3. Photoperiodically entrained flight activity in Halisidota *(Lepidoptera).*

There are many insects which actively run, swim, or fly during a characteristics period of the 24-hour cycle, this activity usually occurring in relation to some other rhythm such as feeding or mate location. In *Periplaneta* and other cockroaches activity begins shortly before the anticipated onset of darkness, reaches a peak some 2 to 3 hours after dark,and declines to a low level for the remaining period of darkness and during most of the light period. *Drosophila robusta* flies actively during the last 3 hours of the light phase but is virtually inactive for the rest of the 24-hour period. Male ants of the species *Componotus clarithorar* are most active during the last 3 hours of the light phase but is virtually inactive for the rest of the 24-hour period. Male ants of the species *Camponotus clarithorax* are most active during the first few hours of the light period but show little activity at other times. The above examples show a well-defined single peak (unimodal rhythm) of activity. Other species, however, exhibit bimodal or trimodal rhythms. For example, females of the silver-spotted tiger moth, *Halisidota argentata,* show two peaks of flight activity during darkness, the first shortly after darkness begins, the second about midway through the dark period. Males of this species, in contrast have a trimodal rhythm of flight activity. Rhythmic feeding activity is apparent in larvae of some Lepidoptera, for example, *H.argentata,* which feed almost exclusively during darkness.

Female mosquitoes, too, show peaks of feeding activity either at dawn or dusk, or during both these periods, though there is some argument with regard to whether feeding activity is endogenous or simply a direct responses to a particular light intensity.

Several good examples may be cited to illustrate the importance of photoperiod in entraining daily endogenous rhythms of mating behaviour. Many virgin female Lepidoptera begin to secrete maleattracting pheromones shortly after the onset of darkness and are maximally receptive to males about midway through the dark period. Equally, males show maximum excitability to these pheromones in the early part of the dark period. The males of certain ant species undertake mating flights at characteristic times within the light period, typically near dawn or dusk. Mosquitoes and other Nematocera form all-male swarms into which females fly for insemination. Formation of these swarms, which occurs both at dawn and dusk, is an endogenous rhythm, entrained by photoperiod, though temperature and light intensity are also involved. For some insect species, egg-laying has been shown to be a photo-periodically entrained endogenous rhythm. In the mosquitoes *Aedes oegypti* and *Taeniorhynchus fuscopennatus,* for example, oviposition is concentrated in the period immediately after sunset and before dawn, respectively. In other mosquitoes, however, no oviposition rhythm exists and egg-laying appears to be dependent on light intensity.

There are several insects which molt to adults during a characteristic period of the day. Many tropical Odonata exhibit mass eclosion during the early evening and are able to fly by the following morning. Corbet suggests that this may minimize the effects of predators such as birds and other dragonflies which hunt by sight. In temperate climates where nighttime temperatures are generally too low for emergence, there may be a switch to emergence during certain daylight hours. In more rigorous climates temperature appears to override photoperiod as a factor regulating emergence, which occurs opportunistically at any time of the day provided the ambient temperature is suitable. Species of Ephemeroptra and Diptera also have daily emergence patterns, which may be associated with immediate mating and oviposition. Though many insect species are known which have a daily emergence rhythm, for only a few of these, mainly Diptera, is experimental evidence available that proves the endogenous nature of the rhythm. In contrast to the previously described rhythmic processes, emergence occurs but once in the life of an insect and results in the appearance of a very different developmental stage, the adult. Nevertheless, this single event, like daily repeated processes, is an endogenous rhythm, entrained by environmental stimuli, especially photoperiod, which exert their effect in earlier developmental stages. For example, populations of many *Drosophila* species emerge at maximum rates 1 to 2 hours after dawn on the basis of photoperiodic entrainment either in the larval or pupal stage. Thus, if a culture of *Drosophila* larvae of variable ages is maintained in darkness from the egg stage except for one brief period of light (a flash lasting as little as 1/2000 of a second is sufficient) the adults will emerge at regular 24-hour intervals, based on the onset of the light period being equivalent to dawn; that is, the beginning of the light period serves as the reference point for entraining the insects' emergence rhythm.

Photoperiodic Effect

Photoperiod affects a variety of long-term physiological processes in insects and, in doing so, allows a species to (1) exploit suitable environmental conditions, and (2) survive periods when climatic conditions are adverse. Some of the ways in which species are enabled to exploit a suitable environment include being in an appropriate developmental stage as soon as the suitable conditions appear, and growing or reproducing at the maximum rate while conditions last. Obviously, to survive adverse conditions, members of a species must already be in an appropriate physiological state when the conditions develop. In other words, organisms must be able to anticipate the arrival of inclement climatic conditions. Thus, among the processes known to be affected by photoperiod are the nature (qualitive expression) and rate of development, reproductive ability and capacity, synchronized adult emergence, induction of diapause, and possibly cold-hardiness. Several of these processes are closely related and are therefore affected simultaneously. Other environmental factors, especially temperature, may modify the effects of photoperiod.

Rate of Development

In some species larval growth rates are affected by photoperiod. For some species growth is accelerated under long-day conditions (when there are 16 or more hours of light in each 24-hour cycle) and inhibited in photoperiods that contain 12 or fewer hours of light; for other species, the converse is true. Often the effect of photoperiod on growth rate is correlated with the nature of diapause induction; that is, species which grow more slowly under short-day conditions tend also to enter diapause as a result of short days. However, it should be noted that the growth rate of many species which enter a photoperiodically controlled diapause is not affected by photoperiod.

Exposure to different photoperiods such as occur in different seasons may result in the development of distinct forms of a species, that is, polymorphism. The physiological (endocrine) basis of polymorphism, and the present discussion will be restricted to a consideration of its induction by photoperiod. Sometimes the forms which develop are so strikingly different that they were described originally as separate species. Beck cites the instance of the European butterfly *Araschnia levana,* described originally as two species, *A. levana* and *A. prosa,* but which is now known to be a seasonally dimorphic species. Caterpillars reared under long-day conditions metamorphose into the nondiapausing black-winged (prosa) form; when they have developed at short daylengths the caterpillars emerge as red-winged (levana) adults which overwinter in diapause. This example shows a typical feature of most dimorphic Lepidoptera, namely, that one form is characteristically found in summer and is nondiapausing, whereas the alternate form is the diapausing, overwintering stage.

Photoperiodically influenced polymorphism is also exemplified by the seasonal occurrence of normal-winged, brachypterous, and/or apterous forms of species of Orthoptera and Hemiptera. But perhaps the best-known example of the effects of photoperiod on development is that of temporal polymorphism in aphids. The life cycle of aphid species is complex and variable but shows beautifully how an insect takes full advantage of suitable conditions for growth and reproduction. A key feature of the life cycle is the occurrence within it of wingless, neolenic females which reproduce viviparously and parthenogenetically. In many species the offspring are entirely female. This combination of features enables aphids to reproduce rapidly and build up massive populations in the spring and summer when weather conditions are good and food is abundant. As a result of the crowding which results from this reproductive activity, winged migratory forms develop, and a part of the population moves on to alternate host plants. From these migratory forms several more generations of female aphids (alienicolae) are produced (again through viviparity and parthenogenesis), which may be winged or apterous. Eventually the allienicolae give rise to winged sexuparae (all female) that migrate back to the original host plant, and whose progeny may be either winged males or wingless females (oviparae). These reproduce sexually and lay eggs which pass the winter in diapause on the host plant.. The following spring each egg gives rise to a female individual, the "stem mother" or fundatrix, normally wingless, that reproduces asexually, and from which several generations of neotenic females (fundatrigeniae) arise. There are many variants of this generalized life cycle, most often through its simplification; that is, one or more of the life stages is omitted as, for example, in species which do not alterate hosts when migrants and whose offspring do not appear as distinct forms. Indeed, in some species sexual forms have never been described and reproduction appears to be strictly parthenogenetic.

The development of seasonally occurring aphid forms is influenced by a variety of environmental factors, including photoperiod. Crowding is the major factor that influences production of summer migrants, whereas the shorter days of late summer and early fall induce development of sexuparae and oviparae. For some species there is a critical daylength for induction of oviparous forms. In *Megoura viciae,* for example, which does not alternate host plants (i.e., it has no migrant form, and the oviparae are produced directly from fundatrigeniae), the critical daylength is 14 hours 55 minutes at].5°C. At greater daylengths continuous production of viviparous, parthenogenetic females occurs; when the daylength is below this critical value oviparae are produced. In some species production of males also is induced by short-day photoperiods, though temperature and age exert a strong influence. For example, in the pea aphid *Acynhosiphon pisum* male offspring are not produced by young females or by females reared under long-day conditions. Old females reared at short daylengths and temperatures from 13 to 20°C produced a large proportion of males. Outside this temperature range the proportion of males declined.

Reproductive Capacity

The effects of photoperiod on reproductive processes are almost all indirect, that is, result from other photoperiodically induced phenomena, especially adult diapause (see below). By its effect on the nature of development, as in aphids, photoperiod may indirectly modify the fecundity of a species. Beck notes one example of an apparently direct effect of photoperiod on fecundity. In *Plutella rpaculipennis,* the diamondback moth, egg production in individuals reared under long-day photoperiods averaged 74 eggs moth, whereas egg production under short-day conditions was only half this value.

Diapause

As stated by Beck the diapause is a "genetically determined state of suppressed development, the manifestation of which may be induced by environmental factors." It is a physiological state in which insects can survive cyclic, usually long, periods of adverse conditions, unsuited to growth and reproduction, including high summer or low winter temperatures, drought, and absence of food. An insect enters of diapause usually some time in advance of the adverse conditions and terminates diapause after the conditions have-ended. In other words, not only does the insect leave itself a margin of safety, but it anticipates the arrival of the adverse conditions. Furthermore, the factor which leads to the induction of diapause (most often photoperiod) is not in itself an adverse condition. Thus, diapause differs markedly from quiescence, which is temporary, nonadaptive form of dormancy, induced directly by the arrival of adverse conditions.

Occurrence of Diapause

Diapause may occur at any stage of the life history, egg, larva, pupa, or adult, though this stage is usually species-specific. Only rarely does diapause occur at more than one stage in the life history of a species. Such may be the case in species that require two or more years in which to complete their development. Anticipation of the arrival of adverse conditions means that the environmental stimuli which induce diapause must exert their influence at an earlier stage in development. Thus, egg diapause is the result of stimuli which affect the parental generations. These stimuli act on the female parent either in the adult stage or, more often, during her embryonic or larval development. In *Bombyx mori,* for example, the daylength experienced by developing female embryos determines whether or not these insects will lay eggs that enter diapause. Specifically, exposure of embryos to long daylengths results in females which lay diapausing eggs, and *vice versa*. For *B, mori* good evidence exists for the production of a diapause hormone by females exposed during embryogenesis to long-day conditions. This hormone, synthesized in the subesophageal ganglion, has as its target organ the ovary which is caused to produce diapause eggs. Whether this scheme is applicable to the induction of egg diapause in other species is not known.

Diapause may occur at any larval stage, though the instar in which it is present is characteristic for a species. In many species it occurs in the final instar and, upon termination, is immediately followed by pupation. In this situation it is referred to as prepupal diapause. In the induction of larval diapause environmental stimuli normally exert their influence at an earlier larval stage, though species are known in which the environmental stimulus is given in the egg stage or during the previous generation. For example, in the pink bollworm *Pectinophora gossypiella* the photoperiod experienced by the eggs, as well as that during larval life, is important in determining whether or not prepupal diapause occurs. In *Nasonia vitripennis,* a parasitic hymenopteran, induction of larval diapause is dependent on the age of the female parent at oviposition, as well as on the photoperiod and temperature to which she is exposed early in adult life.

The pupa in the stage in which a large number of species enter diapause. The environmental signal that induces diapause is generally given during larval development, though for some species the influence is exerted in the parental generation. In the Chinese oak silkworm, *Antheraea pernyi* for example, the last two larval instars are sensitive to photoperiod, whereas in the horn fly, *Haernatobia irritans,* pupal diapause results when the female parent has been exposed to short daylengths. Diapause may also occur in adult insects when it is known as reproductive diapause. Either young adults or larval instars are the stages sensitive to environmental stimuli. Newly emerged adult Colorado potato beetles (*Leptinotarsa decemlineata*), when subjected to short daylengths, will enter diapause. In the boll weevil, *Anthonomus grandis,* short-day conditions experienced by larvae will induce diapause in the adult stage.

Mansingh has subdivided diapause and the events surrounding it into a number of phases. This arrangement is convenient for a description of the sequence in which various processes occur, though it must be realised that these phases normally are not clearly separated in time but merge gradually with one another. In the preparatory phase environmental factors induce changes in metabolic activity in anticipation of diapause, resulting generally in accumulation of reserves, especially fats, but including carbohydrates and in some species cryoprotctants. During this phase the metabolic rate remains normal. Entry into the first phase (induction phase) of diapause is signaled by a great decline in metabolic rate and, in postembryonic stages, in the activity of the endocrine system. For example, in diapausing *Hyalophora cecropia,* a saturniid moth, the rate of oxygen consumption (a measure of metabolic rate) is only about 2% of the prediapause value; in larval European corn borers (*Ostrinia nubilalis*), which have a "weak" diapause, the rate of oxygen consumption falls to about one quarter of the prediapause level. In the induction phase continued production of certain reserves, especially cryoprotectants, probably occurs. What causes the decline in metabolic rate associated with the beginning of diapause is uncertain. It may be due to the continued effects of environmental stimuli, or it may result from the changed metabolism of an insect. For most insects that overwinter in diapause a period of exposure to low temperature is necessary before development can continue, that is, before diapause can be terminated. This is the refractory phase (phase of diapause development) and is perhaps the least understood aspect of the diapause condition. Some authors have suggested that low temperature is necessary for breakdown of diapause-inducing substances (perhaps hormones) or growth-inhibiting substances produced in earlier phases. Others have proposed that this phase is necessary for reactivation of specific systems, for example, the endocrine system, important in postdiapause development. The refractory phase is followed by the activated phase, a period in which insects are capable of terminating diapause but do not do so because of prevailing environmental conditions (especially low temperature). Certain authors consider that once insects reach this stage, when their dormancy is (often) simply temperature-dependent, they must be considered as being quiescent, that is, no longer in diapause. Mansingh, however, points out that, although insects in this phase are capable of continued development, several aspects of

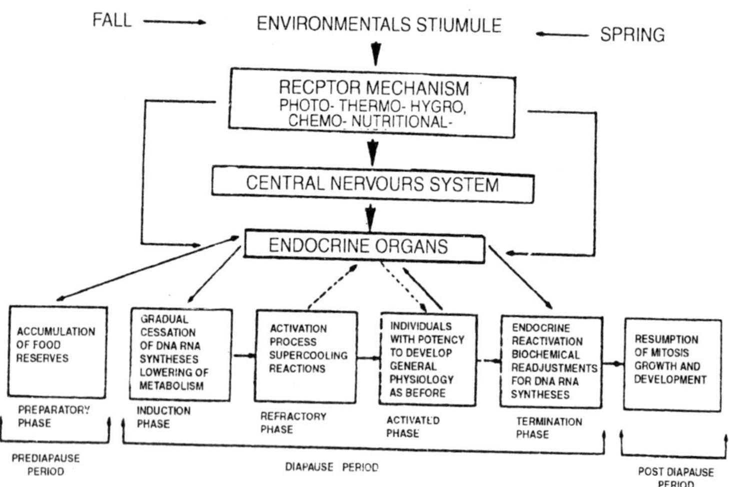

Fig. 2.4. Phases before, during, and after diapause in overwintering insects. Probable (solid arrows) and possible (broken arrows) relationships between the environment, endocrine system, and the various phases are indicated.

their physiology are similar to those of the refractory phase, for example, greatly depressed respiratory rate and presence of cryoprotectants. He believes, therefore, that activated insects should be considered to be still in diapause. In Mansingh's scheme the final phase of diapause is the termination phase which ensues as environmental conditions become favourable for development. In this phase the metabolic rate returns to normal, the endocrine system once more become active, body tissue again become capable of nucleic acid and protein synthesis, and any cryoprotectants present gradually disappear. As a result of these changes post-diapause development can begin.

In view of the varying degrees of severity of climatic conditions that insects in different geographic regions may encounter, it is perhaps not surprising to find that the intensity (duration and stability) of diapause varies. This variability, which is both interspecific and intraspecific, is manifest as a broad spectrum of dormancy that ranges from a state virtually indistinguishable from quiescence to one of great stability in which an insect can resist extremely unfavourable conditions. In each situation the strength of diapause is precisely adjusted through natural selection to provide an insect with adequate protection against the adverse conditions, yet to continue growth and reproduction as soon as amenable climate returns. Broadly speaking, insects from less extreme climates exhibit "weak" diapause (called oligopause by Mansingh, in which development may not be completely suppressed; the insects may continue to grow slowly (and even molt) and feed when conditions permit during the period of generally adverse climate. In weak diapause the induction phase is relatively short, since the biochemical adjustments which an insect makes in order to cope with the adverse conditions .are relatively simple. As a corollary of this, insects that overwinter in weak diapause are not, for example, very cold-tolerant. The refractory phase is short so that the activated phase is entered relatively soon after diapause has begun, and diapause is quickly terminated with environmental conditions return to normal. Conversely, in "strong" diapause, which is the rule in insects from severe climates, there is a lengthy induction phase, after which development is fully suppressed. The refractory phase usually lasts for several weeks or months, and the activation phase usually does not begin until diapause is more than half over. The termination phase is relatively slow, normally spanning 2 or 3 weeks after the return of suitable climatic conditions. Frequently insects which overwinter in strong diapause are very cold-hardy.

Diapause was formerly subdivided into facultative and obligate diapause. Facultative diapause described the environmentally controlled diapause of bivoltine and multivoltine species (having two or more generations per year) in which the members of certain generations had no diapause in their life history. Obligate diapause referred to the diapause found in univoltine species (those with one generation per year) in which every member of the species undergoes diapause. It was incorrectly assumed that in univoltine species diapause was not induced by environmental factors. Careful experimental work on a number of univoltine species has now revealed that in these species diapause is environmentally controlled. Further study may well demonstrate that this is always the case and render invalid the distinction between obligate and facultative diapause.

Induction and Termination

There are many factors influencing the diapause. *Photoperiod is* especially important in the induction of diapause, though ambient temperatures and diet during the preparatory and induction phases may influence the incidence (proportion of individuals entering diapause) and intensity of dormancy. As noted earlier, the refractory phase commonly requires that an insect be chilled for a certain length of time. For some species, however, exposure to long daylengths may supplement or replace the temperature treatment. Diapause is normally terminated spontaneously that is, as soon as temperatures return to reasonable levels after the activated phase has been entered, development continues. In some species, however, photoperiod or availability of moisture are important determinants in the onset of postdiapause development.

For the great majority of insects that exhibit a photoperiodically induced diapause it is the absolute daylength which is critical rather than daily changes in daylength. Most insects studied to date show a long-day response to photoperiod. That is, when reared under longday conditions, they show continuous development, whereas at short daylengths diapause is induced. Between these extremes is a critical daylength at which the incidence of diapause changes abruptly. Examples of insects that show a long-day response are the Colorado potato beetle, Leptinotarsa *decemlineata,* and the pink bollworm, *Pectinophora gossypiella*. In a number of species, including the silkworm, *Bombyx mori,* diapause is induced when the daylength is long, while at short daylengths development is continuous. Such insects are said to show a short day response. The European corn borer,

Ostrinia nubilalis, and the imported cabbage worm, *Pieris brassicae*, have a short-day-long-day response to photoperiod; that is, the incidence of diapause is low at short and long daylengths, but high at intermediate daylengths (14-16 hours of light per day). The ecological significance of such a response is unclear, since under natural conditions, insects would already be overwintering in diapause when the daylength was short. A few northern species of Lepidoptera behave in the opposite manner, namely, show a long-day-short-day response to photoperiod. All photoperiods except those with 16 to 20 hours of light per day, induce diapause. Again, however, the ecological value of such a response is uncertain.

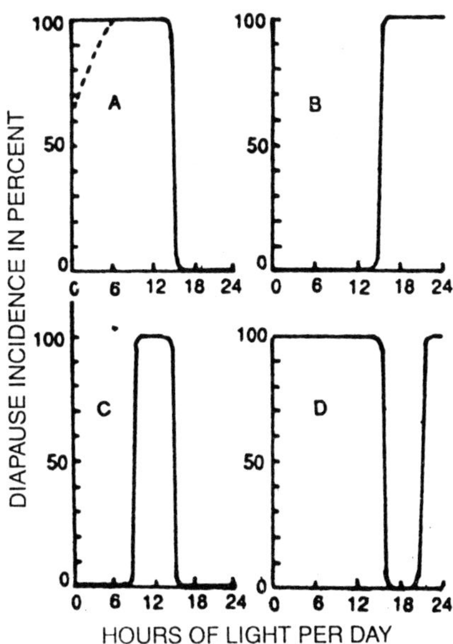

Fig. 2.5. Different types of diapause incidence-daylength relationships in iifsects. (A) Long-day, (B) short-day, (C) short-day-long-day, and (D) longday-short-day.

The precise value of the critical daylength for a species varies with latitude. For example, the sorrel dagger moth. *Acronycta rumicis*, is a long-day, insect which, near Leningrad (latitude about 60°N), has a critical daylength of about 19 hours. In more southerly populations the critical daylength is gradually reduced and is, for example, only 15 hours on the Black Sea cost (43°N). In the dragonfly, *Anax imperator*, and perhaps a few other insects, diapause is induced by daily changes in daylength rather than by absolute number of hours of light per day. *Anax* larvae that enter the final instar by the beginning of June are able to metamorphose the same year. Those which reach the final instar after this date enter diapause and do not emerge until the following spring. It seems that larvae are able' to determine the extent by which the daylength increases. When the daily increment is 2 minutes or more per day larvae can develop directly, whereas at smaller increments or decrease in daylength diapause is induced.

Temperature may profoundly modify or overrule the normal effect of photoperiod on diapause induction. For example, the critical photoperiod depends on the particular (constant) temperature at which insects are maintained: in *A. ntmicis* a 5°C difference in temperature results in a 1-hour difference in the critical daylength. At extreme values the effects of temperature may overcome those of photoperiod with reference to induction of diapause. In long-day insects exposure to constant high temperature may completely avert diapause induction regardless of photoperiod. Conversely, in shortday insects high temperature induces diapause, even under long-day conditions. In nature temperatures normally fluctuate daily about a mean value. This daily fluctuation (thermoperiod) also may modify the influence of photoperiod according to whether or not it is in phase with the light-dark cycle. For example, in *A. rumicis* the incidence of diapause was increased by low nighttime temperatures and *vice versa,* though at very long daylengths (18 hours or more) temperature had little effect. In most species studied diet influences of diapause only slightly or not at all. In *P. gossypiella,* for example, the incidence of diapause induction may be increased by feeding the larvae on cotton seeds whose water content is low and/or oil content high, provided that the daylength is not much greater than the critical value.

For most insects diapause termination is not under photoperiodic control but occurs, under natural conditions, when suitable temperatures for development return in spring. In a few species, however, exposure to appropriate photoperiods will terminate diapause. For example, in *H. cecropia* and *P. gossypiella* long day conditions terminate diapause. Conversely, in some *Limnephilus* species (Trichoptera), which in the adult stage have a summer diapause, diapause is ended by short daylengths.

In some species, especially those which overwinter in the egg stage or in a partially dehydrated condition, contact with liquid water is necessary for the initiation of postdiapause development. In diapausing larvae of O. *nubilalis,* for example, whose water content falls by midwinter to about 50% of the prediapause level, uptake of water (by drinking) is essential before the insect can continue -its development. *Lestes congener,* a damselfly found on the Canadian prairies, oviposits in late summer in dried ,out, dead stems of Scirpus (bulrush). The eggs begin to develop immediately but only to the end of anatrepsis and then enter diapause. Postdiapause development in the spring will not begin until the eggs are wetted, regardless of temperature. Wetting is achieved under natural conditions as the level of the water rises during snow melt and also as a result of wind action, which causes ice movements and subsequent breaking and submersion of the plant stems.

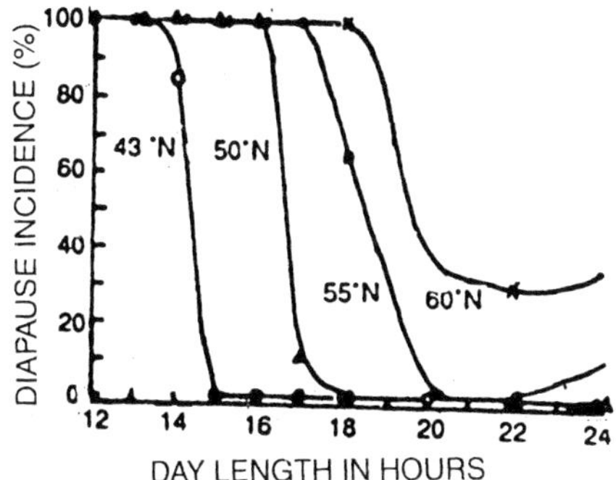

Fig. 2.6. Effect of photoperiod on diapause incidence in Acronycta nunicis *(Lepidoptera) populations from different northern latitudes.*

WATER

Water, is an important as a necessary and abundant constituents of protoplasm. The body of an organism is composed of about 70 percent of water by weight. It represents the most extensive into medium animal life. The division of the habitats and the amount of water present in the terrestrial environmental are based mainly important determinant of the respective environments. Water is an their distribution and abundance. Active organisms must retain within their body a certain proportion of water in order for metabolism to occur normally. Deviation from this proportion for any length of time results in injury or death.

Terrestrial Insects

For terrestrial organisms, the problem generally is to reduce water loss from the body, which occurs as a result of surface evaporation and during excretion of metabolic wastes. Surface evaporation is especially important in small organisms, including insects whose surface area is relatively large in relation to body volume. That insects have been able to solve this problem is one of the main reasons for their success as a terrestrial group. Not only do insects generally possess a highly impermeable cuticle and various devices for reducing water loss from the respiratory system, but they also have an efficient method of excretion, that is, one which uses a minimum of water. Such water loss as does occur is normally made up by drinking or from water in the food, though members of a few species from very dry habitats are able to take up water from moist air should the opportunity arise, or use water produced in metabolism.

The importance of water is not restricted to postembryonic stages; during embryogenesis, also, the correct proportion of water must be present within the egg. Again, the primary problem is to prevent water loss (unlike postembryonic stages of most species, eggs cannot move in search of water or into habitats where loss is reduced !). To facilitate this a female may oviposit in a moist medium and/or surround the eggs with protective material. In addition, the eggshell (chorion) is highly impermeable to water. As a result the egg is very resistant to desiccation and is frequently the stage in which periods of drought are overcome. Dormant stages, especially those in diapause, are sometimes able to withstand considerable water loss without damage, though the deficiency must be remedied before development can continue. As noted above, renewal of the normal water content may serve as the signal which initiates postdiapause development. The example of 0. *nubilalis* larvae has already been cited. Likewise, yellow woollybear caterpillars (*Diacrisia virginica*) enter diapause as mature larvae weighing about 600 mg. During diapause their weight falls to about 200 mg. mainly as a result of the loss of water. This loss must be made up in the spring before the larvae can pupate.

In view of the importance of water, it is not surprising to find that many terrestrial insects behave in a characteristic manner with respect to moisture in the surrounding air or substrate. The response may have immediate survival value for the individual concerned or may confer a long-term advantage on the individual and, ultimately, on the species. The ability to recognize and respond to slight differences in relative humidity enables an insect to move into a region of preferred humidity. Not only does this have immediate survival value, but because other individuals of the species will tend to respond similarly it may also increase the chances for perpetuation of the species. Some insects seek out sites with a preferred humidity, in which to enter diapause. Though this behaviour is of no immediate value to the insect, it increases the chances of survival of the dormant stage. Similarly, female grasshoppers about to oviposit dig "test holes" with their ovipositor to determine the moisture content (and probably other features) of the soil. Eggs are normally laid in moist soil, and a female may retain the eggs in the oviducts for some time if she does not immediately find a suitable site. Again, this behaviour has no immediate value to the female but certainly increases the eggs' chances of survival.

Thus far, the discussion has emphasized the harmful effects of too little water and the mechanisms by which terrestrial insects avoid this problem. On occasions, however, too much moisture may be equally detrimental to insects' survival. The effects of excessive moisture may be direct (viz., causing drowning) but more often are indirect. For example, insects that normally develop cold-hardiness partially as a result of dehydration maybe less cold-hard and therefore less capable of surviving low temperatures of winter if this has been preceded by a wet fall. Wet conditions may also affect a species' food supply. However, the most important way in which excessive moisture affects insect populations is by stimulating the development and spread of pathogenic microorganisms (bacteria, protozoa, fungi and viruses). For example, a long back in the summer in Saskatchewan (Canada) the weather was abnormally humid, with above average rainfall in some areas of the province. These conditions appeared ideal for the fungus *Entomophthora grylli,* which underwent a widespread epizootic, causing high mortality in populations of several species of grasshoppers, especially *Camnula pellucida,* the clear-winged grasshopper, and to a lesser extent *Melanoplus bivittatus* (two-striped grasshopper) *and M. packardii* (Packard's grasshopper). Such was the effect of the fungus on *C. pellucida* that by the fall of 1963 its proportion in the grasshopper species complex had fallen to 7% compared with 64% the previous year.

Finally, the beneficial effects of snow on the survival of insects must be noted. Snow is an excellent insulator and in extremely cold climates serves to reduce considerably the rate of heat loss from the substrate. Thus, the substrate remains considerably warmer than the air above the snow. For example, with an air temperature of –30°C and a snow depth of 10 cm, the temperature of soil about 3 cm below its surface is about –9°C. In the absence of snow the soil temperature at this depth is only a degree or two higher than that of the air. This means that species with only limited cold-hardiness may be able to survive the winter in cold climates provided that there is ample snow cover. In other words, because of snow a species may be able to extend its, geographical range into areas with low winter temperatures. In Saskatchewan, for example, the damselflies *Lestes disjunctus* and *L. unguiculatus* overwinter as eggs (in diapause) laid in emergent stems of *Scirpus*. The eggs can tolerate exposure to temperatures as low as –20°C and remain viable. Below this temperature mortality increases significantly. At Saskatoon, where this study was carried out, the mean temperature for January is, however, about –22°C, though the temperature frequently falls well below this value (the record low being about –48°C !). Field collection of eggs throughout the winter showed that, whereas the viability of eggs from beneath the snow remained near 100%, no eggs collected from exposed stems survived. Thus, the insulating effect of snow is essential to the survival of these species in this region of Canada. In addition, the snow cover may also prevent desiccation.

Aquatic Insects

The most important features of the surrounding medium that affects the distribution and abundance of aquatic insects appear to be its temperature, oxygen content, ionic content, and rate of flow. The ability of insects to regulate both the total ionic concentration and the level of individual ions in the hemolymph is a major determi- nant of their distribution. Typical freshwater insects are restricted to waters of low ionic content because, although they are capable of excreting excess water that enters their body osmotically, they have no mechanism for removing excess ions which enter the body when the insect is in a saline medium; that is, they cannot produce a hyperosmotic urine. Further, members of some species may be unable to colonize some freshwater habitats because these contain certain ions such as Mg^{2+} and Ca^{2+} in too high a concentration.

In contrast, members of many species that normally inhabit saline environments appear to be able to regulate their hemolymph osmotic pressure and ionic content over a wide range of external salt concentrations. In other words, they can produce hyperosmotic urine when it is necessary, in a saline medium, to excrete excess ions, or hypoosmotic urine, when in freshwater when excess water must be removed from the body. As they are normally found only in saline habitats, it must be assumed that their distribution is governed by other environmental factors. The insect fauna of an aquatic habitat may vary with the speed at which the water is moving. Insects in still or slowly moving water are not prevented from moving, for example, in search of food or to the surface for gaseous exchange. In contrast, rhephilic insects (those that live in swiftly moving streams or rivers) have of necessity evolved structural, behavioural, and physiological adaptations to survive in these habitats. Among the' structural adaptations which may be found in rheophilic insects are flattening or streamlining of the body, and the development of friction discs or hydraulic suckers. Flattening may take on differing significance among species, though ultimately its function is to enable insects to avoid being washed downstream by the current. In members of some species, which live on exposed surfaces, flattening enables them to remain within the so-called "boundary layer," a thin layer of almost static water covering the substrate. For members of most species flattening is associated with their cryptic habit, permitting them to live under stones, in cracks, crevices, etc. Streamlining, too, is a modification mainly used by insects to avoid currents by burrowing into the substrate, though members of a few streamlined species, for example, most species of *Baetis* and Centroptilum (mayflies), do live on exposed surfaces and are able to swim against quite strong currents.

The major physiological adaptation of rheophilic species is related to gaseous exchange. Because of the danger of being washed downstream, insects in moving water cannot come to the surface to obtain oxygen; they rely on oxygen dissolved in the medium. Through evolution, members of rheophilic species have become adapted to a medium with a high oxygen content and conduct most or all gaseous exchange directly across the body wall. Further, they depend on the water current to renew the oxygen supply at their body surface. As a result, in many species, gills, if present, are reduced, and the ability to ventrilate, by flapping the gills or undulating the abdomen, has been lost. Their relative inability to move because of the current has, been paralleled, in many rhephilic insects, by the evolution of devices which enable them to obtain food passively; that is, they depend on the current bringing food (especially microorganisms and detritus) to them. These devices include the nets built by many trichopteran larvae, fringes of hairs on the forelegs and/or mandibles of some larval Plecoptera, the fans on the premandibles of blackfly larvae, and the sticky strings of saliva produced by the chironomid *Rheotanytarsus*.

An important factor in the distribution of aquatic insects, and one which is related to the extent of water movement, is the substratum. Members of many species of stream insects are characteristically associated with particular types of substratum. For some insects the significance of this association is easily understood. For example, water pennies [larvae of Psephenidae (Coleopteral)], found in fast-moving waters, require largish rocks to which they can become attached. Similarly, larval Blepharoceridae (Diptera) need smooth rocks, not covered with silt or algal growth, to which to attach their suckers. And some Leuctridae (Plecoptera) require gravel of the correct texture in which to burrow.

WIND

Because of their weight and relatively large surface area/volume ratio, insects may be profoundly affected by wind. By altering the rate of evaporation of water from the body surface wind may be important in the water relations of-the insect. Flight activity (whether or not flight occurs, the direction of movement and the distance traveled) is also directly related to the strength and direction of the wind. Wind action may also exert indirect effects on insect, for example, by causing erosion of soil or snow so that the insects (or their eggs) are exposed to predators, extremes of temperature, or desiccation. Through its effect on the flight activity of winged insects and because insects by virtue of their weight are easily transported on wind currents, wind is an important factor in dispersal, the movement away from a crowded habitat so that scattering of a population results. Though a good deal of insect dispersal is of no benefit, for some species the dispersal is adaptive, that is, confers a long-term advantage on the species by transferring some adult members to new breeding sites. Because of its advantageous nature, physiological, structural, and behavioural features which facilitate adaptive dispersal (= migration) will become fixed in a population through natural selection.

Migration

Johnson describes migration as "essentially a transference of adults of a new generation from one breeding habitat to others." In many species migration begins shortly after the molt to the adult and mass migrations are frequently preceded by highly synchronized adult emergence. In a sense, therefore, migration forms part of a species' development just as do mating and oviposition.

The form of migration varies widely among species. Some of the variables are the proportion of the population which migrates, whether migration occurs in every generation or only in certain generations, the distance travelled, and the nature of the migratory movements (wind-dependent or wind-independent, feeding en route or proceeding directly). For example, the swarming flights of social insects, such as ants and termites, involve only a fraction of a colony's population, may be completed in a matter of minutes, and may take the migrating individuals Only a few yards from the original colony. In contrast, the migrations of locusts are undertaken by all members of a population and may cover several thousand miles. The migrations extend over a number of weeks and are interspersed with short periods of feeding activity. Johnson suggests that all forms of migration may be arranged in three major categories, though there is gradation both within and between each of them. In the first category are included species which, as adults, migrate from the emergence site a new breeding site where they oviposit, then die. Johnson included to in this group species such as the housefly, all of whose members, at *emergence,* leave the old habitat and disperse randomly. After a period of maturation, they seek out new breeding sites. The of also contains species which seasonally produce P P flying migratory individuals, for example, aphids, termites and ants. Migrations are largely wind-dependent and may occur in every direction from the emergence site. The migration time and distance are usually short, and once individuals reach a suitable breeding site, th y remain there for the rest of their lives. Indeed, on reaching such a site some species characteristically shed their wings.

Also placed in the first category, but having migrations which are of a much grander scale, are the migratory locusts. Desert locusts, *Schistocerca gregaria*, for example, may travel thousands of miles as they move from one breeding area to another as each becomes unsuitable because of drought. Like those of aphids, etc., the migrations of desert locusts are wind-dependent. Because they inhabit fairly dry regions, breeding in the desert locust is synchronized with the arrival of a rainly season. As rain comes to different parts of the inhabited area at different times of the year, adults migrate in order to continue breeding activity. It is the winds on which locusts migrate that also bring rain to the new areas. During spring breeding occurs in north and northwest Africa (in conjunction with rain in the Mediterranean region), in the Middle East across to Pakistan, and to the south in East Africa. In the latter regions, local seasonal rains occur at this time. As northern Africa and the Middle East become dry in early summer, locusts migrate southward on prevailing winds to an area which runs across Africa, from east to west, lying just south of the Sahara desert, then northward across southern Arabia and into Pakistan. This area is closely associates with the Inter-Tropical Convergence Zone (ITCZ), where hot, northbound air from the equatorial region meets cooler air flowing south. The mixing of these air masses within the ITCZ results in the production of rain and a reduction of wind speed so that the locusts again become earthbound. Locusts from East Africa, south of the ITCZ, move north and east on prevailing winds to be deposited in southern Arabia and India. These summer migrations may take locust swarms several hundred or even thousands of miles in a relatively short time. In contrast, the fall and winter movements which bring locusts to their spring breeding sites generally consist of a number of shorter migrations made over a longer period of time, mainly because the air temperatures at this time of the year are only intermittently suitable for migration. The north- ward migration results largely from cyclonic weather disturbances that move eastward across Africa every few days. These disturbances bring with them warm southerly winds on which locusts may be carried. As the winds push northward they mix with cooler air, which results in rainfall and temporary cessation of migration. Successive waves of warm air gradually bring the locusts to their spring habitat. The above summary of the annual movements of locusts is of necessity extremely simplified. Nevertheless, it shows how migration, based on wind currents, has evolved as an integral part of locusts' life history to facilitate year-round breeding activity through the exploitation of temporarily suitable habitats.

Finally, category one includes some species (mainly Lepidoptera) whose migrations are independent of wind currents. That is, the insects do not rely on wind to make the migrations, though their movements are undoubtedly influenced by wind speed and direction. An important difference, therefore, between these "active" migrations and the "passive" movements of the form described, say, for locusts, is that, in the former, insects must have *a "sense of direction."* In other words, they must be able to orient themselves with reference to environmental cues, especially the sun. Because the sun's position changes through the day the insects must also have a sense of time so that they may make corrections to account for this change (the light compass reaction). A much-studied example of a species that migrates under its own power is the great southern white butterfly *Ascia monuste* (Pieridae), whose migrations up and down the Florida coastline are well-known. In Florida the species breeds Year round but not in all localities simultaneously. Periodically populations comprising immature females and males of all ages make migratory flights over distances up to 100 miles or more to new areas where *Bans maritima* (maritime salt wort), the primary host plant, is abundant. In contrast to the situation in locust migration, it is not the arrival of adverse conditions that stimulates migration in *A. monuste*. The migrations occur from areas where food and oviposition sites are still abundant. Though the sun has been suggested as a reference point by which the butterflies orient themselves during flight, local cues are also important. For example, the insects may closely follow the shoreline, roads railway tracks, or telephone lines.

In his second category Johnson includes species whose migration is in two parts, an emigration to feeding sites where sexual maturation occurs. followed by a return flight to the original (or a similar) site of emergence where the insects oviposit. Many Odonata, for example, do not remain in the area of the pond from which is other emerge but migrate to nearby wood or hedgerows to prey on other insects until mature. They then return to water, mate, and lay eggs. Some species regularly return to the feeding also have a two-part migration, first to find a host on which to feed and latter to locate an egg-laying site. In some cases, the initial part of the migration is considerably longer than the second. Like that of Odonata, at migratory flight of some mosquitoes is wind-independent.For most migratory species, however, wind determines distance travelled.

The third category includes species which again have a two-part migration. The initial migratory flight takes the species to suitable hibernating or aestivating sites where they enter diapause, after which they return to the region in which they emerged and reproduce. Within this type of migration three subcategories can be recognized. In the first, the sites of diapause are within the general breeding area of the species. Species which adopt this arrangement include the Colorado potato beetle. *Leptinotarsa decemlineata,* and the corn thrips, *Limothrips cerealium.*

Belonging to the second subcategory are species that migrate to a climatically different region prior to diapause. Especially common is migration between warmer lowland areas where the insects have emerged and mountainous regions, either to avoid summer heat or to overwinter. Such migrations are seen in various noctuid moths, for example, the army cutworm, *Euxon auxiliaries,* in Montana, which moves southwest to the Rocky Mountains, and in some coccinellid beetles, such as the convergent lady beetle *Hippodamia convergence,* in northern California. Adult beetles first appear in early May and soon most, migrate, using prevailing winds, to mountain canyons in the Sierra Nevada range where they aggregate under stones, litter,

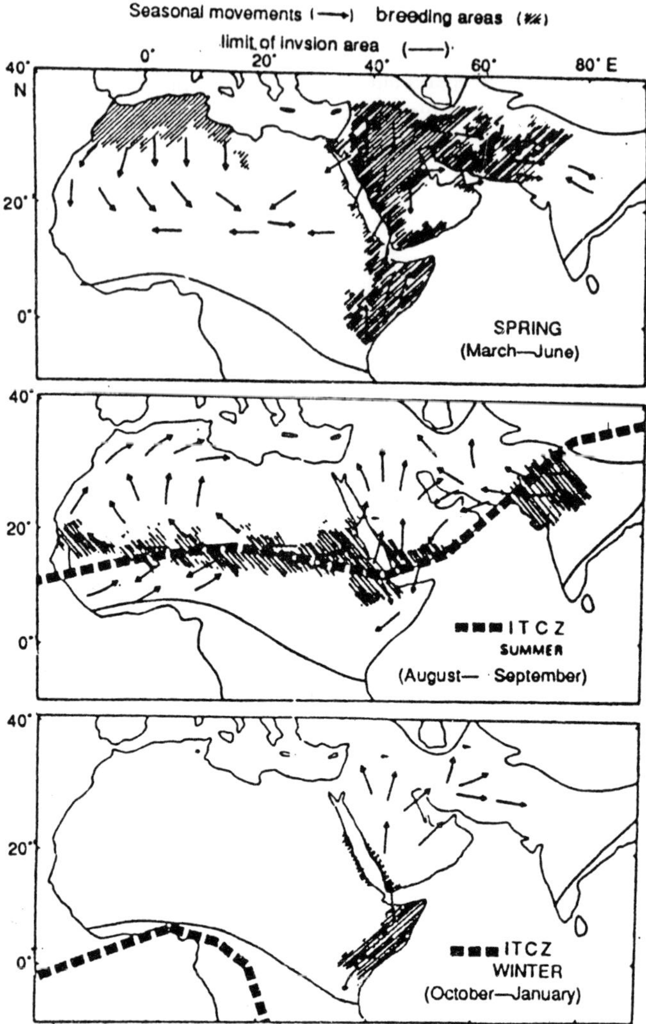

Fig. 2.7. Major movements of swarms of Schistocerca gregaria from spring, summer, and winter breeding areas, in relation to the position of the Inter-Tropical Convergence Zone (ITCZ).

etc., and enter diapause. Diapause lasts for about 9 months, and the following February and March adults, again windborne, return to the valleys where a new generation is produced. Breeding activity is thus closely correlated with mass emergence of spring-breeding aphids. (Interestingly, as a result of Man's agricultural activities, aphids are.

now available on a year-round basis, and some populations of H. *convergence* no longer migrate but through the summer produce several generations of progeny, the last one of which overwinters in diapause at the breeding site).

Migrations included in the third subcategory differ from those of the second subcategory only in terms of the distance covered, especially during prediapause movements. The classic example of a species in this group is the monarch butterfly, *Danaus plexippus,* some populations of which spend early summer in southern Canada, then migrate southward during August to October to overwintering sites in southern United States. Mark and recapture experiments have demonstrated that the butterflies may travel upward of 2000 miles at average speeds of about 20 miles per day. Since on certain days the butterflies may not migrate because of poor weather conditions, the distances travelled on suitable days may be considerably in excess of the average value. Females which migrate south are sexually immature and remain in reproductive diapause until about the end of February when oogenesis begins and butterflies begin to move slowly northward. However, there is some dispute as to whether overwintering insects make the return journey to their original habitat. Some authors believe this to be the case, whereas others believe that the northward migration occurs in a series of shorter steps, each made by successive generations. The latter arrangement would place *D. plexippus* in the same category as the migratory locusts. Like those of locusts the migrations (southward and northward) depend very largely on wind currents.

As the above examples demonstrate, migration can take on many forms among different species, yet its common purpose is to improve a species' ability to survive and multiply. For most species, wind supplies the power for migration, and their physiology and behaviour have so evolved as to make best use of this.

CONCLUDING REMARKS

The distribution and abundance of insects are markedly affected by temperature, photoperiod, water and wind. As poikilotherms, insects have a metabolic rate that within species- and stage-specific limits is proportional to temperature. Their rate of development within these limits is inversely proportional to temperature. Outside these limits insects will survive, but their development is retarded or prevented. The temperature extremes for survival are known as the upper and lower lethal limits. Survival at extreme ambient temperatures may be accomplished by (1) behavioural means, such as burrowing or ovipositing in substrate; and/or (2) entering a physiologically dormant condition (diapause). At below-freezing temperatures insects may also become freezing- tolerant, that is, capable of withstanding freezing of their extracellular fluids, or, when they are freezing susceptible, become supercooled. In both arrangements, polyhydroxyl cryoprotectants such as glycerol, sorbitol, and trehalose are important. In species from habitats whose climate is suitable of development and/or reproduction for a limited period each year, temperature may be an important synxhronizer of development and/or eclosion.

Photoperiod, the naturally occurring 24-hour cycle of light and darkness, exerts both short-term and long-term effects on behaviour and physiology which keep insects in tune with changing environmental conditions. In a few species daily activity are triggered by changing light intensity, that is, are of exogenous origin. However, in most species, diurnal rhythms of activity, for example, iocomotor activity, feeding, mating behaviour, oviposition, and edosion, originate endogenously and are phase set by photoperiod. By responding to seasonal changes in photoperiod insects can exploit suitable environmental conditions for development and reproduction and survive periods when climatic conditions are adverse. Among the long-term processes affected by photoperiod are the nature and rate of development, reproductive ability and capacity, synchronized eclosion, diapause, and possibly cold-hardiness.

Diapause is a genetically determined state of suppressed development. It may occur at any stage of the life history, though this is usually species-specific. Photoperiod exerts its influence at a stage earlier than the one in which diapause occurs. In this way insects are able to anticipate the onset of adverse conditions. Induction of diapause is, in almost all species, a response to the absolute daylength (number of hours of light in a 24-hour cycle) rather than daily differences in the daylength. For a species, there is a critical daylength at which the incidence of diapause (proportion of individuals that enter diapause) changes markedly, Long-day insects develop continuously at all daylengths above the critical daylength (usually about 16 hours of light per day) but enter diapause at shorter daylengths. In short-day insects, development is continuous at daylengths below the critical value (usually about 12 hours). In short-day-long-day insects, development is continuous at short and long daylengths, but at intermediate daylengths (about 14-16 hours of light per day) the incidence of diapause is high. Long-day-short-day insects develop continuously within a narrow range of daylengths (16-20 hours light per day) and enter diapause at all other daylengths. The value of the critical daylength for a species may change with temperature and latitude.

Water is an important determinant of the distribution and abundance of insects. A problem for most terrestrial species is to reduce water loss from the integument and tracheal system and in excretion. In postembryonic stages this is achieved by means of a relatively impermeable cuticle, valves and/or hairs that reduce water vapour movement out of the tracheae, production of highly concentrated urine, as well as by active selection of more humid microclimates. Eggs are covered with a cuticlelike chorion and may be laid in an ootheca and/or substrate. For some species in cold climates snow covcr may be important as an insulator and in preventing desiccation.

3

BIOTIC FACTORS

In nature the presence of other organisms of different species is an unavoidable and also a necessary part of the environment. The existence of other species may be crucially important in the provision of food, shelter, or some other necessity. Various kinds of animals and plants are undesirable neighbours and influence each other's life and also modify the environmental factors. The factors which depend directly on the action of the living organisms or the vegetation are called the *biotic factors*. As most insects eat living organisms, food is probably the most obvious and important biotic factor. However, other interactions are known which, though not as easily recognized as feeding, are nonetheless important regulators of insect distribution and abundance.

FOOD

Quantitative Aspects

Though the amount of food available might be considered as an important regulator of insect abundance, it has been found in natural communities that populations do not normally use more than a small fraction of the total available food. This is primarily because other components of the environment, especially weather but including, for example, predators, parasites, or pathogens, usually have a significant adverse effect on growth and reproduction. Other features of insects may, however, be important in this regard. Many species, especially plant feeders, are polyphagous. Thus, when the preferred food plant is in limited quantity, alternate choices can be used. Among endopterygotes, larvae and adults of a species may eat quite different kinds of food, and in some species such as mosquitoes the food of the adult female differs from that of the adult male.

Two situations may occur in which the quantity of food limits insect distribution and abundance. In the first, there is no absolute shortage of food, but only a proportion of the total is available to a species. Thus, there is said to be a "relative shortage" of food. Various reasons may account for the food not being available. (1) The food may be concentrated within a small area so that it is available to relatively few insects. As an interesting example of this Andrewartha cites the Shinyanga Game-Extermination Experiment in East Africa in which, over the course of about 5 years, the natural hosts of tsetse flies were virtually exterminated over an area of about 800 square miles. At the end of this period one small -elephant herd and various small ungulates remained in the game reserve. However, almost no tsetse flies could be found, despite the fact that. collectively, the mammals which remained could supply enough blood to feed the entire original population of flies. The distribution of the food was now so sparse that the chance of flies obtaining a meal was practically nil. (2) The food may be randomly distributed but difficult to locate. Thus, only a fraction of the individuals searching ever find food. Such is probably the situation in many parasitic or hyperparasitic species whose host is buried within the tissues of plants or other animals. (3) A proportion of the food may occur in areas which for other reasons are not normally visited by the consumer so that, in effect, it is not available.

In the second situation, food may become a limiting factor in population growth when a species' numbers are not kept in check by other influences, especially natural enemies. This may happen, for example, when a species is accidentally transferred (often as a result of Man's activity) from its original environment to a new geographic area where its natural enemies are absent. Under these conditions, the population may grow unchecked, and its final size is limited only by the amount of food available. Occasionally, even in a species' natural habitat, food may limit population growth, when weather conditions are favourable for development of a species but not for development of those organisms which prey on or parasitize it.

The nature of the food available may have striking effects on the survival, rate of growth, and reproduction potential of a species, and much work has been done on insects in this regard. For example, of the insect fauna associated with stored products, the sawtoothed grain beetle, *Oryzaephilus surinainensis,* can survive only on foods with a high carbohydrate content such as flour, bran, and dried fruit, whereas species of spider beetles, *Ptinus* spp., and flour beetles, *Tribolium* spp., have no such carbohydrate requirement and are consequently cosmopolitan, occurring in animal meals and dried yeast, in addition to plant products. For some phytophagous insects, a combination of plants of different kinds appears necessary for survival and/or normal rates of juvenile development. In the migratory grasshopper, *Melanoplus sanguinipes,* for example, a smaller percentage of insects survive from hatching to adulthood, and the development of those that do survive is slower when the grasshoppers are fed on wheat (*Triticum aestivum*) alone compared with wheat plus flixweed (*Descurainia sophia*) or dandelion (*Taraxacum officinale*).

Both the rate of egg production and number of eggs, produced may be markedly affected by the nature of the food available. Many common flies, for example, species of *Musca, Calliphora* and *Lucilia,* may survive as adults for sometime on a diet of carbohydrate. However, for females to mature eggs a source of protein is essential. Pickford showed that *M. sanguinipes* females fed a diet which included wheat and wild mustard (*Brassica kaber*) or wheat and flixweed produced far more eggs (579 and 467 eggs per female, respectively) than females fed on wheat (243 eggs/), wild mustard (431 eggs/), or flixweed (249/), alone. These differences in egg production resulted largely from variations in the duration of adult life, though differences in rate of egg production were also evident. For example, per cent survival of females fed wheat plus mustard after 1, 2 and 3 months was 93, 60 and 13% respectively. These females Produced, on average, 8.4 eggs/ female-day. The corresponding figures for females fed on wheat alone were (1) survival; 87, 27 and 0% over 1, 2 and 3 months, respectively; and (2) rate of egg production; 4.6 eggs/female-day. The metabolic basis for these differences was not determined.

Between Insects and Plants

Deserving of special in a discussion of insects and their food are the relationships which have evolved between insects and higher plants. As might be anticipated in view of the length of time over which they have evolved, some of these relationships are extremely intimate and refined though essentially the relationships have a common theme. Insects gain energy (food) at the expense of plants, whereas plants attempt to defend themselves (conserve their energy) or at least to obtain something in return for the energy which insects take from them. Though the theme remains constant through time, the relationships themselves are always changing as a result of natural selection. Insects strive to improve their energy-gathering efficiency (most often by concentrating on energy in a particular form and from a restricted source and by specialization of the method used to collect the energy) while plants concurrently improve their defenses. There is, as Price puts it, "constant warfare" between the two opponents, and this forms the basis of their coevolution.

The most common method used by plants as defecse against insects (and othe herbivourous animals) is produciton of toxic metabolities. It is possible that orignally some of these metabolites were simply short-lived intermediates in normal biochemical pathways within plants and/or provided a means of storing chemical energyu for later use by the plant. In other words, the original function(s) of these compounds may have been unrelated to the occurrence of herbivores. An example of such a compound might be nicotine produced by the tobacco plant (*Nicotiana* spp;) Raddioisotope studies have shown that, although about 12% of the energy trapped in photosyntheses is used for nicotine production, the nicotine has a relatively short half-life, 40% of it being converted to other metabolites (possibly sugars, amino acids, and organic acids) within 10 hours.

Another possibility is that the chemicals arose as by plant's primary metabolism, and the plant, being unable to excrete the molecules, simply retained them within its tissue. Regardless of the origin and earlier function(s) of these chemicals, animals that fed upon the plants which produced them would create strong selection pressure for the production of greatersu antmight ba chemical or more toxic derivatives of it. This pressure might be especially great on longer-lived plants. Selection would also favour production of greater quantities of a chemical or more toxic derivatives in the reproductive parts of plants, as these parts represent concentrated stores of energy and are therefore especially attractive to herbivores. Price cites several examples in support of this proposal, including *Hypericum perforatum* (Klamath weed), which, like other members of the genus, produces the toxicant hypericin. The concentration of the toxicant is 30 *ug/g* wet weight in the lower stem, 70pg/g in the upper stem and 500,ug/g in the flower.

Thus animals that become adapted to feeding on plants that produce toxins will be at a considerable advantage over animals which do not. Among herbivores, insects show the greatest ability to cope with the toxins. In part, this arises from the enormous period of time over which coevolution of insects and plants has occurred, but it is also due to insects' high reproductive rate and short generation time which facilitate rapid adaptation to changes that occur in the host plant. Through evolution, many insect species have not only developed increasing tolerance to a host plant's toxins but are now attracted by them. In other words, insects locate food plants by the scent or taste of their toxic substance and frequently are restricted to feeding on such plants. For example, certain species of flea beetles, *Phyllotreta* spp., and cabbageworms, *Pieris spp.,* feed exclusively on plants such as Cruciferae that produce mustard oils. Colorado potato beetles, *Leptinotarsa decemlineata* and various hornworms, *Manduca* spp., feed only on Solanaceae, the family that includes potato (*Solanum tuberosum*) (produces solanine), tobacco (*Nicotiana spp.*) (nicotine), and deadly nightshade (*Atropa belladonna*) (atropine).

The method most often used to overcome the potentially harmful effects of these chemicals is to convert them into nontoxic or less toxic products. Especially important in such conversions is a group of enzymes known as mixed function oxidases which, as their name indicates, catalyze a variety of oxidation reactions. The enzymes are located in the microsome fraction of cells and occur in particularly high concentrations in fat body and midgut. (Interestingly, it is these same enzymes that are largely responsible for the resistance of insects to man-made insecticides.) Some insects are able to feed on potentially dangerous plants as result of either temporal or spatial avoidance of the toxic materials. For example, the life history of the winter moth, *Operophtera brumata* is such that the caterpillars hatch in the early spring and feed on young leaves of oak (*Quercus* spp.) which lack the highly toxic tannin. Though, later in the season, weather conditions are suitable and food is still apparently plentiful, a second generation of winter moths does not develop because by this time large quantities of tannin are present in the leaves. Spatial avoidance is possible for many Hemiptera whose delicate suctorial mouthparts can bypass localized concentrations of toxin in the host plant. Some aphids feed on senescent foliage where active concentration on of toxin is less than that of younger, metabolically active tissue.

Price proposes that at least four advantages may accrue to an insect able to feed on potentially toxic plants. First, competition with other herbivores for food will be much reduced. Second, the food plant can be located easily. Related to this, as members of a species will tend to aggregate on or near the food plant, the chances of finding a mate will be increased. Third, if an insect can store within its tissues the toxin ingested as it feeds, it may gain protection from would-be predators. This appears to be the situation with most of the insect fauna associated with plants of the family Asclepiadaceae (milkweeds), many of which produce cardiac glycosides, substances that at sublethal levels, induce vomiting in vertebrates. Most insect species that feed on milkweed are aposematically (brightly and distinctiy) coloured, a feature commonly indicative of a distasteful organism and one which makes them stand out against the background of their host plant. On sampling such insects, a would-be vertebrate predator discovers their unpalatability and quickly learns to avoid insects having a particular colour pattern. Interestingly, a few insect predators have evolved tolerance to the plant-produced toxins stored by their insect prey and are, themselves, unpalatable to predators further up the food chain! The fourth advantage to be gained by tote microorganisms. these plant products is protection against pathogenic example, the cardiac glycosides present in the hemolymph of the large milkweed bug, *Oncopeltus fasciatus,* have a strong antibacterial effect.

The channeling of energy into production of toxic or at least repellent substances is the most often used method by which plants may obtain protection, though others are known. A few plants expend this "energy of protection" on formation of structures which preyon or deer feeding, or even harm would-be feeders. For example, passion flower plants (*Passiflora adenopoda*) have minute hooked hairs that grip the integument of caterpillars which attempt to feed on them. The hairs both impede movement and tear the integument as the caterpillars struggle to free themselves so that the insects die from starvation and/or desiccation. Leguminous plants have evolved a variety of physical (as well as chemical) mechanisms to protect their seeds from Bruchidae (pea and bean weevils). These include production of gum as a larva penetrates the seed pod so that the insect is drowned or its movements hindered, production of a flakey pod surface which shed, carrying the a weevil's eggs with it, as the pod breaks open to expose its seeds, and production of pods which open "explosively" so that seeds are immediately dispersed and, therefore, not available to females which oviposit directly on seeds.

In a curious evolutionary twist, some plants use insects to gain protection from herbivores, in return for which they provide the insects with food and shelter. A well-known example of such a mutualistic relationship is that which has evolved between the bull's-horn acacias (*Acacia spp.*) and ants, *Pseudomyrmex spp.* The aggressive ants guard the plant against herbivores, while the plant produces nectar (in petioles) and protein (in special "Beltian bodies" formed at the tips of new leaves) on which the ants feed. A mutualistic relationship of a very different kind is that in which the plants supply food to insects usually in the form of nectar andpollen, and, in return, insects provide the transport system necessary for effective cross-pollination. The success (importance) of insects as pollinators compared with pollinators from other group such as birds and bats is presumably a result of their much longer evolutionary association with plants. Most of the modern insect orders were well established by the time the earliest flowering plants appeared about 225 million years ago. Thus, insects were able to gain a considerable head start as pollinators over birds and bats, the earliest fossil records for which date back about 150 and 60 million years, respectively.

To achieve effective cross-pollination, two important factors must be taken into consideration in an evolutionary sense. First, plants must produce precisely the right amount of nectar to make an insect's visit energetically worthwhile, yet stimulate visits to other plants, and second, plants of the same species must be easily recognized by an insect. If too much energy is made available by each plant, then insects need visit fewer plants and the extent of cross-pollination is reduced. If a plant produces too little food (to ensure that an insect will visit many plants) there is a risk that the insect will seek more accessible sources of food. Natural selection determines the precise amount of energy which each plant must offer to an insect, and this amount depends on a number of factors. The amount of energy gained by an insect during each visit to a flower is related to both quantity and quality of available food. Thus, until recently, it was considered that many adult insects obtained their.carbohydrate requirements from nectar and their protein requirements from other sources such as pollen, vegetative parts of the plant (as a result of larval feeding), or other animals. Baker and Baker have shown, however, that the nectar of many plants contains significant amounts of amino acids, so that insects can concentrate their efforts on nectar collection. This not only increases the extent of cross-pollination by inducing more visits to flowers, but it may also lead to economy in pollen production, since pollen becomes less important as food for the insects. The amount of nectar produced is a function of the number of flowers per plant. Thus, it is important for plants which have a number of flowers blooming synchronously that each flower produces only a small amount of nectar and pollen, so that an insect must visit other plants to satisfy its requirements.

More nectar is produced by plant species whose members typically grow some distance apart, so that it is still energetically worthwhile for an insect species to concentrate on these plants. Related to this is the fact that the insects which forage over greater distances are larger species such as bees, moths, and butterflies whose energy requirements are high. When nectar is produced in large amounts, it is typically accessible only to larger insects which are strong enough to gain entry into the nectar- producing area or have sufficiently elongate mouthparts. This ensures that nectar is not wasted on smaller insects who lack the ability to carry pollen to other members of the plant species. Temperature also affects the amount of nectar produced, as it is related to the energy expended by insects in flight and to the time of day and/ or season. For example, in temperate regions and/or at high altitudes, flowers which bloom early in the day or at night, or early or late in the season, when temperatures may not be much above freezing, must provide a large enough reward as to make foraging profitable at these temperatures. An alternative to production of large amounts of nectar by individual flowers, is for plants which bloom at lower temperature to grow in high density and flower synchronously. Beyond a certain distance between plants, however, the amount of nectar which an insect requires to collect at each plant (in order to remain "interested" in that species) exceeds the maximum amount that the plant is able to produce. Thus, the plant must adopt a different strategy. Among orchids, for example, about on half of the species produce no nectar but rely on other methods to attract insects. Especially deception by mimicry. The flowers may resemble (1) other nectar-producing flowers, (2) female insects so that males are attracted and attempt pseudocopulation, (3) hosts of insect parasitoids, or (4) insects which are subsequently attacked by other territorial insects. These somewhat risky methods of attracting insects are offset by the evolution of highly specific pollen receptors (so that only pollen from the correct species is acquired) and a high degree of seed set for each pollination.

It is important for both plants and insects that insects visit members of the same plant species. The chances of this occurring are greatly increased (1) when the plant species has a restricted period of bloom, in terms of both season and/or time of day; (2) where members of a species grow in aggregations, though this is counterbalanced by a restriction of gene glow if pollinators work within a particular plant population; and (3) when the flowers are easily recognized by an insect which learns to associate a given plant species with food.

Recognition is achieved as a result of flower morphology (and related to this is accessibility of the nectar and pollen), colour, and scent. The advantage to an insect species when its members can recognize particular flowers is that, through natural selection, the species will become more efficient at gathering and utilizing the food produced by those flowers. The degree of influence that these variables exert is manifest as a spectrum of intimacy between plants and their insect pollinators. At one end of the spectrum, the plant-insect relationship is non-specific; that is, a variety of insect species serve as pollinators for a variety of plants. Neither insects nor flowers are especially modified structurally or physiologically. At the opposite extreme, the relationship is such that a plant species is pollinated by a single insect species. Flower morphology is precisely complemented by structural features of the pollinator; the plant's blooming period is synchronized with the life history and diurnal activity of the insect; and, where present, nectar is produced in exactly the right quantity and quality to satisfy the insect's requirements.

INTERACTION BETWEEN INSECTS AND OTHER ANIMALS

Interactions between insects and other animals ; (including other members of the same species) take many forms, though most are food-related. Insects may be predators (which require more than one prey individual in order to complete development), parasitoids or parasites (which need only one host to complete development). Parasitoids differ from parasites in that they ultimately kill their "host" which is typically another arthropod. Alternatively, insects may serve as prey or host for other animals. In a third form of interaction, insects may complete either with other members of the species or with other animals for the same resource, for example, food, breeding or egglaying sites. Overwintering sites, or resting sites. Between opposite sexes of the same species, the interaction may be for a very obvious purpose, propagation of the species.

Intraspecific Interactions

The nature and number of interactions among members of the same species will depend on the density of the population. These interactions may be either beneficial or harmful. It follows that there will be an optimal range of density for a given population, within which the net effect of these interactions will be most beneficial. Outside this range of density, that is, when there is underpopulation or overpopulation (crowding), the net result of these interactions will be less than optimal for perpretuation of the species. Interestingly, animals have involved various regulatory mechanisms which serve either to maintain this optimal density or to alter the existing density so as to bring it within the optimal range. In the discussion which follows we shall see how these mechanisms operate in some insects.

Underpopulation

Probably the most obvious detrimental effect of underpopulation is the increased difficulty of locating a mate for breeding purposes. For most species, mate location requires an active search on the part of the members of one sex which, under conditions of underpopulation, might present special problem for weakly flying insects. To alleviate this, many species have evolved highly refined mechanisms (for example, production of pheromones, sounds, or light) which facilitate aggregation or location of individuals of the opposite sex. The relatively slight chance of finding a mate is offset to some extent by the fact that one mating may suffice for fertilization of all eggs a female may produce, that is, sperm may remain viable for a considerable period, and a female may produce a large number of eggs.

Andrewartha and Birch suggested that on some occasions the effect of non-specific predators might be much greater when prey density was lower than normal because the chance of an individual prey organism being eaten is increased. In support of this suggestion, they cite observations on the Australian plague locust, *Austroicetes cruciata,* whose population density was high in the period 1960-1980. Drought conditions in the winter of 1970 resulted in a great shortage of grasshopper food and a decline in population density. Only a few small areas of land remained moist enough to support growth of grass and surviving grasshoppers congregated in these areas. But so did the birds which normally fed on the insects and they reduced the population density to an extremely low level.

Lower than-normal densities may also have a serious effect in species which modify their environment, for example, social insects. The temperature and humidity within the nest are normally quite different from those outside, regulatedby the activity of members of the colony. If a proportion of the population is removed or destroyed, those individuals remain may no longer be able to keep the temperature and humidity at the desired level and the colony may die. Another interesting example noted by Andrewartha and Birch is that of the lesser grain borer, *Rhizopertha dominica* (Coleoptera), which is a serious pest of stored grain in the United States. In damaged (cracked) grain beetles can survive and reproduce even at low population density. However, in sound grain only cultures whose density is quite high will survive because the insects themselves, through their chewing activity, can cause sufficient damage to the grain that it becomes suitable for reproduction. The nature of this suitability is unknown. Below a certain level of population the so-called "threshold density," the chances of survival for a population are slim because of the unlikelihood of a meeting between insects of opposite sex and in reproductive condition. This fact is important in two areas of applied entomology, namely, quarantine service and biological control. Quarantine regulations are designed so that for a given pest the number which enter a country over a period of time is sufficiently low that the chances of the pest establishing itself are very slim. In biological control using insects as the controlling agents experience has taught that it is wiser to release the insects in a restricted area, especially if they are limited in number, rather than distributing them sparsely, in order to improve the chances of establishing a breeding population.

Populations of many insect species may be considered as "selfregulating," that is, should the density of the population fall below normal (though not below threshold) it will, in the course of time, return to its original level. There may be various reasons for this. As a species' density falls, its predators may experience greater difficulty in finding food so that they migrate elsewhere or produce fewer young. As a result of the decline in predator density a larger proportion of the prey species may survive to reproduce. If this continues for several generations the original population density may be re-established. Another possibility is that with a decrease in density, there will be a greater choice of egg-laying and, perhaps, resting sites. Selection of the best of these sites will again increase the chances of survival of an insect or its progeny and lead to a population increase. Some species have rather more specific mechanisms for overcoming the disadvantages of underpopulation. For example, females of some species practice faculative parthenogenesis in the absence of males, which serves not only to maintain continuity of the population, but, as the progeny are generally all female, any offspring that do find a mate can make a substantial contribution to the next generation. In the desert locust adult females in the solitary phase live longer, so that the chance of encountering a male is increased and, further, produce up to four times as many eggs compared to gregarious females.

Overpopulation

As population density rises beyond the normal level members of a species will increasingly compete with each other for such resources as oviposition sites, overwintering sites, resting places, and, occasionally, food. Such competition may itself have a regulatory effect, as a proportion of the population will have to be satisfied with less than optimal conditions. Thus, if oviposition sites are marginally suitable, few or no progeny may result. In less than adequate overwintering sites, insects may die if the weather is severe. If insects cannot find proper resting places, their chances of discovery by predators or parasitoids are increased, as are their chances of dying due to unfavourable weather conditions. As noted earlier food is seldom limiting, though under unusual circumstances it may become so.

In addition to the general regulating mechanisms just mentioned, some insects regulate population density in more specific ways. Migration, is a means by which a species may reduce its population density. In such species, it is crowding that induces the necessary physiological and behavioural changes which put an insect into migratory condition. Crowding may also lead to reduction in fecundity. For example, in *Schistocerca gregaria* gregarious females lay fewer eggs than solitary females because (1) their ovaries contain fewer ovarioles (2) a smaller proportion of the ovarioles produce oocytes in each ovarian cycle [as a result of (1) and (2), each egg pod contains fewer eggs)], and (3) they have fewer ovarian cycles. Likewise, in the migratory grasshopper, *Melanoplus sanguinipes,* mating frequency, which is a function of population density, is inversely related to number of eggs produced and longevity.

A few species employ a very obvious means of reducing crowding, namely, cannibalism of either the same or a different life stage. Among larval Zygoptera, for example, cannibalism of earlier instars is common under crowded conditions. For species whose larvae inhabit small and/or temporary ponds with limited food resources, cannibalism may be important in ensuring that at least a proportion of the population reaches the adult stage. Another consequence is that stragglers are eliminated, which results in greater synchrony of adult emergence. In the confused flour beetle, *Tribolium confiusum,* and some other beetle species, all of whose life stages are spent in grain or its products, egg cannibalism occurs. Adults eat any eggs they find, and, therefore, the higher the adult population density, the greater the number of eggs consumed. In some species of insects that inhabit a homogenous environment, population density is regulated by making the environment less suitable for growth. For example, *T. confusum* larvae and adults "condition" the flour in which they live, and as a result a smaller proportion of the larvae survive to maturity, and the duration of the larval stage is increased. The nature of this conditioning is not known. In some species, regulation of population density is achieved by having individuals that dominate others so that the reproductive capacity of the latter is either reduced or totally suppressed. This is seen most clearly in social Heymenoptera where one individual, the queen, dominates the other members of the colony, which are mostly female. In more primitive species, dominance is achieved initially by physical aggression, though in time the subordinates recognize the queen by scent and consequently avoid her. In highly social forms, such as the honeybee, dominance is asserted entirely through the release of pheromones.

In many species, dominance has taken on another form, namely, territoriality, the defense of a particular area. The size of the area defended (territory) may vary, but not below a minimum value, so that a maximum population density is attained. Territoriality is exhibited by insects that belong to a number of orders, both primitive and advanced, and is typically associated with some aspect of reproduction. Most often males establish territories and defend them against other males, usually by chasing and fighting but occasionally by nonaggressive means such as 'chirping in some Orthoptera. Females enter males' territories for mating and oviposition. Among Odonata, where mating immediately proceeds egg-laying, males also protect females as they oviposit.

Territoriality with respect to food availability may be seen in some species, especially parasitoids and social insects. For example, female inchneumons, braconids, chalcids, and scelionids (Hymenoptera) may mark the host either chemically or physically as they oviposit so that other females of the species do not lay in the same host. Such behaviour ensures that the offspring will have adequate food for complete development. (The marks may also be the means by which hyperparasites locate a host !) Social insects defend both their nest and foraging sites against members of other colonies.

INTERSPECIFIC INTERACTIONS

Competition and Coexistence

An important form of interactions is' when an insect competes with other organisms for' the same resources. Grasshoppers, sheep, and rabbits all eat grass, and if this is in short supply the presence of the mammalian herbivores will have a very obvious effect on the distribution and abundance of grasshoppers living in the same area. However, as noted earlier, food is seldom a limiting factor as far as the abundance of animals is concerned, and the other requirements of these three species are so different, that the species can coexist perfectly well. The collection of requirements that must be satisfied in order for a species to survive and reproduce under natural conditions is described as a niche. Thus, a niche includes both physical and biotic requirements, and its complexity varies with the environment in which a species finds itself. For example, the critical daylength for induction of diapause in a species may vary with latitude. Equally, with reference to biotic requirements, the complexity of a niche will differ according to the number and nature of other species utilizing the same resources. The more closely two species are related, the more nearly identical will be their requirements, that is, their niche, and the greater will be the degree of competition between them where the two species coexist. Normally, in this situation the less well-adapted species becomes extinct or restric- ted to areas where it can again compete favourably with the other species as a result of different environmental conditions, a phenomenon known as competitive exclusion or displacement. In the absence of competition, a species' niche will be broader (less complex); that is, a species' requirements will be less stringent and form the so-called "fundamental" niche. Conversely, the niche occupied by a species that coexists with others is known as the "realized" niche.

A well-documented example of competitive exclusion in insects involves three species of chalcid, belonging to the genus*Aphytis,* which are parasitoids of the California red scale, *Aonidiella aurantii,* found on citrus fruits. In the early 1900s, the golden chalcid *Aphytis chrysomphali* was accidentally introduced into southern California, probably along with red scale on nursery stock imported from the Mediterranean region, though it is a native of China. During the next 50 years, *Aphytis chrysomphali* spread along with its host throughout the citrus-growing area and exerted a reasonable degree of control over red scale, particularly in the milder coastal areas. However, a

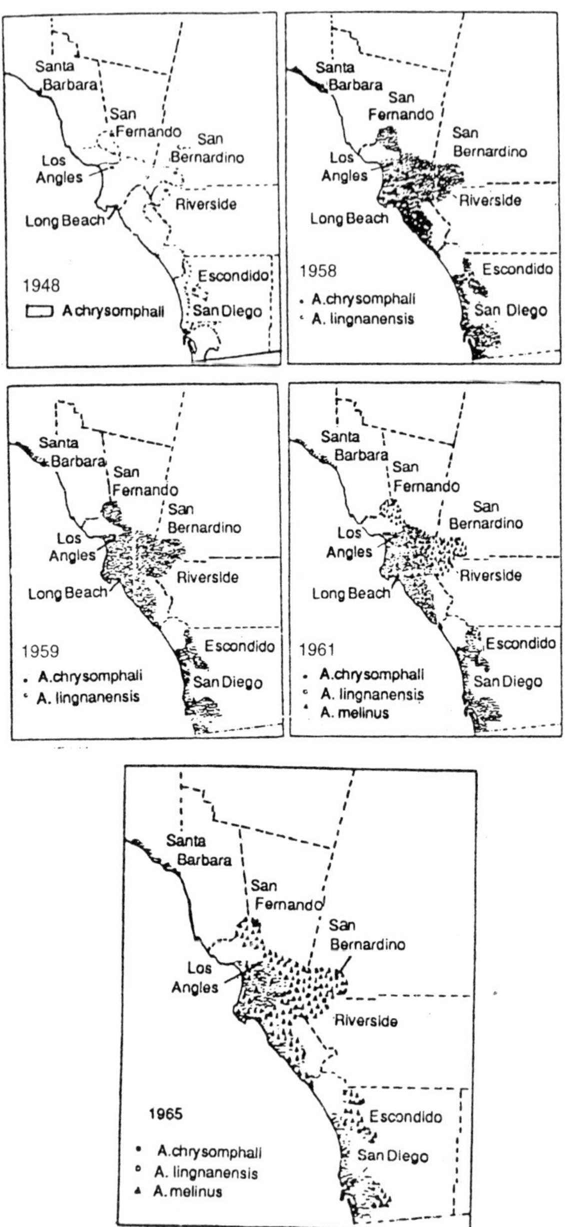

Fig. 3.1. Changes in teh distribution of Aphytis chrysomphali, A. lingnanesis *and* A. melinus *in Southern California between 1948 and 1965.*

second species, also Chinese, *Aphytis lingnanensis,* was introduced in the hope of obtaining even better control of the pest. During the 1970s, *A. lingnanensis* gradually *displaced A. chrysomphali* so that, by 1981, the latter was virtually extinct, being restricted to a few small areas along the coast. However, *A. linganensis was* ineffective as a control agent of red scale in the inland citrus-growing areas around San Fernando, San Bernadino, and Riverside, where annual climatic changes are greater. It was found for example, that periods of cool weather (18 or less for of all stages. Further, even light overnight frosts (-1°C for 8 hours) killed sperm in the spermathecae of females, who did not mate again, and rendered males sterile. Exposure of females to a temperature of 15°C for 24 hours led to an increase in proportion of male progeny. These factors caused a reduction in "effective progeny production" (number of female offspring produced per female) from 21.4 to 4.5 and a resultant inability of the species to control red scale populations. Consequently, a third species, *A. melinus*, was introduced from India and Pakistan in 1970 and 1971. This species rapidly desplaced *A. lingnanensis* from these inland areas, and by 1981 virtually the entire population of chalcids in thse areas was made up of *A. melinus.*

Competitive displacement does not always occur, because closely related organisms have evolved mechanisms that enable them to occupy almost but not quite the same niche. These mechanisms include habitat selection (spatial selection), microhabitat selection, temporal (diurnal and seasonal) segregation, and dietary differences. Two or more of these mechanisms may operate simultaneously to prevent competition between species. As an example of spatial segregation, we may cite the distribution of *A. lingnanensis* an *A. melinus* in southern California which DeBach considers to have stabilized, with *A. lingnanensis* occupying the milder (less climatically extreme) coastal districts and *A. melinus* the interior. Spatial separation is also seen in damelflies (Zygoptera), which inhabit prairie ponds. For example, two species of Coenagrionidae, *Coenagrion resolutum* and *Enallagma boreale,* hatch, develop, and emerge as adults almost synchronously. However, the species can coexist because larval *E. boreale* are restricted to deep, open water, while *C. resolutum* occurs in shallow water with emergent vegetation.

Price provides several examples of microhabitat selection that enable closely related species to coexist. In England, two species of Psocoptera, *Mesopsocus immunis* and *M. unipunctatus,* coexist on larch twigs with no readily obvious differences in their biology. Careful studies by Broadhead and Wapshere revealed, however, that the species oviposited in different microhabitats. *M. immunis* preferred to oviposit in the axils of dwarf side shoots, whereas M. *unipunctatus* selected girdle scars and leaf scars. Tahvanainen observed that the cogenetic flea beetles, *Phyliotreta crucifera* and *P. striolata* were concentrated on different parts of their food plant, *Brassica oleracea* (cabbage and relatives). The former species showed a preference for sunny locations and occurred largely on the upper surface of top and middle leaves, *Phyllotreta striolata* was concentrated on the underside of leaves, especially those near the base of the plant.

Diurnal segregation is exemplified by two species of *Andrena, A. rozeni* and *A. chylismiae,* solitary bees that forage on the evening primrose (*Oenothera clavaefonnis*) whose flowers remain in bloom for less than a day. Flowers open in late afternoon and are visited by *A. rozeni* between about 4:00 p. m. and 7:00 p. m. *Andrena chylismiae is* an early morning forager and visits flowers between 5:00 a. m. and 8:00 a. m., that is, just before they wilt.

Excellent seasonal segregation is shown by the damselflies studied by Sawchyn and Gillott, who were able to arrange the damselflies into three types according to their seasonal biology. Type A species, which included *Coenagrion resolutum, Enallagma boreale* and other Coenagrionidae, overwinter in diapause as well-developed larvae and emerge highly synchronously between the last week of May and mid-June. Sexual maturation takes about 1 week and the oviposition period extends to the end of July. Females lay eggs in the submerged parts of floating plants. Embryogenesis is direct and requires less than 3 weeks; half-grown larvae may be collected before the end of July and mature larvae by mid-September. Included in Type B are three species of *Lestes, L. unguiculatus, L. disjunctus* and *L. dryas,* which overwinter in diapause as well- developed embryos. Eggs hatch synchronously during early May, but the very young larvae are not preyed on by the larger larvae of Type A species either because they are too small, that is, outside the range of prey size, or because the Type A larvae have ceased to feed in preparation for the final molt. Type B larvae developed rapidly and synchronized adult emergence begins in early July and is completed within 2 weeks. Adult maturation requires 16-18 days, and females oviposit in green emergent stems of *Sci pus* (bulrush), which may relate to the requirement of water for embryogenesis. Adults are not normally seen after the end of August, though in mild years they may survive into October. In type C is included one species, *Lestes congener,* which is characterized by the lateness of its seasonal chronology. *Lestes congener* overwinters in diapause at an early (preblastokinetic) stage of embryogenesis. Embryonic development continues in the spring after the eggs are wetted and hatching occurs at the end of May. However, the young larvae are too small to serve as prey for the Type B species. Larval development is rapid in *L. congener so* that synchronized emergence begins in late July and continues for about 3 weeks. Thus, larvae of Type A species generally are not eaten by the much larger larvae of *L. congener.* Sexual maturation in *L. congener* takes about 3 weeks. Oviposition begins in mid-August and copulating adults may be seen until early October. Female *L. congener* oviposit only in dry stems of *Scirpus,* a feature associated with the lack of prediapause embryonic development observed in this species.

Thus, the occurrence of seasonal segregation between types and of microhabitat segregation (e.g., deep versus shallow water for larvae, and oviposition in floating vegetation, or emergent green or dry stems in adults) both between and within types, enables a number of species of Zygoptera to coexist and make use of the rich food Supply (in the form of *Daphnia, Diaptomus* and Diptera larvae) which is found in prairic ponds. Dietary difference also enable closely related species to coexist. For example, larvae of teh caddis flies *Pycnopsyche gentilis* and *P. luculenta* are able to coexist in woodland streams in Quebec because the former prefers fallen leaves. whereas *P. luculenta* feeds on sub-merged twigs or, if these are not available, on detritus or well-rotted leaves.

Predator-Prey Relationships

It will be abundantly clear that the distribution and abundance of a species will be greatly affected by those organisms that use it as food and that the reverse is also true, namely, that the distribution and abundance of prey will determine the distribution and abundance of predators.

Most Insects feed on plant material in one form or another, that is, are primary consumers, and therefore play a major role in the flow of energy stored in plants to higher trophic levels. However, another large group, probably numbering about 10% of known species, feed on other animals, especially insects. Some of these are typical predators or parasites, but the majority arepa sitoi andas belong especially to the Techinidae (Diptera), Strepsiptera, and so-called "parasitic" Hymenoptera (for details of the latter). A parasitoid may be defined as "an insect that requires and eats only one animal in its life span, but may be ultimately responsible for killing many". Typically, a female parasitoid a single egg or larva on each host, which is then gradully eaten as the offspring develop. Adult parasitoids are free-living and either do not feed or subsist on nectar and/or pollen. Thus, a parasitoid differs from atypical predator which feed on many organisms during its life and a parasite which may feed on one to several host individuals but does not kill them. However, as Price points out, the distinction between predator and parasitoid is not always clear. For example, a bird that captures insects as food for its offspring is comparable with a parasito predator lays its egg on a freshly killed or paralyzed host. Further, a predator and parasitoid face the same problem, namely, location of prey (host), and may solve the problem in an identical manner. Of course, from the prey's point of view, it matters not whether the aggressor is predator or parasitoid; for either, it must take appropriate steps to avoid being eaten ! In the final analysis, the population dynamics of predator-prey and parasitoid-host relationships wili be identical, and it is therefore appropriate to discuss these relationships under the same heading. In the remainder of this section, therefore, the terms "predator" and "prey" should be taken to include "parasitoid" and "host," respectively, except where specifically stated otherwise.

Let us consider first the strategies employed by prey species in order to reduce the chances of their members being eaten. Probably the most obvious strategy is for insects to avoid detection. This they may do in various ways by burrowing into a substrate which frequently also serves as food, by hiding, for example, on the underside of leaves, by becoming active for a restricted period of the day, or through camouflage where their colour pattern merges with the background on which they normally rest, or they precisely resemble a twig or leaf of their food plant. Other prey species have opted for other protective mechanisms which depend on initial recognition of the prey by the predator for their effectiveness. Such mechanisms include being distasteful, a feature usually accompanied by aposematic (warning) colouration so that a predator soon learns to recognize that species are distasteful. Related to this is Mullerian mimicry, in which distantly related, distateful species resemble each other, so that if a predator recognizes their pattern of colouration all species are protected. Another form of mimicry is Batesian, in which an edible species (the mimic) comes to resemble a distasteful species (the model). The success of this method of avoiding predation relies on the probability of the predator selecting the distasteful model rather than the edible mimic; that is, the population density of the model must greatly outweigh that of the mimic. Another chemical method of defense is to secrete obnoxious liquid or vapour whose odour repels predators. Other species release poisons, which on contact with skin or when injected by means of spines, hairs, or sting, injure or kill the attacker. Some insects, especially species of butterflies, practice intimidation displays aimed at frightening would be (vertebrate) predators. The butterflies normally rest with their wings closed vertica'ly above the body. On being disturbed, the butterflies rapidly open their wings to reveal a striking colour pattern, often including large "eyespots," intended to evoke prompt retreat of the enemy.

Predators make use of a variety of stimuli in order to locate prey. Some may attempt to capture and eat anything that moves within a certain size range and employ only simple visual or mechanical cues for detection of prey. Most species are, however, relatively preyspecific (feed on only a few or a single species of prey), and prey location is therefore a much more elaborate process. For many of these more specialized predators, the first step is location of the prey's habitat, and this is frequently achieved as a result of attraction to odours released from the food of the prey. For example, females of the ichneumon fly, *Itoplectis conquisitor,* a parasitoid, are attracted by the odour of pine oil, especially that of Scots pine (*Pinus sylvestris*), on which one of its preferred hosts, caterpillars of the European pine shoot moth, *Rhyacionia buoliana,* are found. For some predators, attraction is greater after the food of the prey has been damaged by the prey. The hymenopteran *Nasonia vitripennis,* for example, is attracted to meat, especially when this has been contaminated by the parasitoid's hosts, various muscid flies. Similarly, the ichneumon *Nemertis canescens is* more attracted to oatmeal contaminated by its host, larvae of the Mediterranean flour moth, *Ephestia kuhniella,* then to clean oatmeal.

Having been attracted to the habitat of its prey, a predator must now specifically locate the prey. For many species this involves a systematic search, though this behaviour is initiated only after receipt of an appropriate signal which indicates the likelihood of prey in the immediate area. Usually, such signals are again chemical in nature and include, for example, odours from the prey's feces or from the damaged tissues of the prey's food plant. Final location of prey is commonly achieved by means of its odour (though such odours are effective only over a very short range) or, more often, taste. Some oarasitoids locate hosts by the vibrations or sounds the latter make as they borrow through the substrate.

In some species, location of prey is followed immediately by feeding or, in parasitoids, oviposition or larviposition. In others, additional stimuli must be received before prey is deemed acceptable. These appear to be especially critical in parasitoids for which selection of hosts of the correct age may be important. For example, some parastoids accept only hosts above a certain size; cylindrical host shape improved acceptance in the ichneumon *Pimpla* instigator; hairness of the host (by preference, caterpillars of the gypsy moth, *Lymantria despair*) *is* an important determinant of acceptability in the braconid *Apanteles melanoscelus;* female *Itoplectis conquisitor* probe host larvae with their ovipositor but will lay eggs only if the host's hemolymph has a suitable taste. Movement may be an important stimulant or deterrent of acceptability. Some parasitoids oviposit only if a larval host moves, whereas movement of an embryo within an egg may inhibit oviposition by egg parasitoids. A special feature of many parasitoids is their ability to discriminate between non-parasitized hosts on the basis of physical markings, odours or tastes left by the original parasitoid as it oviposited or larviposited. Such marks render a host unacceptable to the parasitoids that locate it subsequently and ensure that the parasitoid larva, on hatching, has sufficient food for its complete development. Other parasitoids leave trail- marking pheromones as they search for hosts, which inhibit researching of an area and thereby facilitate dispersal of the species.

When given a choice a predator may consistently select a particular species for prey. However, in its natural habitat its survival does not normally depend on availability of that species, and in its absence other species are acceptable as prey. Special mention is made of this point, as it has sometimes been overlooked in attempts at biological control of pests. Some attempts have failed because the introduced predators reduced the pest to low density and then died out because alternate prey was not available in the new habitat. As a result, the pest was able to rebound to an economically important level. In other words, secondary prey species form an important reservoir for the predators at times when the density of the primary prey is low.

INSECT DISEASES

In insects, as well as in almost all other organisms, the great majority of individuals (80-99.99% of those born) never survive to reproduce. Fifty per cent or more of this mortality may be due to predation, while the remainder results from unsuitable weather conditions, perhaps starvation, and especially disease. Diseases may be subdivided into noninfectious and infectious categories. The former includes those that result from physical or chemical injury, nutritional diseases (due to deficiencies of specific nutrients), genetic diseases (inherited abnormalities), and physiological, metabolic, or developmental disturbances. Infectious diseases, which can be spread rapidly within a population of organisms, are caused by microorganisms, including viruses,. rickettsias, spirochetes, bacteria, fungi, protozoa and nematodes. Though infections of many of these pathogens may be directly fatal, other pathogens simply "weaken" an insect, rendering it more susceptible to predation, parasitism, or other pathogens, to chemical and other means of control, or altering its growth rate and reproductive capacity. Most of the time in natural populations, the effects of pathogens are not readily obvious. This is described as the enzootic stage. On occasion, however, conditions are such that the pathogens can reproduce and spread rapidly to decimate the host lation. This is known as the epizootic phase, and the outbreak is described as an epizootic, comparable to an epidemic within a population of humans. Study of the factors that lead to epizootics, epizootiology, is of interest not only from a purely ecological point of view but also in view of the potential use of microorganisms in the biological control of insect pests.

Epizootics

Essentially, there are four primary components in the development of an epizootic; the pathogen population, the host population, an efficient means of pathogen transmission, and the environment, all of which are closely interrelated. Key features of a pathogen are its virulence (disease-producing power), infectivity (capacity to spread among hosts), and ability to survive. Clearly, pathogens (or specific strains of a pathogen) which have both high virulence and high infectivity are the ones that most often cause epizootics, though the susceptibility of the host is also important. Some pathogens may be highly virulent but of low infectivity and, as a result, have a low potential for causing epizootics. *Bacillus thuringiensis,* for example, though pathogenic for many Lepidoptera, seldom causes an epizootic under natural conditions because of its poor powers of dispersal. Indeed, the inability to disperse, together with limited capacity to survive outside a host, are probably the main reasons why epizootics are, relatively speaking, of rare occurrence. Dispersal may be effected either by abiotic or biotic agents in the environment, including wind, rain, running water, snow, host organisms (both healthy and infected), and their predators (both vertebrate and invertebrate) or parasites. Host organisms may disperse the pathogen as a result of defecation, regurgitation, oviposition (that is, the pathogen occurs either on or within the eggs), disintegration of the body after death, or cannibalism. Predators commonly distribute pathogens via their feces, though some insect parasitoids transfer the microorganisms via their ovipositor when they either sting the host or lay an egg on or in it. Pathogens may survive in either the host or the environment, sometimes for considerable periods. Those which survive in the environment typically have a highly resistant resting stage, such as spores (bacteria, fungi and protozoa), inclusion bodies (viruses), or cysts (nematodes).

Members of the host population pick up pathogens as a result of physical contact with contaminated surfaces, or eating contaminated food (including cannibalism), or receive pathogens directly from the mother via transoverian transmission. Contact with a pathogen, however, does not necessarily result in ill effect for the host, as the latter has various means of defending itself. Further, even when some members of a population are susceptible to a pathogen, an epizootic does not always follow because of the difficulty of dispersal of the pathogen referred to above and because other members of the population may have varying degrees of resistance.

Density, distribution, and mobility of hosts are important factors in the development of an epizootic. Generally speaking, epizootics are more likely to occur at high densities, even distribution, and high mobility of hosts, as the chances of dispersal of the pathogen are greater under these conditions. On occasion an epizootic may develop at low host density, as a result of widely dispersed but long- lived pathogens that remain from a previous high-density outbreak. Even at high host- population density, an epizootic may not develop if the host population has a discontinuous distribution and/or poor mobility. The importance of the environment, physical and biotic, in the dispersal and survival of pathogens has already been noted. Environ- mental factors are important in other ways in relation to epizootics. For example, factors which induce stress in an insect, especially extremes of temperature, high humidity, and inadequate food, may lower its resistance to a pathogen. In conclusion it should now be apparent that whether or not an epizootic occurs depends on a variety of conditions relating to pathogen host and environment. Only when knowledge of all these factors is available for a given bost-pathogen interaction can an accurate forecast of a potential disease outbreak be made. Such knowledge is of critical importance in determining the success or otherwise of biological control using pathogenic microorganisms.

Types of Pathogens

It is natural that the best-known pathogens are those which cause epizootics in economically important insects and show potential for use in microbial control of pest species. In this short account, the major features of some of these pathogens will be outlined, as a basis for the discussion on microbial control.

Bacteria

Many species of bacteria have been shown experimentally to be highly pathogenic should they gain access to the hemocoel. However, under natural conditions, the majority of these never cause epizootics (even though their infectivity is high) because of the barrier presented by the integument and lining of the gut. Further, the gut may be unsuitable for survival and multiplication of the bacteria because of its pH or redox potential, or because of the presence within it of antibacterial substances or antagonistic microorganisms. Infection of an individual insect occurs when the integument or gut is physically damaged. The commonest route of invasion appears to be via the midgut. Bacteria are sometimes able to slip between the peritrophic membrane and the midgut epithelium at either the anterior or the posterior end of the midgut, or through ruptures caused by the passage of food.

The subsequent mode of action of the bacteria, that is, how they cause a pathological condition, is variable. Invasion and destruction of the midgut epithelium is typically the first step, and for some bacteria this may be their only activity, their host dying of starvation. More often, bacteria not only destroy the midgut epithelium but then grow rapidly in the hemolymph and tissues, causing a massive septicemia. Others liberate toxins that kill the host's cells. Other bacteria become pathogenic only when they are able to enter thehemocoel via lesions in the midgut epithelium caused by other microorganisms such as protozoa, viruses and nematodes. Bacteria known to be naturally pathogenic in insects can be arranged in two groups, the non-spore-formers and the spore-formers. Included among the non-spore-forming bacteria *is Serratia marcescens,* varieties of which attack a range of insect species and whose presence is recognized by the reddish colour of the dead host. Outbreaks of S. *marcescens* are common in high-density laboratory cultures of insects. According to Bailey, at least five species of bacteria are involved in European foulbrood disease of larval honeybees, though a non- spore-former, *Streptococcus pluton,* is the causative agent. The remaining species are secondary pathogens or saprophytes.

The spore-formers are the most important group from the point of view of epizootics and for their potential importance in biological control, largely because they remain viable for a considerable time outside their host. Further, some species are highly pathogenic should the sporangia be ingested because their sporangia include, in addition to a spore, a crystalline structure, the parasporal body, that contains various toxins and enzymes such as hyaluronidase and phospholipase for digestion of the cement holding together gut epithelia cells. Thus, the bacteria may be pathogenic due to the parasporal toxins, even though, initially, the spore may not germinate because of prevailing conditions of the gut. Bacteria that produce a parasporal body are known as crystalliferous bacteria. Two of the other known, spore-forming, non-crystalliferous bacteria are *Bacillus cereus,* which has been isolated from a range of host species, and *B. larvae* which is the cause of American foulbrood in bee larvae. Only young larvae (up to 55 hours old) are susceptible, suggesting that only in early larval life are gut conditions suitable for spore germination. Despite the availability of antibiotics for treatment of American foulbrood, it continues to be a common disease. Though this is partially due to the long-lived nature of *B. larvae* spores (especially in honey), its appearance is frequently the result of poor management on the part of beekeepers who expose contaminated yet unoccupided supers. Bees from adjacent hives visit the supers to steal honey and in doing so spread the disease.

Of the crystalliferous species, *B. thuringiensis, B. popilliae* and *B. lentimorbus* have been the subject of considerable research, pure and applied, during the past 30 years. *Bacillus thuringiensis* includes an enormous number of highly pathogenic varieties which attack Lepidoptera (more than 100 susceptible species) and representatives of several other orders, including some economically important species such as mosquitoes and houseflies. Honeybees are not, however, susceptible. Extensive field-testing has shown that *B. thuringiensis* has desirable attributes for successful biological control of insect pests and commercial preparations are now available. *Bacillus popilliae* and *B. lentimorbus* cause "milky disease" in larvae of some scarabaeid beetles, including the Japanese beetle, *Popillia japonica,* an important pest in the eastern United States, that feeds on roots of grasses, vegetables, and nursery stock. Mass produced spore preparations of*B. popilliae* are now marketed for control of this pest.

Rickettsias

Only a few species of rickettsias are pathogenic in insects, though some infect pests and may have potential as biological control agents, for example, *Rickettsiella popilliae,* which attacks Japanese beetles. However, almost no work has been done to test this possibility perhaps, as St. Julian *et al.* suggest, because some rickettsias of insects are also pathogenic in mammals.

Viruses

According to David, more than 700 species of insects are known to be susceptible to viral diseases. Of these, about 80% are Lepidoptera, 10% Diptera, and 5% Hymenoptera. Many of these species are economically important, and much research has been and is being conducted to determine the value of viruses in biological control.

Viruses may be arranged in two categories, according to whether the nucleic acid they contain is in the form of DNA or RNA. Viruses in both groups use raw materials in host cells for replicating their nucleic acids, and, by producing viral mRNA, they use the host's ribosomes for synthesis of viral proteins, thereby causing disruption of the host cell's metabolism. The DNA viruses include Nuclear Polyhedrosis Viruses (NPVs), Granulosis Viruses (GVs), and Iridescent Viruses (IVs), while among the RNA- containing viruses the best known are the Cytoplasmic Polyhedrosis Viruses (CPVs). Like bacteria; viruses mainly infects insects when ingested on contaminated food .or during cannibalism, though some may be transmitted on the surface of or within eggs. Initially, they invade midgut epithelial cells, move and, for some, this is the only tissue affected. More often, theyand, into the hemocoel and subsequently attack fat body, to a lesser extent, other tissues.

Some viruses are relatively short-lived outside the insect host and their survival from year to year requires that at least some members of the host population survive. Others, such as NPVs and CPVs are able to survive outside the host for a considerable time under suitable conditions. Cabbage looper NPV, for example, may persist for 9 years in soil. Viruses are relatively stable within the temperature and humidity range that they normally experience. However, they are sensitive to sunlight, especially its shorter (ultraviolet) wavelengths, and are inactivated by a few hours of continuous exposure. Thus, those which are disseminated on the host's food plant may have limited viability. In commercial preparations viability may be increased by additives which screen out ultraviolet radiation. Viruses are also sensitive to pH and need to be maintained in conditions close to neutrality. Again, in commercial preparations such sensitive may be partially overcome by the inclusion of buffers.

The best-studied insect viruses are the NPVs and GVs. The former have been isolated from more than 240 Lepidoptera, and from representatives of other orders, whereas the GVs apparently are restricted to Lepidoptera. Bergold presents a partial list of species susceptible to NPVs, included in which are many pests, among them *Heliothis zea* (corn earworm), *H. viriscens* (tobacco budworm), *Trichoplusia ni* (cabbage looper), *Prodenia* and *Pseudaletia spp.* (armyworms), and *Neodiprion spp.* (sawflies), against which commercial NPV preparations have been developed. Examples of pests with highly pathogenic GVs, which are now being developed commercially and/or field tested, are *Pleas spp.* (cabbageworms), *Carpocapsa pomonella* (codling moth), and *Choristoneura murinana* (fit budworm).

Iridescent viruses have been mainly isolated from Diptera, including mosquitoed and blackflies. Though highly infective whey. injected experimentally into the hemocoel, IVs do not appear to have much future as biological control agents in Diptera, at least, because they are rapidly destroyed when ingested. Further, the peritrophic membrane of dipteran larvae does not have gaps like that of larval Lepidoptera. Almost all of the approximately 150 species of insect from which CPVs have been isolated are Lepidoptera, and a number of these are pests. Relatively little work appears to have been carried out on the potential of CPVs as control agents, perhaps because many of the pests in which they occur are also susceptible to the better-known NPVs and because they are relatively slow-acting.

Fungi

Studies on entomogenous fungi, including their potential as control agents, tend to be overshadowed by the enormous volume of work being carried out on bacteria and viruses. However, as Roberts points out, the first attempt at microbial control used the greenmuscardine fungus, *Metarrhizium anisopliae* and the first large-scale programme, which covered almost the whole of Kansas, used a fungus, *Beauveria bassiana*. Unlike bacteria, viruses, and protozoa, fungi normally enter insects via the integument rather than the gut, whose conditions (especially pH) are unsuitable for fungal spore germination. Apart from suitable temperature and pH (in soil-dwelling fungi), high humidity or even liquid water is essential for spore germination, an observation which accounts for the frequent occurrence of fungal epizootics during periods of rainy or humid weather. After germi- nation, access through the cuticle is probably achieved through the secretion of chitinase and proteinase enzymes by elongating hyphae. Initially, the hyphae which penetrate colonize the epidermis but then spread to other specific body tissues. Some tissues are not attacked until after the host's death when the fungus becomes saprophytic. Death may result from the mere physical presence of a mass of hyphae which disrupt tissues or inhibit hemolymph circulation. Alternatively, fungal secretions may cause histolysis or be toxic to the host. At the end of an epizootic a fungus may survive in various ways. It may persist at low incidence in remaining members of the host population or it may infect other, less susceptible, species. It may enter a facultatively saprophytic phase, for example, in soil. Or, most commonly, it may produce spores that can survive outside the host for some time. The longevity of spores varies among species and in relation to weather conditions. Low humidity and temperatures a few degrees above freezing point appear to result in greatest longevity. Spores are also susceptible to sunlight, though whether this is due to ultraviolet radiation is uncertain.

Several hundred species of fungi are known to attack insects. Some of these are very common and can cause epizootics. It is natural, therefore that these are the best studied, with emphasis on their potential as microbial control agents. Species of *Metarrhizium* (especially *M. anisopliae* which has over 200 host species, mostly soil inhabitants) and *Beauveria* (*B. bassiana* and *B. tenella* in particular) appear to be the best prospects for control agents. Spores of *M. anisopliae* and *B. bassiana* are readily producible on a commercial scale, and field testing is underway, *Coelomomyces* species are aquatic fungi which are obligate parasites almost exclusively of larval mosquitoes, and which, under natural conditions, are probably important regulators of mosquito population density. Roberts notes, however, that laboratory culture of these fungi is proving difficult, so that studies on them are hindered. The genus *Entomophthora* includes more than 100 species of fungi, many of which cause epizootics among grasshoppers, aphids, caterpillars, mosquitoes and houseflies. Though *Entomophthora* species are usually highly specific with reference to their insect host, many are facultative parasites and are amenable to culture on a mass scale.

Protozoa

Protozoa pathogenic to insects are typically acquired by hosts as they ingest food, though a few species may be passed on to subsequent generations in the host's eggs. In some species the midgut epithelium is the first tissue attacked, and only later are other tissues, especially fat body, invaded. In other species the protozoa migrate through the midgut wall to specific tissues in the hemocoel. Disease is caused by the general debilitating effect of the protozoa as they reproduce, by toxins released from the protozoa, or as a result of secondary invasions of viruses or bacteria. Protozoa are disseminated as spores or cysts, some of which may survive for long periods outside the host.

Most disease-causing protozoa in insects are Sporozoa, including Coccidia, Gregarinia, and especially Microsporidia for which more than 200 host species are known. The protozoa probably play an important role in regulation of insect populations, though in only a few instances has this been authenticated. Species of the microsporidian *Nosema* are agents for a number of well-known insect diseases, two examples of which are pebrine disease of silk worms caused by *N. bombvcis* and nosema disease of honeybee (pathogen *N. apis*). Other species of *Noseina* known to be highly pathogenic include *N. lymantriac* [primary host, the gypsy moth (*Lyntantria despair*)], *N polyvora* (imported cabbageworm (*Pieris brassicae*)], and *N. locustae* (various species of grasshoppers). Though pathogenic protozoa would seem to be good candidates for biological control agents, would seem to be is proceeding slowly, primarily because, research into this possibility with few exceptions, the pathogens cannot be cultured outside their host. As a result obtaining sufficient spore material for testing is some what slow.

Nematodes

Though obviously not microorganisms *sensu stricto*, nematodes are generally included in this term in discussions of insect pathogens. Nematodes enter into a viriety of interactions with insects. but hthose that are pathogenic largely belong to two families. Mermithidae and Neoaplectanidae. Nematode pathogens exert various effects on insects but in most istances do not directly cause death but, rather, protracted larval development, abnormal morphology (including wing shortening), and reduced fecundity. Manyb of the effects noted can be attributed to debilitation of the host as the nematode feeds on its tissues, especially fat body. Other effects result from more "specific" activities on te part of the pathogen. For example, some morphological abnormalities probably result from endocrine imbalances, indeced perhaps by toxins released when juvenile nematodes enter a host. As the bacterium develops within the host (whose death it rapidly causes as result of septicemia), it is fed upon by the nematode which ultimately produces up to 10 progeny. Infection of new hosts may occur passivley when nematode eggs are ingested on contaminated food and hatch within the gut, or actively where juvenile nematodes search out a suitable host whose body they enter via the integument.

Pathogenic nematodes have been found in representatives of at least 15 insect orders, including mosquitoes, blackflies, grasshoppers· weevils, ants, and various caterpillars and probably they are important natural regulators of insect populations. Howevebe difficult, obligate parasites, their large-scale culture has proved consequently few studies have been made on biological control using nematodes. Some field tests have been made using beetle, tobacco against codling moth, corn earworm, Colorado potato budworm , and other pests, but the results were variable.

CONCLUDING REMARKS

The biotic environment of insect is composed of all other organisms that affect insects' survival and multiplication. Food is not normally an important regulator of insect abundance because other environmental factors have a significant adverse effect on insect growth and reproduction. In addition, many insects are polyphagous, and larvae and adults may eat different food. In two situations the quantity of food may be limiting: (1) when only a proportion of the total food is available, and (2) when insect population density is not kept in check by other factors. The nutritional quality of food also markedly affects survival, rate of growth, and fecundity of insects. Through solution complex interactions between plants and insects have developed based on the theme that insects feed on (gain energy from) plants, while plants attempt to defend themselves (conserve this energy) or obtain service (most .often cross- pollination, rarely protection) from insects in exchange. Some plants protect themselves by producing toxins. However, some insects have become able to cope with these toxins and may even accumulate them for protection against predators and, possibly, microorganisms. Other insects have become adapted to feeding on parts of plants that lack toxins (spatial avoidance) or when plants have a low toxin content (temporal avoidance).

4

INTER-RELATIONSHIP

It is the relationship between the individuals of different species. The inter-relationship may be either temporary or life long. It may be beneficial, harmful or. without any apparent effect. An individual insects carries with it a small community of other organisms. §ome are merely phoretic passengers, but others live more or less intimately in or outside their hosts. In the high mountains large flightless weevils live amidst mosses in humid forests. The backs of the long-lived, slow-moving weevils are camouflaged with living fungi, algae, lichens, and liverworts. The integumental surface and setae, plus a secretion, encourage plant growth. Mites, nematodes, rotifers, diatoms, and psocid insects live and feed among the plants, causing no harm to the weevils. Less viable but no less interesting or important are the microbes and occasional helminth worms that are associated with all other insects. Lower forms of life were present before insects evolved. We can speculate that as scavengers in decaying vegetable matter the early insects would have been immersed in a microbe-rich environment and would have ingested and excreted saprophytic forms. Inside the insect's gut, some were digested and absorbed, and some persisted harmlessly or as injurious parasites. In time, some microbes evolved a beneficial partnership such that their hosts could exploit foods that were otherwise nutritionally deficient.

The mobility of insects and their resistance to desiccation allow their less hardy associates to survive and be dispersed in the terrestrial environment. When insects began feeding on the vascular fluids of higher plants and vertebrates, certain viruses and microbes were introduced into the wounds. Some proved to be highly dangerous to their new hosts. Insects also became involved as intermediaries in the natural cycles of other disease agents. Although insects alone rarely cause death of plants and vertebrates, as vectors of disease they can have catastrophic effects on entire populations.

SYMBIOTIC RELATIONSHIPS

Broadly defined, symbiosis is the living together of dissimilar organisms, regardless of the possibly injurious or beneficial interactions. In our present discussion, the microbes are called *symbionts* and insects are the *hosts*. Symbionts may live parasitically at the host's expense. If the host's vitality is impaired, the symbiont is called a *pathogen*. Agents causing fatal diseases of insects include certain viruses, bacteria, protozoa, fungi, and probably most parasitic helminths. Some of these pathogens can be used effectively in controlling pest insects. Insect hemocytes defensively phagocytize the smaller agents and encapsulate the larger ones. Insects do not produce specific antibodies against pathogens, but lysozymes in the gut, fat body, and hemolymph can destroy microbes by enzymatic action.

A coevolutionary tendency exists for the hosts and symbionts to become mutually adjusted. Parasites that kill their host also die, whereas those causing less harm to their host survive. Hosts that are susceptible to parasitic damage are selectively eliminated, leaving z esistant hosts in the majority. Thus, the relationship evolves towards benign parasites and resistant hosts.

Symbionts that cause no harm to their hosts are *commensals,* such as the fungi Laboulbeniales. *Mutualistic* symbionts have evolved a reciprocally beneficial relationship with their host. When the symbionts are outside the insect's body, e.g., the fungus gardens of insects, they are called *ectosymbionts*. *Endosymbionts* are mutualistic microbes sheltered inside the insect's body. Buchner recognized that certain groups of insects were dependent on symbionts because the insects diet lacked essential items. For example, the vascular fluids of both higher plants and vertebrates, and wood are deficient as food insects.

Phloem-sucking Homoptera obtain carbohydrate in surplus, but the diet is inadequate in protein; all possess symbionts that supply missing nutrients. Predatory Hemiptera lack symbionts but phytophagous Pentatomidae have them. Larvae of *Dashyelea* flies (Ceratopogonidae) and *Nosodendron* beetles (Nosodendridae) live in sap and have symbionts.

Vertebrate blood is notably lacking in B vitamins. Phthiraptera, Cimicidae, *Triatoma* (Reduviidae), *Glossina* (Muscidae), and crawling ectoparasitic flies are parasites that feed exclusively on blood in all feeding stages and have symbionts. Adult parasites with scavenging larvae, i.e., Siphonaptera and biting flies, lack symbionts. The larvae of these insects obtain B vitamins sufficient for the rest of the life cycle from bacteria-rich food.

Wood feeding insects depend on ectosymbionts such as the fungus gardens mentioned above or on endosymbionts in the intestine. Scarab grubs contain bacteria; anobiids and certain cerambycids contain yeasts; and certain termites contain protozoa or bacteria. Certain pests of seeds and stored grain have symbionts; *Nysius* (Lygaeidae), *Lasioderma* (Anodbiidae), *Sitophilus* (Curculionidae), *Rhizopertha* (Bostrychidae), *Orzaephilus,* and *Coccotrypes* (*Scoly-* tidae). Oddly, the Bruchidae apparently lack symbionts. Symbionts also occur among insects with a variety of other food habits. Many phytophagous weevils harbour bacteria. *Bromius, Cassida,* and *Donacia* are chrysomelid beetles whose larvae feed on green plants and have bacterial symbionts; other chrysomelids lack them. Tephritid flies and lagriine tenebrionid beetles feed in fresh or decayed plants. Both have bacterial symbionts. Many species of scavenging cockroaches have bacterial symbionts, as do certain ants of the genera *Camponotus* and *Formica*. The yeasts of nonpredatory *Chrysopa* adults have been described previously.

Microbes commonly gain entrance to the insect's body through the mouth as a part of the food. It is not surprising to find most endosymbionts still reside in the gut, having evolved the ability to live in the intestinal environment. They are often transmitted from generation to generation, or among individuals simply by ingestion. For example, the cellulose-digesting protozoa and bacteria of termites are passed' among the colony members by anal feeding. Insects without overlapping generations infect the eggs. Phytophagous Pentatomidae defecate on the eggs and the nymphs acquire symbionts after hatching. Some insects have special organs for smearing bacteria on the egg as it is deposited. The female *Donacia* covers the egg with a secretion that encloses a mass of bacteria near the larva's head. On hatching, the larva eats through the mass and ingests the bacteria. The host's intestine may be modified to accommodate endo- symbionts. The hindgut of certain scarab beetle larvae is greatly enlarged as a fermentation chamber containing bacteria and wood particles. Lateral saclike chambers, or caeca, are characteristic of insects with intestinal endosymbionts. Crane fly larvae may have a large diverticulum on the hindut. Phytophagous Hemiptera-Heteroptera characteristically have many bacteria-filled caceca along the posterior portion of the hindgut. Malpighian tubules may also serve as bacterial crypts. Presumably the localization of endosymbionts in blind chambers reduces their loss in feces, allows a longer time for them to act on food, and increases the insect's absorption of nutrients derived from the microbes.

A significant coevolutionary step is seen in those endosymbionts that become intracellular. In addition to other possible advantages, thc microbes thus sheltered are protected from phagocytosis. Intermediate stages have been observed iii intestinal caeca and Malpighian tubules where symbionts are both in the lumen and inside the insect's cells. Cells containing yeast or bacterial symbionts are called *mycetocytes.* These may be part of the epithelium or may be clustered in discrete organs in the hemocoel called *mycetomes.* Mycetocytes and mycetomes containing one to several kinds of symbionts may occur in various places within a single insect. The number of symbionts are regulated by the insect host. Often the symbiontcontaining tissues are associated with or modified from the gut, Malpighian tubules gonads and genital ducts, or the fat body. Some mycetomes are easily visible, even from outside. Early microscopists Robert Hooke and Jan Swammerdam saw the yellow mycetome on the gut of the human louse.

In contrast to those symbionts associated with the gut and transmitted to the next generation via feces, the symbionts residing in internal organs are moved to the ovaries by their mycetocytes or by the hemolymph. Depending on the structure of the ovary, the symbionts are transferred into the egg and later included in the embryonic mycetocytes.

The identities of intracellular symbionts in terms of microbial classification remain controversial. Earlier they were sometimes considered waste products or normal cell organelles, such as mitochondria. It is now certain that many intracellular symbionts of insects are actually microorganisms. Now we are uncertain whether mitochondria are derived from ancient symbionts ! For critical analysis, the symbionts must be culturcd, but unfortunately this has rarely been achieved. Judging by other eviqence and observations of their anatomy with the electron microscope, insect symbionts include yeastlike, bacteriumlike, and rickettsialike organisms.

INSECTS AS VECTORS OF DISEASE

Vectors are the carriers of disease causing agents or pathogens. Among the most devastating diseases of crop plants, domestic animals, and humans are those carried by insects. Insects that transmit disease agents are called *disease vectors*. The life history, host selection, and feeding behaviour of the vector largely determine the epidemiology of the disease. By controlling the insect, it is sometimes possible to break the link in transmission and to stop the spread of disease. Microbes causing disease in plants and animals rarely also cause disease in the vector even when they live and multiply in the vector. An exception is Western X mycoplasma, which reduces the longevity of its leafhopper vector. Yet certain agents of plant disease actually seem to be beneficial to the vector by favourably changing the host plant's structure or functioning. Experiments have shown that vectors may feed or oviposit more frequently on diseased plants. A comparable relationship between animal diseases and their vectors is not known.

The nature of the transmission, of pathogenic organisms by insect vectors to plant hosts may be *mechanical or biological*. Mechanical transmission involves the contamination of the body or mouthparts, or at most the foregut, after feeding on an infected host. The pathogen is transferred to a new host when the vector next feeds or makes contact. Infectivity is lost when the supply of pathogen is depleted or at ecdysis if the vector is immature. For example, mosquitoes function literally as flying pins in the transmission of the myxoma virus among rabbits. Similarly, the nonpersistent plant viruses are rapidly spread by aphids during their brief and repeated probing behaviour in search of suitable plant hosts.

Biologically transmitted pathogens, acquired after prolonged feeding, enter the vector's gut, hemocoel, or various organs. Infectivity is not immediate, but occurs only after *a latent period* during which the pathogen moves about in the cost or further develops or reproduces. Once infective, the vector tends to rent am infective for life. The persistent circulative plant viruses, such as the aphid- transmitted pea nation mosaic, do not replicate in the vector, but circulate in the body. On thg other hand, helminths causing animal diseases undergo developmental changes but do not multiply it their intermediate insect hosts. This is called *cyclodevelopmental* trans- mission of animal pathogens. When the pathogen multiplies in the vector, the transmission is called *propagative*. Persistent prc Pagative plant pathogens, such as the aphid-transmitted lettuce necrotic yellows, and plague bacteria in fleas, are examples. If the multiplication is accompanied by cyclic development, as in the case of malaria plasmodia in anopheline mosquitoes, the term is *cyclopropagatne*.

In some cases, the insects and acarines acquire infections as immatures remain infective after one or more ecdyses. This is called *transstadial* transmission. Some transmit pathogens to their offspring by *transovarial* transmission, a feature already described above for endosymbionts. Certain arboviruses and rickettsiae are transovarially transmitted by ticks, but few insects have been shown to transmit animal pathogens similarly top their offspring.. Plant pathogens, however, can be transvarially transrmtted. Some persistent viruses, rickettsialike pathogens, and mycoplasmas are transmitted in this way by leafhoppers.

INTER-RELATION WITH VIRUSE AND MYCOPLASMALIKE DISEASE AGENTS

Viruses are highly variable, submicrosccPic particles consisting of either deoxyribonucleic acid (DNA) or ribonucleic acid (RNA) and usually, but not always, with a protein cover. Viruses multiply or replicate only in living cells, primarily those of bacteria, plants, insects, and vertebrates. The best-known viruses associated with insects are those are pathogenic to insects, higher plants, or vertebrates. From the standpoint of numbers of species of insects, the most important patho- gens are the DNA-containing nuclear polyhedrosis viruses (NPV), DNA granulosis viruses (GV), and RNA cytoplasmic polyhedrosis viruses (CPV). Lepidoptera caterpillars .and larval sawflies are most susceptible to these viruses. The polyhedrosis viruses are characterized by polyhedral crystals. Carter lists 261 viruses that are transmitted to plants by insect vectors. Aphids transmit the largest number of viruses, mostly those producing the mottled "mosaic" diseases. Aphids also rank first in numbers of species of vectors. Some species may vector numerous viruses, for example, *Myzus persicae* is the vector of more than 100 viruses.

Leafhoppers rank next in importance and are noted as vectors of persistent propagative viruses. Recently, one group of diseases called the "yellows diseases" has been discovered to be caused not by viruses, but by organisms called mycoplasmas in the phloem that resemble minute bacteria. Like bacteria, mycoplasmas are procaryotes, i.e., the nucleus lacks a membrane. The cells are highly variable in shape and uniquely lack a cell wall. Mycoplasmas were previously known as pathogens of mammals and birds, but not associated with arthropods. It has been estimated that as many as 350 species of plants may be involved in the natural cycle of aster yellows disease and its vector, the aster leafhopper, *Macrosteles fuscifrons*.

Of historical interest is the tulip "breaking" virus that causes the petals of red or purple flowers to be beautifully striped. The first record was published in 1576, making this the oldest known plant disease. Broken tulips became greatly admired in Europe. Paintings of the sixteenth and seventeenth centuries often depict the attractive blossoms. Demand was heightened because the bulb of a strikingly patterned flower might degenerate or rapidly die. Various methods of cultivation were alleged to increase breaking, but the capricious cause was unknown. A colossal gambling craze developed in Holland in 1634-1637 called "tulipomania." Fortunes were traded for single prized bulbs. The episode was finally stopped by the government. We now know that the virus is transmitted mechanically by several aphids, including *Myzus persicae.*

Viruses pathogenic to vertebrates that are transmitted by arthropods are collectively called *"arboviruses,"* an abbreviation of "arthropod-borne viruses." These contain RNA as the nucleic acid. Out of more than 200 arboviruses, 50 infect humans. Yellow fever, dengue, and various encephalitis viruses are the most important. Mosquitoes are the vectors for the great majority of arboviruses, followed by ixodid ticks, *Culicoides* flies (Ceratopogonidae), *Phlebotomus* flies (Psychodidae), and possibly laelapid mites. Yellow fever is an arbovirus transmitted by the mosquito *Aedes aegypti.* This disease may be fatal in up to 10 per cent of human cases. Hundreds of thousands have died, especially in tropical Africa and South America. The yellow fever mosquito was originally from Africa, but now occurs worldwide as a vector in urban environments. Although controlled in cities and towns, the virus persists in tropical forests. Here it is transmitted among monkeys by forest mosquitoes such as *Haemagogus* in the New World and various *Aedes* in Africa. Jungle yellow fever is transmitted to humans living in forest clearings and working in forests.

INTER-RELATION WITH BACTERIA

Among procaryotes broadly called the bacteria are distinctive groups closely associated with arthropods: certain true or eubacteria, spirochetes, rickettsias, and mycoplasmas. The last group was mentioned in the preceding discussion of viruses because, until recently, insectborne mycoplasmas have been confused with certain persistent plant viruses. The procaryotes in this section all have cell walls. Eubacteria are commonly found on the integument, in the gut, and in mycetocytes. Endosymbiotic bacteria occur in Orthoptera, Isoptera, Phthiraptera, Hemiptera, Coleoptera, Hymenoptera, and Diptera. Certain larval calliphorid flies, known as "surgical maggots," are exceptional in that the gut is sterile. A bactericidal substance, allatonin, kills bacteria in the midgut. Napoleon's surgeon. Larrey, noted that healing was actually enhanced when neglected battle wounds were infected with maggots. Maggots were later used medically because they ingest bacteria and necrotic tissues.

Bacteria pathogenic to insects have been reviewed by Faust Infection is usually through ingestion. Important examples of bacterial diseases are milky disease of Japanese beetles, caused by *Bacillus papiliae* and *B. lentimorbus;* and the honeybee diseases. American foulbrood, caused by *Bacillus larvae,* and European foulbrood caused by *Streptococcus pluton, Bacillus cercus* and its variant, *B. thuringiensis,* produce crystals toxic to more than 182 species of pest insects, mostly Lepidoptera caterpillars. Commercial preparations of bacteria and crystals are applied with regular spray equipment to trees and crop plants in the control of pests. Bacterial diseases of plants are mostly transmitted mechanically by insects, but some seem to be endosymbionts of the gut and may be transovarially transmitted. Fire blight of pears, apples, and some 90 kinds of other trees is caused by *Erwinia amylovora* and mechanically transmitted by many insects, especially bee pollinators.

Human diseases caused by bacteria and mechanically transmitted by insects are dysentery bacteria, *Shigella* and *Salmonella,* carried by muscid filth flies, and tularemia, caused by *Francisella tularensis* and transmitted by the bite of tabanid deerflies. The organism causing plague, or Black Death, *Yersinia pestis, is* transmitted biologically by fleas. Plague bacilli are naturally transmitted among wild rodents by rodent fleas. While hunting or camping human beings may acquire infections by handling diseased rodents or rabbits. Urban populations are endangered when the pathogen infects domestic rodents such as the black rat, *Rattus rattus,* and its ectoparasite, the oriental rat flea, *Xenopsylla cheopis*. Bacteria multiply in the flea's gut, forming a gelatinous plug in the proventriculus. *A "blocked flea" is* unable to pass blood to the midgut and repeatedly attempts to suck. The result is that plague bacilli are regurgitated into the wounds. As the disease spreads among rats, the susceptible rats die. Fleas leave cold rats and transfer to live rats or humans. Following infection of a human by flea bites, the lymph nodes become inflamed -hence the name `*bubonic plague,* " referring to the swollen buboes. In the most deadly phase of an epidemic, bacilli are rapidly spread from human to human by inhalation of infected respiratory droplets.

Plague has devastated the populations of entire countries since ancient times and has played a decisive role in history. In addition to the staggering statistics of human deaths, the impact of this disease is reflected in works of art and literature. In the *Decameron*, Giovanni Boccaccio (1313-1375) describes plague in Florence in 1348. This was at the beginning of the great epidemic that swept away 25 million Europeans and contributed to social change in the fourteenth century.

The terror of plague is shown in art beginning in 1348. Reproduced here is an engraving. *"The Pest,"* by Pierre Mignard (1610-1695). The scene was created from Biblical accounts of the plague of David (II Samuel 24 and 1 Chronicles 21) and Thucydides's description of the plague in Athens. Accurately illustrated are symptoms of unquenchable thirst (fountains in center background), instanity (delirious patient at left being restrained), and axillary buboes ruptured or lanced (armpit of woman in center foreground). The angel in the sky is pouring sulfurous fumes as a disinfectant. Smoke from torch and brazier were also intended to be purifying.

Spirochetes are slender, motile bacteria of spiral configuration. Some are associated with insects. Termites of the advanced Family Termitidae may depend on spirochetes as intestinal endosymbionts. In the same genus as the spirochetes of syphilis. *Treponema,* are pathogens causing human skin diseases called pinta and yaws. These are transmitted mechanically from lesions by *HippelaWs* (Chloropidae) eye gnats.

Rickettsiae are small, nonmotile bacteria that are spherical or rod-shaped. All the associated with arthropods at some point in their natural cycle. Diptera, Hymenoptera, and ticks possess commensalistic or mutualistic forms. The best known rickettsiae are pathogens of vertebrates that are transmitted by bloodsucking fleas, lice, ticks, or mites. Epidemic, or louse-borne, typhus lever is caused by *Rickettsia prowazeki* and transmitted by human body lice, *Pediculus humanus* (Pediculidae). The microbes multiply in the louse's gut, passing out with feces. Human infection results when infected feces are inhaled or lice are crushed and the pathogens are introduced by fingers into skin abrasions or the eyes. Louse-borne typhus spreads rapidly during times of social strife. Crowding and poor sanitation, as in war or famine, favour louse infestations. Typhus was partly responsible for the collapse of Napoleons's army in 1812.

Murine, or *flea-borne typhus is* caused by *Rickettsia typhi.* The disease is transmitted among rats by rat fleas such as *Xenopsylla cheopis* (Pulicidae) and others. Humans acquire infection in the same manner as in louse-borne typhus, i.e., through infected flea feces and crushed fleas. Other important rickettsial diseases are transmitted by acarines: Rocky Mountain spotted fever caused by *Rickettsia rickettsii* and transmitted by ticks; and. scrub typhus, caused *by Rickettsia tsutsugamushi* and transmitted by chiggers. Until recently rickettsias have been considered confined to insect or vertebrate hosts. Several diseases of plants, previously thought to be persistent viruses, are now associated with rickettsialike organisms; Pierce's disease of grapes, phony peach disease, and clover club leaf. All are transmitted by leafhoppers. Clover club leaf has been shown to multiply in both the plant and insect.

INTER-RELATION WITH PROTOZOA

Protozoa are *endosymbionts* in nearly all orders of insects but are best known in Orthoptera and Isoptera. Extraordinary quantities are found in termites, where flagellates constitute up to one-third of a nymph's weight. Protozoa enter insects via the mouth, and many types remain associated with the gut, but others become intracellular parasites or live in the hemocoel. They may be pathogenic, commensalistic, or mutualistic in relation to the insect host. Pathogens causing several major diseases of vertebrates are transmitted by insects, as are a few minor protozoan pathogens of plants.

The geologic record gives no clues to the antiquity of insectsYmbiont relationships. That these associations can be quite old is inferred from the distribution of flagellates among the primitive termites and *Cryptocercus* roaches. Cleveland and his associates found 25 species of flagellates in *Cryptocercus*. Several species of the flagellate genus *Trichonympha* are found in both the roach and various termites. Because few opportunities for exchange of endosymbionts now seem to exist between the two orders of insects, we infer that both probably derive their *Trichonympha* from a common ancestor in the Mesozoic Era.

Protozoa pathogenic to insects have been reviewed by Brooks. The most important are the microsporidians, which are parasites of many, if not most insects, especially of Lepidoptera and Diptera. The pebrine disease of silkworms, caused by *Nosema bombycis* and nosema disease of honeybees, caused by N. *apis,* are examples. The coccidian *Adelina is* pathogenic in Coleoptera and Diptera. Relatively harmless are the eugregarines that are also known from many insects, especially Coleoptera, Orthoptera and Diptera. Some are easily seen with the unaided eye because they may be up to 16 mm long. *Mattesia grandis is,* however, highly pathogenic to the boll. *weevil.Anthonomis grandis,* and may prove useful in its control. At one time malaria was considered the most important disease of humans. It is caused by four species of sporozoans in the genus *Plasmodium* and transmitted by mosquitoes of the genus *Anopheles*. Persistent chemical insecticides, especially DDT, and antimalarial drugs have substantially reduced mortality. The prospect was so encouraging that in 1955, the World Health organization resolved to undertake a worldwide eradication programme. The use of residual insecticides continues to be the main strategy, but a variety of other methods are being developed to control resistant populations of the vectors. Unfortunately, malaria is now increasing in several parts of the world.

The biological transmissin of plasmodia is of the cyclopropagative type. Female *Anopheles* ingest microgametocytes and macrogametocytes along with blood from infected humans. In the mosquito's midgut, the microgametocytes produce male microgametes that seek and penetrate the female cell, now enlarged and called a macrogamete. The resulting zygote develops into a motile ookinete. This enters the midgut epithelium and encysts as an oocyst between the epithelium and the outer tissues of the gut. Within the oocyst the cell undergoes mitotic and meiotic divisions, ultimately producing thousands of haploid sporozoites. The oocyst bursts, releasing the sporozoites in the hemocoel. The sporozoites invade various tissues, but those reaching the salivary glands are passed into another human's blood when the mosquito feeds. In the human, the sporozoites first enter cells of the liver, then produce merozoites that enter red blood cells. Merozoites develop into trophozoites that destroy the blood cell and release either more merozoites or gametocytes. The release of merozoites and their toxins occurs at regular periods according to the species of *Plasmodium.* This is the cause of the recurring favours and chills that characterize malarial attacks.

Other important diseases of humans in tropical regions are caused by flagellates of the genera *Tryponosoma* and *Leishmania.* Several kinds of diseases are produced by the latter, including kala azar and espundia. *Phlebotomus* flies (Psychodidae) are known as vectors. Trypanosomes cause trypanosomiasis, or sleeping sickness. In Africa, both sexes of tsetse flies, *Glossina* (Muscidae), feed on blood and ingest flagellates. Some mechanical transmission may occur immediately by infected mouthparts, but cyclopropagative transmission flows. The flagellates multiply in the gut, and moving anteriorly to the salivary glands, they are passed to new hosts when the fly feeds. Trypanosomiasis in America is called Chagas' disease. The vectors are blood-sucking reduviid bugs of the Subfamily Triatominae. The transmission is also cyclopropagative in the insect's gut, but infection of new hosts is by feces. The bug defecates after feeding. Humans accidentally rub the contaminated feces into the wound or into the eyes or mouth.

Flagellates of the genus *Phytomonas* infest plants, especially those with latex. Vectors are various phytophagous HemipteraHeteroptera.

INTER-RELATION WITH FUNGI

Fungi have many interesting relationships with insects as commensals, mutuals, and pathogens. Many fungal diseases of plants are transmitted by insects, but apparently no pathogens of vertebrates. The laboulbeniales are fungi that live almost exclusively on the integument of Coleoptera, Diptera and Neuroptera. As commensalistic ectosymbionts, they are transmitted from insect to insect by contact. The insect hosts are rarely killed by the fungi.

A mutualistic relationship exists between *Septobasidium* fungi and various scale insects in the Southeastern United States. Patches of fungus grow in concentric, annual rims on the bark of trees. Inside are tunnels and chambers enclosing scale insects. Thus embedded and protected, the scales feed on the plant with their long sucking mouthparts. The fungus apparently derives nourishment parasitically from the living insects and may kill the insect. Mutualistic ectosymbionts among the fungi are frequently cultivated in *"fungus gardens."* The insects are gall midges (*Lasioptera*) wood wasps (Siricidae), ambrosia beetles, fungus ants (*Atta*), and fungus termites. Nutritious food is obtained from fungal saprophytes that grow on cellulose-rich wood or vegetable matter. Some fungus is carried by the adult insects to new locations. Queen *Atta* ants carry a pellet of fungus in a pouch in the mouth when they fly forth to establish new colonies. Wood-boring ambrosia beetles and wood wasps have special integumental cavities called *mycetangia*. Here the fungus is protected from desiccation and is nourished by a secretion. The mycetangia are filled with fungus before the insect leaves its infected gallery. When the beetles bore into a new host or the wasps oviposit, the fungus is inoculated in the area where the progeny will develop.

Blue-stain fungi of the genus *Ceratocystis* are associated with certain scolytid bark beetles. The spores are carried on the body, in mycetangia, or passed with feces. Sawood moisture of the infected tree is reduced, making the tree more favourable for beetles. The stain lowers the commercial value of the wood. *Dutch elm disease* is caused *by Ceratocystis ulmi.* First discovered in Ohio in 1930, this European disease has killed or has made necessary the destruction of elm trees in many urban areas. It has been recently recognized in California, *Scolytus multistriatus* and *Hylurgopinus rufipes* are vectors. The former feeds on twigs of healthy trees after emergence from infected trees or logs. The beetle then seeks sick trees or freshly cut elm wood to construct its breeding galleries. The healthy trees are infected with spores that cling to the insect. The fungus blocks water-conducting tissues, causing limbs or the whole tree to wilt. The affected parts then become suitable breeding sites for more beetles.

Endosymbiotic fungi and yeasts are found in the mycetomes of Hemiptera-Homoptera and intestines of anobiid and cerambycid beetles. Fungi that are pathogenic to insects normally invade through the integument, but a few enter via the gut. Warm humid environments favor fungal attack. The fungal filaments and reproductive structures are often evident on the body surface. Species of *Entomophthora* and *Beauveria* are common pathogens. In the past, the latter caused serious losses of silkworms in China and Europe. *Beuveria globulifera* was early noted as causing a contagious disease of the chinch bug *Blissus leucopterus* (Lygaeeidae). Near the end of the last century, the fungus was mass-produced and distributed to farmers for control of the pest. *Entomophthora* infects all life stages of insects, especially Diptera, Hemiptera, Lepidoptera, Coleoptera and Orthoptera. In the fall, *Entomophthora muscae* causes epidemics among flies, leaving them attached in lifelike postures inside houses or on plants.

Insects mechanically transmit fungal pathogens of plants, but this does not preclude intimate biological relationships. The Dutch elm disease mentioned above is an example. Spores of *Fusarium moniliforme,* causing the disease endosepsis of figs, are transmitted when the fig wasp pollinates the flowers. A honeydew-like secretion is caused by the ergot fungus *Claviceps,* when it attacks grasses and cereals. The secretion, infected with'spores, is rich in amino acids and attractive to Diptera. The insect visitors spread disease by carrying the spores externally or by passing them in feces.

INTER-RELATION WITH HELMINTHS

Helminths are the worm like triploblastic animals belonging to Platyhelminthes, Aschelminthes and Acanthocephala. Among the flatworms, or Platyhelminthes, are two classes that involve insects as intermediate hosts. The digenean fluckes of the class Trematoda usually depend on snails as the first intermediate host, then enter a second intermediate host (snails, crustaceans, or fish) or encyst on aquatic plants before being ingested by the definitive vertebrate host. The fluke *Prosthogonimus spp.*, however, seeks dragonfly naiads as the second intermediate host after parasitizing snails. The parasites enter the anus while the naiad takes in water during respiration. Birds eat the infected naiads or adult dragonflies and become the definitive hosts.

One of the most remarkable effects of a parasite on its vector has been observed in the case of the fluke *Dicrocoelium spp.* Eggs are released by the adult flukes in the definitive host and excreted. The eggs are then ingested by land snails and parasites later expelled from the snails respiratory pore in a ball of slime. Hundreds of parasites may be protected in each ball. The balls are collected by several species of ants in the genera *Formica* and *Proformica.* In the nest, the slime balls are eaten by the colony, resulting in a high rate of infection. Most parasites encyst in the ants' abdomen, but one or two often migrate to the brain, where a lesion develops. In the evening, ants usually descend from vegetation, but those with brain lesions remain on the vegetation until warmed by the next. day's sun. Ruminants grazing early in the day ingest the infected ants, thus completing the cycle.

The tapeworms, or Cestoda, depend primarily on arthropods as intermediate hosts. Crustaceans are the usual hosts because most tapeworms are marine. The adults occupy the intestines of vertebrates. Some tapeworms in the terrestrial environmental utilize insects as intermediate hosts. Eggs of *Dipylidium caninum,* the dog tapeworm, are ingested by larval dog fleas, *Ctenocephalides canis;* cat fleas, *C. fells;* human fleas; *Pulex initans;* and the dog louse, *Trichodectes canis.* The larval fleas and the biting lice have chewing mouthparts. They are able to ingest eggs, whereas the adult fleas cannot. Dogs and cats and their wild relatives acquire tapeworms by eating adult fleas or lice that were infected in earlier costars. Humans are occasionally hosts.

Various species of *Hymenolepis* infect aquatic crustaceans, earwigs, dung and scavenger beetles, millipeds, meal moths, and fleas. *Hymenolepis nana,* the dwarf tapeworm of humans, mice, and rats, and *H. diminuta,* another tapeworm of mice and rats, both depend on insects as intermediate hosts. Coprophagic scavengers, including larval fleas and the mealworm beetle, *Tenebrio molitor,* ingest infected rodent feces. The insect is eaten in turn by the definitive vertebrate hosts.

Humans may be parasitized also. A number of other genera of tapeworms involve beetles, grasshoppers, larval and adult flies, and ants in their life cycles. The *spiny-headed worms, orAcanthocephala,* also live as endo-parasitic adults in the intestines of terrestrial and aquatic vertebrates. On land, the eggs are ingested by insects, and in water probably by both insects and crustaceans. The intermediate hosts are later eaten by the vertebrate. *Macracanthorhynchus hirudinaceus is* a parasite of pigs and their wild relatives, and occasionally humans. The insect hosts are coprophagic beetle larvae of the Families Scarabaeidae, Tenebrionidae and Hydrophilidae. They acquire eggs of the parasite by eating pig feces. The pigs then eat the infected larvae in the course of rooting in the soil.

The Aschelminthes include two classes of worms that infect insects; roundworms or Nematoda, and hairworms or Nematomopha. The immature stages of the latter are endoparasitic in insects and crustaceans. Adult hairworms are free-living in saltwater or freshwater. The complete cycle in terrestrial and freshwater habitats is not well-known. The adult worms copulate, lay eggs, and die in water. Larval worms emerge and may either penetrate soft-bodied aquatic invertebrates or be ingested by aquatic and possibly by terrestrial insects. Some hosts are not suitable for further development. In these the larvae encyst. Development proceeds, however, in larger terrestrial insects that acquire infection directly from water or by eating intermediate hosts infested with encysted larvae. The parasite enters the hemocoel, feeds and matures. When the host is near or in water, the adult worm emerges from the host quickly and becomes free-living. Heavily parasitized hosts may have the reproductive organs reduced in size. Emergence of the worm is fatal to the host.

May (1919) found up to 20 per cent of tettigoniid grasshoppers, infected with Gordius robustus. Paragordius various was found in gryllid crickets. May believed the parasites were obtained directly from water. Inoue traced part of the life cycle of Chorodes. Mayfly naiads ingest the larvae, and these encyst. The infected adult mayflies are eaten, in turn by larger predators such as the praying mantis. The cyst is digested, freeing the larva to penetrate the host's gut. Development is completed in the hemocoel. The most numerous helminths associated with insects are nematodes. Much remains to be learned about the relationships between the largest group of animals, i.e., the insects, and what is possibly the second largest group, the nematodes. Nematodes have essentially five kinds of relationships to' insects: (1) phoresy, (2) facultative parasitism, (3) obligatory parasitism that depends only on insects as hosts, (4) parasitism involving both insects and plants as host, and (5) obligatory parasitism with insects as intermediate hosts and vertebrates as definitive hosts. Insects are vectors of important nematode diseases of humans and other animals, but they are curiously not vectors of nematodes causing plant diseases.

Insects regularly serve to transport nematodes in a phoretic relationship. Juvenile stages of rhabditoid nematodes in decaying matter or beetle galleries in wood attach themselves externally to insect scavengers or borers and are carried to new habitats. Some harmlessly enter the insect's body, effectively avoiding desiccation. The internal phoretic relationship becomes one of facultative parasitism when the nematode feeds on the host's tissues, but is also able to complete its life cycle without an insect host. The effect on the host varies from no apparent harm to death. Species of Neoaplectana have an odd relationship to their insect hosts that defies classification. The juvenile worm penetrates the insect's body like a true endoparasite. Specific bacteria are released by the worm after it enters the hemocoel. The bacteria rapidly kill the host, and the nematode completes up to several generations, feeding on the dead host's tissues and bacteria. Neoaplectana is probably obligatorily associated with insects in nature, yet can be reared on artificial media such as dog food. Is it a facultative parasite, predator, or saprophyte? Regardless of label, the nematodes are among the most promising organisms for use in the control of insect pests.

Obligate parasites feed only on insects. The juvenile stages of obligate nematode parasites of insects develop in the host's hemocoel, intestine, or reproductive organs. Adults may be free- living or remain in the host. One important family are the mermithids that infest aquatic insects and terrestial insects in moist habitats. The host is killed when the nematode emerges. Infection is sufficiently high in some areas to reduce significantly or to eradicate the host populations. Nematodes influence the host's development by destroying organs, removing nutritional reserves, or possibly producing toxic effectss on the corpora allata. Altered behaviour, reduced fecundity, sterilization, intersexes, and intercastes of social insects may result from parasitism. Juvenile nematodes of the genus Deladenus infest the hemocoel of siricid wood wasps. The adult parasites mature outside the host. Two types of females are produced. One type does not feed and after mating, penetrates a new host. The other type feeds on a fungal symbiote of the wood wasp. Female wood wasps inoculate the fungus where they oviposit. Both sexes of the wood wasps are sterilized by the parasites, but the female continues to fly to new trees for oviposition. The fungus-feeding nematodes are deposited during the futile oviposition in new places where other wood wasps are present. A related nematode is parasitic on weevils and mustard plants.

The last group of nematodes involve species whose definitive hosts are vertebrates. These are mainly the filarial worms, some of which are, host specific to humans. The adult worms feed on lymph and tissue fluids. The young or microfilariae are produced viviparously. Blood-sucking Diptera ingest the microfilariae. These penetrate the insect's gut and become intracellular parasites in fat, muscle, or Malpighian tubule cells. In 1 to 2 weeks, they metamorphose into an infective stage that migrates to the proboscis. When the insect feeds, the parasites migrate into the wound. The grossly swollen legs, breasts, or genitalia characteristics of elephantiasis are caused by *Wuchereria bancrofti. Culex pipiens quinquefasciatus is* the principal sector, but various species in other mosquito genera are also found infected. Species of *Simulium* transmit *Onchocerca volvulus, a* blinding disease of the Tropics. Another eye disease in Africa, caused by *Loa loa, is* carried by deerflies of the genus *Chrysops.* Other nematodes combining insects and vertebrates as hosts include the ascaridoid *Subulura spp.* that infects beetles and cockroaches, and then galliform birds. Many genera of spiruroid nematodes utilize coprophagous scarab beetles, cockroaches, termites, and anthomyiid flies as intermediate hosts. Definitive hosts are domestic animals and birds and then wild allies.

Carnivorous Insects

Carnivorous insects are those insects that kill or injure one or more other invertebrates before completing their life cycle. Most of these carnivorous insects feed on other insects and are said to be *entomophagous*. Snails, earthworms, millipedes, mites, and other terrestrial and freshwater invertebrates are also eaten by insects. Victims are called *prey* if killed directly, *hosts* if fed upon while still living. Entomophagous insects are divided into three major groups according to their mode of feeding. (1) *predators* kill and consume more than one prey organism to reach maturity; (2) *parasitoids* require only one host to reach maturity, but ultimately kill the host; and (3) *parasites* feed on one or more hosts, but do not normally kill the host.

Parasitoidss insects are intermediate between predators and parasites in the sense that they live at first parasitically at the host's expense, but ultimately kill the host. In entomological literature the word "parasite," alone and in combinations (e.g., hyperparasite), if often used loosely for an insect that lives at a host's expense, regardless of the host's fate. From an ecological viewpoint, predators and parasitoids both act to eliminate individuals in the prey or host population, whereas true parasites permit the host to continue functioning in the community, though often at a subnormal level. This is an important distinction, especially when predators and parasitoids are used to control pests. Whenever possible in this text we have used the word "parasite" only for those insects that normally do not cause host mortality. However, we use the term "endoparasite" indiscriminantly for both parasites and parasitoids that are physically inside the body of the host.

Although the three modes of feeding defined above can be easily distinguished among most insects, the spectrum of entomophagous habits is actually continuous. For example, within a species an individual of a normally predaceous insects such as a ladybird beetle, might complete its life cycle by eating only one large host and thus be technically, according to number of victims, a prasitoid. Alternatively, the host of a parasitoid might survive attack, or the host of a parasite might be fatally injured. These abnormal relationships make distinction somewhat arbitrary, but are instructive by indicating how one mode of feeding might evolve into another.

Before further discussion of predators, parasitoids and parasites, some additional kinds of behaviour should be mentioned in which an insect consumes food collected at the energetic expense of the host. Although the insect may not be directly entomophagous, the net result is a reduction in the number of host. offspring and an increase in the offspring of the insect that benefits *Cleptoparasites,* or "cuckoo" parasites, lay their eggs in the nests of other species, in the manner of cuckoo birds. The cleptoparasitic parent or the larva may kill the egg or larva of the host immediately, or the host larva dies of starvation after the cleptoparasite larva eats the nest provisions. In the former instance, the young cleptoparasites often possess enlarged mandibles suited for attack. *A social parasite* is a female that enters the nest of a social host and takes over the role of the queen. The social parasite's offspring are fed by host workers .at the expense of host offspring. The host is usually a closely related species. Parasites that spend much of their life their host's nests are known as *inquilines.* Slavery is practiced by certain ants. Worker pupae of another species are taken by slavemaking workers. The resulting adult slaves then become members of the colony and do most of the work. Nest robbing also involves social species. The robbing species enters the nest of another colony and removes the stored food. *Phoresy* is the transport of an insect on or, physically inside the body of another insect. The insect that provides the transportation is usually not harmed. When the passenger is an adult female parasitoid or predator, however, the usual result is that. the passenger remains aboard until the host lays its eggs. The passenger then oviposits on the host's eggs. This habit occurs frequently in the wasp family Scelionidae. The first instar larvae of meloid and rhipiphorid beetles, stylopid parasites, and eacharitid wasps are commonly phoretic on adult of their favoured hosts. By this means the larvae gain entrance to the nests of the hosts.

Resistance of hosts or prey to attack

Hosts or prey insects may avoid or·actively prevent attack by entomophagous insects. Enemies may be exclude by tough cocoons, 'hard puparia, nests of mud or leaves, or by the inaccessible position of the insect in burrows in soil or plant tissues. Some still succumb to parasitoids and predators that are suitably equipped with strong mandibles or long, powerful ovipositors. Exposed insects may violently resist attack or quickly escape. When approached by an enemy, an aphid may drop from the plant, walk away, or kick and secrete oily droplets from its siphunculi. The odour of the siphuncular secretion alarms other aphids, and they drop off or walk away. Larvae and pupae of Lepidoptera or Coleoptera thrash about when contacted. Larvae may bite, or regurgitate or secrete defensive fluids. One of the advantages of social behaviour is mutual defense against insect enemies. It seems possible that some of the defensive strategies to avoid predation by vertebrates are also effective against insect enemies. Certain aphids are distasteful and are avoided by insect predators after an initial contact. The gustatory senses and learning ability of the predator are therefore important to the success of this defense. The role of protective colouration and behaviour, however, is generally- less effective because many insect predators, unlike vertebrate predators, do not depend on vision-to find prey.

In some cases the insect hosts are able to respond defensively to endoparasite; by a reaction called *encapsulation*. Hemocytes collect around those foreign bodies that are too large to be engulfed by a single cell. A capsule forms as the inner layer of cells flatten over the object's surface and new cells are added outside. The inner layer secretes an envelope of connective tissue. The capsule may remain clear or become darkened by melanization. If the foreign body is an endoparasite, it is killed by the encapsulation. The process may take only a day to complete. Fourteen orders of insects are known to encapsulae foreign bodies, endoparasitic worms, and parasitoids. Among the parasitoids, larvae of certain species definitely stimulate encapsulation in hosts that are not the normal hosts; maggots of Tachinidae and some, but not all, wasp larvae of Ichneumonidae, Braconidae, Chaleidoidea (Encyrtidae, Eulophidae). Proctotrupoidea and Cynipoidea. Yet in their normal hosts, the parasitoids usually escape encapsulation. How do they succeed?

There are certain species of wasps, attack only eggs. By rapidly completing their growth before the host's hemocytes develop, they avoid encapsulation altogether. Rapid destruction of a larval host also avoids encapsulation by simply killing the host quickly. If the parasitoid lingers for a while and allows the host larva to grow, a larger food supply becomes available, but at a greater risk of encapsulation. Certain parasitoids insert their eggs precisely into an organ of the host where the endoparasite will be separated from the host's hemolymph by a layer of connective tissue. This prevents encapsulation. Others first invade the alimentary canal and are sheltered from the host's hemocytes. When the host is suitably larger, the parasitoid feeds voraciously and so debilitates the host that it is unable to react in time. Some parasitoids are initially invested in cellular membranes the cells of which become dissociated, enlarged, and circulate in the host's hemolymph. Apparently the cells absorb nutrients and similarly act to reduce the host's ability to muster an encapsulation.

It has been shown that the eggs and first instar larvae of the wasp *Venturia coneseens* (Ichneumonidae) are coated with a particulate layer that inhibits encapsulation by the hemocytes of its moth host, *Anagasta kuehniella* (Pyralidae). The layer is first deposited on the egg by a specialized region of the wasp's oviduct and later is somehow transferred from the egg shell to the wasp larva once it is inside the moth larva. If the coating is disrupted, encapsulation ensues.

EVOLUTION OF ENTOMOPHAGY

Among the earliest insect fossils in the Upper Carboniferous Period are Odonata. Today the dragonflies are exclusively predaceous, and we assume they were also in ancient times. Predatory habits have apparently evolved repeatedly throughout the orders from scavenging and plant-feeding Acestors. Parasitoids and entomophagous parasites did not appear until the holometabolous life cycle was evolved. Thus, we can conclude that predation is the oldest mode of the entomophagous habits. Other living orders present as fossils in the Paleozoic Era that were mostly predatory are the Neuroptera and Raphidioptera. Certain extinct orders have been suspected to be prdatory. The *Mischoptera* of the Meganisoptera had stout, raptorial forelegs. Were these used to capture prey or to cling to vegetation? The giant *Meganeura* of the Meganisoptera had biting Miles and large eyes. These insects resembled dragonflies and were doubtless predatory. Many fossils are merely wings without the body parts from which we could infer food habits.

The early evolution of *parasitoids* and *parasites is* not well documented by fossils. Most parasitoids are Hymenoptera and Diptera. These orders must have evolved diverse forms during the Mesozoic Era following the first appearance of fossils of both orders in the Triassic Period. The parasitoids were probably part of this radiation. Fossil chalcidoid wasps are known from the Cretaceous Period. In contrast to most predators, parasitoids are host-specific. Presumably as a consequence of coevolutionary interactions with their hosts, parasitoid taxa also tend to have many more species than predatory taxa. The parasitic Strepsiptera are known from primitive forms preserved in Baltic amber. They may have existed no earlier than than Tertiary Period.

TABLE 5.1

Major Taxa of Entomophagous Insects

Predaceous as both immatures and adults

Collembola
- Isotomidae (*Isotoma*)

Diplura
- Japygidae

Odonata (all)

Mantodea (all)

Dermaptera
- Arixeniina (probably)
- Forficulina (most)

Orthoptera
- Gryllacrididae*
- Gryllidae (*Oecanthus*)
- Tettigoniidae (*Conocephalus*)

Psocoptera
- Caeciliidae (*Caecilius*)

Hemiptera (Heteroptera)
- Anthocoridae (*Anthocoris*)
- Belostomatidae
- Enicocephalidae
- Gelastocoridae
- Gerridae (occasionally)
- Hebridae
- Largidae (*Euryopthabmus*)

- Lygaeidae (*Geocoris*)
- Miridae (some)
- Nabidae
- Naucoridae
- Nepidae
- Notonectidae
- Ochteridae
- Pentatomidae (some)
- Phymatidae
- Pyrrhocoridae (*Dindymus*)
- Reduviidae (except Triatominae)
- Saldidae (occasionally)
- Veliidae (occasionally)

Thysanoptera

- Aeolothripidae (*Aeolothrips*)
- Phlaethripidae (*Leptothrips*)
- Thripidae (*Scolothrips*)

Neuroptera (most)

Raphidioptera (all)

Coleoptera (Adephaga)

- Amphizoidae
- Carabidae
- Cicindellidae
- Dytiscidae
- Gyrinidae

Coleoptera (Polyphaga)

- Anthicidae (*Anthicus*)
- Anthribidae (*Brachytarsus*)
- Cantharidae (many)
- Cleridae
- Coccinellidae (most)
- Cucujidae (*Cryptolestes*)
- Elateridae (some)
- Histeridae
- Lampyridae
- Malachiidae

Melyridae (many)
Nitidulidae (*Cybocephalus*)
Nosodendridae
Orthoperidae
Phengodidae
Silphidae (*Xylodrepa*)
Staphylinidae (many)

Diptera (*Brachycera*)
Asilidae
Dolichopodidae
Empididae

Diptera (*Cyclorrhapha*)
Anthomyiidae (*Hylemya*)

Hymenoptera (Apocrita)
Chalcidoidea
Chrysididae
Formicidae
Ichneumonoidea
Vespidae

Predaceous primarily as immatures

Ephemeroptera
Siphlonuridae (*Isonychia*)

Plecoptera
Setipalpia (most)

Megaloptera (all)

Neuroptera
Chrysopidae (*Chrysopa*)

Coleoptera (Polyphaga)
Dermestidae (*Thaumaglossa*)
Drilidae
Hydrophilidae (some)
Lycidae (most)
Meloidae
Rhipiphoridae (most)

Diptera (*Nematocera*)
Cecidomyiidae (*Aphidoletes*)

Ceratopogonidae
Culicidae (*Chaoborus*)
Chironomidae (Tanypodinae)
Culicidae (*Megarhinus*)
Mycetophilidae (*Platyura*)
Tipulidae (Hexatomiini)

Diptera (*Brachycera*)
Bombyliidae (most)
Mydaidae
Rhagionidae
Tabanidae (*Tabanus*)
Therevidae
Xylophagidae

Diptera (*Cyclonhapha*)
Anthomyiidae (some)
Calliphoridae (*Stomorhina*)
Chamaemyiidae
Chloropidae (*Siphonella*)
Drosophilidae (*Gitonides*)
Lonchaeidae (*Lonchaea*)
Otitidae (*Elassogaster*)
Phoridae (*Syneura*)
Sarcophagidae(Sarcophaga)
Sciomyzidae
Syrphidae (most)

Lepidoptera
Blastobasidae (*Hokocera*)
Cosmopteryidae (*Stathmopoda*)
Cyclotornidae
Heliodinidae
Lycaenidae (some)
Noctuidae (*Eublemma*)
Lyonetidae (*Ereunetis*)
Psychidae (Platoeceticus)
Pyralidae (*Laetilia, Macrotheca*)
Sesiidae (*Synathedon*)

Tineidae (*Dicymolomia*)
Tortricidae (some Tortrix)
Trichoptera
Hydropsychidae (*Hydropsyche*)
Polycentropodidae
Rhyacophilidae
Hymenoptera (Apocrita)
Proctotrupoidea
Sphecoldea (some)

Primarily as adults

Cotcoptera (Polyphaga)
Cerambycidae (*Elytroleptus*)
Scarabaeidae (*Cremastocheihis*)
Mecoptera
Bittacidae (some)
Diptera
Anthomyiidae (some)
Blephariceridae
Calliphoridae (*Bengalia*)
Ceratopogonidae (some)
Hymenoptera (most Symphyta)
Hymenoptera (Apocrita)
Bethylidae
Dryinidae
Mutillidae
Tiphiidae

Parasitoids

Coleoptera
Carabidae (*Lebia, Brachinus*)
Colydiidae (*Deretaphrus*)
Meloidae
Rhipiceridae
Rhipiphoridae
Staphylinidae (some Aleocharinae)
Diptera
Acroceridae

Agromyzidae (*Cryptochaetum*)
Anthomyiidae
Conopidae
Nemestrinidae
Phoridae (*Megaselia*)
Pipunculidae
Pyrgotidae
Tachinidae

Lepidoptera
Cyclotomidae
Epipyropidae

Hymenoptera
Bethyloidea
Chalcidoldea
Chrysidoldea
Evanioidea
Figitidae
Ibalidae
Ichneumonoidea
Magalyroidea
Pompiloidea
Proctotrupoidea
Scolioidea
Sphecoidea (some)
Trigonaloidea

Insect ectoparasites of insects

Diptera
Ceratopogonidae (some)
Chironomidae (*Symbiocladius*)

Hymenoptera
Scelionidae (*Rielia*)

True insect endoparasites of insects

Strepsiptera (all)

Hypermetamorphic taxa

Neuroptera
Mantispidae

Coleoptera

Carabidae (*Lebia, Brachuuus*)
Colydiidae (a few)
Drilidae
Meloidae
Rhipiceridae (*Sandalus*)
Rhipiphoridae
Staphylinidae (Aleocharinae)

Strepsiptera

Diptera
Acroceridae
Bombyliidae
Calliphoridae (some)
Nemestrinidae
Tachinidae (some)

Lepidoptera
Cyclotornidae
Epipyroidae

Hymenoptera
Chalcidoidea (some)
Ichneumonoidea (some)
Proctotrupoidea
Trigonaloidea

This list of taxa is intended to be representative, not exhaustive. The listing of a family without qualification does not necessarily mean put all species in the family have the same food habits. Well-known or exceptional genera are given in parenthesis.

PREDACEOUS INSECTS

Predators are usually larger in body size than other entomophagous insects, and more than one and often many prey are eaten. The greater need for prey also makes predators dependent on prey populations of higher density than other entomophagous insects. Prey are usually smaller than the predator but proportional to the predator's size. Irr other words, larger predators take larger prey and smaller predators take smaller prey. Wasps with stings and ants in groups can kill prey larger than themselves. Victims are rapidly subdued, and except when the predators are wasps that store prey for later consumption by their larvae, the prey are eaten immediately.

The same terminology can be used here as in describing the choice of foods by *phytophagous insects. Monophagous predators* feed on one specie of prey; oligophagous predators take several prey species; and *polyphagous predators* take many kinds of prey. The last type are the "generalists." They take individuals of prey species largely in proportion to their relative abundance. Thus polyphagous predators, by continually shifting to the most abundant prey, tend to stabilize populations of prey in the community. Furthermore, if mobile, they are able to thrive in disturbed communities where prey species vary in abundance as ecological succession proceeds. At the other extreme, monophagous predators are density-dependent on one species of prey, and may regulate the prey at lower levels than polyphagous predators. Monophagous predators tend to be associated with undisturbed communities where their host maintains continuous, stable populations. Persual of Table 6.1 leads to the conclusion that a majority of predaceous taxa are carnivorous in all feeding stages. This does not mean they are always exclusively carnivorous; exact diets vary species by species. Adults of some of these visit flowers for nectar, as do certain adults of taxa that are predaceous only as immatures. Scavenging, honeydew, symbionts, and plant foods also may supplement a predator's diet.

Some of the complexities of diet are revealed in the following example. Hagen and his associates have carefully examined the diets of lacewings of the genus *Chrysopa* (Chrysopidae). Adults of about half the species have larger mandibles and are predaceous like the larvae. Adults of other species have shorter mandibles and feed only on honeydew and pollen. The foreguts of the second group contain yeast symbionts and are supplied with larger tracheal trunks for increased respiration. By this means the essential amino acids are acquired even though the adult diet lacks animal prey. Predaceous adults of the first group lack the yeast and tracheal modifications. Females of both groups of *Chrysopa* require substantial amounts of food before eggs are produced. As a consequence, females lay eggs only near abundant food sources that will later supply the 'acewing larvae. An advantage to the honeydew-feeding species is that prey of the larvae may include not only aphids but a variety of other insects attracted to honeydew.

In contrast to other entomophagous insects, predators of both sexes must repeatedly find and subdue prey. They may be active during day and night. The eggs of predaceous insects are usually deposited by the females in close proximity to or at least in the vicinity of suitable prey. In this way the adult's well-developed compound eyes. Chemoreceptive organs, and ability to fly are used to search for prey-rich habitats within which the less well-equipped immatures can forage. Plants of a certain height, odours of honey-dew, odours of decay, and even the pheromones of prey are attractive to searching predators. The adult may eat prey or other attractive foods when they are found or only lay eggs near the prey.

Strategies of Insect Predators

Several kinds of strategies are used by insect predators in finding and capturing prey, (1) *random searching,* (2) *hunting,* (3) *ambush,* and (4) *trapping.*

Insects belonging to the first type roam in the appropriate microhabitat and seize prey after physical contact. Their orientation to objects in the microhabitat and their movements may increase the probability of encountering prey. For example, the predator may patrol leaf edges, veins, or stems and eat insect eggs or sedentary Homoptera. Random searchers may have either monophagous or polyphagous habits. The prey is accepted if proper incitants are detected by receptors on the forelegs, mouthparts, or antennae. The vitim is then devoured by use of mouthparts that are usually specially adapted for predation. After an initial contact or meal, further searching often involves more frequent turns so that the predator stays in an area of previous sucess. While seemingly inefficient, the random searchers are probably the most common type of insect predator And include species highly effective in regulating prey populations.

Most predatory Coleoptera, are random searchers. Predatory carabids are distinguished by long, sharply hooked mandibles that contrast with the broad, blunt jaws of plant-feeding relatives. Coccinellid beetles, syrphid larvae, and neuorpteran predators that feed on aphids also search at random. The mandibles of predaceous coccinellids may be incisors with one or two apical teeth and a basal tooth or they may be small with ducts for sucking prey juices. Neuopteran larvae have sickle- shaped jaws each formed by the mandible and maxilla locked together to create a tube through which body fluids of prey are sucked.

The Lepidoptera are almost exclusively *phytophagous*. Caterpillars of certain moths retain their close association with plants but attack other phytophagous insects such as coccids'and leafhoppers as well as mites. Caterpillars of the lycanid butterflies may be phytophagous or partly or wholly predaceous on ant larvae and pupae or aphids. The relatively small size and high nutritive value of insects eggs make them vulnerable to predation by insects of varied food habits. Scavenging, phytophagous, predatory, or parasitoid insects may consume eggs. Collectively they are called ***egg predators*** when more than one egg is consumed. These predators are of special ecological importance because the prey never function in the, community. For example, the large clustered eggs of Orthoptera are subject to frequent attack by many predatory larvae; clerids, meloids, bombyluds, rhagionids, anthomyiids, calliphorids, otitids, phorids, sarcophagid and eurytomids. The adult female of the predatory species finds the eggs, lays her own eggs, and the larvae feed essentially as random searchers.

The hunting insects differ from random searchers by utilizing sight or other stimuli to orient to prey at a distance. Visual hunters have enlarged compound eyes with overlapping fields of vision that permit distance perception. Mandibles may be sharply toothed, and the legs may be strong and spiny for seizing elusivc prey. Strong fliers often carry their prey to perching places or nests. Conspicuous examples of such aerial huntes are the adults of dragonflies, asilid flies, and the aculeate or stinging wasps. Stinging wasps are able to subdue prey such as katydids or spiders that are physically larger than themselves by injection of paralyzing chemicals with their sting. Dragonflies such as *Anax* (Aeschnidae) fly almost continuously, *"hawking"* for prey, while *Libellula* (Libellulidae) remain perched until approaches, then quickly dash in pursuit. Asilids commonly perch and await flying prey, then return to the perch after the victim is caught. Adult cicindelid beetles pursue their prey by running fast on open ground.

Stimuli other than visual may be used by hunting predators. Although blind, the famous army ants (genus *Eciton*) of the New World Tropics are enormously successful predators. Odour and movement of prey are detected by chemical and tactile receptors while the colony is on one of its periodic raids. Prey many times larger than the individual worker ants are attacked by massive swarms. Cooperative foraging by "packs" of other kinds of ants also subdues large prey. The back swimmers (Notonectidae) are voracious aquatic predators. They flush and stalk prey by sight and are able to detect the vibrations of prey movements with receptors situated along the forelegs. The water striders (Veliidae) also perceive prey by sight and vibrations.

Insects that ambush prey conserve,energy by simply waiting for prey to approach within striking distance. Reduviid and phymatid bugs often remain motionless on flowers awaiting flower visitors. Such predators are exposed to predation by vertebrates and have either concealing or warning colouration. Concealing colouration may also prevent detection by alert prey. Raptorial or clasping forelegs are frequently characteristic of insects that ambush, especially among the Hemiptera. Some reduviids aid prey. capture by smearing sticky secretions or plant resins on their legs. The beaks of predatory bugs are stout and inject saliva that contains proteolytic enzymes. This is why their bites are painful to human in contrast to the mild bites of bugs that are parasites of humans. Some reduviids also have a potent toxin that quickly renders prey helpless. Once the tissues of the victims are digested, the resultant fluid is sucked by the bug.

The praying mantis is a familiar predator that strikes prey from ambush. The co-ordination of the depth-perceiving vision, mobile head and prothorax, and toothed, raptorial fore-legs has been carefully analyzed by Mittelstaedt. The complete strike, timed by high-speed photography, takes 50 to 70 milliseconds. According to Roeder, a fly or cockroach would require about' 45 to 65 milliseconds to respond if startled by the first movement of the mantis; alas, too slow to escape the strike already in motion. The dragonfly naiad similarly grasps prey with quick strikes of its extensible labium. Cicindelid larvae seize prey that pass near the entrance to their burrows in soil. Only a few kinds of insects trap prey. The *"ant lion"* larvae of Myrmeleontidae (Neuroptera) excavate conical pits in fine, loose sand. The larva wails motionless and buried at the bottom until a small insect ventures into the pit. The ant lion fliks sand toward the victim to cause the unstable sand to slide down. Once the prey is seized, the ant lion extracts the body fluids with its sickle-shaped jaws. Larvae of the fly *Vermileo.* (Rhagionidae) also construct pits and trap prey. Wheeler aptly describes these insects as *"demons of the dust."*

Larvae of the glowworm, *Arachnocampa luminosa* (Mycetophilidae) live in moist caves. They spin slimy webs that dangle from the ceiling. They spin slimy webs that dangle from the ceiling. The larvae glow in the darkness, attracting small flies that become entangled in the sticky webs. Larval mycetophilids of the genus *Platyura* also secrete webs that entangle prey and contain a toxic fluid. Even though silk is secreted by various insects, webs are surprisingly rarely used to trap prey in the manner of spiders. The aquatic caddis fly larvae of the Hydropsychidae spin webs that filter small prey and other food from passing currents. Though they do not spin their own webs, one group of slender reduviid bugs, the emesines, wait in ambush at spider webs to attack trapped prey.

PARASITOID INSECTS

The larvae of holometabolous insects, especially, *Diptera* and Hymenoptera, are *parasitoids*. Their unique attributes combine certain features of true parasites and predators. Parasitoids differ from predators in the following features: (1) only one host is required, (2) the host is larger than the parasitoid, (3) parasitoids are frequently host-specific, attacking one or several related host species, (4) a lower density of host population will sustain a parasitoid population, and (5) the victim is usually searched for and selected by the diurnally active, adult female. A species of parasitoid may be specific not only in the choice of host species, but also in the choice of the life stages of the host to be attacked. Eggs or young or both are most frequently attacked, but pupae and sometimes adult hosts are also eaten.

Parasitoids may fed externally as ectoparasitoids or internally as endoparasitoids. Exposed hosts are usually attacked by endoparasitoids, whereas hosts in protected situations such as leaf mines, falls, or nests, are attacked by either endoparasitoids, or ectoparasitoids. When the larva of a species characteristically develops in the ratio of one to a host, the species is termed *a solitary parasitoid.* When several larva of the same species normally develop in a single host, the species normally develop in a single host, the species is called *a gregarious parasitoid.* If the host is a phytophagous insect, the parasitoid is *a primary parasitoid.* Parasitoids that attack other parasitoids are called *hyperparasitoids* or secondary parasitoids. *Multiple parasitoidism* occurs when two or more species of primary parasitoids attacks one host individual. *Superparasitoidism* occurs when a host is attacked by more larvae of the same species than can reach maturity in the one host. Adult parasitoids are free-living, and most of them are winged except for female velvet ants (Mutillidae) and certain other scolioid wasps. Energy for their activity and egg production is derived from food stored by the larva or by feeding as an adult. In the latter case, nectar and honeydew are frequently consumed. Some parasitoid wasps feed on the body fluids that are released from the host's body when it is punctured by the parasitoid's ovipositor. This is called *host feeding.* In some instances, the host is inside a cocoon or for some other reason can be reached only by the parasitoid's ovipositor. A tube of coagulated host's hemolymph, or possibly of a secretion produced by the parasitoid, forms around the ovipositor. When the ovipositor is withdrawn, the parasitoid is able to suck the host's hemolymph as it wells up in the tube.

The adult parasitoid searches first for the habitat in which the appropriate hosts exist. Primary parasitoids are often attracted mainly by the plants that shelter favoured insects host. In this behaviour the parasitoids respond like phytophagous insects to shapes, colours, and odours of plants. Yet they do not feed on plant tissues. Once near the host, female Hymenoptera usually search for suitable individuals on which to oviposit, using their tactile and . olfactory senses. Their movements may be essentially random or somewhat systematic in response to stimuli detected at a distance. Female Diptera lack the well-developed antennae of wasps and the needlelike ovipositor for precisely inserting eggs in hosts. Consequently, the flies commonly depend on first instar larvae to actually locate hosts after the eggs are laid in the proper habitat. Insects that have two or more successive larval instars specialized for different modes of life are *hypermetamorphic*. Among the hypermetamorphic parasitoids, the first instar larva is specialized for active host finding and the subsequent instars specialized for feeding.

In Hymenoptera the ovipositor plays an important role in selecting the host, sometimes in paralyzing it, and in delivering the egg to the host. Dethier demonstrated that chemoreceptors on the ovipositor tip responded to a variety of chlorids, aliphatic alcohols, and hydrochloric acid in much the same way as taste receptors on the anterior appendages. These receptors function in the final discrimination of hosts before the egg is laid. Hosts inside tough cocoons or sclerotized puparia, in leaf mines, or even deep in burrows in solid wood can be reached by parasitoids equipped with ovipositors of suitable length and strength. By alternate movements of the sharply ridged valvulae, parasitoids can drill through resistant substrates. Receptors at the tip sense the presence and suitability of the host. The highly elastic eggs then pass down the minute channel inside the ovipositor by becoming greatly elongated. After deposition in the host, eggs of some species increase in size by as much as 1000 times. Some wasps temporarily or permanently paralyze or kill the host before ovipositing. For example, the venom of *Bracon hebetor* (Braconidae) causes permanent paralysis of host caterpillars when diluted up to 1 in 200 million parts of host hemolymph.

Superparasitoidism and *multiple parasitoidism* may be advantageous to the parsitoids in that the host's encapsulation reaction is dissipated. The resulting competition among larvae also may be disadvantageous. First instar larvae of certain wasps are specialized to compete successfully in such situations. Some have large sickle-shaped mandibles and kill competitors; others release inhibitory toxins or, if larger, deprive smaller competitors of oxygen. Competition is also commonly reduced by the behaviour of the female wasp. For example, *Trichogramma* (Trichogrammatidae, Chalcidoidea) reject hosts on which other females have walked. Some wasps seem to be able, by means of sensilla on their ovipositors, to. select healthy host indviduals from among those already parasitized.

Endoparasitoids are immersed in the body tissues and fluids of their hosts. Many synchronize their development with that of the host by responding to the host's hormones. Some obtain food in the normal manner via the mouth, but others, especially those in eggs, are greatly simplified and absorb food through thc outer integument. Endoparasitoid wasp larvae commonly exchange gases through their outer integument with or without a tracheal system and rarely with open spiracles. Respiration may be aided by caudal filaments, analles, or an averted hindgut. Endoparasitoid fly larvae usually have at least a metapneustic tracheal system. Some perforate the host's or integument and obtain atmospheric air. Others take age of the host's encapsulation reaction and mold a respiratory "funnel" or tube of host tissue connected to a trachea or the integument.

Among the parasitoids, Hymenoptera have several features of reproductive biology that are noteworthy. Recall that sex is determined in this order by a *haplodiploid mechanism.* The ratio of sexes is often unbalanced in favour of females. A peculiarity of Aphelinidae (Chalcidoidea) is that the female may select the host according to the sex of the egg to be laid. Furthermore, the sex of the larva may influence its feeding behaviour; males may be regular hyperparasitoids. Some wasps are exclusively parthenogenetic, in contrast to other entomophagous insects that are rarely so. The unusual phenomenon of polyembryony and parasites; it occurs in some endoparasitoid Hymenoptera and a few Strepsiptera. As many as 1500 embryos in a single caterpillar have been counted after oviposition by one female of *Litomastix* (Encyrtidae).

PARASITES

A parasite is the organism that lives at the cost of other. True parasitic relationships between one insect and another are surprisingly rare. As we have seen in the previous sections, the usual result of attack is the death of the victim. Entomophagous parasites may be divided into ectoparasites and endoparasites. Adult biting midges of the genus *Forcipomyia* (Ceratopogonidae) and several other genera are ectoparasites that take blood from both vertebrates and insects. When feeding on the latter, the flies puncture the wing veins or intersegmental membranes. The flies visit the host only during feeding.

The small wasps of the family Scelionidae lay their eggs among the freshly laid eggs of host insects. Females of several genera have been observed attached phoretically to the bodies of female hosts. After the host's eggs are laid, the wasp immediately oviposits. Young winged females of the French *Rielia manticida* (Scelionidae) search for and attach themselves to mantids of both sexes. Female hosts are more frequently selected. Once attached by their mandibles, the wasps shed their wings and await the host's oviposition, which may not take place for. several months. In the interim, the wasp feeds as an ectoparasites on the mantid's hemolymph. When the mantid's ootheca has been deposited and is still soft, the wasp leaves the mantid to lay its own eggs. The wasp is said then to attempt to return to its host's body. An unusual instance of ectoparasitic behaviour is provided by the aquatic larvae of the midge *Symbiocladius* (Chironomidae). The larvae attach themselves behind the wing buds of mayfly naiads and feed.

Strepsiptera are the only entomophagous insects that are true endoparasites. Numbering about 300 species, they probably evolved in the early Tertiary Period from some group, as yet unknown, of parasitoid Coleoptera. Fossils have been found in Baltic amber. Hosts include insects in the orders Thysanura, Blattodea, Mantodea, Orthoptera, Hemiptera, and Diptera, but most of them are aculeate Hymenoptera. The infested hosts are said to be "stylopized," because the name of a common genus is *Stylops*.

The life history of *Stylops pacifica* (Stylopidae) was studied by Linsley and MacSwain near Berkeley, California. The hosts are two species of bees in the genus *Andrena* (Andrenidae). On bright warm days in February and early March, adult bees emerge from their burrows in soil and visit flowers of the buttercup, *Ranunculus*. As many as 16 per cent are parasitized. The visible evidences are the puparia that protrude from the body, commonly between the fourth and fifth terga of the abdomen. The male *Stylops* is winged and less than 3 mm long. On emergence from the puparium, it immediately begins a rapid, vibrating flight in search of a female. The latter is reduced to virtually a sac of reproductive organs inside the puparium. Females release a sex attractant while the host flies-from flower to flower.

Males by upwind, tracking the odour, until the female is located on the dorsum of a feeding bee. The male *Stylops* lands and inserts the aedeagus by puncturing the female's puparium. Once inseminated the female no longer releases the attractant. Males probably die the same day as they emerge and mate but once. Except during copulation their intense flight activity never ceases and they rarely feed. The, tarsi even lack claws for clinging to objects. Linsley and MacSwain were able to capture the rare males by putting bees with virgin female parasites in cages and placing the cages among flowers. The first-instar larvae are triungulins, and they develop from the fertilized eggs while still inside the female's body. During the next 30 to 40 days, the female dies and the larvae move into a median brood passage in preparation for their exit. A large female *Stylops* probably produces [illegible]000 to 10,000 triungulins. On warm days while the host is visiting flowers, the active larvae emerge through the ruptured puparium. Parasitized hosts move more rapidly among flowers than normal hosts. The triungulins are brushed singly or several at a time onto the flowers.

In contrast to the triungulins of Meloidae, Rhipiphoridae, and possibly other Strepsiptera, those of *Stylops pacifica* do not readily attach themselves to new hosts, but are ingested with nectar by bees. The bee returns to its nest and prepares a ball of pollen mixed with regurgitated nectar. In this way the triungulin is deposited in a nest cell with the bee's egg. The triungulin penetrates the egg, transforming as it does into the second instar, and becomes an endoparasite. As the host feeds and grows, the *Stylops* larva feeds on the host's nonvital tissues and passes through an unknown number of instars. When the bee pupates, the *Stylops* protrudes the anterior portion of its body through the intertergal membrane and also pupates. The last larval skin is not shed, but forms a tanned puparium.

Strepsiptera have no known natural enemies. Major causes of mortality are the initial losses of triungulins that fail to find a female host of the proper species, and superparasitism. Linsley and MacSwain noted that usually only the larger female bees with a solitary female parasite lived long enough for the triungulins to escape. Smaller male hosts, those with several *Stylops,* or those with *Stylops* plus nematode parasites, usually died before the cycle was completed. . Bees that' survive parasitism are variously affected. The genitalia of both sexes may be reduced. Secondary sexual characters, especially in the female, may be shifted toward the opposite sex. Stylopized females may have more malelike yellow colour and reduced pollen-collecting hairs on the legs.

PLANT EATING INSECTS

The ability to macerate plant tissue or to imbibe plant fluids as well as the ability to digest these tissues and to utilize them for energy, growth, and reproduction is called *phytophagy* or *herbivory*. Oddly, insects have limited abilities to digest cellulose, the major substance of which plants are constructed (although some have symbiotic microorganisms that assist in its breakdown). Plant tissue is a source of sugars, proteins, fats, salts, water and vitamins. Most plant tissue provides adequate nourishment for insects, although different species, do have different nutritional requirements. That insects are to varying degrees discriminating feeders reflects a long and fascinating history of plant-insect coevolution, which we shall explore briefly in this chapter and the following two. Insects feed on leaves, buds, stems, roots, fruits, and seeds, as well as on plant tissue in various stages of decay. They feed externally or internally, a borers or leaf miners; they produce galls and others distortions; sucking insects imbibe plant juices and may cause weakening and yellowing. Many insects, even non-phytophagous species, also use plants as shelter, and some make still other uses of plants that are outside the scope of this chapter. Leaf-cutter bees, for example, use pieces of leaves to line their nest cells and leaf-cutter ants harvest bits of leaves that they use as a substrate for growing fungi in their nests.

Returning to more strictly phytophagous insects, we find scarcely any plant immune to attack. Clover is fed on by some 200 insect species; corn, by over 300. Over 200 species attack citrus trees; 400 or more, apples. Among forest trees, elms harbor at least 600 species, while oaks hold the record with nearly 1500 insect enemies (many of them gall formers). Out of its normal habitat, a plant may sometimes be relatively free of insect pests. Eucalyptus grown in Mexico or California, for example, shows little evidence of insect attack; yet in its native home in Australia, eucalyptus harbours a great number of insects. Obviously its foliage is perfectly edible for adapted insects; but insects elsewhere have not evolved mechanisms for overcoming the repellency of eucalyptus oils. Ginkgo trees are seldom if ever subject to insect attack wherever they are grown (they no longer exist in the wild). These trees are relics of a very ancient group of plants that have evidently survived as a result of repellent substances in their tissues that deter both insects and disease. The degree to which a plant species is immune to insect attack is, in general, a reflection of the defenses it has evolved and the evolved abilities of insects to overcome these defenses. These are matters to be explored in the next chapter.

Among the insects inhabiting a particular plant, some may restrict their feeding to that plant species alone and are said to be *monophagous*. Others may be general feeders and include a diversity of plants in their diet; such insects are said to be *polyphagous*. White oak, for example, plays host to several species of gall wasps that not only form gall on white oak alone but even form a distinctive type of gall on only one part of the tree. White oaks may also be attacked by gypsy moth caterpillars, which are decidedly polyphagous insects, attacking a wide variety of broad-leaved trees and even, at times, conifers. Under artificial conditions these caterpillars have been reared on over 400 plant species; but they reject certain plants (such as larkspur) and in nature will feed preferentially on a limited group of shade and forest trees. Some of the Orthoptera are strongly polyphagous; Hungry migratory locusts will gnaw on wooden fence posts, and crickets will consume clothing. Indeed crickets, many ants, and some other insects are essentially *omnivorous,* including both plant and animal tissue and sometimes detritus in their diet.

Much more commonly, insects may be described as moderately discriminating in their tastes. Such insects are said to be *oligophagous*. The Colorado potato beetle feeds on plants of the genus *Solanum;* the imported cabbageworm on various Brassicaceae; the monarch butterfly, on various kinds of milkweeds. We shall consider the chemical basis of host selection in a later section of this chapter. In behavioural terms, a phytophagous insect may reach its host in one of three ways:

1. The host may be selected by trial and error - that is, by moving about and tasting several plants before settling to feed. Many grasshoppers fall in this category.

2. The host may be selected by the mother, who lays her eggs in response to some particular cue, often chemical. Most Lepidoptera find their host in this way.

3. The insect may live in an aggregation that extends through several generations, so that emerging young find themselves already settled on their host plant. Aphids are an example. However, aphids also have a Type I phase in their life cycle. Many aphids (and some other insects) have alternate hosts that are occupied seasonally; often the winter is spent on a woody, perenial plant; the summer, on an herbaceous annual.

TYPES OF PLANT FEEDING

Chewing Insects

Consumers of plant tissue commonly have mouthparts of generalized biting type, with stout, strongly musculated mandibles. Caterpillars may consume many times their own weight in plant tissue in the course of their development. Much fibrous tissue passes through the gut undigested and forms a major part of the large fecal pellets.

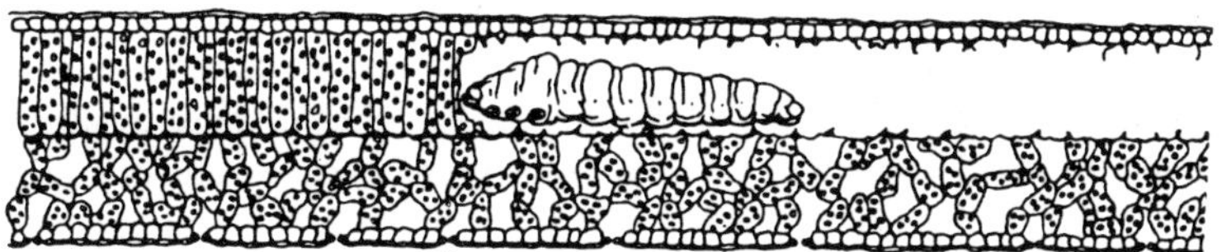

Fig. 6.1. Cross section of leaf being mined by a beetle larva.

Many insects begin feeding at the margin of the leaf, while others feed on either the upper or, more commonly, the lower surface. The leaf may be eaten all the way through, or the insect may scrape off the epidermis and parenchyma, leaving one layer of epidermis and its supporting veins intact. Such insects are said to be leaf skeletonizers. Others mine the interior of the leaf, feeding on the parenchyma and leaving both the upper and the lower epidermis intact. Such *leaf miners* tend to be small larvae that are pale in colour and flattened, and whose mouthparts project forward (prognathous) rather than downward (hypognathous); most of them are legless or nearly so. The patterns they form are often intricate and diagnostic of the species. There are two general types. Some leaf miners chew out a broad patch, forming *a blotchmine,* while others move along a slender path, forming *a linear mine,* which is often quite tortuous. Linear mines tend to be very slender when the larva is small, but the broaden gradually, eventually ending in a small blotch. In North America there are more than 100Q species of leaf-mining insects, belonging to four orders of Endopterygota (Lepidoptera, Coleoptera, Diptera and Hymenoptera).

Leaf tiers, leaf rollers, and *leaf folders* belong primarily to the order Lepidoptera. These insects use silk to hold leaves together in various ways to provide a retreat in which they molt or spend other inactive periods. Sometimes several such larve life together, forming a large, often unsightly mass of leaves and silk; one such species is appropriately called the uglynest caterpillar. Tent caterpillars build communal retreats primarily of silk, and they build silken trails that they follow to and from the nest during foraging trips.

Borers in stems, trunks, and roots have some features in common with leaf miners: They tend to have larvae that are pale in colour, prognathous, and more or less legless. Borers in trees have particularly powerful mandibles as well as a proventriculus capable of grinding the hard particles to a usable size. Even so, much undigested material is passed off in the dry feces. Many borers have intestinal symbionts that assist in digestion, while others feed not on wood but on fungi that grow in the galleries. Larval insects of several orders live in fleshy fruits; others live in nuts and seeds, which like fruits provide a rich source of food, but unlike fruits provide a very dry environment. Thus, the many species of insects that infest seeds, grains, flour, and the like have mechanisms for conserving the limited water available in their food. The feces of such insects are exceedingly dry as a result of water extraction by the rectum, and much of the required water is obtained through the metabolism of starches.

Sucking Insects

The mouthparts of Hemiptera, are admirably adapted for piercing tissues and extracting fluids. Through muscular action, the four very delicate stylets are able to penetrate leaves, stems, and even the bark of trees. They are sufficiently flexible to pass between fibrous elements and, after considerable probing, reach the phloem or 4ascular bundles. Here the pressure of sap within the plant may induce a flow up the food channel between the stylets; or the flow may be assisted by the pharyngeal pump. At the same time saliva is being injected via the salivary channel in the stylets. Many sucking insects produce two kinds of saliva, from different parts of the salivary glands. One is a thin fluid that mixes with the sap and initiates digestion; the other, a more viscous substance that combines with fluids from accessory glands to form a sheath around the stylets. This sheath is formed of lipoproteins that gel on contact with air as a result of the formation of hydrogen and disulphide bonds. Evidently the function of the sheath is to prevent the loss of sap and saliva. Sucking insects must imbibe much fluid in order to obtain their requirements of protein, minerals and vitamins. Much of this fluid chiefly water, carbohydrates, and some amino acids-is passed from the anus unmodifed, and in fact in some Homoptera it bypasses the midge by means of a filter chamber. The sweet, watery excrement of aphids, leafhoppers, and scale insects forms a stricky deposit on foliage, on the ground, and on the tops of automobiles parked under infested trees. This *honeydew is* fed on by bees, wasps, ants, and other insects, and it is also the medium on which a sooty fungus grows, often causing disfigurement of ornamentals. The honeydew of certain scale insects of the Near East is sometimes so abundant that it has been used as food by humans-the "manna from heaven" of the Israelites.

Gall Insects

Galls are abnormal growths on the buds, leaves, stems, or roots of plants. They result from the action of bacteria, fungi, nematodes, mites, or insects of several groups. Gall midges (Diptera, Cecidomyidae) and gall wasps (Hymenoptera, Cynipidae) are most frequently involved, but there are also gall makers in the orders Coleoptera, Hemiptera, Diptera and Lepidoptera. Of the approximately 2000 species of gall makers in North America, about 1500 are gall wasps or midges. Although gall midges attack plants of more than 50 families, gall wasps largely restrict their attacks to two groups: Rosaceae and the genus *Quercus* (oaks) in the family Fagacae. Some 800 species of gall wasps in North America form galls on oaks. These occur on roots, buds, twigs; leaves, flowers, and nuts, and are so diagnostic of species that identification based on the galls is often simpler than that based on the wasps themselves. The simplest galls are mere swellings that involve no major distortion or discolouration; these are said to be *indeterminate galls*. In some cases these are expanded to form *pouch galls,* which are often open to the outside and are especially characteristic of aphids and related Homoptera. The majority of gall midges and wasps make *determinate galls,* which have a form and colour quite different from that of the host plant; good examples are provided by the willow cone gall and the oak apple gall. These exist in such variety that many different terms have been employed to describe them, and guides have been written for their identification. Yet these elaborate structures consist entirely of tissue supplied by the host plant under stimulation by invading insects. Often they resemble abnormal fruits (cones on willows), but rather than containing plant embryos, they provide insects with a rich source of food as well as protection from predators and from the elements. Galls may continue to grow as long as the stimulation persists, even though normal leaf or stem growth may have ceased for that season. Galls begin as small swellings at the point of oviposition by the female. In a sawfly gall of willow, studied by William Hovanitz, of the California Institute of Technology, the egg hatches in about five days, during which time the gall grows slowly. When thc egg hatches and the larva begins to feed, growth of the gall continues. Dr. Hovanitz found that a fluid injected at the time of egg laying initiates gall formation. However, after about eight days the presence of the larva is required for continued growth. When the larva is removed from a gall, growth stops in about two days. Evidently both the mother, at the time of oviposition, and the larva secrete a growth-promoting substance though whether the two substances are same has not been determined.

It has often been proposed that plant growth hormones are involved in gall formation, since abnormal growths produced by these hormones are similar to the cells and tissues in natural galls. Studies of needle galls of pinyon pine (*Pinus edulis*) by J. Wayne Brewer and his associates at Colorado State University have revealed levels of auxin and gibberellin in these galls many times higher than in normal needles of the same age. Extracts of the midge larvae that form the gall did not contain auxin and showed only traces of gibberellin, and it seems likely that the plants themselves produce these abnormal amounts of hormones under stimulation by the larvae. The substances secreted by the insects have so far defied full analysis. They must surely contain some components that differ from species to species, since the resulting galls are so different, even when related species make galls on leaves of the same plant. It is possible that a fuller understanding of gall formation will shed light on processes of cell differentiation in all living things. What little we know of the gall-producing secretions of insects suggests that they contain adenine and other amino acids as well as nucleic acids. It is even possible that they may shed light on the origin of cancer in humans.

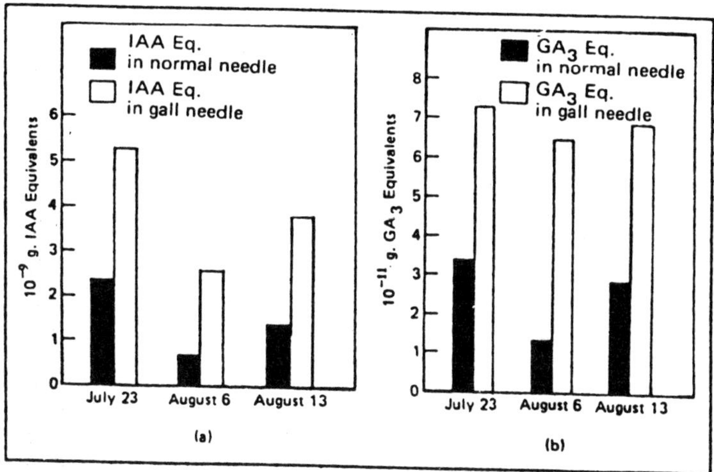

Fig. 6.2. Auxin (a) and gibberellin (b) levels in normal needles of pinyon pine as compared with those in needles having galls. Auxin was measured in terms of its equivalent in indole-3 acetic acid (IAA): gibberellin, in terms of its equivalent in gibberellic acid (GA).

HOST PLANT SEARCHING AND ACCEPTANCE

How does an aphid or a butterfly locate an acceptable host plant for settling or for oviposition? How does a grasshopper "decide" which plants in the environment provide the most suitable food? These are questions of considerable importance, but only partial answers are available. The reactions chains may involve several sensory modalities and highly specialized receptors. It is useful to recognize four stages in host finding:

1. Search for a suitable habitat;
2. Settling on a plant and the most suitable part of a plant (either for oviposition or prior to feeding);
3. Initiation of feeding ("tasting");
4. Feeding to satiation.

The insect may fail to receive appropriate stimuli or may actually be repelled, at any stage, necessitating a return to an earlier step in the sequence. Starvation or failure to lay eggs on a suitable substrate may result if the insect is unable to complete the series.

Search for a Suitable Habitat

As we have seen, apple maggot flies are attracted to yellow surfaces. Similarly, winged aphids can be collected in yellow-painted pans filled with water. In both cases yellow is probably not distinguishable from the green of the host plant, but yellow has higher reflectance properties than green and is thus a supernormal stimulus. Form as well as colour may be involved. Immature desert locusts are attracted to patterns of vertical stripes, evidently because these stimulate the grassy habitats they prefer. During dispersal, insects may become increasingly hungry and increasingly responsive to specific cues likely to guide them to a desirable habitat. These cues are evidently largely visual, but olfactory cues may also play a part, at least at short range.

Settling

It is probable that visual cues often continue to play a role as the insect settles on a plant within a selected habitat. Female pipevine swallowtail butterflies (*Battus philenor*) alight on any leaves that resemble in shape those of their host plants, *Aristolochia,* but they lay their eggs only when, after drumming the leaves with their fore tarsi, they detect specific odor cues. According to Lawrence Gilbert, of the University of Texas, *Heliconius* butterflies locate their passion fruit vine hosts in tropical forests partly in response to their characteristic leaf shapes. These relatively long-lived butterflies return to the same roosting site each night and learn the location of the widely dispersed plants that provide them with nectar and with oviposition sites, returning to these regularly.

Learning probably plays little if any role in host finding in most insects. Most evidence suggests that olfaction is involved and that the insects respond innertly to sign stimuli in the form of odours of plant essential oils. In most cases these odours are attractants only within a range of a few centimeters to a few meters. They are difficult to demonstrate experimentally, since insects often are responsive only for a short period following dispersal. However, there is a growing body of evidence as to the reality of such *sign* (or "token") *stimuli.* Sweet clover weevils are attracted to coumarin, an odorous constituent of *Melilotus,* their normal host plant. Adult females of the imported cabbageworm lay their eggs on cabbage, broccoli, mustard, and other members of the family Brassicaceae, all of which produce odorous mustard oils. Instances such as this have given rise to the statement that insects are often "good botanists," capable of selecting plants that are taxonomically related. However, similar essential oils sometimes occur in quite different groups of plants. For example, methyl chavicol, anethole, and anisic aldehyde occur both in citrus and in members of the parsley family, and members of the black swallowtail butterfly group will oviposit and the larvae will feed on members of either group of plants which may in fact be more closely related than is usually appreciated.

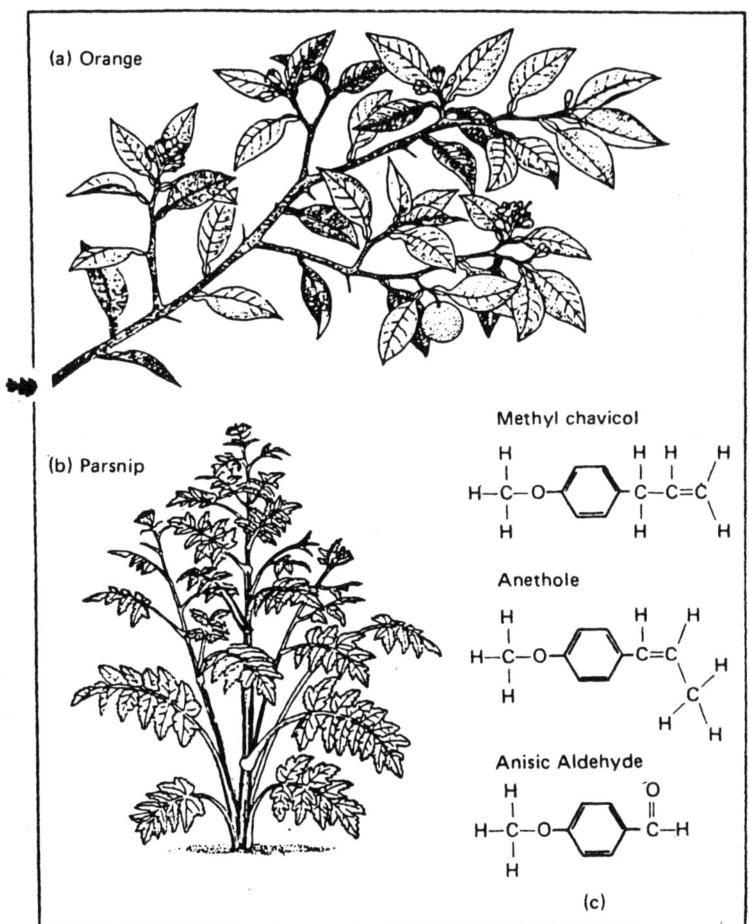

Fig. 6.3. Plants of the citrus family (a) and the parsnip family (b) produce the same three essential oils (c). These substances are phagostimulants for larve of black swallowtail butterflies, which will feed on members of either plant family and will attempt to fed on filter papter soaked with these substances.

There are certain chemical substances that attract and stimulate attack are often called *kairomones*. These are also defined as interspecific messages that benefit the receiver rather than the sender. Thus, they stand in contrast to allomones, which benefit the sender and with pheromones, which are *intraspecific* messages. As we have seen, the olfactory receptors of insects reside mainly in the antennae, and there is evidence that insects are frequently able to distinguish between the odours of many plant species, even when the volatile substances are closely related chemically. Vincent Dethier, now at the University of Massachusetts, has shown that black swallowtail larvae do not confuse six essential oils, each of which is characteristic of one of the food plants of the parsley family. When specific odours reach the antennae of caterpillars, the 16 olfactory receptors respond differentially: Nerve impulses in some increase and in others decrease, producing a pattern characteristic of each substance. These are "generalist receptors" differing from the specialist receptors for pheromones. Response to a particular set of molecules is programmed in the central nervous system, and the behaviour released is best described' as a chemokinesis or chemotaxis leading to reduced locomotion when the source is reached.

While these remarks apply to many *monophagous* and *oligophagous* species, it is probable that *manypolyphagous* species respond to more generalized cues and accept plants on the basis of the presence of phagostimulants (see below) or the absence of feeding deterrents or toxins. Polyphagous species feeding below ground, such as white grubs and w reworms, may respond to respiration products plants, chiefly CO_2, but selective feeders such as cabbage and onion maggots may respond both to CO_2 and to volatile odours of the host. The identification of attractants may have great practical value. The oriental fruit fly, a major pest of many tropical fruits, is known to be strongly attracted to plants containing methyl eugenol. Oddly, it is mainly the males that are attracted to this host plant odor, which is believed to serve as a "rendezvous stimulant," bringing the sexes together for mating. Traps baited with methyl eugenol have been used for many years to monitor populations of oriental fruits flies. On the island of Rota, the fly has been eradicated by dropping fiberboard squares impregnated with kairomone mixed with insecticide.

Food Plant Acceptance

A food plant is finally accepted or rejected as a feeding or oviposition site through stimuli received on actual contact with the plant. These may be visual, relating to the shape or colour of the substrate, but are more often tactile, olfactory, or gustatory. A. J. Thorsteinson, of the University of Manitoba, Winnipeg, showed that female diamondback moths lay eggs more readily on rough than on smooth surfaces. When the rough surfaces are coated with mustard leaf juices, oviposition is further increased. In nature the moths lay eggs on various members of the mustard family, but to varying degrees, depending on the combined effects of tactile and olfactory cues. The initiation of feeding is commonly mediated' by gustatory stimuli. In caterpillars, taste receptors are located primarily on the maxillary palpi. Removal of the palpi (along with the antennae) often causes these insects to accept plants they would normally refuse. Tobacco hornworms feed only on solanaceous plants in nature, but when the palpi and antennae are removed, they will accept such plants as dandelions and plantains.

Any substance that induces feeding is said to be *a phagostimulant.* Experimental evidence of the importance of phagostimulation has involved placing the substance to be tested on an abnormal plant or on agar or filter paper and. recording the amount of feeding that occurs. As long ago as 1910, the Dutch entomologist E. Verschaffelt showed that imported cabbageworm larvae (*Pieris rapae*) would eat nonhost plants when these were smeared with the sap of cabbage plants or with sinigrin, a glycoside that is characteristic of members of the cabbage family. These substances serve both as attractants for ovipositing females and as stimulants for larval feeding. Eastern tent caterpillars restrict their feeding mostly to Rosaceae, especially to wild cherry. According to Vincent Dethier, the leaves of wild cherry contain hydrocyanic acid (HCN) in sufficient quantity to poison cattle. Yet HCN, in combination with benzaldehyde, constitutes an odorous substance often called oil of bitter almonds, which is a mild attractant and a feeding stimulant for tent caterpillars. When the juice of wild cherry leaves is sprayed on filter paper, the larvae readily eat the paper; they also respond to emulsions of equal parts of HCN and benzaldehyde.

Chemical sign stimuli with similar effects have been identified with respect to many insects. Feeding by certain leaf beetles of the *bonus Chrysolina* (Chrysomelidae) occurs only in the presence of hypericin, a substance present in the leaves of Klamath weed. As a result, the beetles have been used effectively in the biological control of these noxious weeds with little danger of them attacking desirable plants. The examples we have cited so far have involved *secondary plant substances,* which play no role in the basic metabolism of plants and have no apparent nutritive value for insects. In some cases these have evidently evolved as feeding deterrents. Mustard oils, for example, deter feeding by many polyphagous insects, although *Pieris* hutterflies, diamondback moths, and some other oligophagous insects ...tve evolved mechanisms not only for accepting these substances but also for using them as cues for host finding and feeding.

Phagostimulants are, however, by no means always secondary plant substances. Nutrients, including minerals, amino acids, and especially sugars, often elicit feeding behaviour. European corn borers, for examples, show a preference for substances containing certain levels of sucrose. Most insects that have been studied have sucrose receptors but are capable of rejecting high concentrations of sucrose, which may be toxic. Often other plant substances are synergistic with sucrose. In diamondback moth caterpillars, for example, sinigrin acts synergistically with sucrose, and in *Pieris* ascorbic acid enhances the effects of sucrose. The silkworm of commerce, *Bombyx mori,* is one of the best studied of insects, and many experiments with artificial diets have been performed with these insects by Japanese workers. In this instance, substances such as morin and inositol synergistically increase the response to sucrose, although by themselves eliciting no feeding response at all. Ysuji Hamamura, of Konan University, Japan, has identified substances involved as attractants and in the biting and swallowing responses of silkworms. Some of the results of his experiments demonstrating feeding stimulants, the number of fecal pellets being used as a measure of feeding. When all necessary substances know to elicit attraction, biting, and swallowing are added to agar, along with known necessary growth substances, the larvae can be reared successfully in the total absence of the normal host, mulberry leaves. However, the resulting cocoon shells do not have the normal wight of silk, and development is retarded. It is evidently the diet of the first-instar larva that is critical. Thus silk producers do best to add mulberry leaves to the diet or to use them exclusively, at least until all dietary elements have been identified.

TABLE 6.1

Feeding Activity of Silkworms on Certain Diets

Diet	*No. of feces*
Basic diet (BD) only	
BD + Sitosterol + Ri	89
BD + Sitosterol + Inositol + Ri	200
BD + Sitosterol + Inositol + Morin + Rt	254
BD without sucrose + Sitosterol + Inositol + Morin + Rt	60

It is obvious from these and similar studies that even though plant tissue generally provides a suitable diet for many insects, many species require certain specific substances for normal development. Much progress has been made in the study of insect nutrition in the past two or three decades, and it will pay us to look at this important field of study at least briefly.

Nutritional Factors

Like insects, many vertebrate animals also subsist largely or entirely on plant tissue, and it is interesting to compare the two groups. As we have said, insects have limited ability to digest cellulose, although some have intestinal microorganisms that break down cellulose so that it is available to them. Grazing mammals, on the other hand, have complicated digestive processes that take advantage of bacterial fermentation to break down cellulose into digestible fatty acids. If we compare silkworms with cattle, for example, we find that both are about equally efficient at utilizing the protein in their diet; but cattle (with the aid of symbionts in their rumen) digest over 70% of the crude fiber in grass, while silkworms pass nearly all of the fiber of mulberry leaves undigested in their feces. Insects also differ from vertebrates in being unable to synthesize cholesterol and therefore requiring this or a similar sterol in their diet. Also, they do not require vitamins D and K, which vertebrates need for bone development. They do require several vitamins of the B group. They also require vitamin C. This is normally available in fresh plant tissue, but some insects are able to synthesize vitamin C. Vitamin A deficiency has been shown to result in reduced visual function in moths; apparently this vitamin is essential for the full development of visual pigments, as it is vertebrates.

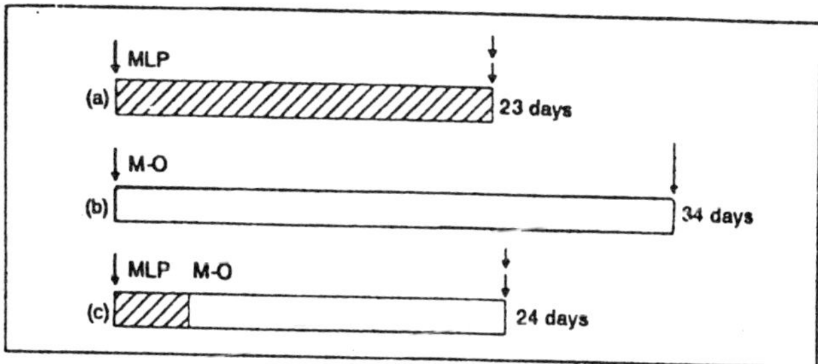

Fig. 6.4. Length of larval period of silkmoths from hatching (arrow) to cocoon spinning (double arrow): (a) when reared throughout on artificial diet enriched with Mulberry Leaf Powder (MLP); (b) when reared on a similar diet without mulberry leaf powder (M-O); (c) when reared on MLP during the first instar only.

Insects also require water, nitrogen, carbohydrates, amino acids, lipids, and minerals such as iron, phosphorus, zinc, magnesium, and sometimes sodium and others. In a recent review by J. M. Scriber, of the University of Wisconsin, and F. Slansky, Jr., of the University of Florida, it was pointed out that larvae of Lepidoptera show superior relative growth rates on leaves with a water content of from 60% to 90% and levels of nitrogen between 2% and 6%. However, species adapted for feeding on tree leaves subsist on somewhat lower levels of water and nitrogen than do those feeding on forbs. Leaves show seasonal trends in the percentages of water and nitrogen, which may be accompanied by other changes in nutrients and in defensive mechanisms. Qualitative variations in nitrogen may be as important as variations in quantity. In young, moisture-rich tissues, nitrogen is available in amino acids and soluble proteins, and in nitrates, vitamins, and other substances. However, in older tissues it is largely in the form of insoluble proteins. Much work has been done on the amino acid requirements of insects. Apparently most insects require the ten "essential" amino acids also required by vertebrates. Various amino acids regarded as "non-essential" in the diet are commonly synthesizhd by insects. However, proline is required by silkworms, cystine by pale western cutworms, and others not among the ten essential amino acids by still other species.

Balance of nutrients is of overriding importance in any diet. Dietary deficiencies may restrict the laying down of sufficient food reserves, in the form of fat body, to carry the insect through the pupal and adult stages; or they may cause reduction in the size and functioning of the endocrine glands, resulting in abnormal development or the suppression of ovarian function. In extreme cases, they may of course; cause starvation and death. Even accepted food plants may not always provide a perfect diet if foliage is old, for example, or deficient in water, or if the plant is growing in soil deficient in certain minerals. Rates of food intake by aphids are known to be affected by the levels of nutrients (sucrose, amino acids) in the plants. Varieties of peas more resistant to pea aphids, *Acynhosiphon pisurn,* are those containing lower concentrations of amino acids at stages of growth corresponding with the period of aphid attack in the field. Clearly there are advantages to plant breeders in knowing what factors retard the feeding and development of insect pests.

Adults of many insects, such as butterflies and moths, require carbohydrates in the form of nectar; but many also obtain amino acids from nectar. Adults of some insects do not feed at all (giant silkworm moths, for example) subsisting for their short lives entirely on fat stored in the larval stage. Sucking insects, since they do not imbibe the fibrous parts of plants, are able to digest most of their intake; but as we have seen, they frequently discharge a large part of the water and sugars as liquid feces. Nutritional changes in plants, such as those occurring in senescence, may result in the production of wingeu morphs of aphids that disperse to other hosts. Diverse insects have symbiotic microorganism, either in the gut or in special organs called mycetomes, which play various roles in nutrition. In the case of aphids and similar sucking insects, symbiotic bacteria are believed to supply nitrogen, which is not obtainable in adequate quantities in plant sap. In other instances symbionts are known to synthesize B-group vitamins, which cannot be obtained from foods such as dried grains. In termites and some other wood-eating insects, intestinal protozoa and bacteria play important roles in the breakdown of cellulose.

Artificial Diets

In the past 30 years much progress has been made in developing artificial diets for insects. These provide a tool for investigating the precise dietary requirements of insects. By omitting substances of altering the quantities of substances and determining the effect on development, number of eggs laid by the resulting females, and the like, one may determine the balance of nutrients required in nature. For precise nutritional studies, one must provide a diet in which the chemical nature of all ingredients is known. A basic diet must contain the following: water, carbohydrates, fatty acids, the 10 essential amino acids, cholesterol, choline, pantothenic acid, nicotinamide,,thiamine, riboflavin, folic acid, pyridoxine, biotin, vitamin B12, vitamin A, vitamin C, and several minerals. For chewing insects, it must also be made of the right consistency, usually by adding agar or cellulose (both nutritionally inert). Sucking insects require a liquid diet, which must be imbibed ,through a membrane. In every case the artificial diet must be sterilized and/or supplied with a substances that inhibits microbial growth.

Quantities of these ingredients must be adjusted appropriately, and phagostimulants and additional nutrients added as required-the latter may depend on the ability of the species or its symbionts to synthesize the substance. Research on precise dietary requirements is a very active field at the present time. It was found, for example, that a diet satisfactory for pea aphids was not adequate for rearing green peach aphids. R. H. Dadd and T. E. Mittler, of the University of California at Berkeley, found that the addition to the diet of small amounts of iron, zinc, and manganese, as well as greater care to prevent loss of vitamin C, permitted rearing green peach aphids through many generations. Discoveries of differences between species in their requirements for minerals, amino acids, vitamins, and other substances, combined with knowledge of phagostimulants and the ability to resist or detoxify plant defensive substances, provide the basis for a biochemical definition of an insect's food niche, a matter of much potential importance in the effort to control insects without resort to insecticides. The development of artificial diets has also been a boon to mass rearing of insects for experimental studies of many kinds, as well as for the rearing of predators and parasitoids of phytophagous insects for biological control. For mass rearing, it is cheaper and more convenient to use diets of unrefined substances such as wheat germ or soyabean meal, which contain protein, fatty acids, minerals, and other essentials. To these water, sugars, and other more specific requirements must be added to provide a balanced diet. Artificial diets for many phytophagous insects are now available commercially, and "cook-books" for diverse insects are now available.

The Advantages of Polyphagy and Monophagy

Polyphagous insects are able to take advantage of the nutrients in a variety of plant species, since they are not cued into specific attractants and phagostimulants. Their food is available with limited searching, and they are in no danger of food shortage if a particular plant is decimated. (We live in a time when many plant species are regarded as endangered, and some are already extinct, carrying with them any insects that are closely tied to them.) A polyphagous species may be able to extend its range widely, even to other continents if opportunities are provided. Some of our worst imported pests -are polyphagous - the Japanese beetle and the gypsy moth, for example. So why be monophagous? *Monophagy* involves close adaptation to a single host species. The plant is easier to locate, since the sense organs and nervous system of the insect are programmed to respond to specific cues. Mate finding may also be enhanced, since many phytophagous insects mate on the host plant. On its host, the-insect is able to compete successfully with other, polyphagous species, since it is able to resist or detoxify the substances the plant has evolved to deter its enemies. Toxins in the plant may even be used by the insect to deter its own enemies, as has happened in the case of the monarch butterfly and other insects. Many of the plants utilized by monophagous oc narrowly oligophagous insects are, in fact, avoided by generalist feeders because of their toxic or repellent properties. A good example is provided by ferns, which are generally avoided by grasshoppers and other generalists but exploited by a small group of specialists belonging to several orders of insects. There is, incidentally, little evidence that specialized feeders us their host plants with greater physiological efficiency than generalists. For the most part, the advantages they gain are ecological rather than physiological.

Despite the advantages of close adaptation to a specific host plant, it is probable that insects so adapted have limited capacity to reverse the process or to broaden their host acceptance. Their receptors may have evolved so as to perceive only certain molecules, and they may lack the capacity or the necessary symbionts to digest a different plant tissue. They may be able to detoxify (at some metabolic expense) a plant substance that would deter another insect, but that ability would not serve them well on another plant. It should be added that monophagous species can sometimes be put to use in the biological control of weeds; in this instance one must be sure that the insects lack the capacity to switch readily to another host. Clearly it is not

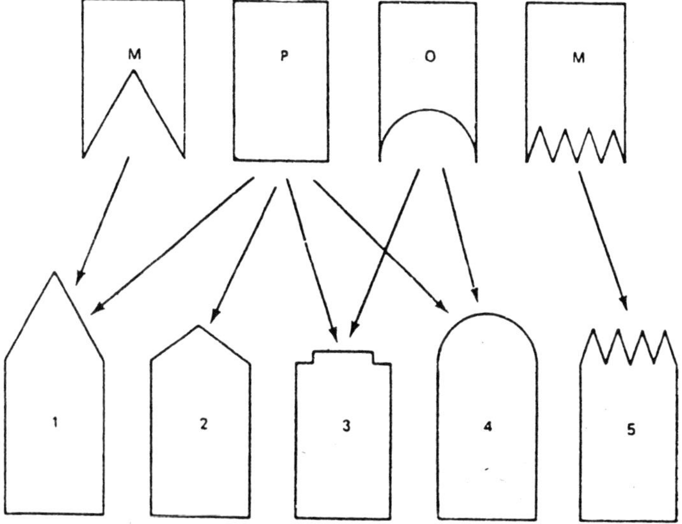

Fig. 6.5. Diagrammatic representation of the relationships between insects (top) apd their host plants (bottom). M = monophagous; P polyphagous; 0 = oligophagous. Plants 1-5 are assumed to produce chemical signals that impinge on receptors in the insects. Plant 5 produces substances to which only one monophagous species responds positively; to the remainder the substances are repellent.

correct to approach these questions from a purely entomological point of view. Plants undergo their own evolution, which is directed by many environmental influences. The development of secondary plant substances, of particular types of foliage or bark, of repellents or toxins-all of these require specific genetic events and many of them are energetically expensive, requiring physiological commitments that influence other events. Under certain conditions it may be advantageous for a plant to protect itself against insect attack or against disease at a certain cost in seed output. When this occurs, there are likely to be groups of insects that themselves find it advantageous to develop mechanisms for overcoming of the plant's defenses, even though it may have disadvantages from other points of view.

In the many tens of millions of years in which insects and plants have been on earth, associations of many kinds have evolved. As a general rule, most plants are attacked buy a somewhat limited number of pests, and most insects attack a somewhat limited number of hosts -that is, most are narrowly to broadly oligophagous. Natural selection, like politics, is often a matter of compromises that compound themselves to a degree of complexity that is often hard to fathom. Since polyphagy is prevalent among groups of insects that are usually considered more primitive - brisletails, cockroaches, crickets, grass-hoppers, earwigs, and the like-and most of the more advanced groups of insects show varying degrees of food specialization, it does appear that in the course of time the trend has been toward more intimate associations with specific food sources.

TRANSMISSION OF PLANT DISEASES

The effect of insects on thei, host plants often goes well beyond the actual consumption of plant tissue. This is especially true of sucking insects. As the stylets reach the vascular tissue, salivary fluids are released and may have localized toxic effects or toxic effects that are carried throughout the plant. Insects may also pick up pathogenic microorganisms from one plant and carry them to another. An insect whose feeding produces symptoms of disease is said to be *toxicogenic,* and the condition is spoken of as a *phytotoxemia.* An insect that transmits disease organisms is called *a vector.* A variety of insects, chiefly those with sucking mouthparts, may serve as vectors of plant diseases. This is very large subject we can pursue only briefly here.

Phytotoxemias

Little is known of the chemistry of the salivary secretions of sucking insects; they are believed to contain enzymes such as *amylase* but may also contain inhibitors of plant growth substances. Plugging or localized destruction of vascular tissues may also produce disease conditions. The reasons why certain insect-plant associations result in disease and others do not remain obscure. Several kinds of phytotoxemias are recognized, and we shall consider each briefly in the following paragraphs:

1. Localized lesions at the feeding site, resulting in spoting or stippling, Leafhoppers and mealybugs have been indicated as causative agents of leaf spotting on citrus, pineapples, sunflowers, and other plants. Spots may be paler or darker in colour than the surrounding tissue, or in some cases reddish in colour. Size of the spot may depend on the time spent feeding at that site, since there is little diffusion of toxin from the point of insertion of the stylets and only localized damage to tissue.

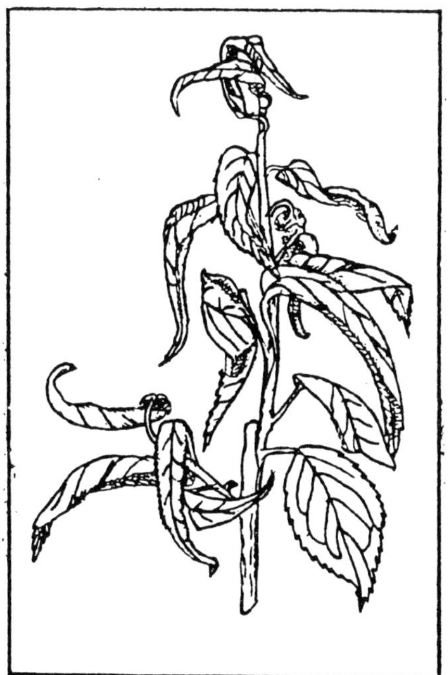

Fig. 6.6. Leaf curl on plum produced by the feeding of large numbers of green peach aphids.

2. Localized lesions with development of more general symptoms. Two-lined spittle bugs (Cercopidae) may cause initial spotting followed by streaking and browning of leaf blades; tarnished plant bugs and

other members of the family Miridae often produce disfiguring blotchs on leaves or fruits. In these instances vascular tissues carry the toxins some distance from the point of feeding.

3. Malformations of plants, including leaf curling production of witches' brooms, shortening of internodes, and other distortions. One of the most common examples of this is a browning and curling of leaf edges produced by the feeding of leafhoppers (Cicadellidae) and often called "hopperburn." Several crop plants are subject to hopperburn, such as potatoes, melons, and lettuce. Gross malformations of plants are sometimes caused by sucking insects as well as by mites;, they are sometimes difficult to distinguish from certain microbial diseases or from true galls.

4. Systemic conditions, including yellowing, wilting, reduction in growth, or killing of part or all of the plant. These conditions result from translocation throughout the plant of toxins produced by sucking insects. Aphids, leafhoppers, mealybugs, and other Homoptera have been indicated, and crops attacked include celery, sugar beets, corn and others. Psyllid yellows of potatoes is one of the best known of systemic toxemias.

PHYTOPHAGOUS INSECTS IN THE PALEOZOIC ERA

As stated already that first insects were probably scavengers in the moist debris that accumulated beneath early land plants. Living plant tissues, i.e., reclining stems and rhizomes along the ground, were also within range of the litter dwellers. As plants evolved greater height and tree-like forms in the Devonian Period, a new habitat was created fer terrestrial animals. The spores of these plants may have been an important items in the diet of insect scavengers. Measuring less than 200 μm in diameter, spores of the Lower Devonian plants could have, been easily ingested when found singly or in windrows on the ground. At the tops of the sporophyte plants spores also could be found fresh and concentrated in exposed sacs or sporangia. An arboreal insect faces greater risk of desiccation than an insect that lives in moist litter, furthermore it must cling, while walking, to smooth and sometimes vertical surfaces, and it risks greater exposure to predators and parasitoids. Exposure to aboreal or aerial predators, however, was not a problem for Devonian insects because none existed. Nor were any other organisms in competition for food borne high on erect plants. It is likely, therefore, that some of the insect scavengers acquired the resistance to water loss and the tarsal modifications necessary to climb

Devonian plants. The shift from scavenging to feeding on vegetative parts of plants also probably required physiological adjustments to the new diet.

The Carboniferous swamp forests would have provided an abundant food supply for phytophagous insects. Among the fossils preserved in the Upper Carboniferous Period are insects already highly specialized for external plant feeding. Thc paleopterous orders Palaeodictyoptera, Megasecoptera, and Diaphanopterodea had mouthparts prolonged in a break. The beak seems most suited for feeding on plants, but it is a matter of speculation whether the insects took tissue fluids by piercing and sucking, or probed for spores, pollen, and seeds in reproductive cones. The abrupt decline of the plant taxa that dominated the Carboniferous Period may explain the extinction of these breaked Paleoptera. Direct feeding on vascular phloem probably began with the evolutionary appearance of leaves. Feeding on stems probably did not take place until after the appearance of the arborescent gymnosperms known as the Cordaitales. The cambium and phloem of these plants were close to the surface and accessible by piercing mouthparts. The stems of other common plants had a thick cortex around the vascular tissue. The evolution of hemipterous piercing-sucking mouthparts, therefore, is correlated with the increasing availability of phloem tissue in the Carboniferous. Numerous' fossils of Hemiptera (Sub-order Homoptera) are known in the next period, the Permian. These are the oldest surviving insects that are exclusively phytophagous. When the number of species of breaked Paleoptera and Homoptera are compared with the number of other fossil insects, Carpenter estimates that nearly half the Paleozoic insects had piercing-sucking mouthparts. This is some measure of the amount of plant food available and the extent of its utilization by insects. The proportion of insects that are phytophagous has apparently remained approximately the same up to the present.

The feeding habits of Faleozoic insects with chewing mouthparts are less easily associated with plant feeding. Some may have been predators or scavengers. The jumping Orthoptera were present in the Permian Period and probably were mostly phytophagous, as they are today. The first possible evidence of insect damage to leaves was found in early Permian rocks in South Africa. Leaves of the ancient fern *Glossopteris* were discovered with marginal scallops resembling the notches made by edge-feeding, chewing insects today. Fleshy fruitlike or berrylike reproductive structures and nutlike seeds of gymnosperms have been found in the lower Permian. The flesy fruits were probably eaten and dispersed by reptiles which then dominated the vertebrate scene. These fruits were probably also a surface of food for insects long before the origin of the fruits and nuts of angiospersms. Recall that the first endopterygote insects appear in the Permian. Among other advantages, larval insects were able to penetrate the tissues of plants and fleshy fruits for the first time. We do not know when mining and boring in living plants began. The earliest insects capable of such activity may have been Coleoptera which were present in he Permian and which today exhibit these habits. The miners and borers may have evolved repeatedly from scavengers that bored in dead wood or decaying vegetable matter, or from external phytophagous forms that extended their feeding into the plant from the surface. Today the endoptery- gotes are the most numerous of the phytophagous insects.

THE FLOWER-VISITING INSECTS

Angiosperms are among the dominant land plants today. It is generally agreed that they owe the origin and much of their diversification directly to the behaviour of insects. The earliest flowering plants are known only from pollen grains. Like the fossil spores of the Paleozoic, pollen is more readily preserved than plant fragments. The pollen of gymnospersm and that of early angiosperms are so much alike that no sharp distinction can be made. The first fossil grains with predominantly angiospermous features occur near the end of the Lower Cretaceous Period. Latter, at the close of the Cretaceous, angio-sperms pollen exceeds that of gymnosperms and fern spores. The evolution of angiosperms was so rapid that an astonishing 67 families are represented at this time. What are some of the events which led to the origin of this successful group? During the evolution of the gymnosperms, fertilization by swimming sperm was replaced by the growth of a pollen tube. Although the need for moisture or special fluids at fertilization was thus eliminated and drier regions became habitable, the pollen grains must lodge in contact with the ovule. Sexual outcrossing among gymnosperms is assured because individual plants are unisexual, producing either pollen or ovules, but not both. Large quantities of wind-borne pollen are needed in order for a small fraction to land by chance in the correct sport for fertilization. The transfer of pollen from male to female structures is called *pollination.*

Large pollen sacs, seeds, and other edible tissues probably attracted insects to the cones of Paleozoic gymnosperms. A polleneating insects that moved only among male cones would not bring about pollination. Bisexual cones having both sexual organs, howevef, would be suited to benefit from such an insect. Attractive food would be combined with the receptive ovules. An insect would be able "to transport pollen from the male organs to the female organs, increasing the likelihood of correct placement of pollen of the same species next to the ovules. The total amount of pollen needed would then by greatly reduced. Such an insect is called *a pollen vector*. The first pollen vectors may have included terrestrial or flying reptiles or early birds, but the most important were probably the flying insects. Among these, the Coleoptera are though to be the most significant. They were probably well diversified in the Mesozoic Era. Interest in them is heightened by the fact that a number of primitive angiosperms today are beetle-pollinated. However, many beetles consume the ovules of the plants that they pollinate. For this reason, certain flower structures such as carpels can be explained as defensive measures initially evolved against the powerful, chewing, jaws of these insects.

Other features seem designed to aid pollinators in locating and recognizing flowers. The coloured petals aid visual recognition and orientation. Odours are emitted which are attractive to insects at a distance. The first floral odors may have initiated odours of fruits or decay that were attractive to scavenging beetles. Thus, the early flowers presumably had both pollen and ovules, sowy petals and odours, and their pollinators came mainly for pollen. The addition of nectaries, (glands that secrete nectar) probably came after beetles had established insect pollination as a regular part of angiosperm reproduction. Primitive beetle flowers generally lack floral nectar. Nectaries are lacking among all gymnosperms, but are present on new fronds of the fern *Pteridium*. *A* small amount of sugary fluid is secreted from the ovule of certain gymnosperms as a part of the pollination process, but this may or may not be significant in the evolution of angiosperm nectaries. Nectar is an aqueous fluid rich in sugars. Recently Baker and Baker demonstrated the presence of other nutrients of value to pollinators amino acids, proteins and . lipids. Other substances include ascorbic acid, possible serving as an antioxidant, and alkaloids, which might be toxic to certain unwanted flower visitors. Nectaries are associated with the vascular phloem system of plants.

The first nectaries of angiosperms may have been outside the flower, i.e., extrafloral nectaries, and they may have served a role different from that of floral nectaries. Although nectaries were rare before the appearance of angiosperms, insects had access to a fluifl of comparable composition beginning at least in the Permian, if not earlier. This is the honeydew excreted by the phloem-feeding Homoptera. The Homoptera living today are wasteful feeders, ejecting the phloem sap largely unaltered and in quantity. Among the -insects attracted to honeydew are natural enemies of phytophagous insects such as ants, predatory and parasitoid wasps, and lacewings, as well as other insects such as bees and moths. In some cases this is a regular or major part of their diet.

Fossil ants are known from the Cretaceous, and we conjecture that they were as fond of honeydew as are their descendants. Ants and certain Homoptera have evolved mutualistic associations in which the ants protect the Homoptera from natural enemies in return for honeydew. The host plants also benefit by the feeding of ants on phytophagous insects. Even vertebrate herbivores are discouraged by ants on foliage. The first nectaries, therefore, may have been the plants' device for supplying imitation honeydew as an attractant for beneficial ants and other predaceous insects, without the injury of phloem-feeding Homoptera. The secretion of nectar inside the flower was an incentive to actively flying insects in need of carbohydrate fuel such as Lepidoptera, Diptera and Hymenoptera. Floral nectar differs in composition from both honeydew and extra-floral nectar in ways that suggest it is secreted expressly for the food needs of favoured pollinators. Advanced families of plants have higher concentrations of amino acids than primitive families, and butterfly-pollinated flowers have higher concentrations than beepollinated flowers. This is associated with the inability of most butterflies to ingest, proteinrich pollen, whereas bees obtain their amino acids from pollen. *Heliconius* butterflies, however, collect pollen on their galeae and digest it there, taking up free amino acids. Flies which feed on protein-rich dung are attracted to the nectars of fly-pollinated flowers that are high in amino acids.

Now let us turn our attention to the insect visitors of flowers. The most common pollinators are Coleoptera, Lepidoptera, Diptera and Hymenoptera. They have several features in common all are actively flying adults of neopterous endopterygote insects. Their scarch for mates, oviposition sites, and plant or animal food is aided, by a strong flight apparatus, highly developed senses, and, in some groups, learning ability. These same attributes aid pollinators, as they search for and remember flowers. Individual insects which visit flowers of the same plant species during a single flight or longer period are said to be*flower-constant*. When all individuals of an insect species are restricted to visiting a single species of plant for food (nectar, pollen, other substances), the insect is said to be *monotrophic*. If several, possibly related, plant species are visited the insect species is *oligotrophus* and if many are visited, the term *polytrophic* applies. An individual bee may be flower-constant to each of a series of plant species during successive time periods and be a member of a polytrophic species. When visits are for pollen, the terms *monolectic, oligolectic* and *polylectic* are used. Flower constancy is beneficial to both plants and insects. It is advantageous for a plant to attract flower-constant visitors because they are the most effective cross-pollinators. It is advantageous to insects to become temporary or permanent specialists because they reduce competition for food and forage more efficiently, learning to recognize a given flower and operate its floral mechanism. In a general way, the flower size, shape, position of reproductive parts, colour patterns, odour, nectar composition, and time of flowering can be matched with the sizes, anatomies, diets, sensory physiologies, rhythmic activity, and foraging behaviours of its pollinators. Even among related species of plants, different species may depend on quite different kinds of pollinators.

TABLE 6.2

Major Taxa of Terrestrial Phytophagous Insects

External feeder on foliage, stems, roots, fruits, and/or seeds

Exposed feeders

- Isoptera (some)
- Dermaptera
- Plecoptera (some)[3]
- Orthoptera
    - Acrididae
    - Gryllidae
    - Gryllotalpidae
    - Tettigoniidae

Phasmatodea (all)

Hemiptera (Heteroptera)

- Coreidae
- Largidae
- Lygaeidae[4]
- Miridae
- Pentatomidae
- Piesmatidae

Table 6.2 Contd.

Pyrrhocoridae[4] Tingidae

Hemiptera (all Homoptera)

Thysanoptera (most)

Coleoptera (Adephaga)

Carabidae (some)

Coleoptera (Polyphaga)

Anthicidae (some)[3]

Anthribidae (some)[3]

Byrrhidae (some)[3]

Byturidae

Cantharidae (some)[3]

Cerambycidae (some)[3]

Chrysomelidae

Coccinellidae (*Epilachna*)

Curculionidae

Elateridae (some)[3]

Meloidae (some)

Scarabaeidae (Melolonthinae, Rutelinae)[3]

Lepidoptera[2]

Bombycoidea

Geometroidea

Hesperioidea

Noctuoidea

Notodontoidea

Papilionoidea

Sphingoidea

Hymenoptera (Symphyta)[2]

Tenthredinoidea

Leaf rollers and makers[2]

Coleoptera

Attelabidae

Lepidoptera

Gelechiidae

Gracilariidae

Lasiocampidae

Table 6.2 Contd.

Pyralidae
Tortricidae (Torticinae)
Yponomeutidae
Hymenoptera (Symphyta)
Megalodontidae
Pamphilidae
Case bearers[2]
Coleoptera (Polyphaga)
Chrysomelidae (Clytrinae, Cryptocephalinae)
Lepidoptera
Coleophoridae
Incurvariidae
Psychidae
Tineidae
Open galls
Thysanoptera (some)
Hemiptera (Homoptera)
Aphididae (some)
Internal feeders on foliage, stems, and/or roots[2]
Borers
Coleoptera (Polyphaga)
Brentidae
Buprestidae
Cerambycidae (some)
Curculionidae
Languriidae
Platypodidae
Scolytidae
Diptera
Agromyzidae
Anthomyiidae
Chloropidae
Ephydridae
Lepidoptera
Cossidae

Table 6.2 Contd.

Hepialidae
Noctuidae
Pyralidae
Sesiidae
Tortricidae (Olethreutinae)

Hymenoptera (Symphyta)

Cephidae
Siricidae (some)
Syntexidae
Xiphydriidae

Leaf miners

Coleoptera

Buprestidae
Chrysomelidae
Curculionidae

Diptera

Agromyzidae
Anthomyiidae
Cecidomylidae
Chironomidae
Drosophilidae
Ephydridae
Lauxaniidae
Psilidae
Sciaridae
Syrphidae
Tephritidae

Lepidoptera

Coleophoridae
Cosmopterygidae
Cycnodiidae
Elashistidae (some)
Eriocraniidae
Gracilariidae
Heliodinidae

Table 6.2 Contd.

Heliozelidae
Incurariidae
Lyonetidae
Nepticulidae
Noctuidae
Opostegidae
Pyralidae
Tischeriidae
Tortricidae (a few Oleuthreutinae)
Yponomeutidae (Argyresthiinae)

Hymenoptera

Argidae
Tenthredinidae

Closed galls

Coleoptera
Buprestidae
Cerambycidae
Curcullionidae

Lepidoptera

Cosmopterygidae
Gelechiidae
Tortricidae (Olethreutinae)

Diptera

Agromyzidae
Cecidomyiidae
Hymenoptera
Cynipidae
Eurytomidae
Tenthredinidae

Flower feeders

Flower-tissue feeders[3]

Coleoptera (Polyphaga)

Anthribidae
Buptrestidae
Cantharidae

Table 6.2 Contd.

Cerambycidae
Chrysomelidae
Curculionidae
Elateridae
Meloidae
Melyidae
Nitidulidae
Scarabaeidae
Lepidoptera
Lycaenidae (some)[2]

Pollen feeders

Colembola (some)
Blattodea (some)
Dermaptera (some)
Plecoptera (some)[3]
Hemiptera (Heteroptera)
Anthocoridae
Miridae
Thysanoptera (some)
Coleoptera (Polyphaga)
Cephaloidae[3]
Meloidae[3]
Mordellidae[3]
Nitidulidae
Oedemeridae[3]
Phalacridae[3]
Diptera (probably many)[3]
Anthomyiidae
Bibionidae
Bombyliidae
Calliphoridae
Mycetophilidae
Muscidae
Scatopsidae
Syrphklae

Tachinidae

Lepidoptera

Micropterygidae

Nymphalidae (*Heliconius*)[5]

Floer feeders

Hymenoptera

Apoidea[6]

Vespidae (Masarinae)[6]

Xyelidae[2]

Nectar feeders

Neuroptera

Chrysopidae

Mecoptera

Panorpidae (Panorpa)

Diptera (many)

Lepidoptera (most)

Trichoptera (some)

Hymenoptera (most)[6]

Internal feeders in fruit and/or seeds on living plants[4]

Coleoptera (Polyphaga)

Bruchidae Byturidae[2]

Chrysomelidae

Curculionidae

Nitidulidae

Scarabaeidae[3]

Diptera[2]

Cecidomyiidae (*Cauarinia*)

Tephritidae (*Ceratitis, Rhagoletis*)

Lepidoptera[2]

Gelechiidae (*Pectinophora*)

Incurvariidae (*Tegeticula*)

Lycaenidae (*Strymon*)

Mpctiodae (*Heliothis*)

Nolidae (*Celama*)

Pyralidae (*Ostrinia*)

Tortricidae (*Laspeyresia*)

Hymenoptera[2]

Agaonidae (*Blastophaga*)

Eurytomidae (*Bruchophagus*)

---

[1]This list of taxa is intended to be representative, not exhaustive. The listing of a family without qualification does not necessarily mean that all species in the family have the same food habits. Unless otherwise indicated, both the immature and adult stages are believed to have the same food habits. Wellknown or exceptional genera are given in parenthesis.

[2]Feeding is mainly by larvae.

[3]Feeding is mainly by adults.

[4]Feeding is mainly on seeds.

[5]*Heliconus* adults ingest nutrients from pollen that have been dissolved in nectar.

[6]Adult females of Apoidea and Vespidae (Masarinae) also store pollen and nectar in their nests as food for their larvae.

This specificity attracts effective pollinators and tends to reduce losses of pollen and nectar to nonpollinating visitors. The reward given to pollinators is thereby more closely regulated to promote cross-pollination. Commonly nectar is situated deep within a floral tube so that casual visitors are unable to reach it. Elongation of the mouthparts into a sucking tube is consequently a frequent adaptation among specialized flower-visiting insects. The elongation is achieved in many ways and often independently. Curiously, the Hemiptera, with their long sucking beaks, never. became regular flower visitors for nectar.

The largest group of efficient pollinators are the bees, or Apoidea. About 20,000 species are known in the world. Bees evolved from visually hunting, predaceous wasps that frequently visit flowers for nectar. Both sexes of bees take nectar as flight fuel. Females eat pollen as a source of the protein used in producing, their eggs. All females, except the cleptoparasites and social queens, also collect pollen and nectar for their larvae. Either this is stored in the nest as provisions, or, in certain social species, the pollen is fed directly to the 'larvae.

The adaptations of bees that are associated with flower visitations are plumose or featherlike hairs; special pollen- transporting devices; modifications of the tongue, or glossa, for extracting nectar; a diet of pollen and nectar; and, in the honeybees, a highly developed system for communication. A few species of bees are monotrophic, but most bees are oligotrophic or polytrophic. Among the latter are honeybees which visit an enormous variety of flowers, including those designed to attract insects other than bees. During times of food scarcity, honeybees collect honeydew or fruit juices as nectar substitutes. When pollen is scarce, honeybees have been observed to collect flour or even inert dust. Certain primitive bees, such as *Hylaeus* (Colletidae), are relatively hairless, like wasps. They eat pollen and later regurgitate it with nectar while preparing the nest provisions. But most bees have abundant, plumose hairs which retain pollen grains brushed on the body during flower visits. Female bees methodically groom themselves

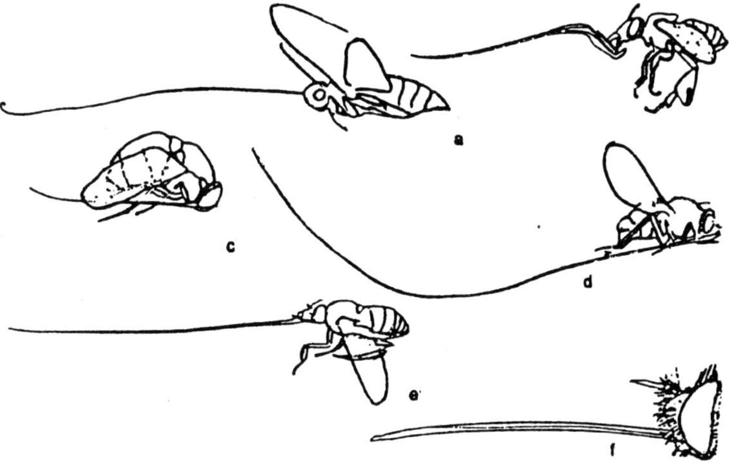

Fig. 6.7. Extreme modifications of mouthparts of flower-visiting insects (length of proboscis in parentheses): a, sphingid moth, Manduca quinquemaculato-proboscis *(12* cm*)* is coiled under head when not in use; b, male apid bee Euglossa asarophora-proboscis *(3cm) is folded between legs when not in use; c, acrocerid fly,* Lasia *kletti-proboscis (2.4 cm) is swung forward in used, nemestrinid fly,* Megistonhynchus longirasdiss-proboscis *(8.4 cm) is swung forward in usere, tabanid* fly, philoliche longwostns-proboscis *(5.8 cm)* is carried in light as shown; f, head of bombylud fly, Bomylus lancife-proboscis *(9.7 mm) is carried as shown.*

and pack the pollen into special devices for transport to the nest. These are of two kinds: (1) pollen brushes, or *scopae,* of long, dense hairs on the hind legs of most bees or on the underside of the abdomer in Megachilidae; and (2) pollen baskets, or *corbiculae,* which are created by a circle of stiff hairs on the outer surface of the hind tibiae of honeybees, bumblebees, and their relatives. Andrenidae, Colleticae, and Halictidae have short tongues suited to take nectar from exposed nectaries or flowers in which the bee can bodily enter. These are considered less specialized than the long-tongued

Megachilidae, Anthophoridae, and Apidae, which can reach nectar hidden in the inner recesses of specialized flowers. The expansible crop carries nectar back to the nest and also functions on outbound flights as a fuel tank.

"Bee flowers" characteristically open at certain times during the day, emitting sweet or aromatic odours and presenting their pollen and nectar. Petals of bright blue, purple, yellow and other colours within the bee's range of cdlour vision are common. Recall that red is invisible to bees; it is an uncommon colour of bee flowers. Patterns reflecting ultraviolet are seen by the bee but are invisible to us. Separate petals which create a broken outline are suited to detection as a mosaic image by the bee's compound eyes. The two-lipped form of certain bee flowers; such as those of legumes or mints, provides a landing platform. This places the bee in a position favouring acccss to the food and pollination. Distinctive stripes of spots serve as nectar guides which orient the bee to the food. Two other large groups of pollinating insects show conspicuous modification for flower visiting: certain Diptera and most Lepidoptera. In both orders, the special modifications are mainly elongation of the mouthparts to reach hidden nectar. The mouthparts of butterflies and moths are suited only to sucking fluids. Most species take nectar, but some moths do not feed at all as adults. The longest tongue of any insect is the 22.5-cm proboscis of the Madagascar hawkmoth. *Xanthopan morgani predictor* (Sphingidae). The moth is apparently the sole pollinator of the orchid *Angraecum sesquipedale, a plant* with nectar situated in an equally long tube and accessible only to this moth.

Although the mouthparts of flies are variously modified for blood-sucking or sponging, the general ability seems to be retained to ingest nectar and small particles such as pollen grains. Certain species in each of several families of flies have developed exceptionally long mouthparts for probing deep flowers. Some species with long mouthparts are found in Bombyliidae, Apioceridae, Nemestrinidae, Acroceridae and Tabanidae. Shorter, but distinctly specialized, mouthparts are also seen on species of *Rhingia* (Syrphidae), Conopidae and Tachinidae. The long-tongued flies visit the same kinds of flowers that bees visit. The so-called "fly flowers" are mainly adapted to less specialized, short tongued insects which normally feed on fluids from dead animals, feces, or plant juices. The flowers depend more on odor than their appearance to attract these insects. The shallow flowers are often white or dull-coloured; the nectar is exposed; and the smell is often musty or rank.

Flowers attractive to butterflies open during the day, have sweet odors, and often have nectar at the base of a deep tube. The flowers are erect and have a horizontal surface for landing. Red is visible to butterflies and is common colour of *"butterfly flowers,"* such as carnations or the butterfly weed. *Asclepias tuberosa.* "Moth flowers" bloom in the evening or night; most of them have heavy, sweet scents; and they are often a highly visible pale or white colour. Hawkmoths (Sphingidae) characteristically hover in front of a flower and take nectar by extending their long probosces. Flowers visited by hawkmoths are horizontal or drooping, with the reproductive pats situated to contact the hovering moth. The Coleoptera which visit flowers are active fliers that frequent open, sunny places, in contrast to their terrestrial, cryptic relatives. Beetles tend to linger in flowers, feeding on pollen and flower parts with their powerful mouthparts, and sometimes taking nectar. Elongation of the mouthparts has occurred in only a few cases. The heads of the cerambycids *Strangalia spp.* and *Cyphonotida laevicollis* are prognathous, with the anterior portions somewhat elongated.

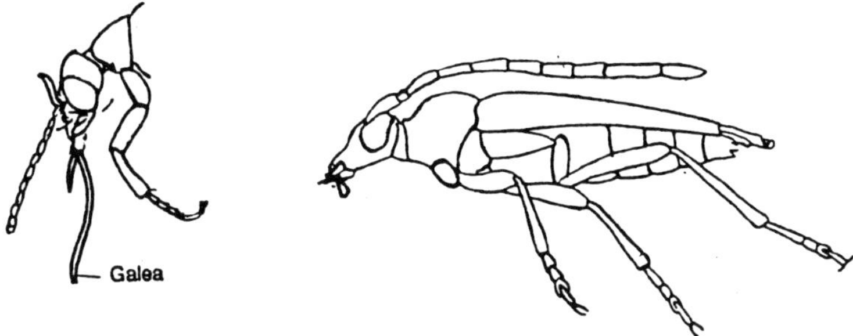

Fig. 6.8. Adaptations of flower-visiting Coleoptera: a, meloid beetle. Nemognatha *sp., with elongate galeae 73 mm long,* b, *cerambycid beetle,* Cyphonodda laevicollis, *with prognathous elongate head.*

The most spectacular adaptations of this sort in the Coleoptera are the greatly elongated galeae of *Nemognatha* (Meloidae), which form a sucking tube. Turning now to certain examples of extreme interdependence between plants and their pollinators, we find in these associations that pollen and nectar are not the prime incentives for the insects. The host specificity is compounded by the specificity of the larvae which feed on the plant tissues: the fig wasps and yucca moths lay their eggs in the ovaries of their hosts. Initially they probably were only accidental pollinators. Seed production, however, is advantageous to both the plant and the seed-infesting insects. The relationships now are completely mutualistic. The largest group of highly specialized pollinators are the tiny wasps of the Family Agaonidae which pollinate figs. The genus *Ficus* (plant Family Moraceae), found in tropical regions, includes about 800 species. Virtually every species of wasp is confined to a single species of fig. The fig that we eat is actually an inflorescence composed of an enlarged receptacle which encloses many small flowers.

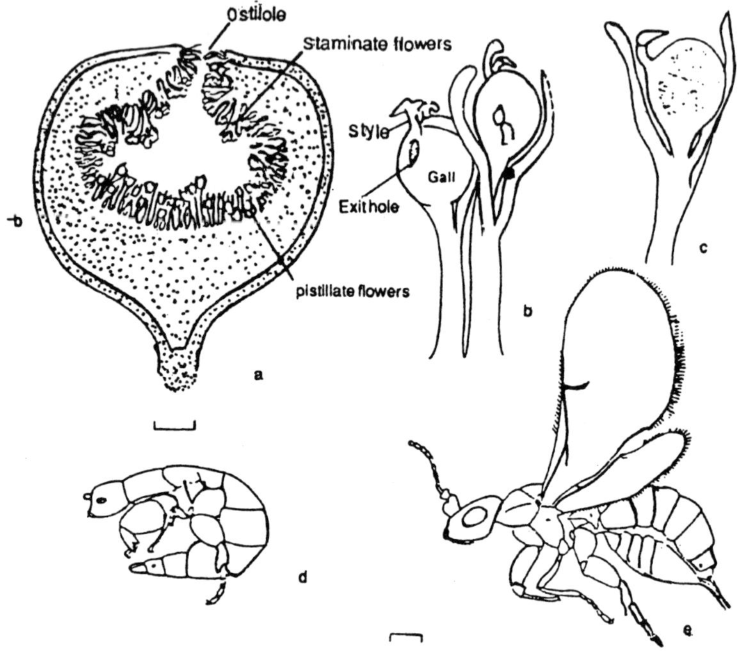

Fig. 6.9. Pollination of caprifig by Bllastophaga wasps: a, caprifig at time of emergence of wasps (scale equals 5 mm); b, gall flower with male wasp inside and another with exit hole; c, gall flower with female wasp inside. d, male Blastophaga, e, female Blastophaga.

In general, the pollination of the caprifig, *Ficus canca,* by the wasp *Blastophaga psenes* takes place in the following manner. The fig has flowers of two kinds: pollen-producing male florets and female florets with short styles. The female wasp flies to a fig in the proper state of maturation and forcibly enters it through the narrow opening, or ostiole, which is guarded by scales. The restricted opening presumably excludes nonpollinating insects. In the process she loses her wings and antennal flagella. She penetrates deeply in the fig to reach the female florets. There she inserts her ovipositor through the short style of a floret to the ovarian region, where she lays an egg. She also is seen to remove some fig pollen with her front legs from special pouches on her body and brush it on adjacent stigmas, thus pollinating the female florets. After laying her eggs, she dies, still in the fig. Each wasp large feeds inside a floret, causing a tiny gall. At maturity, the adult males are fightless and have reduced legs, eyes, and antennae. They chew their way out of their galls first and seek the galls containing adult female wasps. A hole is bored in the gall by the male, and he copulates with the female by means of an extensible abdomen. The male wasp then dies. The inseminated female emerges from her gall and seeks the pollen contained in the male florets nor

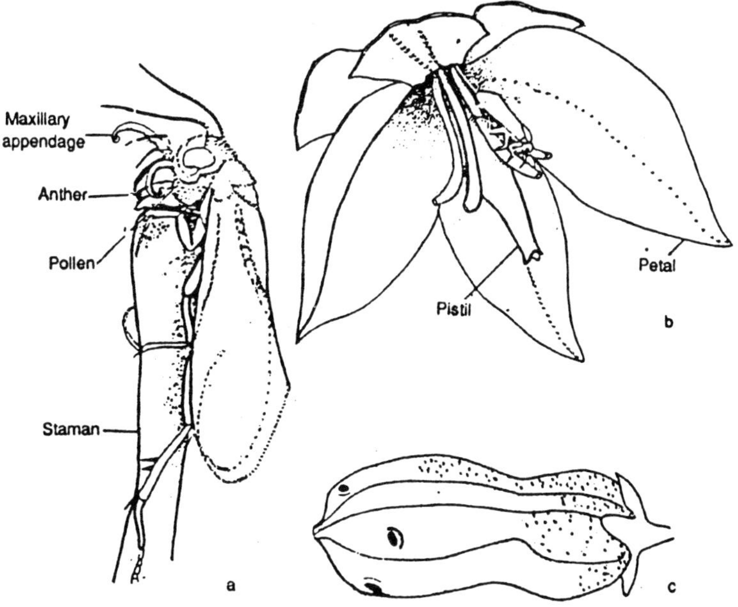

Fig. 6.10. Pollination of Yucca sp. by Tegedcula moths q female of Teg eticula yuccasella collecting pollen from anther, b, position of female of the during oviposition in ovary of Yucca c, mature pod of Yucca showing emergence holes.

the ostiole. She packs pollen into special cavities on her body, leaves the fig, flies to another fig in the proper state of development, enters it, and the process is repeated. The exact cycle varies with the species of wasp and fig. When edible figs were introduced in California in the late 1800s, the Smyrna variety failed to produce fruit. An enterprising grower traveled to Turkey to learn the secrets of successful fig culture. After some difficulty, including an epidemic of plague, he returned with the knowledge that special pollination is necessary. The Smyrna variety has only female florets with long styles. The wasps and suitable pollen must be obtained from the caprifig, in which the normal cycle can be completed. Caprifigs fruits, containing pollen-laden females of *Blastophaga,* are hung in perforated bags among the limbs of Smyrna fig trees. The *Blastophaga* emerge and enter the Smyrna figs. They are unable to lay eggs because their ovipositor is too short for the long-styled florets. The fig is nevertheless pollinated and normally ripens with seeds into an edible fruit. Another group of host-specific pollinators are the Yucca moths, *Tegeticula* and *Paralegeticula* sp. (Incurvariidae). All species of *Yucca* (plant Family Agavaceae) are American in origin, but they have been introduced elsewhere in the world. More than two dozen species of *Yucca* east of the Rockies and the Mojave Desert are pollinated by one moth species. *T. yuccasella.* In the West, *Yucca brevifolia* is pollinated by *T. paradoxa, Y whipplei* by *T. maculata;* and YY *schottii* by *Paralegeticula polleniferae,* as well as *Tegeticula yuccasella.*

The eastern moths are active at night, the time at which flower scent is also strongest. The female *T. yuctasella* enters the white flower, climbs up the stamens to the anters, and gathers the pollen in a ball. The pollen mass from one to four anthers is carried under her head, clasped by a prehensile elongation of the maxillary palpi and the bases of the forelegs. She then flies to another flower in 'the proper state of ovarian development. After inspecting the ovary, she bores in - with her sclerotized, elongate ovipositor and lays an egg. Climbing the style, she packs some pollen on the stigma. This behaviour is often repeated after each egg is laid. On the average one egg is inserted into each of three compartments of the ovary. A few of the many seeds in pollinated flowers server as food for the moth larvae. Unpollinated flowers do not develop seeds. When fully fed, the larvae leave the seed pod and pupate in the ground. Emergence of the adults is timed to coincide with the flowering season.

A final example is provided by the male euglossine bees of the American Tropics, which visit orchids. Males take nectar as flight fuel from various flowers, but they visit orchids to obtain odours. The floral odours are created by species-specific blends of volatile compounds such as benzyl acetate, cineole, eugenol, methyl salicylate, and methyl cinnamate. Males of species of *Euglossa* and *Eulaema* are each attracted to certain odours. The males brush the odour-producing surfaces and apparently store the fragrance in special cavities in their large hind tibiae. The bees' use of the odour is not clear, but they seem dependent on an adequate supply. Possibly it is metabolized or converted to attractants for either or both males or females. During their contact with the orchid, the male bees become intoxicated. When disabled, they fall into a trap device. During their escape, a packet of pollen is attached to a specific place on their body. At their next visit to an orchid of the same species, the packet is removed by the orchid thus achieving pollination.

Modern Phytophagous Insects

An adequate classification of phytophagous feeding habits would be overly complex for our purposes. Here we shall divide insects by their taxonomic groupings and by their general mode of feeding. The mouthparts and other characteristics of the immature and adult insects should be kept in mind when considering each group and its food habits. Orthoptera and Phasmatodea have chewing mouth-parts in all stages and feed externally on plants. The phytophagous species among the endopterygote orders Hymenoptera, Coleoptera, and larval Lepidoptera also have chewing mouthparts. Some of these feed externally, and some bore bodily into the plant tissues. The rasping mouthparts of all stages of Thysanoptera are applied externally to disrupt cells and suck cell fluids. The piercing-sucking mouthparts of all stages of Hemiptera and the fruit-piercing moths take vascular or tissue fluids by penetrating the plant while the insect remains outside. Mouthparts of larval Diptera vary from the normal chewing type to hooklike structures which tear loose and ingest plant tissue and fluids. Larval flies are able to feed internally by boring. Adult Diptera, whether of the biting or sponging type, ingest only liquid food and particles in suspension. They feed externally and probably take fluids which are freely available without further damage to the plant. Nectar and pollen, as well as saps and juices from previously injured tissues or fruits, are eaten. The sucking mouthparts of adult Lepidoptera pass fluids of the same kinds, but not particles.

Insects which tat the vegetative parts of plants can be broadly divided into external and internal feeders. During the life history of some species, especially small moths, the larvae may feed first inside then outside. External feeders may be freely visible to predators and parasitoids. Such *exposed feeders* are usually protectively coloured and patterned if they are large enough to be edible by vertebrates. The manner of feeding is characteristic of the species. Many caterpillars and sawfly larvae feed along the leaf edge. Surface feeders with chewing mouthparts may ingest whole pieces of leaf, leaving holes or notches. Others remove most of the photo-synthetic tissues, leaving a delicate skeletonized vascular network. The cellulose-rich feces are called *frass*. Exposed feeders simply drop frass from their feeding stations.

The feeding injuries of leaf-feeding Hemiptera are often recognized as small, discoloured spots where the. inner palisade and spongy mesophyll cells are broken down and emptied. The insect's saliva sometimes has physiological effects on the leaf which are also injurious. Thysanoptera also remove the contents of the inner leaf cells, resulting in silvery air, spaces inside the leaf. Damaged leaves and stems may wither, discolour, or fall prematurely. Some external feeders gain protection by feeding on roots or within enfolding leaves. Those that are able to spin silk may bind together leaves in a sheltering cluster. The *leaf rollers* are caterpillars and sawfly larvae which roll or fold leaves to create a tube. The larvae hide in the tube, feeding at its edge or on nearby leaves. Some moth species pupate in the roll. Adult attebrid weevils cut the leaf bearing their egg, and the leaf forms a roll naturally. The weevil larva feeds inside. Parenthetically, we 'should note that the predaceous gryllacridid cricket *Camptonotus carolinensis* also rolls leaves and fastens them with an oral secretion. The leaf roll is used as a retreat.

Insects that feed inside the plant, completely surrounded by living tissue, are exclusively endopterygotes and usually the larval stages of the life history. *Leaf miners* are small larvae that eat some or all of the mesophyll tissues. between the outer layers of leaf blades or needles. Female insects select the host and lay their eggs on the leaf surface, or inserted in the mesophyll, or nearby on the plant. Usually mature leaves are mined. The larvae feed in a manner characteristic of the species, leaving a "signature" which is sometimes beautifully serpentine. Larvae of Diptera are cylindrical but soft-bodied and adaptable to the restricted mine. The other larval miners are highly flattened, usually colourless, legless, and with a flattened, wedgelike head which slopes, forward. No adult insects are leaf miners. Linear mines begin as a tiny channel and progressively widen as the larva grows in size and appetite. The direction of the mine may be altered when vascular bundles are encountered. Blotch mines are created when the larva feeds in various directions, eating both cascular and mesophyll tissues. The frass is often deposited in the mine or ejected through an opening. Lepidoptera may lay frass inside in a continuous line, or pack it at one end or plaster it randomly on the minefloor, while Diptera lay two rows. Hymenoptera scatter the frass about the cavity or in piles.

Some miners pupate in the mine, while other species leave to form a cocoon elsewhere. Plant *borers* are insets that burrow in living or dead plant tissues other than leaves. The xylophagous scavengers discussed in the previous section are borers in dead plants. Their life-span is usually long because of the lower nutrient value of the food, variable and sometimes low moisture content, and the stable environment. We are concerned here primarily with larvae that bore into living buds, stems, roots, fruits, seeds, nuts, or grains. Life-spans of these borers may be short, not only because the living plant tissues change.

Although this is a heterogeneous group, the larvae share several similarities arising from their sheltered mode of life. The bodies are often cylindrical, pale, legless, and with bumps or rough areas of skin which provide traction against the burrow walls. The mouthparts, mounted on a retractable head capsule, excavate tissue bit by bit. Antennae are short and retractable into grooves. These specialization give borers access to food rich in nutrients: newly developing leaves, cambium tissue, the flesh of fruits, and endosperm of seeds. Frass is often packed behind the larva as it advances. Certain secretions of insects and mites stimulate abnormal development of growing plant tissue, resulting in misshapen leaves or in swellings called *galls.* These are usually initiated in the spring and early summer when the meristematic tissue is active. Aphids feeding on the underside of a new leaf can cause the leaf to curl around them and enclose a favourably high humidity. Homoptera and mites create galls by their feeding secretions. The gall is typically a hollow cavity which remains open to the exterior and consequently is called an *open gall.* A group of insects or mites or several generations may live inside the gall, feeding and taking shelter. The galls of endopterygote insects are usually, but not always, occupied by a single larva. Either the ovipositing female or the larvae or both seem to be responsible for the biochemical stimulants. The galls do not have a permanent opening and are called *closed gall.* The host plant responds with a growth of specific colour and design such that the insect can be identified by the gall it makes. The larva is surrounded by moisture and food and is largely protected from natural enemies. Some wasp parasitoids, however, are able to lay their eggs in or near the gall-making larvae so that several kinds of insects may emerge from a single gall.

HOST SPECIFICITY

How specific are insects in their choice of food? Some exposed feeders accept a great variety of plants as food. The larvae of the gypsy moth, *Porthetria despair* (Lymantriidae), are known to feed on 458 species of plants in the United States. Such insects that accept a wide variety of plants for food are called *polyphagous, Oligophagous* insects feed on a few species of plants, often reated to one another or having certain similar biochemical constituents. *Monophagous* insects feed . on only one species. Insects with the more restricted range of hosts are usually the leaf miners, borers, and gall makers which are surrounded by plant tissues, or insects adapted to toxic plants. The early plantfeeding Neoptera are assumed to have been polyphagous, exposed feeders, that are exemplified now by Orthoptera. The oligophagous and monophagous taxa evolved as specialists, with occasional reversions to polyphagous habits. What factors favour the evolution of host specificity? To answer this question, we must consider in detail the coevolutionary nature of insect/plant relationships. Part of the explanation lies, on the one hand, in the defense strategies of plants against attack. We have seen that all parts of a plant may be eaten; roots, stems, leaves, sap, flower, parts, fruits and seeds. Plant growth is affected by loss of food when photosynthetic tissue is eaten or phlouem sap is drained. Damage to roots and xylem deprives the plant of water and minerals. Chemicals in insect's saliva or secreted by the ovipositor may have general or specific effects on the host's physiology. Injured cambium or meristematic tissue results in abnormal growth. These influences lead to stunting, lowered production of seeds, or death. Damage to flowers, fruits, and seeds directly affects the population growth of plants. Phytophagous insects also transmit plant diseases.

In the coevolution of insects and plants, the plant evolves a protective measure, then insects evolve effective means to overcome the plant's defense which in turn selects for new plant defenses, and so on. In the context of this interaction, a plant which is less damaged because of heritable characteristics is said to be *resistant*. Three basic kins of resistance have been identified by Painter; (1) Resistant plants may be *nonpreferred* for oviposition, shelter, or food; e.g., some chemical or physical feature of the plant either is lacking and fails to attract insects *or* some feature is present which is repellent. (2) Resistant plants may adversely affect the biology of the insect. Physical or chemical properties of the plant may result in the insect's early death, abnormal development, decreased fecundity, or, other deleterious conditions. For example, toxins, repellents, copious sap or pitch, or tissue which is nutritionally inadequate for insects could reduce or eliminate attack. This kind of resistance is called *antibiosis*. (3)

Resistant plants may be *tolerant* and survive even when infested by insects at levels that kill or injure susceptible plants. Rapid replacement of lost parts, excess production of seeds, rapid wound healing, and detoxification of insect salivary toxins are some of the possible ways a plant might survive damage.

The non-preference and antibiotic properties prevent or reduce attack. These properties vary (as do other genetic traits) from plant species to species, geographically with the ranges of species, locally depending on ecology, and from individual to individual (see discussion of alkaloids in lupines). For example, the oleoresins or pitch of conifers traps, expels, or is toxic to boring insects in needles or bark. The variation in physical and chemical composition of oleoresins gives almost every tree a unique individuality. Angio-sperms have so-called secondary plant substances such as essential oils, alkaloids, and glycosides whose primary function seems to be in chemical defense, although some may be otherwise integrated into the plant's metabolism. This toxic, biochemical shield has partially protected flowering plants against herbivorous, both insect and vertebrate. These chemicals, incidentally, also give us spices and flavourings. The plant-feeding insects, on the other hand, compete for food. The resistance factors evolved by plants further limit the number of kinds of plants available to eat. Insects which are able to survive the antibiotic properties and develop a preference for a nonpreferred host will acquire not only food but also some relief from interspecific competition. Those able to bore into plant tissues must tolerate immersion in the host's chemical environment ad physical constraints, but here also are food and relief from competition, plus escape from certain enemies and protection against desiccation, freezing, etc.

Some insects store toxic plant substances and thereby acquire a defense for themselves against vertebrate predators. Thus a number of advantages accrue to the monophagous or oligophagous insect that is adapted to the special condition of life associated with one or a few kinds of plant hosts. Some insects may be secondarily polyphagous because they are able to tolerate a variety of resistance factors in plants. Their adaptation to biochemical stresses also may permit them to resist or detoxify insecticides manufactured by humans.

The defensive mechanisms of plants and host specificity of insects have evolved in response to essentially two periods of contact; (1) the period of oviposition, during which the female seeks suitable host plants on which to lay her eggs; and (2) the period of feeding, during which the immature and sometimes adult insects eat the plant. Oviposition behaviour involves recognition and orientation to a host plant at some distance, the search for specific sites in the plant, and finally, the deposition of eggs, followed by dispersal. The behaviour is a series of complex events and involves many of the insect's sensory receptors. Any heritable physical or chemical feature of the plant which reduces the numbers of eggs, and thus ultimately the number of feeding insects, will be selectively favoured. This is resistance of the nonpreference type and is achieved either by failing to attract ovipositing females or by providing some inhibition.

Feeding behaviour of insects on plants is similarly complex. Beck identified four steps; (1) host recognition and orientation; (2) initial biting or piercing of the plant; (3) maintenance of feeding; and (4) cessation of feeding, usually followed by dispersal. The behavioural response at act step depends on releasing stimuli provided by the plant and on the insect's response thresholds, which vary with its physiological state. Resistance of the non-preference type would be given a plant which lacked the appropriate releasing stimuli or which discouraged feeding at some step. Physical and chemical stimuli have been classified according to the response they elicit from insects. During orientation to a host plant at a distance, certain stimuli may act positively as *attractants* or negatively as *repellents*. When in close contact with the plant, positive stimuli may stop further locomotion, i.e., be *arrestants,* or act as repellents to hasten the insect's departure. At the initiation of feeding, positive stimuli are *suppressants*. Feeding is maintained by *stimulants* or terminated by *deterrents*.

The sensory apparatus and orientation behaviour of insects are finely tuned to the characteristics of the desired host plants. Secondary plant substances which are repellent to most insects are, in fact, often the feeding stimulants for the appropriate monophagous insects. Nutrients, including sugars, amino acids, phospholipids, and ascorbic acid, can also be stimulants to certain insects. The sensory receptors on the antennae and maxillae of cater- pillars are chiefly involved in discrimination. When such receptors are experimentally removed, oligophagous caterpillars often accept as food a broader range of plant species. Although the female usually selects the host plant when she lays her eggs, the caterpillar must select the parts of the plant to eat, avoiding concentrations of toxins and finding the riches; food.

Since phytotoxemias, especially when systemic, often resemble diseases caused by viruses, it is useful to recall that there are several fundamental differences:

Toxemias	Virus diseases
1. Toxin does not reproduce in plant	1. Virus reproduces in plant
2. Symptoms subside when insects are removed	2. Symptoms persist when insects are removed
3. Recovery common	3. Recovery uncommon
4. Degree of injury related to number of insects and length of time they. feed	4. Degree of injury not necessarily related to number of insects or length of time they feed
5. Disease not perpetuated by vegetative propagation or transmitted by grafting	5. Disease can be perpetuated by vegetative propagation and transmitted by grafting

Vectors

Insects are involved in the transmission of bacterial, fungal, viral, and mycoplasmal diseases of plants. Some of these are all too well known; Dutch elm disease, a fungus disease transmitted by bark beetles; fire blight, a bacterial disease of fruit trees, transmitted by flies and other insects; and potato leaf roll virus, transmitted by aphids. Note that vectors need not be sucking insects, although these insects are especially well suited for inoculating plants, especially with viruses. Insect transmission of plant diseases is a large subject we can treat only briefly here.

Disease organisms may be spread in one of two ways:

1. Transmission may be *mechanical;* that is, the organisms are borne on the surface of the insect, usually the mouthparts, and in this way carried from plant to plant. When sucking insects are involved, this type of transmission is spoken of as *stylet borne.* It is also spoken of as *nonpersistent* since the microorganisms survive only a short time unless deposited on or in a plant.

2. Transmission may be *circulatory;* that is, the organisms are ingested by an insect, circulate in the body, and are later discharged in salivary fluids. In some cases the microorganisms multiply in the insect. This type of transmission is *persistent,* in the sense that it may occur over a considerable period of time. Transmission may be by *inoculation,* in the case of sucking insects, or by surface *deposit* of pathogens, which must then invade the tissue, often through a wound made by the insect. In some cases the relationship between insects

and pathogens is *obligate,* which means that the pathogens are transmitted only in this way. In other cases the relationship is*faculative,* since the pathogens can be transmitted in other ways, for example, by wind; rain, or other organisms. We present here a single example of a disease caused by each major type of pathogen. Throughout the world several hundred plant diseases have been reported to be transmitted by insects and mites, and several thousand insect species have been incriminated as vectors. The brief overview given here will serve only as the briefest of introductions to this field.

Bacterial Diseases

Plant parthogenic bacteria are rod-shaped bacilli, usually nonspore formers, which are able to enter plant tissue only through wounds or by inoculation. They have little capacity to live outside their plant host, and transmission is usually mechanical and non-persistent. Obligatory relationships between the bacteria and a particular insect host are unusual; more commonly a number of different insects and sometimes other agents are involved in transmission. However, the example we select does involve specific vectors.

Cucuurbit wilt is caused by *Erwinia tracheiphila,* a bacillus that invades and blocks the vascular bundles of cucumbers and to a lesser extent those of cantaloupes, squash and pumpkins. The first symptoms are localized wilting; when stems are cut a milky ooze emerges. Eventually the entire plant may wilt and even die, a condition resembling dehydration resulting from drought. This disease occurs in many parts of the world and may be devastating if not controlled. Experiments have shown that when plants are protected from the attacks of two species of leaf beetles, the striped and the spotted cucumber beetle, the plants are also protected from cucurbit wilt. Apparently these beetles carry the bacteria from infected to noninfected plants on the mouthparts or in their fecal pellets, the bacteria gaining entry via feeding wounds.

Fungus Diseases

Relationships between insects and fungi are common and often complex. The relationship may be intimate and mutually beneficial, as in the case of fungi cultivated by certain ants, termites, and ambrosia beetles, or it may involve the casual transmission of spores from one plant to another. A great variety of rots, wilts, cankes, and root infections are produced by fungi that may be transmitted by insects. Unlike bacteria, fungi are often able to penetrate plant tissues directly, without requiring a wound. Transmission is usually mechanical, and sometimes several kinds of insects, or even physical agents such as wind or water, may serve as vectors. The example we select is, however, one involving a specific vector and a mutualistic relationship between insect and fungus.

Blue stain of conifers is caused by fungi of the genus *Ceratostomella*. These fungi cause discolouration of felled timber, reducing its value, and they also invade living trees via holes through the bark made by invading bark beetles. The relationship in beneficial to both beetles and fungi. The latter proliferate in the new host, weakening and eventually killing the tree. This renders the tree more suitable for development of the beetle larvae. When these complete their development, they fly to another tree while carrying the spores. The result is an expanding group of dead and dying trees. The mountain pine beetle of the Rockies and southern pine beetle of the Gulf states are especially notorious vectors. Both are members of the genus *Dendroctonus*. Bark beetles employ a complex chemical signaling system that enables them to attack trees en masse. The trees, in turn, have evolved chemical defenses.

Virus Diseases

A great number of plant diseases are produced by viruses; in Walter Carter's book *Insects in Relation to Plant Disease,* a partial listing of these occupies 38 pages,, while a list of the insect vectors occupies 41 pages. Symptoms of virus disease are diverse; they include blotching and mottling of leaves (termed *mosaic*), leaf curl, tumours, rosettes, distortions of flowers and fruits, yellowing, and necrosis. Symptoms are produced by destruction of tissue cells, often accompanied by abnormal growth of other cells resulting in disturbances in respiration and photosynthesis. Various inclusions are sometimes visible in prepared sections; these represent accumulations of virus, particles. Like all viruses, they are unable to survive apart from host tissue. Transmission may, however, sometimes be mechanical and nonpersistent, in which case either chewing or sucking insects may be involved. The more usual vectors are sucking insects such as aphids, leafhoppers and thrips. Transmission is frequently circulative and may involve relationship with a specific vector and multiplication within the vector. In some cases the virus is transmitted form one generation to the next transovarially.

Curly top of sugar beets is transmitted by the beet leafhopper, an insect occurring in the southwestern United States but undertaking seasonal migrations into the beet-growing regions of the Great Basin and the western Great Plains. Symptoms include leaf curl, stunting, and distortions of the roots. The only important mode of transmission is by the feeding of beet leafhoppers. The virus is retained within the blood of the leafhoppers through molts, but there is no multiplication within the body. The virus overwinters in various wild plants and in beets that have been left in the field. It is picked up by leafhoppers feeding in the spring and transmitted to seedlings.

Mycoplasmal Diseases

Before 1967, mycoplasmas were classed as viruses, since like viruses they pass through capable of retaining bacteria. However, they are now regarded as quite a different group of organisms having some features in common with bacteria: They can be cultured on agar media apart from the host, and they are suscep- tible to certain antibiotics, especially tetracycline, Mycoplasmas are pleomorphic, the cells undergoing changes in form through their life cycle. The most common disease symptoms are yellowing, stunting, and the development of "witches' brooms." At least 15 plant disease are now attributed to mycoplasmas, all of them transmitted by leafhoppers.

Aster yellows occurs in many parts of the world and infects not only asters but also plants of at least 40 families, including vegetable crops such as potatoes, carrots, lettuce and spinach. In addition to yellowing, plants may slow dwarfing or various malformations. The common vector in North America is the aster leafhopper, Macrosteles fascifrons. Transmission is circulative, with multiplication occurring in the body of the vector. Leafhoppers are not infective until at least nine days after the mycoplasma has been ingested.

7

LIVING IN GROUPS

Social life is the highest development of intra specific interrelationship. From simple animal aggregations there may evolve complex animal societies composed of specialized types of individuals such as the colonies of bees, ants and termites. Although ants (like termites) live solely in organized societies, bees and wasps may have either a solitary or a social way of life. Sometimes the boundary between the two is hazy. Various simple forms of family life are shown by a few mining bees of the genus *Halictus,* as described earlier, and by a few vespid wasps. Vespid wasps of the genus *Stenogaster* include both solitary species and species whose members live in united families. Among the latter, the females reared by the mother remain in the nest for a short time giving help. After their departure, they are replaced by younger sisters. Frequently such offspring, instead of establishing their own nests at a distance, attach them directly to the maternal structure, forming a home that contains a loose federation of families.

THE WORKERS

In other social bees and wasps, the female progeny do not leave the home, but continue to live there. They participate, as workers, in the care of the brood, in building activities, in the preservation of hygienic conditions in the dwelling, and in sentry duty. Domestic tasks include cleaning out of empty cells, removal of walling off of foreign bodies, and temperature regulation an renewal of air by fanning the wings in the vicinity of the nest entrance and air vents. This last is done in concert and mostly silently, except by bumblebees. Early in the morning a single bumblebee, dubbed a "trumpeter," takes a position immediately beneath the roof of the nest and ventilates it, with a loud buzzing.

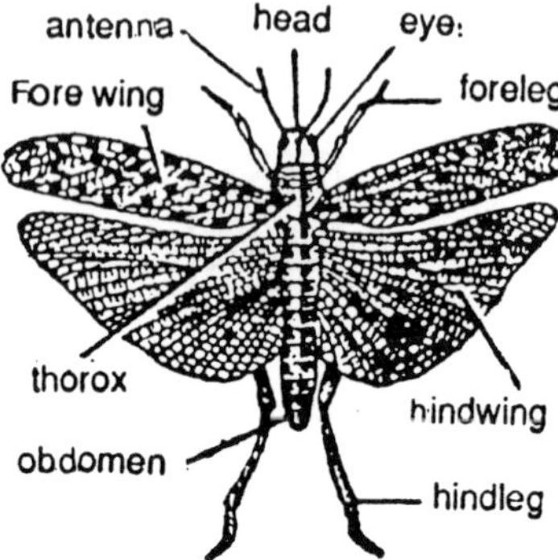

Fig. 7.1. Locust (Schistocercagregaria)

Another chore of the workers is receive food and building material fetched home by their foraging sisters. The food is eaten by the workers and fed to the larvae right away or is first stored in special provision cells. The building material is used at once. An especially important job is the care of the brood and, for honeybees and ants, care of the nest mother or queen. Without proper attention the eggs may die. The larvae, which live in groups within the structure, have to be shifted again and again from chamber to chamber, according to the temperature and the humidity. Even newly matured insects may need to have the cells opened for them when they emerge, or may have to be freed from the pupal skin, as happens with ants.

Aside from these chores, nursing is confined to distributing food adapted to the age of the brood. In general, wasps and ants proffer food prepared from captured insects, spiders, or even fresh meat; the wasps provide it in the form of little balls saturated with saliva, the ants usually as droplets of predigested juice. Bees, on the contrary, feed the brood only with pollen and honey. Just as young songbirds, apparently by means of their strikingly bright-coloured and widely opened gullets, keep alive and augment the urge of the old birds to continue feeding them, the larva of wasps and many ants (but not of bees again and again offer a drop of secretion on their extended mouthparts. This is freedily licked off by the older insects and thus indirectly stimulates them to feed the larvae. Such exchange of food, called trophallaxis, may also induce a swarm to rear as many offspring as possible.

Moreover, many ant larvae do not produce this delicacy from the mouth, but instead exude it from peglike processes or even from the entire body surface. In the vespids of the genus *Belonogaster* the assisting daughters are just like the mother. Since their urge toward nest construction and search for food awakens only with sexual maturation, they are occupied during their first week solely with cleaning operations and with distribution of food in the nest. Then they begin to lay eggs, gather food and enlarge the nest as needed. Nevertheless the family still needs the original mother, for if she were lost the daughters would finally devour their own brood, and the entire society would gradually die off. But otherwise the family gets bigger and bigger, and males, too, are developed. For four to five days the males are fed in the nest with stored up honey by their sisters or else, pilfering on the sly, lead a parasitic life, as is also the case with various species of the *wasps Polistes. If* the members of the community become so numerous that for technical reasons the structure no longer can be enlarged sufficiently, some of the wasps depart and found a new home. But they do this in a most indelicate manner. They not only bite off material from the old home for use in the new one, but even pillage it of the larvae, feeding them to the new brood, with the result that old nest soon is destroyed. *Polistes* wasps are of a rather predatory nature anyway, and occasionally they plunder one anther's nests.

In other wasps, such as *Ropalidia* and.some species of *Polistes* the worker caste begins to show some of the differences that among the rest of the social bees and wasps make it a clearly distinct form. The offspring of the nest mother are smaller females and have reduced fertility or lack it entirely. This results from a restricted supply of food. Except in honeybees and ants, the later offspring, as the family grows in size and the amount of feeding becomes larger, develop into bigger and bigger individuals. With wasps such as *Polistes* and occasionally even with bumblebees (*Bombus*), the later-emerging females scarcely can be distinguished from the mother any longer, but with the other wasps and hornets (*Vespa*) they always are clearly smaller than the queen. The tasks of the workers in the nest frequently are determined by their age-that is, by the degree of maturity of definite internal organs and thus the life cycle of the individual unfolds in a predetermined sequence. Such a sequence of duties has been best studied in honeybees and, with some exceptions, follows the schedule described here.

LIFE CYCLE OF THE HONEYBEE

For the first two three days of their life, honeybees take care of cleaning tasks and the regulation of warmth. By means of community cooperation, they maintain a continuous brood temperature of about 95° F to 97° F (35° C to 36°C). Ventilation and cooling are accomplished by means of whirring the wings, in case of need even by fetching water and pouring it over the combs. On the other hand, heating results from vibratory activity of the flight muscles, from wAhich the wings have been uncoupled, and thus from burning the carbohydrate that has been derived from the honey. From the third to the sixth day of their adult life the bees use pollen and honey to feed the medium-sized to full-grown larvae, which are four to six days old, Both of these foods are stored, carefully separated, in different groups of cells in the combs. From the seventh-day onward, for about a week, two large glands develop in the bee's head. These are vitally important to the colony in that they secrete an extremely growth-promoting, predominantly protein-containing fluid, the royal jelly. This flows from the worker's mouth and is fed to the young larvae and the queen. Unlike them, she is given royal jelly continuously, for to ripen about 100 eggs every hour of the day and night her body must have an enormous metabolic turnover. The "royal court," whose members feed and lick their queen, consists of individuals of various ages.

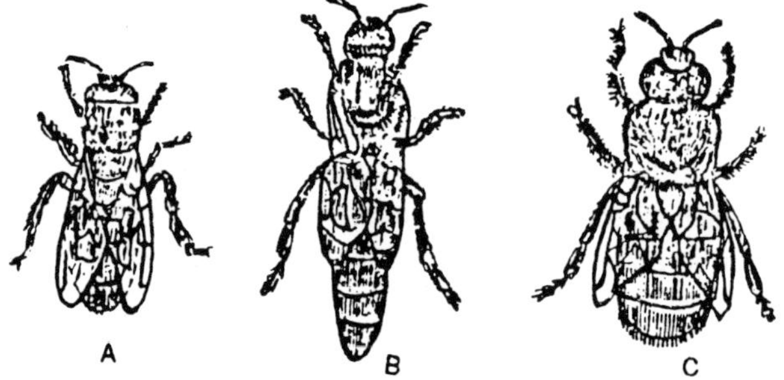

Fig. 7.2. Types of honey bees ; A, Worker, B, Queen; C, Drone.

The queen does nothing but deposit an egg at the bottom of each cell prepared for it. Every day she lays over 2,000 eggs, with a total weight more than her own. At any one time the bees in a colony have perhaps 10,000 larvae to feed, and each of these may receive several thousand feeding visits during the six days it takes to mature. In a strong hive with 10,000 to 80,000 individuals, the 2,000 to 3,000 males (drones) that develop are also fed with royal jelly. But gradually the males come to be regarded as useless parasites, are starved to death

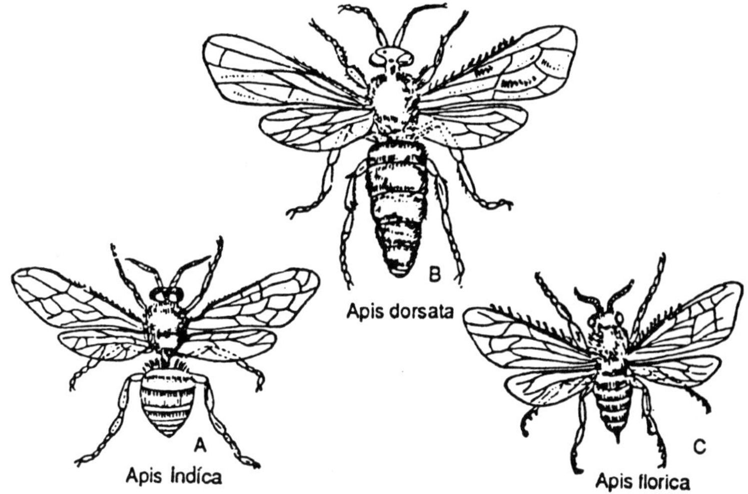

Fig. 7.3. Workers of three species of honey-bee

or killed by stinging, and are thrown out. During the twelfth to eighteenth days of a bee's existence the wax glands begin to function; in addition to construction tasks the workers have much to occupy them during this second period of their life. Above all there is the reception of the honey and pollen brought home by the other bees, the feeding of the larvae with it or the storing of it, and finally the assumption of sentry duty at the hive entrance. In defense of the nest, the bee is ready to sting an intruder, whether it is a larger animal, another insect, or even a bee from another society.

Particularly when times are bad, bees turn into honey thieves. If they succeed in overpowering the guard at the gate, they fetch their companions and raid the nest. Among the stingless honeybees (meliponines) there is even one species whose societies specialize organized predatory invasions of other nests. There they pillage the honey stores and also steal wax for use as building material. The phase of a bee's 'ife, beginning at an age of about three weeks, is of active service in the field. The worker prepares herself by taking several preliminary orientation flights in which she impr upon herself the location of the nest and its immediate surroun Now she begins her food collections, and when she finds sources food learns how to pass on information about them to her comrades. After perhaps ten days of this, the bee's life is at an end; the average age is 30 to 35 days, with a probable maximum of 55 days.

One might be tempted to regard the division of labour within the bee society as merely an automatic consequence of various glandular functions. But experiments have shown that such conduct can be repressed or can be forced ahead of schedule if conditions so demand. In other words, the requirements of the social organization are the moving force of all behaviour. Thus, if a hive happens to lose its normal building workers, old bees whose wax glands have regressed with experience a redevelopment of these glands and will begin to produce wax again. Or suppose a hive is divided into two nests, one with only young bees and the other with only older ones. In the first of these the catastrophe of starvation seems about to take place. And yet many of these young bees go flying out betimes to gather food, although this is not their job, and they do this in spite of their active royal jelly glands, which then degenerate prematurely. On the other hand, in the older bees' nest, these glands continue to function in a number of-bees longer than normally, simply because, for lack of young nurse bees, this has become a vital necessity.

ANT WORKERS

In an ant society, though brood care and division of labour are more highly organized, the type of work seems to be less definitely regulated than it is with bees, and its individual facets are only slightly dependent on the age of the individuals, or not at all. So the society is much more adaptable. In place of females that merely are reduced in size and more or less sterile, there are workers with distinctly different body structures specially suited to the tasks at hand. The workers of a given ant species may be more or less uniform in size and shape (monomorphic), may be variable (polymorphic), or may appear as two distinct types (dimorphic). These last, known usually as *"workers"* and *"soldiers"* may represent the extremes of an originally continuous chain of variations, the intervening links of which no longer exist: In genera with a single type of worker, only one variant, usually a smaller one, has remained, with ants low in the evolutionary scale such monomorphism may be a primary mani-festation.

Where a species has different types of worker, the large ones are designated as *"soldiers,"* yet by no means are they always the defenders or the warriors of the society. Big heads and mandibles of extraordinary shape may be based upon other biological prerequisites, for instance, they may be necessary for mincing up seeds or animal prey. In some species the nest entrance is closed off by the head of a "porter" stationed there; in certain genera the porter's head is so constructed that the door is not only barricaded but is concealed besides. Various worker forms, ranging from about 0.08 to 0.6 inch in length, are found among the leafcuting, ants (*Atta*). As in other ant societies, the different tasks appear to be parceled our to the types best fitted for them. The dwarfs take care of the mushroom garden, the middle-sized individuals gather leaves and work them over in the nest, and the big workers guard and defend the nest.

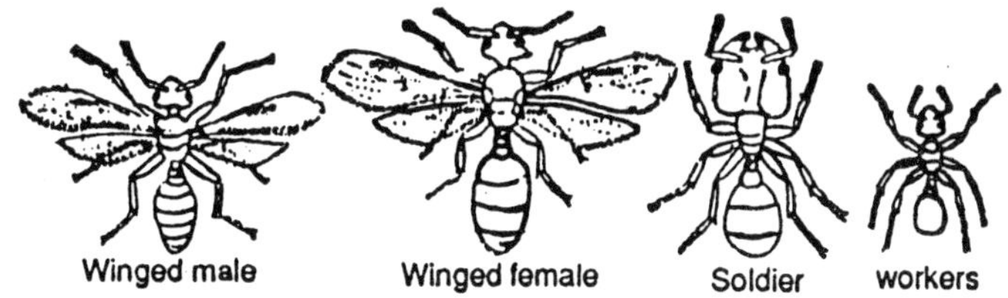

Fig. 7.4. Various castes of the Ants.

In general, the different tasks in the nests of ants all can be carried out by any worker, and usually a single worker executes a particular job only for a limited length of time. Nevertheless, the small individuals seem to devote themselves preferentially to the actual care of the brood. Both the eggs and the larvae are licked over and over and put in piles, arranged according to their age, and the pupal coccons (often mistakently called *"ant eggs"*) are also separated and heaped up in different chambers. Ants mostly feed their larvae, as they do their queen, their fellows, and their guests, from mouth to mouth with drops of nutritive juice from a "crop" or "social stomach" that, like the honey stomach of bees, lies in the fore part of the abdomen. But more primitive species, such as many ponerines, proffer chopped-up insects; and a few genera offer balls of minced tissue as food, in some cases from a special oral pocket.

FORMS OF SOCIAL LIFE

After this consideration of the worker caste and its duties, we return to the forms taken by family and civic life. In the tropics the life span of families of vespid wasps and bumblebees (*Bombus*) does not depend on portion of the hive together with one or several queen - or else, as in other wasps, simply by individual fertilized females. These *Polybia* wasps, moreover, have the strange peculiarity of flying soundlessly, and are particularly prone to attack intruders within a circumference of about two years of their nest. The bleeding puncture made by their sting is very painful and makes the affected part of the body whiten at once, yet causes only a slight swelling. The frequently large societies of the "stingless" honeybees (*Melipona, Trigona*), which do have a sting, though an ineffective one, seem more primitive than the societies of *Polybia*. For these honey-bees close off their brood cells, as do the solitary bees, after providing them with honey paste and an egg. Further feeding, with consequent relations between larvae and workers, does not occur at all. But again, the queen of the nest is more highly specialized than the queens of bumble bees and wasps. With shortened wings, small aggregations of pollen on the legs, a little head, and weak mouthparts as well as reduced brain, she is greatly dependent on the assistance of workers.

With a single queen, stingless honeybees form societies that endure for several years. The queen tolerates the presence of other, virgin queens. Where they are lacking, the colony dies after the death of the queen, for another queen cannot be reared, from such larvae as are present, through special feeding by the workers, as can be done by honeybees (*Apis*) and by the more highly organized among the wasps. On the other hand, the queen by herself is unable to establish a colony. This has to be accomplished through the formation of a swarm led by a young female. In fact, among meliponines such young females usually are immature initially; later, the great swelling of their abdomen makes flying out impossible.

SWARMING

After the sexual forms-males and females (queens) - have been reared, swarming occurs. Since in many species, including the honeybees, these forms are larger than the workers, sometimes far larger, they have to be reared in special large cells. One might imagine that honeybees would construct their cells of a size proportional to their own body mass. But where do honeybee workers get the proper measure for their fatter brothers, the future males (or drones), which they have never seen before in their lives? what signal suddenly causes these bees to build larger cells in the comb, and impels the queen to deposit eggs that are unfertilized and that therefore produce males? Truly they have great power over the life of their folk, these workers. Ultimately, too, they determine the number of the young queens. These are reared with special food in the few big, pendant, peg-shaped queen cells, which strangely enough bear on their surface the comb. Inside the cells the young larvae hang head downward. When they are ready for pupation, their cradles are closed over with waxen covers. The worker caste is then gripped by that feverish, pervasive agitation, the swarming mood. This leds to the departure, as if on order, of about half the population, after each of the individuals has filled up on honey from the plentiful stores in the nest.

In the course of only a few minutes, they fly of from the perhaps some 30,000 of them, together with the old queen. Not being an especially good flier, she soon settles some where on a branch, and the whole billowing swarm of bees gathers around her like a bunch of grapes. From this place, usually a few hours later, they make off to a new nesting place that has been explored mean while by scouts. Or perhaps the swarm is packaged up by a beekeeper and given a home in his apiary. It is precisely this situation that has enabled man to culture bees a practice known to the Egyptians over 5,000 years ago.

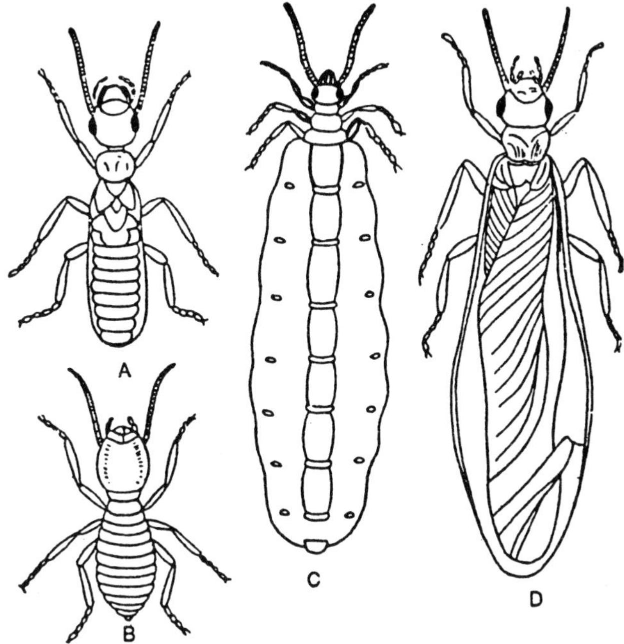

Fig. 7.5. X Queen of termites without wings after nuptial; B, wingless sterile worker, C, mature queen; D, the winged male before nuptial.

Among the ancestral stock that stays behind when the swarm leaves, there emerges after about a week the first of the young queens. Excitedly singing "tu-tu" she opens the remaining queen cells and stings to death her rivals who lie within them and respond with hollow sounds to her call, for in the bees' society such a rival cannot be tolerated. But frequently the swarming mood among the colony has not yet subside, and this murdering of her sisters is prevented by the workers, for a second swarm is about to break forth, perhaps still others are to follow, and each of these supplementary swarms, smaller than the first, requires a queen. Often two or several queens fly along, but only one of them is left alive. The South African honeybees do not absolutely have to have a queen, for with them the workers are capable of producing female progeny. Since a queen, who lives to be four to five years old, is not able all by herself to found a new bee colony, the swarm constitutes the only possibility of increasing the number of the season, but in the temperate zone they die out toward the end of the year. Here, only the new, fertilized queens live through the winter and found new societies in the spring. But, thanks to their higher degree of organization, the societies of honeybees and ants are able to persist continuously even in the north; ant colonies have been observed to last for over eighty years.

Many wasps and bumblebees have simpler and more similar forms of social life, and an example will describe their normal course. A bumblebees queen, after overwintering, fords a site that appeals to her and prepares it for nesting. After plastering a spot on the ground with wax, she mixes a lump of pollen and honey, builds a circular wall of wax on top of it, lays some 7 to 16 eggs inside, and closes the cell with a wax rood. From the same material she builds a storage vessel for pollen and honey to one side, placing it where she can reach it without leaving the waxen cell. Sitting on the cell, she keeps the eggs inside war, and they soon hatch into larvae. These are fed from time to time be the mother, who bites a hole through the lid of wax and then closes it afterward. The larvae also eat the mass of pollen and honey on top of which they were born in the cell, which the mother enlarges as they grow bigger, until finally they spin cocoons that hang together; in these they pupate.

The queen then attaches more waxen egg chambers here and there to the old cell, using in part material from it, so that the lightercoloured cocoons now lie bare. After the first bumblebee workers emerge, these cocoons are used as storage vessels. The workers help the mother, and the more numerous they become the less she works herself, until she perhaps has become nothing but a producer of eggs. Thus the number queen in two ways embodies the transition from the solitary to the social bees. First, she gathers food like the solitary bees and closes off the cell after laying eggs, but on the other hand constantly feeds the young through openings. Second, in he beginning she carries out all the tasks, but later merely lays eggs like a queen bee.

In midsummer, when the family has become numerous and food is plentiful, new queens are reared. Bigger and bigger workers develop, and some lay unfertilized eggs. If there are excess eggs, the bumblebees frequently feed on them. The unfertilized eggs always develop into males, as is everywhere the case among social Hymenoptera. Thus males may be descended from workers. But more often they are produced by the queen, who is able voluntarily to prevent access of semen to the egg she is laying. This seemen, which suffices for the entire duration of her life, was received from the male with whom she mated in the preceding year. The emerging males, fed by their sisters, remain in the nest for a few days until their hairy covering, at first a whitish-gray, has gained its full colour. Then they fly off, visit flowers and mate.

In the tropics bumblebee societies may last for years; then, instead of a single queen, a whole group of them is active in the nest. In the far north, there frequently is another variant. During the very short period of the year when flight is possible, the mother's offspring may not develop into workers but instead directly into males and new queens, as is customary in the solitary bees.

The family life of many vespid wasps corresponds in great measure with that of the bumblebees, apart from the wholly different manner of constructing the nest and feeding the young. In both groups, the mature insects imbibe nectar and sweet or fermen plant substances, as well as honeydew. But the vespids, with the apparent exception of the nectarines, feed their with a paste of chewed-up insects. In the spring two or several vespid queens occasionally found a nest in common. In *Polistes* wasps, this urge for sociability may even extend to where a female will leave her own nest and her still-young brood in the lurch and will attempt to join a distinct family. Whether she succeeds is another matter. For the majority of species drive away intruders, even those of the same line of descent; the cause of this is nothing else than that very possessiveness toward the brood that to some degree has been lost by the worker caste in correlation with their degenerate sexuality, a loss that has made possible the selfless cooperation of the individuals in a society. Through this loss a certain loosening of the rigidly established instinct for the care of the brood also entered and brought with it space for other, new tasks.

The most highly developed social organizations among the wasps are those of certain species of *Polybia* in South America. They are said to surpass in this respect even the social organizations of honeybees, which are very similar. With one and the same *Polybia* species the establishment of new colonies can take place in very different manners according to the circumstances. It can take place by swarming, as in honeybees—that is, through the departure in flight of a bee populations and thereby preserving the species. Lack of food or any kind of disturbance or menace an also provoke bees into swarming; such migratory swarms then represent merely a change of dwelling place and not a fractionation of the population. The honeybee*Apis mellifica,* originally from the Old World, has been spread by man over the entire arth. Until recently its races were not products of intentional breeding, but were primal geographic forms. Today, at all event, crosses can be produced by artificial insemination of queens. 0= the remaining three *Apis* species (*dorsata, flora* and *indica*), all of which live in South Asia, only the last has been domesticated.

A quite different kind of swarming is seen among ants. Excited workers appear before the nest entrance and get more and more numerous. Finally, there appear the winged, sexually mature individuals, which usually are reared in large numbers only years after the society is founded. First come the males, and then the females. They rise into the air, perhaps like clouds of smoke, later to cover the earth with a layer of ants. This is no swarming in the sense of the bees, for these are mating flights. In many genera the males and females, which as a rule are equipped with huge wings, are almost equal in size, but in other genera they are very different. One may even see a tiny male riding about on his partner's abdomen as if on a dirigible. Verging on the incredible are the differences in size between sexually mature forms and workers, especially in legionary ants (dorylines). Here, a male may measure 1.2 inches, and the smallest worker a mere 0.08 inch; or a worker 0.12 to 0.16 inch long may have a queen more than 2 inches long.

The males are of no use in a hymenopterous colony. After mating, they die. The fertilized females then found their purely female societies, as queens with a final cohort of many myriads of workers. There are ant socities with over a million individuals, and one population may hold sway over an area of hundred, even thousands, of square yards. Certain *Formica* ants pile on top of their nests heaps of earth more than a yard high and perhaps four yards in diameter. Such digging by ants is of great benefit to man in loosening and aerating the soil.

On the average the workers live to be about three years old. Thus they have much more time than bees, for instance, to gather impressions and gain experience, and their adaptability is decidedly greater than one might credit insects with. The queens may live for as long as three decades, not as rulers, it is true, but merely as producers of eggs, for among ants even more exclusively than among bees it is the colony that does the deciding. In the simplest case, a fertilized female founds a colony by enclosing herself in a hole she has dug or in some other hiding place, after shedding her wings, which is facilitated by a performed line of rupture. Here the ant remains closed off from the world at large until the emergence of her first workers, which may take a year. She ingests nothing but moisture, living on her bodily reserves, a good part of which come from the breaking down of the thoracic flight musculature. This source of nourishment also enables the queen to rear her first larvae on glandular secretions in spite of the long period without food. The queen may eat some of the eggs she lays, but they, of course, are products of her own body.

When the larvae are fully grown, the mother helps them in the spinning of their cocoons by providing them with bits of dirt, which they incorporate in the structures. Later, she helps the workers emerge from the cocoons. At this point her instincts for the care of the brood usually disappear, since subsequent brood care is taken over by the workers; only in the smaller societies of certain ponerines and *Leptothorax* does the queen continue to help. Soci'ties of a few of the primitive ponerines may be no larger than ten individuals. In founding them the queen does not enclose herself, but goes on the hunt, fetching food for her brood in the manner of the solitary wasps. Frequently several females work together in establishing the nest, but when the first brood of workers appears, the mothers battle one another until only a single one survives. But several or even many of them are tolerated when spatially more extensive societies are concerned. The young queens then settle down in outbuildings after their mating flight. This procedure is also followed by species in which the queens have lost their capacity for digging or for some other reason are unable to found a society by themselves. By remaining within the existing society, they have ant helpers at their immediate disposal.

A young queen of the genus *Carebara* solves this problem by taking along with her on her mating flight a number of tiny workers from the nest; these cling fast to her en route. Or a female of *Formica sanguinea,* a species that is particularly many-sided in its methods of establishing colonies and its ways of life, first joins forces for founding a common nest with a female from the company of one of her slave species; then, as soon as the latter's first workers appear, she kills her. When females that are not self-sufficient but are dependent on worker ants establish branch settlements of a flourishing colony, there frequently are schisms and estrangement between the original population and its offshoots. On the other hand, the adoption of young queens is by no means limited to populations of their own species, but strangers of the same genus are accepted, resulting in mixed communities. These occur frequently, especially in the genus *Formica,* and also in *Lasius* and others. They are only temporary, however, if the queen of the original population dies, and often enough she is beheaded or murdered by the adopted stranger or the latter's workers. In this case, a pure stock of the adopted species gradually arises.

Communities that have lasted a long time frequently consist of several mixtures and a confusing diversity of interrelationships. For instance, a female of a third species may establish her nest in a *Formica* colony that already consists of two species; and, in addition, the workers may sally forth to capture slaves, bring home pupae of still another species, and let the ants that hatch from them likewise become servants of the state. Such mutual associations of different species stretch through countless possibilities, including mere neighbourly activity, the mutual benefits of symbiosis, hospitality, and larceny. They range in one direction to slavery (in which only the ruling ants produce males and new colonies, while the helping ants are allowed to produce only workers), and in the other direction to parasitism (in which species that have become incapable of feeding themselves or are no more than wretched cripples have to be supported by the others).

SLAVERY

The custom of capturing slaves seems to have developed from the dependence of those queens that are able to establish a nest only with the help of workers. The pupae of foreign societies are stolen, and a permanent supply of the enslaved working a population that emerges from them is assured to the society by forays repeated annually. But occasionally the slaveholders cradicate all the potential sources of slaves in the area and have to return gradually to self-sufficiency. Slave hunts may be extended over such great distances that the soldiers establish guarded camps at intervals of a day's march from home.

The dependence on slaves varies from one society to another. The saberlike mandibles of the Amazon ants (*Polyergus*) make them fine fighters, but also make them so incapable as workers at home that they are fully dependent on their slaves, which usually far outnumber them. On the other hand, many *Formica* communities are not unconditionally dependent on slaves, and keep only a modest number of them; in fact, the larger the community and the greater its own resources, the fewer slaves it maintains. The species of *Formica* that steal slaves, although they are less capable soldiers than *Polyergus,* thus remain good workers. But the Amazon ants must depend on their slaves even to feed them, for their daggerlike jaws, tailored for piercing the head of adversaries, do not permit them to chew their food. In addition, these implements are no good for caring for the brood or for construction, and apparently this formal specialization is accompanied by a degeneration of the corresponding instincts. Thus, the true masters in the *Polyergus* community are the slaves, which happen to be *Formica* species. These would by no means exchange their life of slavery for one in the maternal nest, for among the warrior-folk they are better protected, quite apart from the fact that ants (and not only these ones) feel at home in the place where they were born. And more than ample food is at hand, for during the summer the daily slave-hunting expeditions yield an abundance of captured larvae and pupae that can be eaten.

The predatory attacks of Amazon ants on *Formica* communities are carried out with refined tactics adapted to prevailing conditions, and are uncannily abrupt. After the return of scouts sent out to ascertain the route to be followed for attack and the proper initial dispositions of the forces, the soldiers assemble before their nest, excitedly drumming each other's heads with their antennae. As if responding to an order, part of the population, numbering from many hundred to perhaps 2,000 warriors, sets out in a close column, marching directly at full speed and perhaps straight through heavy grass to the gathering place near the selected nest. When the attackers have consolidated here, they carry out an assault so suddenly and with such concentrated force that the *Formica* community is caught by surprise and in a few minutes is sacked. Nevertheless, in the first confusion of battle, *many Formica* ants succeed- in fleeing to a place of safety, carrying ' part of the. brood in their mandibles. *A Polyergus* colony has been observed to undertake 44 expeditions in 33 days, collecting a booty estimated at 40,000 slave pupae.

In addition to various species of *Formica* and *Polyergus,* the myrmicine genera *Strongy lognathus* and *Harpagaxenus* take slaves. *Strongly lognatnus* ants have saberlike mandibles, but unlike the Amazons are capable of feeding themselves. And they have different tactics or battle methods. Thus certain *Stronglylognathus* communities maintain throughout the duration of their attack, a constant liaison between their own nest and the *Tetramorium* nest they have assaulted; their aim is to intimidate the inhabitants of thee latter, namely to render them more or less defenseless by pinching them suddenly from behind with the mandibles. But if battle is joined, nonetheless, fights break out between the robbers slaves, participating in this expedition, and the similar workers of the besieged community, from which it is possible that slaves themselves have descended, having been captured in an earlier raid. Consolingly, however, such an occasion may end in reconciliation, with attacker and attacked giving up the battle and joining forces. The methods of slaveholders vary. Colonies of *Harpagoxenus sublmevis* drive *leptothorax* societies out of their own nest, set themselves up in it, and obtain the indispensable helping ants from the *Leptothora pupae* left behind. For these slaveholders, which even try to make workers out of already-hatched queens by biting their wings off, are unable to rear their own brood.

NEIGHBOURS, GUESTS AND THIEVES

Composite nests also are shared by very different groups of ants and even by ants and termites. Frequently societies of this sort are brought together by such things as the presence of favourable dwelling places.-for instance, hollow branches or the hours made by termites. Each of the species, more or less forced by circumstances into a beighbourly existance, has its own dwelling, but with a common entrance to the nest. This may result in various forms of symbiosis. A defenseless species may live with a species capable of defending itself and may bear a deceptive resemblance to it. The combined defenses of two or more populations living in a given habitat may enhance the safety of each. In the outer parts of the ant gardens of a *Componotus* colony, for example, a population of *Cremastogaster* may establish itself. Under moderate menance only the latter takes the appropriate measures of defense, but when seriously threatening attacks occur, the fundamental owners appear from the depths of their specherical nest.

A few genera of tiny ants live as obligatory lodgers; they build their little cities and dwellings in the middle of the nests of much larger species, being tolerated as friends of the latter and fed by them on solicitation. Certain *Leptothorax* species are ant guests of this sort. They often ride on the backs of their host ants, licking them. Other such guests include a few *Formicoxenus* and *Symmyrmica* ants, the males of which, as a rare exception, are wingless. Except in human society, hospitality probably is nowwhere manifested in so varied and interesting ways as among ants (and, to a much lesser extent, among termites). In addition to welcomed and uninvited ants, guests include certain mites and isopods (soe bugs). One may estimate at several thousand species the number of living forms that, by craft or by friendly means, overcome the natural standoftishness of ants and profit directly from them in one way or another.

There are a great many thieving ant species whose workers settle among other ants as bad, antagonistic neighbours or even as lodgers, frequently in numbers nearing the hundreds of thousands. They are dwarfs only about 0.04 to 0.08 inch long, almost too small to be taken hold of, and some also have a bad smell. Masses of them will attack their much larger hosts, if these put themselves in the way, and by stinging them especially in the antennae and the mouth, make them incapable of fighting. These tiny devils eat the host's brood and get into the hosts' chambers by making fine passageways that course like a network throughout the structures of the host ants; the hosts cannot possibly pursue them through these little tubes. *Soienopsis* and many other genera are thief ants of this sort, and they dwell also among termites. Since the smallest workers are best adapted to this way of life, these species have developed from originally larger forms, as is still shown by the sexual individuals, above all by the queens, which frequently are veritable giants in comparison with their tiny workers. Thus, the workers of *Carebara,* which live with termites, seem like lice hanging to the legs of their queen. Less harmful thieves are those highway men that settle in the vicinity of another nest with the intention of plundering the ants that are bringing foodstuffs home. Both robbery and quarrels over boundaries can lead to open war or perhaps to feuds lasting for years between different stocks.

Contests of a more ritual nature also occur among ants. *Camponotus* ants, for example, run headlong against one another, with the abdomen audibly beating the ground. But ants in general engage at once in mortal combat. The principal weapons are the mandibles and, among the more primitive ants (ponerines, myrmicines), the toxic sting. In lieu of stinging. *Formica* curls the abdomen forward between the legs and sprays out its poison, formic acid. Certain species disseminate repugnant odours (for example, many *Lasius*), and dolichoderines plaster the enemy's antennae with a sticky, ill-smelling secretion from the rear end. And finally, the soldiers of many species are able to blockade the nest entrance with their head.

ANT HARVESTERS, FARMERS AND HUNTERS

The food of ants consists of plant juices, nectar and honeydew, as well as insects (ants not excepted), worms, and other small animals. Insect-eating ants can be highly useful to man. A large community of , wood ants of the genus *Formica,* for example, destroys about 100,000 insects daily. In specializing on certain types of food, some ants have developed unusual organizations and ways of life. Ants that feed on honeydew, a sweet excretion of aphids, are a good example. These ants in their own nest raise aphids, feeding them leaves or roots and even building special chambers - stalls, so to speak - for such "milk cows." The ants comprehend to an astounding degree the essentials of aphid care, a capacity that has probably developed in great part from the instincts for the care of their own brood.

Fig. 7.6. Harvester ants gather seeds in provision for the dry season.

Fig, 7.7. Leafcutting ants require green leaves on which to grow their jungle food (enlarged).

Instead of letting "domestic animals furnish a continual supply of desired juice, certain ants (such as *Mymecocystu; Prenolepic, Leptomyrme r, Melophorus,* a few *Camponotus* and *Plagiolepis*) of warm, dry countries store it in the bodies of their own workers. A number of such workers are fed by their sisters until their expandable abdomen inflates into a gigantic, amber-coloured, shimmering sphere, upon which the normally contiguous segmental sclerites are widely separated from one another. These "walking honey jars" can creep forward only slowly and with difficulty, and usually remain hanging calmly in groups on the ceiling of a cavity in the nest; particularly when food is scarce they dole out their store from the mouth drop by drop to their entreating sibs.

Man gathers and eats the bodies of such honey ants, or at least their contents, rating them as a delicacy that surpasses the honey of bees. Incidentally, the honeydew of aphids is not the sole constituent, for these ants frequently also gather nectar and exudations from plant galls, in America particularly those from oaks. Quite different specialists are the harvest ants, especially *Messor, Pheidole, Holeomyrmex,* and *Pogonomyrmex,* the last of which strings energetically. These collect plant seeds, preferentially those of grains and grasses, and accumulate them in their nests. The seeds, later to be broken up and eaten, are laid out in the sun to dry; if they nevertheless sprout, the sprouts are often bitten off. Certain species throw such unwanted seeds out of the nest, and surrounding the nest entrance there soon grows a dense fringe of grass, a phenomenon that has led to the erroneous designation of these ants as *'farmer ants."* The harvest ants are not only eaters of seeds, but also hunters of insects; in addition, a hard-stinging American species (*Solenopsis geminata*) eats fruit and cultures aphids.

In contrast, the well-known leafcutting ants (*Atta*) of tropical and subtropical America are one-sided specialists that grow "vegetables." There vegetables are the protein-containing bodies that grow on the mycelia of certain fungi. And the majority of these fungal species will flourish only in the gardens of certain leafcutting ants. The culture medium in which the fungi grow is prepared by these ants and consists of a fermenting mass of chewed-up leaves carefully manured by the ant's own excrement. The amount of plants that an *Atta* community will cut up in a very short time and carry into the fungal chambers is so great that the result is frequently as destructive as a catastrophe of nature. The nest workings, which may be many yards below ground and spread over a wide area, may perhaps have a volume of several hundred cubic yards.

No matter how familiar the illustration showing the ants transporting sections of leaves, direct contact with the processions out of doors is always an overpoweringly impressive experience, especially when almost every "banner" borne is of a different colour. Rocking and reeling, the ants hustle nervously along their routes, stumbling past their fellows coming the other way, who draw aside for them, and, falling suddenly into the aperture of a nest entrance, are swallowed up by the earth, one after the other,. or even two at a time, over and over again. On her flight into new country, a young queen, as founder of a colony-to-be, brings with her not only the instrict for tending a fungus garden but, in a special pouch of her head in back of the mouth, a tiny wad of fungal mycelia from the maternal home. In the new little brood chamber the ant puts this down, deposits five or six eggs on it, and manures the fungus by pushing little*bits of it* beneath her anus and then returning them to, the pile. The wad grows, and yet the young queen takes none of it; instead she eats some of her own eggs and also feeds her first hatching larvae exclusively on these.

The tiny workers that after a few weeks have developed from these larvae are the first to consume the "vegetables" that have grown on the fungus plant, which now is about 0.8 inch in diameter. The mother and brood still partake only of eggs. The workers also manure the precious fungus, open the bropd chamber perhaps some ten days later, and gather and chew up pieces of leaves. This now permits the vitally important vegetable to develop adequately.

Certain attines are not leaf cutters, but culture their fungus on insect feces, especially that of caterpillars, or on all sorts of decaying plant tissues. In great contrast to these vegetarians are two groups of warlike carnivores. First, there are the primitive Australian ponerines of the genus *Myrmecia,* known as bulldog ants and notorious for their stings and furious attacks. Like certain other ponerines *(Odontomachus, Harpegnathos),* they are able to leap upon their adversary by snapping themselves backward from the ground with their powerful mandibles. Otherwise, ability to jump has been seen.among Hymenoptera only in a few chalcids, and here is done with the legs. In their organized predatory raids, the bulldog ants hunt mostly termites. The second group of carnivores are the driver, or migratory, ants (dorylines). They also prey on termites, as well as on other ants. In tropical America the driver ants are represented especially by the genus*Eciton,* and in Africa by*Anomma.* Their sexual individuals are gigantic, the males resembling wasps more than ants, the females wingless from the beginning. The workers, remarkably unequal in size, have saber-shaped mandibles. In large-headed individuals these are awesome and in certain *Eciton* species take on grotesque, dimensions.

The driver ants travel in well-organized formations that differ according to the species of ant. Some columns may be more than 100 yards-long and several yards wide. At times, the workers with the most formidable mandibles march on each. side of a column. Biting, stinging, murdering, and pillaging, these armies move over the countryside, some travelling more through open territory, others through woods and thickets. Whatever is unable to flee from them is tom to pieces and carried forward in little bits. The ground, vegetation and trees, holes caves, nests, even houses are in a short time completely cleared of every living thing, and even larger animals and people take flight. Clamoring antbirds accompany these horrifying processions and eat their fill of the insects fleeing before them. Many driver ants migrate below ground, and others under the protection of leaves and fallen debris. In case of need they may even build uninterrupted tunnels above ground over open stretches. The driver ants build no nest, but in a sheltered place crowd together in a heap, leaving cavities that constitute the brood chambers. These satisfy all requirements for the care of the brood.

In the nomadic life of these ants, resting intervals approximately twenty days long alternate with slightly shorter migratory periods, a rule that is determined by the rhythm of egg-ripening in the queen, for she hardly could take part in the march with her abdomen swollen with ripe eggs. In a circle of as much as a mile around the resting places, everything edible is soon eradicated, yet the signal for a new migration apparently does not stem from a shortage of food, but rather from the 25,000 or so larvae produced from the previous egg-laying period. In fact, this signal seems to emanate from their secretions, which are licked up by the attending workers and stimulate them. Because of their social effects, these secretions are called *"social hormones."* Certain other insects go along as undisturbed guests on the expeditions of migratory ants. Rove beetles (Staphylinidae) frequently accompany the ants. That they are allowed to do so may seem odd, for they rarely resemble the hosts in appearance. But with the exception of the males, the ants have no compound eyes, and at most have ocelli; the majority are blind and gauge their environment exclusively by the senses of smell, taste and touch. Evidently, these guests meet the specifications covered by these senses deceptively well. Along with such adaptation, the guests have developed to an astonishing degree the ability to respond satisfactorily to antenal "fingering," the so-called "antennal language," despite the difference in the structure of the host's and guest's antennae. When the migratory ants raid termite houses, frequently some of the accompanying guests get into the termite chambers, perhaps lose touch with the ants when these withdraw, and are left behind, usually to starve to death or to be killed. But certain of these guests are able to make themselves acceptable to the new hosts and live henceforth as guests of the termites.

COMMUNICATION

The ability of insects to live together in communities rests on the means of communication among them. Such communication is based first of all on the odours of the species and nest, which are perceived through the antennal sense organs. Sentries at a nest entrance admit no individuals contaminated with the odour of a strange nest, and populations refuse to accept them. But if strangers somehow succeed in taking on the community odour, they are adopted without further ado. Some ants regularly use this "fifth column" system to gain entrance to a nest, and certain others are rendered inconspicuous naturally by the possession of deceptive body odour. Mother and children (or workers) recognize one another by smell, even after long separation, at least up to a certain age; after that, recognition may fade, for older workers often change. Odours serve not only for recognition, but also for marking pathways. By their odours, for example, honeybees become direction signs for their companions returning homeward. In front of the hive entrance, bees stand and do a waggle dance, during which fragrance is emitted from an exsertile, membranous organs between the last two segments. The odour is disseminated to the winds by means of continual fanning movements of the wings. In the same way bees that have discovered a source of food call in their fellows. Or the fragrance of the flowers, clinging to a bee that returns home successful, can induce her nest-fellows likewise to scour the vicinity in search of such blossoms.

The simple urge for imitation may play an especially large role in ant communities; it seems that there the older workers, leading the way in all actions, set an example for the younger ones. When a large prizeis being transported by several individuals, for instance, there is a constant participation of new individuals, that, attracted by what is going on, hasten up apd crowd into the work. Thus, there is a constant succession of more or less compulsory relief of those already on duty, and the object passes through many "hands" before it is finally fetched home. Such community transport takes much longer than that engaged in by individual ants, principally because the differing temperaments and intentions of the participants are likely to be a mutual hindrance. Quite similarly, any moods or conditions of excitement may be disseminated, via imitation, throughout the population, yet ants also have at their disposal concrete means of expressing themselves. As one instance, there is the capability of many species of producing high-pitched chirping notes by rubbing two abdominal segments together. And, of course, there is the "antennal language," which is rooted in the sense of touch. Definite signs and signals are given by antenal movements, which include stroking, tapping, and drumming; with these may be included similar motions of the forelegs, as well as blows with the head. Added precision frequently is given the communications not only by the varying intensity of the movements, but also by the production or transmission of odorous materials. Within the community, the most frequent signs of this sort no doubt are connected with the mutual solicitation of food. This situation also may render more comprehensible the astounding initiation and acquisition of such signs by many ant guests that belong to different insect orders.

BEE LANGUAGE

The honeybees (*Apis mellifica*), and quite similarly a few advanced wasps, have developed an incredibly highly differentiated sign language. For if a honeybee has found a source of food in the immediate vicinity of the nest, say up to 50 or even 100 yards distant, once home she executes a small circle on a comb, first to the left and then to the right, and so on. This is done in the midst of her sisters, both busy, and idle, and they, carried away by the display of so much zeal in their immediate vicinity, are infected by her spirit and join the leader in her circular dance. Thereafter ' the bees fly out and round about the hive until, by means of the particular flower odour on the leader of the dance, they have located the source of honey or pollen she has announced so ingratiatingly by her dancing.

But this is only part of the story. For if the flowers are farther away, then the discoverer, still dancing alternately to the left and to the right, changes from a single circle to a broad figure eight, the longer middle portion of which is a straight line. Every time the dancing bee runs over this stretch, she waggles her abdomen, surrounded and followed by her sisters, who are not just looking on but are taking the message in. For the more slowly the dancer runs, the more her waggling movements over the middle part of the course are accentuated, and the farther is the distance to the source of food. Not just an approximate distance but the precise one is communicated and comprehended, measured by the bees no in units of length but in terms of the required expenditure of flight energy, which has to be greater in a head wind, for example.

Yet the most incredible feature of the dance is that it communicates the exact compass direction. As is well-known, the sun serves as a compass for bes, even when hidden behind clouds, as long as clear patch of blue sky is visible. If the dance takes place on the "flight board" in front of the hive entrance, then the mid-stretch of the dance points straight as an arrow to the food source. But this direct indication of direction is impossible in a dance within the nest on the comb, which hangs vertically. Here the straight part of the path is run through from below to above when the location to be indicated is in a compass direction exactly toward the sun, and from above to below when it is away from the sun. But if the source of food, as viewed from the hive, lies to the right or left of the sun, the bee dances the straight stretch upward at the same angle to the right or left of the vertical by which the direction of the discovery site departs from that of the sun. Hence, vertical direction on the comb is equivalent for the bees to the position of the sun, which signifies a translation of the direction learned through orientation in sunlight into perception of the force of gravity. Astonishingly, the dancing bee also indicates the precise compass direction when the place she has found cannot be reached in a straight line of flight, but only by means of side excursions, such as flight around a mountain. But since the bees reading her message are oriented by the dance as to the distance, they now produce the required amount of exertion in flight and, after flying around the obstacles but always holding to the proper compass direction, they arrive at the goal.

The dance expresses, in addition to distance and direction, the productivity of the source of food, which is communicated by the degree of liveliness. After a rich discovery the dance is a correspondingly excited one, and even an arousing one. The dance is also used by swarming bees in searching for a new home. Each bee returning from the search dances on the hanging mass of the swarm. She communicates not only the location of the place she has found but also how good it is. The discoverers of the best situation prove to be the most infectious dancers and induce more and more of their comrades to fly out and inspect the place. These return, dance with equal elan, and soon the other scouts, which are behaving less convincingly, are ignored and either give up or simply join with the rest. Thus finally all are doing the same dance, the decision is made, the swarm breaks forth, and, led by the many dancers, they fly off to the new home. In this way, the swarm is likely to select the best hollow tree even though it may be miles away.

WINTER SWARMING

Bees swarm densely not only not only when seeking a new home, also when passing the winter in the hive. A single inactive bee, like all resting insects, has inappreciable body warmth of its own and is therefore at the mercy of the environmental temperature. When the temperature drops to about 46°F (8°C), the bee is incapable of moving and soon dies. Nevertheless, together in the hive, bees are able to survive a rigorous winter. They cluster in a thick spherical mass around the empty inner combs, and individual bees inside the cluster produce heat by vibrating their wing muscles. In this way they are able to maintain a temperature in the center of the swarm of 68°F to 86°F (20°C to 30°C) even when it is as cold as -4°F to -22°F (20°C to - 30°C) outside. The temperature of the outer layer of the swarm is

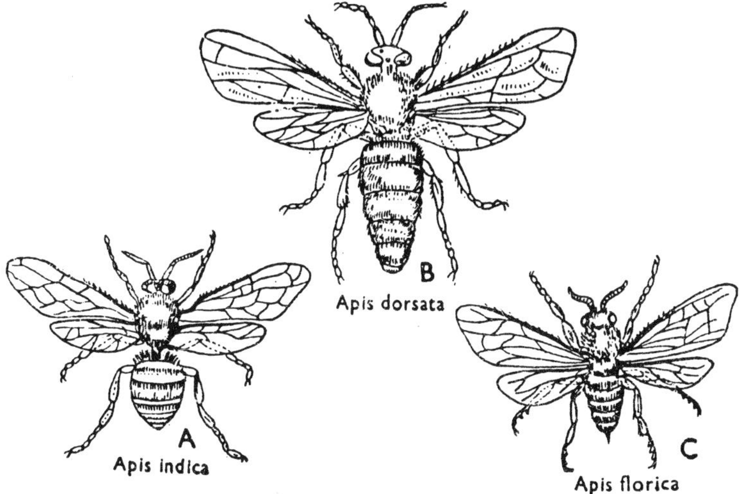

Fig. 7.8. Honeybee dances. On the comb at the left is a round dance, on the right band one a tail-wagging dance, in which the leader is vibrating her abdomen. Below, with the odour-producing organ in front of the bind end uncovered, two wagging bees ate dispensing scent (clarification in drawing at the top).

about 45°F to 46°F (7°C to 8°C). When raising a winter brood, the bees raise the cluster temperature to 95°F (35°C). Ants spend the cold season of the year in deeper chambers or in special winter nests. A few house ants-such as the notorious yellow pharaoh's ants (*Manomorium pharaonis*), which have been spread all over the world and which establish their colinies everywhere, even in the handle of a table knife-live in comfort in the heated houses of humans and avoid the problem of overwintering altogether.

SOCIAL PARASITES

Among certain bumblebees, wasps, and ants, individual social species have become parasites. They differ from their hosts in that they have lost their worker caste and, in part, their own instincts for brood care. Whereas a few *Polistes* and *Vespa,* which resemble their wasp hosts almost to the last hair, live quite peaceably in the latters nests and lay their eggs in the comb, the female parasites of bumblebees and ants are compelled to gain possession of foreign workers for rearing their own brood. With some exceptions,' this can be accomplished only by disposing of the host's queen. This is done usually with naked force, but among certain ants with treacherous guile. A parasitic bumblebee (*Psithyrus*) forces her way into the nest of her host (*Bombus*), intimidates the workers with her bites, slaughters the queen, Ad destroys eggs and larvae. In some cases, *Psithyrus* will spare the life of the bumblebee queen, which then no longer pays any attention to her own progeny. In either event the bumblebee colony perishes.

In rare instances a genuine bumblebee (*Bombus*) adopts the despotic methods of *a Psithyrus,* kills a relative, and with the latter's workers founds her own community. But *Psithyrus* founds no new community, merely rearing a few new males and females. In ants, ,social parasitism may transpire in a significantly more peculiar manner. Parasitic queens frequently have arisen from former slaveholders, whose own workers,

Fig. 7.9. Food sharing between workers of the ant, Fomtica fusca The worker on the left is receiving food from that on the right which has regurgitated a drop of liquid from its crop and offers it between the outstretched mandibles.

instincts for brood care, and even ability to feed themselves independently became superfluous and gradually were lost altogether. Some of these ants are pitifully reduced creatures, unable to rear their offspring, yet they are endowed with the refined cunning needed to compel others to carry out these tasks. The female of a Bothriomymiex for instance, climbs onto the back of the much larger queen of a Tapinoma community, bites her head off, and nov usurps her place in the society, to which she gained access thanks to her similar body odour. Other parasitic females are not in so simple a position; first they must patiently make friends in the outlying quarters with the workers, and attempt to accustom these to themselves, until their own body odour has become imbued sufficiently with the family smell.

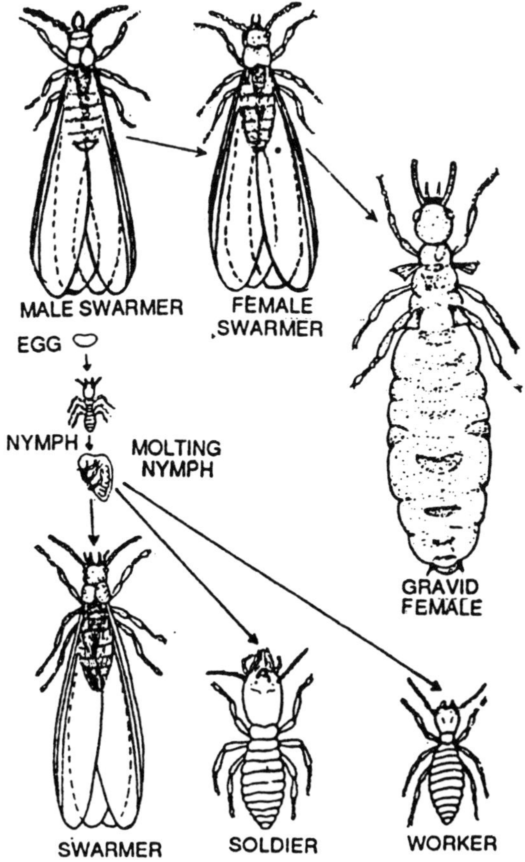

Fig. 7.10. Stages in the life-history of Termite or white ant.

Still another procedure is used by the female of Epimyrmex stumperi; she takes a firm seat, from which she cannot be dislodged, on the back' of a worker of the selected Leptothorar colony, and for a long time brushes the worker as well as herself with her bristly forelegs. Thus the crafty Epimymtex perfumes herself with the *Leptothorax* odour. And then finally, being unrecognized in the darkness of the passageways and chambers of the nest, she comes upon the queen, rolls her over, and bites a firm hold in the throat of her victim, who is much larger but does not defend herd£ There the Epimyimex hangs for days, until the queen dies or is completely exhausted.

Workers are in the vicinity no doubt, but none offers help against the perfumed strangler; no one knows of the drama that is being played out silently in the middle of the community. Finally their own queen, perhaps still alive though paralyzed, is not heeded any further and must slowly starve to death, while the monster sets out after another queen, if there is one, but leaves her unmolested if she is young and has not been fertilized. What a horrible triumph of bare natural instincts. How friendly, in contrast, seems the relationship of *Teleutomynnex schneideri* with their hosts ants *Tetramorium caespitum.* For their these little invaders are tolerated, and hence, as *a* rare exception in ant communities, the queens of two different species dwell in peace side by side. Not literally side by side, it is true, for the parasites, themselves pitiably incapable figures, ride upon the host queen and are tended by her royal court.

TERMITES ORDER ISOPTERA

Termite populations run into the millions. They forge the complexion of a landscape like no other organism except man. Their secretive activities result in almost uncanny accomplishments; these grow out of their remarkable social organization, species although they

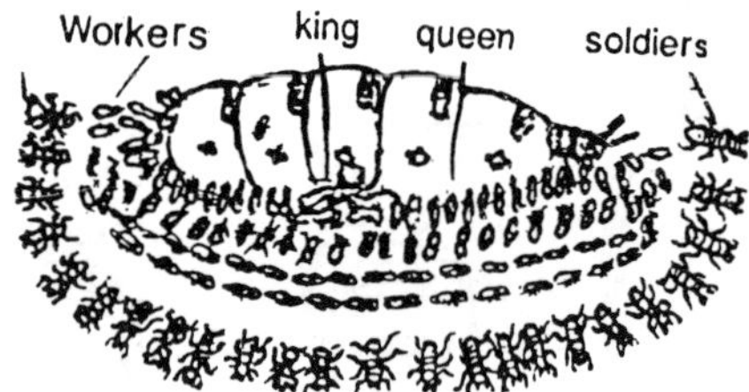

Fig. 7.11. A scene of the royal chamber inside a termitarium.

make inroads not on the brood but on the food stores. As remarked earlier, termites and ants sometimes live together, and even certain bees (*Trigona, Hemisia, Acanthopus*) set up their societies unmolested in the arboreal nests of termites. The same is done by a few parrots;

and in Africa the great Nile lizard (*Varanus niloticus*) lays its eggs in a hole it has clawed out of a termite hill, where the constant temperature and humidity are favourable for brooding.

Termite guests include members of the most varied insect orders, as well as mites and spiders. Many insect guests that are greatly desired and well-tended by the termites have strongly swollen, often grossly misshapen abdomens (physogastry), as in the wingless flies *Termitoxenia,* which live in the fungus gardens, and in numerous beetles of the family Staphylinidae, among which there is a viviparous species from Brazil (*Corotoca melantho*) that deposits first-stage larvae instead of eggs.

BROADER RELATIONSHIPS

Practically all insect-eating organisms are active as enemies of the sexual individuals, which swarm in huge numbers, and during such swarming even man traps termites as food. But the pursuit of termites within their structures requires specialists. Among vertebrates these include the armadillos, anteaters, and a few others usually adept at digging. Among birds the woodpeckers take precedence. But none of these is as destructive as bulldog ants, migratory ants, and a few others. These decimate the termites, emptyping an entire house at a time and then frequently taking possession of it, or even eradicating the termites from whole localities. In general termites cannot cope with these enemies. But the so-called "nasute" forms are exceptions. The sticky excretions rom their "nose" gum up beyond repair the antennae and mouth of the attacking ants and thus are much more effective than implements for biting.

Humans that inhabit the warm countries must be on guard against the termite hordes, for these insects devour almost anything and everything, even (possibly with the help of their solvent saliva) metal and ivory. Coming from the ground, they penetrate into the wooden parts of the houses, hollowing everything out yet leaving the outer layers deceptively untouched, and in the same way get into furniture and utensils of all sorts. In addition to nonliving materials, they attack trees and other plants. As proof of their destructiveness, man has been forced to establish institutions for testing termite-proof materials, of which there are incredibly few. A problem everywhere in the tropics, termites also threaten to become one in the temperate zone. Notorious pests there are *Kalotermes minor* and *Reticulitermes* in North America, and *Kalotermes flavicollis* in Europe. Although considered destructive by man, the armies of termites have inestimable value in the natural economy of the tropics. Their dissolution of dead materials, above all fallen timber, and their loosening up of the soil enable new generations of plants to grow. On the other hand, in certain districts the secretions given off by termites during the activities.of building can harden the ground to such an extent that it becomes unsuitable for cultivation.

CLASSIFICATION

About 2,000 tropical and subtropical species of termites are known. They range from about 0.08 to 0.9 inch long (large queens up to 4 inches). Of the three to five families of termites, the kalotermitids and the mastotermitids seem the more primitive; the latter are represented only by the single Australian species *Mastotennes danviniensis,* which has been designated the most primitive of all. Rich in species and more advanced in their organization arc the termitids and rhinotermitids. Only among them is there, strictly speaking, a true worker caste, namely fully developed workers and soldiers no longer capable of transformation. Those of the other groups are merely nymphs of different stages. Such nymphs can be developed into workers, soldiers, or sexual individuals by special feeding applied at a definite period of their development. At first glance, insect societies may seem strangely similar, or at least comparable, in some ways to human societies. But it is well to keep in mind the infinite distance that separates the two. Our social existence is based on the family as a unit, has been developed by human intellect, and depends upon the free will of the participants. Insect societies, on the other hand, recognize no unit other than the population as a whole, are governed by instinct, and have compulsory memberships. There is really no need to make comparisons; the life of social insects is marvelous enough in itself.

8

POPULATION OF INSECTS

The need for more research, and more adequate research, on natural populations of insects is frequently stressed by both economic entomologists and population theorists. The harmful side-effects of many insecticides and the development of resistant strains of insect have discouraged the search for a panacea that would solve all problems, irrespective of an understanding of individual species orof ecological principles. Instead, there is a growing emphasis on developing forms of population management to suit particular life systems. Although the need is widely accepted, the possibility of gaining an adequate understanding of natural populations is still sometimes questioned, largely because of the multiplicity of ecological events and processes in the life system of any subject species that could conceivably affect its population numbers. Many other elements in a life system may be known to influence natality or mortality, but with net effects that are either too small or not variable enough to influence population trend measurably from generation to generation. Although the study of natural populations requires more time and staff then the study of confined laboratory populations,especially when difficult sampling problem are involved, it is safe to conclude that the limited results achieved to date reflect only the lack of adequate effort and means, not the lack of possibility.

In this chapter, recognizing both the necessity and the possibility of securing and adequate understanding of natural populations, we shall outline the objectives and some of the approaches that appear to be promising for future work. Methodology will be discussed only in very general terms, both because it requires so much modification to suit individual problems, and because it has been discussed recently in detail by Southwood. The treatment will be perspective rather than retrospective, with the emphasis on the life system as a whole instead of on particular processes, and particularly on the possibilities offered by mathematical modelling.

THE OBJECTIVES

The main objective in studying the life systems of natural populations is to learn enough about their functioning to devise efficient ways of manipulating them as desired. The successful management of insect populations calls for: (i) the effective integration of what is learned about species characteristics, environmental influences, and ecological processes, in particular life systems; and (ii) the integration of these individual syntheses into a body of useful ecological principles. The synthesis made to describe the functioning of particular life systems are called models. Like other words that are used extensively, the term 'model' has acquired a wide meaning. Ziman wrote '...this is objectionable, because one does not like the sense of the word 'model' diluted until it becomes synonymous with theory. There ought at least to be a remnant, a reminder of the idea of a mechanically interacting systems, and at least a suggestion that the system is amenable to mathematical analysis.' In this broad sense, models may be verbal, diagrammatical, or mathematical in form.

Graphs and other forms of mathematical analysis were used extensively in the investigations concerned, but the various relationships demonstrated or inferred were not fitted together in an overall mathematical summarization. Verbal models, based on wellconceived observations and experiments, are very useful and much of our present knowledge of the characteristics of life systems is based on them. Sometimes they are all that is needed to solve a pest problem; in other cases, they are all that can be produced with the means and time available. However, verbal models do not provide the *quantitative* integration which is needed if we are to progress much further in or understanding of population dynamics and pest management. Such integration can be provided only by mathematical formulations. A mathematical model is simply '... a mathematical formulation (preferably one that makes biological sense), which mimics numerical changes taking place in natural populations and by means of which quantitative predictions can be made.' The effects of additional independent variables, such as predation, were clearly recognized, but were expressed only indirectly through the slopes of regression lines. Further work, including experimentation, is necessary before the effects of other variables, particularly weather, can be modelled in a more informative way. However, the equations describe more efficiently what is understood about the insects concerned than could purely verbal integrations, and the amount of variance explained satisfactorily provides assurance that most, if not all, of the 'key' process effecting numerical change during the period of study have been detected. An *adequate* explanatory mathematical model for a natural insect population, e.g., the population of a pest species, would have the following uses, some of which have been described in more detail by Watt:

(i) It would provide the only *quantitative* means of showing how much is understood about the life system of the subject species in terms of the influences and process involved and the interactions between them. Such interactions have received little attention to date, but it can be shown that the actual impact of any variable on population trend is partly dependent upon the form and degree of its interaction with other variables, especially those operating contemporaneously.

(ii) It could be used, together with experimentation, in the development of ecological principles. Computers could be operated to predict. probable outcomes as parameters in the model are modified or removed, or new parameters added. The accuracy of predictions could be tested by field and laboratory experimentation. As physics has taught us, an exciting prospect for the theorist is that a possible consequence of model-building is the discovery of new principles.

(iii) It could be used by the economic entomologist in population management. The model could be used, with the aid of a computer, to optimize management procedures and tactics. Models complete enough for this purpose have yet to be devised, but Watt has presented an example of a computer programme which illustrates the approach.

SUBJECT SPECIES

The insect to be studied is usually determined by economic considerations, and government agencies tend to support population work on pests rather than on innocuous species. This is reasonable because the sooner there are adequate models for important pests, the sooner can better management be implemented. It is suggested, however, that more attention should be given to inocuous species because, in confining so much of our work to pests, we are dealing mainly,with atypical species and this introduces a bias in attempts to derive general population principles. Population studies on innocuous species assume additional value, both theoretical and practical, if man-made changes in the environment or accidental introductions to new environments raise such species to the status of pests. When a major pest is being studied it is often possible to count associated arthropod species on the same samples of foliage, etc., and to measure some of the independent variables that may affect them. Although the data are a 'by-product' obtained with little additional work, they can be very revealing, *Acleris variana* was one of several insects studied in this way during intensive studies on *Choristomneura fumiferana and* it is interesting to observe that the models for the former species, although crude and empirical, give a higher degree of predictability than the more detailed models for the latter. The life system of *A. variana* in the Green River area is more typical of Canadian forest insects and less dıfficult to model satisfactorily. This approach, when carried far enough, can also produce valuable data on community ecology. For example, it turned out that the two species of budworm were affected by some mutual parasites and predators and that the serve outbreak of C *fumiferana* had repercussions on the population changes of *A. variana.*

The Time

With respect to time, our recommendation is for more time, better continuity, and a level of initial planning which recognizes the fact that useful descriptive models cannot be build by studying a natural populations in one place for a few generations. Those who study confined laboratory populations, where most variables are held constant, are commendably reluctant to reach conclusions until the population has been studied through a considerable number of numerical oscillations. Yet those who study natural populations, where complex processes are acting and interacting, often discontinue the programme and publish analyses before the population has passed through even one oscillation or fluctuation. For populations that oscillate in a more or less regular manner, it is difficult to see how even a preliminary model can be developed without studying at least one complete cycle in numbers. Then the preliminary model should be tested through at least a second oscillation, for three reasons:

(i) to learn whether or not the course of events in the first oscillation appears typical of the population behaviour of the species;

(ii) to test the predictive powers of the model on freshh data not involved in its derivation, thereby losing no degrees of freedom; and

(iii) to refine the model with the aid of concomitant experimental work so that empirical parameters and functions can be changed to forms that are more satisfying biologically.

For populations that fluctuate irregularly, the preliminary model should similarly be based on a sequence of numerical increases and decreases long 'enough to define the pattern of fluctuations in time and space, then tested and refined on an additional sequence.

Once sampling techniques have been worked out and one or two oscillations or sequences have been followed, there is a considerable investment in a project and the decision to discontinue should not be made lightly.Tf the original investigators find themselves growing stale by following one population too long, it is often helpful if the project is turned over to new investigators who may bring fresh ideas and enthusiasm to it. *Diprion heryniae was* studied during an outbreak in central New Brunswick and through subsequent fluctuations, involving some fifty generations. The work was about to be discontinued when a new and unexpected variable, namely the insecticide DDT, was added temporarily to the system. This is providing an exciting opportunity to test the model and to learn whether population numbers will return to the previous mean level of abundance after the severe disturbance caused by the insecticide.

The Place

The corresponding suggestion with respect to place is for more places and for a more careful selection of places than has been usual in the past. One reason for studying a population simultaneously in different places (study areas) is simply to get replication so that adequate data are available for multi-variate analyses within a reasonable period of time. This is especially necessary for species that have only one generation a year. A more important object, however, is to replicate in very different places so that a model can be developed which includes not just the attributes of time that determine insect numbers but also the attributes of place, such as forest composition and age; meteorological differences associated with region, topography; or vegetation type; type of resource management being practiced; differences in the complex of natural enemies or in their efficiency; and so on. As it is mainly the environmental influences associated with place that can be modified by man, it is not feasible to develop a model that will be generally useful for population management by studying a pest species in one place, however long the study is continued. Similarly, the only comprehensive theories of population dynamics are those which attempt to explain not only fluctuations in one place but differences in mean density from place; so that a model developed for one place will not be adequate for developing and testing population principles.

The criteria to be used in the selection of places are extremely important and will depend, of course, upon the hypotheses that have been formulated about the population behaviour of the subject species. This will be discussed later. For statistical reasons, the places selected should include not only modal values of the variables in question but also rather extreme values. Some investigators seem to prefer natural 'unspoiled' environments for the conduct of population work, but Geier and Clark have pointed out: The higher man's economic development of the environment the greater are the possibilities for protective management. Where land use is primitive and agriculture extensive, protective management is necessarily reduced to its simplest form by lakc of financial resources and limitations of technique. ... As the level of economic development rises, so do the potentialities of protective management. The more man has altered the environment, the greater are the chances that some new or old environmental factor could be modified critically to the disadvantage of a pest without adversely affecting crop production. As one example, the development of more intensive forest management in Canada will afford better opportunities to create conditions unfavourable to outbreaks of *Choristoneura fumiferana,* providing that the pertinent variable associated with place have been correctly modelled.

PRELIMINARY STUDIES AND HYPOTHESES

It is assumed that there is now a clearly defined objective, a subject species to work on, and a decision to follow the population through a sufficient number of generations and in sufficiently different places to produce and test models that will satisfy the objective. At this stage there is a natural urge to initiate measurements of population numbers and of all recognizable variables that may conceivably affect them. However, even if the resources should be available for such a programme, the history of science shows that rapid progress is seldom made by such a diffused approach. Therefore, the next step is to form some preliminary working hypotheses about the life system of the subject species. In the case of certain well-known pests, sufficiently good ecological information may already be available for this purpose; in other cases it may be necessary to carry out preliminary studies various kinds. It is difficult to discuss hypotheses separately from methods because the forming, discarding, modifying, and strengthening of hypotheses is a continuous process in population studies. However, the subject is sufficiently important to merit individual attention and the present section is concerned largely with preliminary working hypotheses — on the understanding that they will be subject to frequent revision as more detailed data accrue.

In the experimental sciences, a problem is chosen or a question asked and a working hypothesis to explain it is propounded and tested. Or better still, as proposed by Chamberlin, alternative hypothese are set up and experiments are devised which lead to the exclusion of incorrect explanations through an accumulative method of inductive inference. The selection of multiple hypotheses avoids the sterility that often develops through mental fixation on one solution, and is especially useful in experimental biology where there is sometimes more than one explanation of a phenomenon. In the study of populations, good use can be made of experimentation, but generally we have to rely more on the direct analysis of observations made on events which occur naturally within life systems. By definition, all variables in the life system of a subject species have some effect on its population numbers. However, from recent studies on numerical change in natural populations, it appears that the effects of most variables will be inconsequential. The object, then, is to formulate hypotheses as to the key influences and processes determining the rate of population change and mean numbers, both in time and in space, and to test them by finding how much each suspected key influence contributes to the degree of population predictability. Two sorts of working hypotheses are necessary and will be discussed separately

(i) What are the probable key influence determining the temporal population changes in one place and differences in abundance from place to place? Working hypotheses are selected by reviewing critically everything that is known about the species. In the case of important pests, there is often much relevant information in the literature. Historical data on the pattern of outbreaks in time and space, information on the type of area that consistently favours increase to high population numbers, data on natural enemies, and many other types of information are helpful in narrowing the choice of hypotheses.

Equally useful information may be available for other species in countries which have annual surveys of insect abundance and natural control, based on the collecting and rearing of many species. For example, the distribution, relative abundance in different environments, pattern of oscillation, and parasitism of *Hyphantria cunea* over the past thirty years, as revealed by annual records of the Forest Insect and Disease Survey of Canada, were used along with other historical data in formulating working hypotheses about the key influences involved. If information of neither sort is available, it is necessary to conduct some broad-scale, necessarily superficial, studies on the abundance of the species, its ecological characteristics, and the environmental influences involved. The object is to learn at least enough to permit the selection of appropriate places for more intensive studies.

(ii) What is the probable mode of action of the suspected key influences? Is their intensity of action influenced by population density? What processes are likely to serve as stabilizing mechanisms? Hypotheses about mode of action and function are important if we are to measure the right attributes of the influences in question, measure them in the best way, and gain useful concepts about possible interactions and the form of the model which we hope to produce. Hypotheses of this sort should be based on a thorough knowledge of population theory, and on the form of models constructed to date for ecological processes. In the formulation of the hypotheses about key influences and the ways in which they operate, we cannot assume that the average quality of the individuals of a subject species will remain constant during the course of numerical changes in a population. For example, Wellington has shown that the quality and quantity of food in the maternal generation of *Malacosoma pluviale* affect the amount of egg yolk and the quality and survival rate of the progeny. This is an influence on population quality that is transmissible, but not heritable in the, usual genetic sense. There are also heritable changes in quality from generation to generation, associated with the fact that the natural selection pressures operating at high densities may be very different from those operating when numbers are low. Recent work by Ford and others demonstrates that changes in the nature of selection, operating often through polygenes, can vary population quality considerably during the course of numerical fluctuations. Consequently, in order to construct models that will explain variance arising from this source, it is necessary to be familiar with these possibilities when hypotheses are being formulated, and to remain alert throughout an investigation for possible changes in the reactions of individuals to environmental conditions.

MEASUREMENT OF VARIABLES

In the places selected for detailed studies, the first requirement is the development of a sampling technique to record population numbers.

Population density, or its rate of change, will be the only dependent variable in the model that we hope to construct, and the lower the sampling error, the greater the chance to obtain good predictability of density through the independent variables.. There are many points to be considered in developing sound techniques, selecting appropriate confidence limits, and reaching logical decisions as to the optimum allocation of sampling means.

A study of the distribution of individuals in space is an integral part of the development of sampling methods. The frequency distribution for most insect populations tend to be 'over-dispersed'. They often approximate th negative binomial and variance can be stabilized to some extent, but not perfectly, by logarithmic transformations. The negative binomial distribution, however, can be approximated by a number of different explanatory models, some with two parameters and some with more than two. As Waters has pointed out, it is affected both by statistical elements, such as the size of the sample unit, and by biological elements, such as the oviposition and dispersal habits of the species and population density. More basic research on insect distribution than has been done to date, aimed at the development of explanatory models, might well contribute useful biological information on the species and might lead to new and more efficient sampling designs. Shiyomi and Nakamura describe an interesting approach in which individuals are stocked on plants in a known distribution pattern and changes in the form of the distribution are measured as the insects multiply and disperse.

The dispersal and migration habits of the subject species should also be examined at this stage of an investigation. Dispersal influences the distribution pattern and hence the size and location of sample units and of the selected study plots. Also, if displacement is found to be a primary event of considerable importance (e.g., as in *Phaulacridium vittatum*), early recognition of this fact can lead to appropriate developments in the design of the study.. The movements of insects can be studied in various ways, e.g., by capturing, marking, and releasing individuals, and then recapturing some of them. Mathematical models based on the assumption of random displacement can be used in the analysis of movements; they can be elaborated with the aid of computers of imposing restrictions on the initial postulates of randomness. Finally, a very practical aspect of the investigation of population density in which rarly exploratory work may pay large dividends later is the development of mechanical or chemical techniques for separating insects from foliage or other substrates. The factor that most often limits the amount of sampling that can be done by existing methods is the number of man-hours of tedious and often error-prone labour involved in ']hand-picking' the samples.

We have stressed the need for adequate measurement of the dependent variable, population density, but measurement of the independent variables that affect density is no less important. For example, after very intensive studies on *Choristoneura fumiferana,* it surprised all of the investigators to learn that the principal factor limiting the value of predictive models was failure to measure all the pertinent independent variables, or to measure them in the best way. The measurement of independent variables is too specific to the individual species and to the hypotheses that have been formed about the functioning of its life system to be discussed here in general terms. It should, however, be recognized at the beginning of an investigation that there are tow different ways of handling independent variables and that this will influence the form of the models that are developed. One way is to measure the independent variable itself, say temperature, to learn by regression analysis whether it appears to influence population trend, and to find by process studies the causal pathways through which it affects survival or reproduction. The other way is to measure the *effect* of the variable on the population, for example the percentage of individuals parasitized or the extent of mortality. Mathematically, it is better to measure the variable itself, but in practice it is sometimes easier to measure mortality. For example, it is easier to measure the degree of parasitism than to measure the population of adult parasites available to attack the host population, although this tells us less about the functional response of the adult parasites to host density. Both methods, or combinations of them, are commonly used, and the direct measurement of total mortality during one age interval is often used to estimate the population density at the beginning of the following age interval. The development of field techniques for measuring both the dependent and independent variables, and the frequency with which the measurements are taken,' are influenced by the type of mathematical model which is going to be produced. In general terms, the three possibilities are:

(i) models based on life-table studies, in which it is desired to model the change in population density for each developmental stage or age interval of the insect as a function of the independent variables operating during watch age interval;

(ii) models in which the change in population from generation to generation, measured at one specific point in the life cycle, is modelled as a function of the key variables determining numerical change, irrespective of the particular stage or stages affected by them; and

(iii) models in which the main objective is to describe ecological processes, that is, the modes of operation of particular independent variables.

There are recent examples of all three types in the literature and, in the following three sections, it is proposed only to mention their relative advantages and disadvantages. Although the models are different, at least in mathematical form, it should be recognized that the three approaches are complementary as far as the field methods of study are concerned, with no sharp dividing lines between them. Where a choice is available, i.e., where the form of the model is not dictated by the difficulties inherent in studying a particular population, age-specific studies should generally precede or accompany the development of models based on one specific point in the life cycle, and in either case concomitant process studies are required. This will become clear in the following sections.

'LIFE-TABLE' STUDIES

Age-specific studies leading to the construction of life tables require the measurement of population density at a number of points in the life cycle during each generation of the insect. This permits the calculation of age-specific mortality or survival rates for each developmental stage or age interval. If only population densities are listed, as in the demographic life tables, an adequate series of tables will reveal, through regression methods or even graphical methods, how much each age interval contributes to variation in total generation survival, and hence changes in population trend. In developing life tables for insect populations, however, the studies generally include data on the independent variables operating in each age interval, the mortality that they contribute, and additional data on both primary and secondary ecological events. Thus life-table data permit the construction of sub-models for each age interval showing how population change is determined during each age interval, and these sub-models may be combined, sequentially, into a complete model for the whole generation.

The main advantage in developing life tables of one form or another is that the 'comprehensive' approach involved provides more complete data on population dynamics than do other approaches and affords greater scope for detailed modelling. Life tables are highly desirable for important economic pests, where resources are available to permit the construction of an adequate series of them. The agespecific data accrued in this way include the effects of both the key variables and other variables, and are ideal for use in population management. The models produced would permit us to test the consequences of manipulating variables that operate in different age intervals, and to attempt to reduce environmental favourableness at different points in the life cycle. Where sustained resources are not available for long-term studies of this sort, or where comprehensive age-specific studies are either unnecessary or difficult to carry out with existing techniques, it is still desirable to collect as much age-specific data as possible for a few generations at least. In this case, the purpose is mainly to tabulate and analyze ecological events in the life system of the species, and to detect critical age intervals and key influences that deserve detailed study. In fact, if the historical data on the species or the preliminary survey studies have not led to the formulation of satisfactory hypotheses, preliminary age-specific data of this sort are essential. In this situation, as contrasted to that described above, the age-specific methods are used on a short-term basis as a step towards the use of more abbreviated methods, rather than for the construction of detailed age-specific models.

A major difficulty in the 'comprehensive' approach that yields life tables is the sampling problem. It sometimes takes several years just to develop satisfactory techniques, especially where it is desired to sample all developmental stages on a comparatable basis, and where different stages of the same insect occur in different sampling universes such as the foliage of trees and in the ground. It is no easy task to develop comprehensive sampling techniques even for species which occur in high population numbers Their development is much more difficult in the case of species which remain at low levels of abundance for much or all of the time. Ives has reviewed work on the development of life tables for a number of forest, orchard, agricultural pests and drawn attention to the problems that are most frequently encountered. Where it is desired to sample in many different places, precise phenological timing also presents a problem.

The survivorship curve for one generation of an insect slopes downwards, but more steeply in some parts than in others. When our aim is to produce life tables, we arbitrarily divide the survivorship curve into a number of sections and try to get population 'fixes' for sections that are relatively flat. Small errors in timing which result in sampling during periods of rapid numerical decrease can be disastrous. It is not surprising that the most successful application of life table guides to date has been in the latitudes where most "insect species have only one generation per year, with relatively little overlapping of developmental stages. Widely overlapping stages and generations, giving rise to the simultaneous occurrence of recruitment, death, and dispersal in the subject species make the problem more difficult. However, considerable progress has been made in devising mathematical procedures for analyzing numerical trends in such species.

'KEY-FACTOR' STUDIES

'Key-factor' methods require a measurement of population density at only one point in the life cycle, the same point being used in successive generations. The resulting models are designed to predict population density from generation to generation by means of the key influences which largely determine population trend. This approach was proposed because it was found to provide good predictability in the analysis of certain long-term population data in which there was only one density measurement per generation, and because the analysis of life-table data revealed the existence of key intervals and key influences, so that the study of all age intervals seemed unnecessary for some species. The advantageous are that less sampling is required than for the preparation of life tables, and the sampling needed can be confined to a stable section of the survivorship curve where rapid methods are suitable and where exact phenological timing is not crucial. The analysis is much simpler than that of life-table data, but it permits separation of the effects of density-independent and density-related processes, and provides a method for modelling difference in mean density from place to place. However, unless preliminary life-table work or adequate historical data have provided strong hypotheses as to the key influences in a life system, this approach is something of a gamble. Except for the reduced sampling, the actual field methods do not differ very much from those of life-table studies which represent the other extreme in terms of scope. There are many exampless of studies in which the approach is intermediate in scope between the two. Both approaches, or approaches intermediate between them, require work on ecological processes. Without such work, we cannot hope to understand the functioning of life systems.

THE STUDY OF ECOLOGICAL PROCESSES

Under this heading are included all studies directed towards the elucidation of particular processes, such as intraspecific competition or predation, as well as studies on the mode of action or effect of abiotic influences such as temperature or rainfall. Ideally, process studies should yield. mathematical formulations in the from of sub-models which should fit into and refine an overall mathematical model describing the functioning of a life system. The results obtained in the study of particular processes must be integrated in some way, preferably mathematically, because ascertaining the existence and mode of action of a process in the laboratory, or even in a natural population, does not demonstrate its role in the fluctuation and stabilization of population numbers. For this an overall model is required, showing how all key influences contribute to the variance.

To give a few examples of process studies: the work of Nicholson on intraspecific competition and that of Park on inter-specific competition are well-known; as also are various investigations leading to the development of models in population genetics. Holling's general studies on predation have produced both simple models that can easily be used with field data, and complex explanatory models with many parameters. The latter models, when programmed for a computer, can be used to calculate the properties of an 'ideal' predator, and are therefore very instructive. There are many laboratory studies of host-parasite interactions, designed to learn whether numerical oscillations are inherent in a system and what conditions are required to stabilize numbers. Unfortunately, the results have not been modelled mathematically and field workers are still using either the purely deductive model of Nicholson and Bailey or the deductive-inductive model of Watt.

Process work on abiotic influences and on the quality of such resources as food has lagged far behind and no useful models are available. A promising approach is the development of life tables under laboratory conditions where such influences as temperature, humidity, and food quality are controlled over a wide range of favourable and unfavourable values. In this work, the continuation of rearing through a second or third generation a necessary because the effects of these influences are not necessarily immediate, but may manifest themselves during subsequent developmental stages of the insect or even during subsequent generations. It is desirable to study physical influences and food quality together because of the high degree of interaction between them. The attempt to construct detailed population models from field data ' on *Choristoneura fumiferana* would have benefited greatly if laboratory models had been available to show the effects of food quality, temperature, etc., on survival.

Process studies have been undertaken not only in the laboratory but also under semi-natural and natural conditions. For example, Burnett carried process studies to a semi-natural environment in his study of host-parasite interactions in large cages on a lawn. Wellington carried them to the field in hisy study of changes in population quality in relation to natural population changes. Clark studied in the field the mode ofkaction of many processes affecting the numbers of *Cardiaspina albitextura,* with particular attention to density relationships. When many influences are being studied, a great deal of judgment is required in deciding how far to go with the analysis of processes. The investigator may find himself with an interesting host-parasite interaction that calls for experimental work, a need for laboratory models covering physical factors and food, and an interesting sequence of events in the field which appear to 'be due to genetic variability and require inbreeding and crossbreeding experiments for elucidation. Under these conditions, process studies can only be carried to the point where predictability is satisfactory, and cause and effect are demonstrated.

The advantage of process studies is that they can demonstrated the biological pathways through which influences affect population density. Spurious relationships can be obtained in the multi-variate analysis of field data, especially in the case of meterorological variables where the investigator has so many choices. Experimental work on the ecological processes involved not only discloses spurious relationships, but shows also how valid relationships can be modelled efficiently. It reveals the pertinent attributes of the independent variables, and the way in which they should be measured to provide maximum predictability. There is a great advantage in having life-table or key-influence studies and process work develop together, because each gives direction to the other. This is, in fact, the soundest way to proceed in population studies. Theobservational field work reveals key influences, probably including some new ones not covered by preliminary hypotheses, and provides the final test of relationships and functions derived from field and laboratory experimentation, the research on ecological processes reveals causal pathways, discloses spurious relationships, and suggests forms of modelling observational data that are biologically satisfying. If the hypotheses suggested by historical data and/or extensive surveys are supported by a large percentage of explained variance in a mathematical model and a high degree of population predictability, and if this again is supported by process studies on cause and effect, we are getting about as close as we can to proof in population dynamics.

MODELLING

Although modelling is listed here as the final step, it should not be left until all of the field and laboratory work is completed. As suggested earlier, it is advantageous to construct preliminary models as soon as a reasonable amount of information has accumulated. In fact, the possible form of the model should receive attention during the period when preliminary hypotheses are formulated and field techniques are selected or developed.

The construction of mathematical models for insect life systems is in its infancy. Therefore, although the possibilities offered by modelling are obvious, it would be premature at this time to attempt a critical assessment of the value of the models which have been used. The few models published to date, although preliminary and crude, have demonstrated that a high degree of population predictability is possible. Various weaknesses which they contain, both mathematically and otherwise, have been pointed out both by. their originators and by others, and numerous suggestions have been made which should lead to vast improvements in the future. For example, the team of investigators who developed age-specific models for outbreaking populations of Choristoneura fumiferana devoted much time to critical assessment of their efforts and to suggestions for improving both the design of their work and future attempts at modelling. And subsequently Watt pointed out a source of mathematical bias in one phase of the analyses. Careful examination both of the models published to date and of the assessments which have been made of them should be helpful to beginners and other workers who decide to attempt mathematical synthesis.

Approaches to modelling have been covered in a series of papers by Watt which will also provide valuable leads to the literature on this subject. The techniques developed for modelling and computer programming, both in entomology and in other fields of science, are far in advance of the quality and quantity of entomological data available. Therefore, until more field projects are completed and the results are modelled, we will not know what formulations are the most appropriate for describing life systems. How complex and detailed should models become? In the order of amplexity we can go from empirical predictive equations (which can sometimes be very simple if predictability rather than inter-pretation is the main object), to descriptive models incorporating major causal pathways, and finally to comprehensive models of great complexity. It is difficult to draw dividing lines between these different stages of what is really a continuum. Initial field models will be empirical and simple; they can be refined progressively to whatever extent is necessary. The criterion for deciding how far to go is usefulness in describing, interpreting, and applying the results of a study. Although mathematical models can only approximate to reality, they yield more useful summarizations of quantitative studies than any other form of synthesis.

INSECT POLLINATION

Pollination is the transfer of pollen grains on the stigma of female flower. One of the most highly developed and fascinating associations in biology is that between insect pollinators and flowering plants. The association has been instrumental in the evolution of many plant and insect species and has resulted in the development of numerous intimate and specialized relationships between members of the two groups. In many cases the insect and plants involved have developed elaborate structural or behavioural mechanisms that ensure pollination. While these mechanisms are interesting from a scientific standpoint, their practical value cannot be overstated. Without these plants and the insects that pollinate them, the basic quality of our environment and lives would be greatly altered. In this chapter we shall first discuss the coevolution of this association and the advantages it conveys on the partners involved; then we shall consider the mechanisms, results, and importance of pollination; lastly we shall describe the biology and attributes of the basic pollinator groups.

Insects and Flowering Plants

Plant pollination by insects is a coevolutionary process that has been ongoing for over 200 million years. Fossil records show that winged insects were abundant in the Carboniferous period, long before any flowerlike structures were present. The earliest flowering plants were probably fertilized by lightweight, wind-borne pollen. Such pollen would have been difficult to collect by insects and may not have been an important food source for them at that time. Early insect pollination was undoubtedly accidental, with plant-feeding insects bumbling into anthers, becoming contaminated with pollen, and transporting a few grains to the next plant visited. Since these plantdirected vectors were much more efficient than the randomly directed wind, there must have been enormous selective pressure on plants toward the development of new and more effective pollinating mechanisms. An early step in this direction was probably the development of sticky pollen grains that adhered to the insects and thus would have been carried more readily on the insects' bodies to other flowers where some would have been transferred to the sticky or feathery stigmas of those flowers. Insects would also find this sticky pollen more accessible as a food source. The flowers eventually began to secrete small amounts of sweet fluid (nectar), and thus floral visitation by insects was more encouraged. Later, or perhaps concurrently, the flowers also developed attractive odours that increased insect visitation, and it was probably then that insects become important pollinators. With time the flowers acquired colours that made them stand out from the green plant and allowed them to be more easily seen by insects. Paralleling these changes, of course, was an evolution in the senses and behaviours of associated insects, especially with regard to the perception of colours and odours and in the ability to associate these characteristics with food.

In general, insects' perception of colour differs from that of humans in that their visual range is shifted toward the shorter wavelengths of the electromagnetic spectrum. Although they cannot perceive long red wavelengths, they do see shorter ultraviolet ones quite well. Honey bees, and presumably many other insects, distinguish fewer colours than humans do. They normally respond to only four area of the spectrum; yellow-green (650- 500 mμ), blue-green (500-48mμ), blue-violet (480-400mμ), and ultraviolet (400-310mμ). Since honey bees and probably other bees do not perceive pure spectral red, it is not surprising that few pure red insect-pollinated flowers are found in Europe and Asia, where bees are the majorpollinators. The native flowers of that area are mostly yellow, blue, or purple-red-colours readily perceived by bees; deep red flowers, like the field poppy, are visible to be only because they reflect large amounts of ultraviolet. On the other hand, most pure red flowers are pollinated by birds, especially hummingbirds, which are confined to the Americas. Birds are known to have vision especially sensitive to the red wave-lengths. An exception is a group of red flowers pollinated exclusively by butterflies, which are among the few insects tested that have been shown to perceive this colour.

Ultraviolet colours appear to be an important characteristic of insect-pollinated plants. Recent investigators of pollination biology have discovered that there is a whole world of ultraviolet in the plant kingdom, invisible to humans but clearly of great importance to plant-visiting insects. When plain flowers are photographed, with film sensitive to ultraviolet light, many are seen to have striking colours and/or patterns that probably act to attract bees. Specialized floral patterns called *nectar guides,* which appear to be used by insects in locating the nectar source of a particular flower, have been recognized for many years. However, the use of the phogographic technique' described above has revealed that ultraviolet nectar guides are quite common and are probably more important in encouraging floral visitation by insects. Obviously, floral colors and other characteristics have evolved in conjunction with insect senses, and we shall not completely understand this complex association until floral characters can be considered from the stand- point of what insects perceive. Continue coevolution of insects and plants has resulted in a broad range of relationships between the two groups, from accidental visitation to very intimate associations between some members. In extreme examples the relationship becomes a form of obligate symbiosis, in which both the plant and the insect are completely dependent on each other for survival.

The Yucca Moth

A famous example of the latter is the obligate association between the Spanish dagger, or yucca plant, and the yucca moth. All species of yucca are American, and those east of the Rocky Mountains are pollinated exclusively by a single species of moth, *Tegeticula* (*Pronuba*) *yuccasella.* The only food of the larva of this moth is provided by the yucca ovules, which grow abnormally large in the neighbourhood of the moth's egg. Because an unpollinated yucca flower soon dies, pollination of the flowers by the moth is necessary for survival of the larvae. Pollination by casual insect visitors does not occur, because the plant's vaselike style requires that pollen be carefully placed for fertilization to occur. However, the yucca moth has developed a behaviour pattern that results in pollination of the yucca flowers and survival of her offspring. After these small, undistinguished nocturnal moths mate, the female visits the large, creamy white, pendulant yucca flowers to collect pollen. Through evolution the mouthparts of the moth have been greatly modified into curved tentacles that cannot be used to feed on either the plant's pollen or its nectar. Apparently the adults do not feed at all and live only a short time. The curved tentacles of the yucca moth are used instead to collect the sticky pollen from the open anthers of a yucca flower and to form it into a ball. The female moth holds this under her head with her tentacles and front legs, and generally carries the pollen ball to a second flower.

Fig. 9.1. Cross section of a yucca blossom, showing a female pronuba moth stuffing a mass of pollen (gathered from another blossom) down the style.

There she examines the plant's ovary, and if she determines it is suitable, bores into it with her ovipositor and lays an egg. She then climbs up the vaselike style and thrusts some pollen down the tube, thus pollinating the flower. This process is repeated several times per plant. Since the moth usually moves to a second plant before applying the pollen, greater genetic diversity is ensured for the yucca through cross-pollination than if the moth had pollinated flowers of the same plant. An individual female will repeat this process of egg laying and pollination on a number of flowers, apparently laying only a few eggs in each, with the result that there are normally more developing seeds than the moth larvae can consume. When full grown, the larvae leave the seed pod and enter the soil, where they overwinter as pupae, and the "excess yucca seeds ripen and disperse. The emergence of adults from one season's moth brood occurs over a three-year period after pupation, thus ensuring survival of some individuals even if the yuccas fail to flower, as happens some years. In this relationship the moth pollinates the plant and ensures seed production, while the plant provides food and shelter for the insect larva.

Fig Insects

A similar obligate symbiotic association is found between plants of the genus *Ficus* (fig trees) and their exclusive chalcidoid wasp pollinators of the genus *Blastophaga.* The fig "flower" actually consists of numerous tiny imperfect flowers arranged inside a pear-shaped receptacle, the small opening of which is frequently closed with flexible scales. In the wild fig there are three types of receptacles, each associated with the reproductive cycle of the plant's pollinators, which can only develop in the fig flowers. The first type of receptacle is formed in winter. It contains many neuter (modified female) flowers and a few male flowers, the latter located at the entrance of the receptacle. Females of the fig wasp enter the receptacle; lay eggs in the neuter flowers, and die. The larvae develop in the flowers' ovaries, maturing to adults in the spring. The wingless, nearly blind males emerge first, and individuals crawl about until they locate the pupal cocoons of females. The male chews a hole in the cocoon and inseminates the female before she emerges. He dies in about a day, never laving the flower. The female emerges shortly after copulation and leaves the receptacle, acquiring pollen from the male flowers at its entrance. A second type of receptacle has now appeared on the fig, containing either a mixture of neuter and female flowers or flowers of the female type only. Wasps that enter the fig lay eggs on both types of flowers, but only those in the neuter flowers develop. Oviposition activities also result in the accidental pollination of the female flowers, and these develop seed. Wasp development in the neuter flowers occurs as before, but this time with the inseminated females emerging in the fall and going to the third type of receptacle. This small receptacle contains only neuter flowers, in which the females lay their eggs. The larvae develop successfully in these flowers, emerging in the winter, and the cycle continues. The fig tree has developed a number of unusual characteristics that promote the survival of its wasp pollinators. For example, the flexible scales located at the entrance to the receptacle probably discourage entry by predators and parasitiods and thus increase the survival of the wasps. The plant has also evolved special flowers (the neuters) in which the developing larvae feed, with the winter receptacles entirely devoted to this use. Generally each species of fig is pollinated by a single species of fig wasp. This species-to-species relationship offers strong evidence for the coevolution of these plants and their insect associates.

Flower Constancy

Another effect of coevolution is the flower constancy exhibited by some pollination especially bees. Where flower constancy is high, the pollinator restricts foraging to one plant species during single trips or for longer periods of time. A major result is to increase the probability of fertilization, in that pollen deposited in a flower by a visiting bee

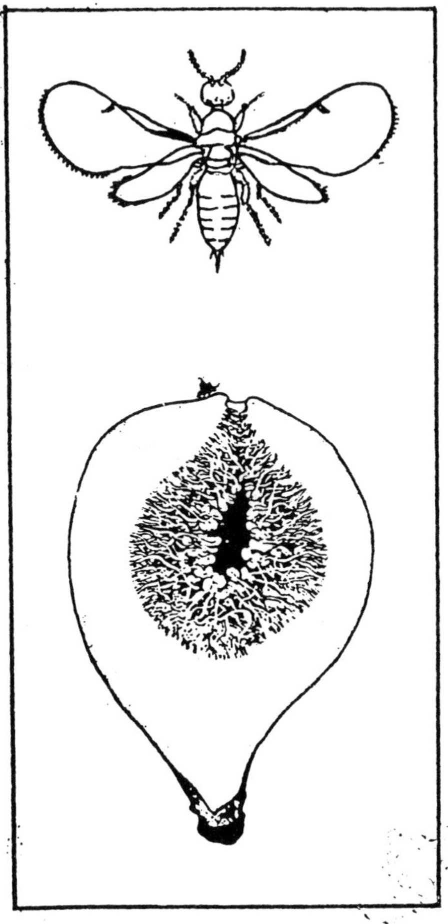

Fig. 9.2. Schematic drawing of a fig inflorescence, with a female fig wasp at the entrance. An enlarged drawing of the female wasp is shown at the top.

is likely to be from the same species rather than from an "alien" species of plant. High levels of flower constancy may be seen in the behaviour of individuals and colonies of honey bees, although other bee species exhibit similar behavioural patterns. The constancy of a bee is best estimated by examining, the types of pollen on the bees body after a foraging trip, and such studies reveal an amazing fidelity for several bee groups. Not only do individual bees work the same flower species on separate trips, as indicated by their pollen loads, but entire honey bee colonies, or groups of colonies, may work one flower species for 10 to 11 days or until the source is depleted. Such constancy must influence the plant species composition in an area, since flowers visited selectively by the bees would be more productive and thus eventually out-compete less favoured plants. Plant communities and bee populations have become established in patterns similar to the coevolution of individual flower species and their insect pollinators.

Flower constancy is of value to both the plant and insect, and there is likely to be a coevolutionary trend in that direction. The general pattern seems to have been the evolution of floral structures that favour certain types of efficient pollinators and discourage less efficient ones. Natural selection has also favoured the pollinators with more efficient food-gathering behaviour. A bee's fidelity to a plant species whose whole local population is synchronously providing nectar and pollen is more efficient than random flower visitation. Bees can readily learn to go to the food source without wasteful efforts and are thus able to visit more lowers per unit time. In extreme cases of constancy, developing larvae are thought to have specialized in metabolizing floral products of individual plant species and are able to utilize the resources more efficiently and develop more quickly.

TABLE 9.1

FLOWER CONSTANCY AS INDICATED BY THE PERCENTAGE OF INDIVIDUALS IN A SAMPLE CONTAINING POLLEN FROM ONE PLANT SPECIES

Genus of bee	*Percentage pure pollen loads*
Andrena (a solitary bee)	54.0
Apis (honey bee)	81.0
Anthophora (a solitary bee)	20.0
Bombus (bumble bee)	55.0
Halictus (a solitary bee)	80.5
Megachile (leafcutter bee)	65.0

Structual plant adaptations that facilitate pollinator constancy are selected for in that nectar and pollen production can be more efficient, since fewer insect groups must be *'fed"* to achieve pollen transfer.

Nectar and pollen sources are usually partially protected by floral parts, and this conserves the food resources for the specialized pollinators of the plant species. An early development in flower constancy is thought to be the fusing of petals, or other floral parts, into a tube around the stamens. This reduces the number of general insect visitors and lowers competition in favour of those that have special adaptations to enter the blossom, thus reinforcing flower constancy. Insects that are genetically programmed to exploit only certain species of flowers are said to be *oligolectic* (as opposed to *polylectic* species, which exploit flowers of many kinds). Such insects tend to have emergence times synchronized with the flowering periods of their hosts, and there are often intricate behavioural and morphological adaptations for gathering pollen from the host plants. Oligolectic bees tend to be plentiful in and regions, when many plant species flower simultaneouly following rains.

POLLINATION

In plants the sexual organs are found in the flowers. Flowers that carry both the female pistil and the male anthers are said to be *perfect*. *Imperfect* flowers, on the other hand, may possess either the pistil or the anthers, but not both. Plants that possess imperfect flower of only one sex, either male or female, are called *dioecious*. Those having imperfect flowers of both sexes on a single plant are called *monoecious*. As one would expect, insects and other pollen vectors are generally most important to plants that have imperfect flowers, particularly those that are dioecious. However, many perfect flowers also profit from insect pollination and have evolved mechanisms to ensure that it occurs. Pollination refers only to the transfer of pollen from anther to stigma and technically does not include fertilization, since the latter indicates the successful union of two gametes to form a zygote. Pollination can occur, and frequently does, without fertilization. There term *pollinator* refers to the *vector* bee, for example that carries the pollen from flower to flower. *Pollinizer,* on the other hand, refers to the *plant* that produces the pollen.

There are two basic types of pollination in nature. In *self pollination,* pollen is transferred from the anther to the stigma of the same flower, to other flowers on the same plant, or to flowers of another plant having the same genetic makeup. The latter situation frequently occurs in the fruit industry, where an entire orchard may theoretically be composed of plants reproduced vegetatively from single parent and that are thus genetically'identical. Self-pollination may occur without any external agent involved, or as a result of some vector. *Cross-pollination* involves the transfer of pollen from the anther of one plant to the stigma of another having a different genetic makeup, and it always involves an external agent, usually wind or insects. Cross-pollination may take place between varieties of the same species, as frequently occurs among the several closely related varities of blueberries, or between less closely related plant I varities, such as cauliflower and cabbage. However, if pollination occurs between species with greatly different genetic compositions, fertilization does not occur. Self-pollination is generally thought to result in less genetic diversity and plant vigour and thus in many instances is less desirable than cross- pollination.

When pollen with the proper genetic components is placed on a stigma, the pollen grain produces *a germ tube* that grows down through the style to the *embryo sac* in the flower's ovary. There it discharges two male cells, one of which fertilizes the female egg cell, or *ovule*. The second male cell unites with sterile female cells, called *polar bodies,* to form the *endosperm* nucleus. The result of this second union is the formation of the seed endosperm, which is the nutritive tissue used by the fertilized egg during seed germination. *Fruit* formation is stimulated by fertilization and is a result of secondary growth in the ovary and nearby floral structures. In most cases pollination and fertilization are necessary for fruit formation to occur, although plant growth hormones and other artificial materials have been used successfully in some plantss to stimulate fruit development without seed formation. In some species normal fruit formation is the result of the combined development of several, or even many, ovules, and fertilization of all ovules is necessary. Fertilization of only a portion of the ovules results in lopsided, deformed, or stunted fruits. In these cases adequate pollination is very important, and sometimes several visits by pollinators are necessary to ensure proper fruit development.

IMPORTANCE OF INSECT POLLINATION

Plant succession, animal diversity, and soil composition are all interrelated facets of plant survival and reproduction. The role of insects in plant reproduction is far-reaching, involving not only plants and their insect associates but in the longer term the whole ecology of an area. Here we shall consider the value of insect pollination to the insects themselves, to plants, and to ourselves.

Importance to Insects

A number of insects, but especially bees and adult Lepidoptera, have developed total dependence on floral products for food. Nectar, which is composed mainly of the sugars glucose, fructose, and sucrose, with traces of other materials such as proteins, salts, and acids, provides the sole energy source for many flower visitors. Some nectar-feeding insects obtain protein from plant foliage, meat, excrement, or blood, but bees are totally dependent on pollen for this cell-building component of their diet. This dependence has led to many specilaizations in structure and behaviour, both of the bees and the flowers, as will be discussed below. These specializations have given rise to frequent speciation in the evolution of insect pollinators, and many of these insects could not survive without the plants which they evolved. Some insect-pollinated flowers provide advantages to their visitors in addition to food. Peter Kevan, now at the University of Guelph, Canada, demonstrated that flowers of the arctic plants *Dryas integrifolia* and *Papaver radicatum* act as solar reflectors, the corollas focusing heat on the plants' reproductive structures. These flowers track the sun during the day, following it at the rate of 15 degrees of arc per hour as it moves across the sky. Both flower species have open bowlike corollas in which several anthophilous insects commonly bask. Kevan's research showed that all basking insects developed considerably higher body temperatures than would be expected, and he suggested that the extra warmth is valuable for increased metabolism and greater mobility. The insects also obtained food in the form of nectar and sometimes pollen from the plants, and transported pollen from flower to flower during their foraging trips.

Importance to Plants

Without insects as pollinators, many plant species in natural areas would eventually become extinct, ultimately reducing animal as well as plant diversity. It is known that insect pollination is extremely important to the continued survival of forbs of the grasslands, to shrubs and herbs of temperate forests, and to desert flowering plants. Utah, has pointed out that the most drastic effect of the elimination of pollinating insects would be in uncultivated areas, where many plants that act to enrich and hold the soil would soon die out. The value of this association is especially great in the and western United States, where even minor plant damage can cause serious soil erosion. Peter Kevan notes that although there is only meager information on the relationships between native pollinators and plant species, it is clear that disruption of the pollination mechanism would have far-reaching consequences to whole ecosystems. For example, without pollination seeds and fruits of some species would be eliminated, thus ;educing food levels for animals dependent on these structures and, of course, preventing reproduction of many plant species. Department of Agriculture, notes that hundreds of wild flowers, weeds, trees and other noncrop plants are apparently insect pollinated, with such complex interrelationships that a serious estimate of the value of insect pollination in native areas is almost impossible. Martin concludes that without such pollination we would live in a very different, less productive, and less interesting world.

Importance to Humans

Many of the world's food crops, such as rice, wheat and corn, are wind pollinated and do not benefit from insect visitation. However, most fruits, vegetables, and nuts cannot be produced commercially without insect pollination. In addition, many of the animal products that we consume, including beef, pork, poultry, and dairy products, are produced by using insect-pollinated legumes, such as alfalfa, clover, and trefoil, as major food sources for the animals. It has been estimated that when all sources are considered, about one-third of our total diet is directly or indirectly dependent on insect-pollinated plants. It is generally believed that modern agricultural practices in the United States, especially the widespread use-of pesticides, have reduced native pollinator levels to the point that they are no longer adequate for proper pollination of these plants. As a result, fruit, vegetable, and seed producers commonly rent honey be colonies to place in their fields during the blossom period to ensure adequate pollination. In many cases crop yields have been drastically increased by such practices. For example, researchers in Michigan demonstrated that blueberry yield can be increased as much as 200% by providing additional pollinators in the form of honey bees, as compared with yields obtained under normal conditions.

Insect pollination may provide advantages other than increasing crop yield. When pollinators are abundant, a greater proportion of early flowers set fruit, which results in earlier and more uniform ripening. With high pollinator levels approximately 90% of a blueberry crop may be harvested after two pickings, when under normal conditions the 90% level is not reached until the fifth harvest. It is apparent from numerous studies that without insect pollination, many foods we take for granted would not be available, because the articles either could not be produced at all or could only be produced at prohibitive costs.

POLLINATORS

Hymenoptera

Insects play a very important role in pollination. Here we are taking the various groups of pollinators under the following heads :

Bees. The most important pollinating insects in temperate areas are the bees, which collect pollen and nectar throughout the summer to feed themselves and their young. This group, which is totally dependent on flowers for survival, has developed a number of structural and behavioural modifications to facilitate the collection of these plant products. Most bees have abundant branched setae, or hairs, on their bodies that act to collect and hold pollen during floral visits. Often these occurs in localized patches, forming a specialized pollen-collecting area, or *scopa,* with the location on the body varying according to the group. For example, solitary bees in the genera *Colletes* and *Andrena* have scopal hairs on the propodeum, hind trochanters, femora, and tibiae, while leafcutter bees have the scopa located on the underside of the abdomen. The most intricate specilization is the *corbicula,* or pollen basket, with its associated structures, found in bumble bees and honey bees. The corbicula consists of the broad hind tibia, which has its smooth, slightly convave surface surrounded by a fringe of long, curved/ hairs. An associated *"tool,"* the pollen comb, consists of a row of spines at the lower end of the tibia. Below the pollen comb, on the first tarsal segment, which is also broad and flat, is a dense "brush" of hairs on the inner surface. With this device pollen is brushed from various parts of the bee's body and mixed with a bit of nectar. It is then removed from the brush with the pollen comb on the opposite leg. The pollen-nectar mixture is next pressed upward into the corbicula by means of a long "spur" at the upper end of the broad tarsal segment. The process continues until the baskets are filled with the sticky pollen-nectar mixture when the bee returns to her nest.

There is a long, tonguelike *proboscis* to collect nectar in bees. The bee proboscis is not a permanent structure as in most sucking insects, but instead is a temporary organ created by bringing together the galeae, labial palpi, and glossa to form a tube for ingesting liquids. When the proboscis is not in use, it is withdrawn by pulling the basal parts up behind the head and folding the distal structures back against the prementum. The activity of social bees centers around the collection of nectar and pollen. The abilities of bees, especially honey bees, to tell time, distinguish colours and shapes of flowers, communicate with their sisters, and in general find their way about evolved as means of increasing foraging efficiency. These and other characteristics make social bees the most important and effective pollinators of flowering plants. In the section below we shall discuss examples of social and solitary bees in some detail.

Honey Bees

Honey bees are probably the most important pollinators of commercial crops. They are maintained by humans because they produce and store honey in large quantities and, in recent years, because of their value as pollinators. Honey bees are especially valuable because the entire colony, except for the males, survives the winter, and thus high populations are available in early spring when pollination requirements are high. During the summer a honey bee colony normally consists of 15,000 to 100,000 sterile female workers, a single fertile female queen, and a few hundred males, or drones. These bees live in a nest made of parallel wax combs of hexagonal cells that contain the larvae and stores of honey and pollen. In nature colonies occur in hollow trees, caves, or similar protected areas.

Three different types of individuals are found in a colony of honey bees. *Males,* or drones, inseminate virgin queens but otherwise seem to serve no useful function for the colony; they are driven from the hive or killed by workers in the fall. They cannot even defend the hive since they have not sting, which, being a modified ovipositor, is found only in females. The *workers* develop form larvae that received *royal jelly* (often called "bee milk"), a high-quality food produced by hypopharyngeal glands of worker bees for the first two to three days of larval life; thereafter they are fed a pollen-honey mixture called *bee bread.* Workers are reared in normal wax cells later used to store honey or pollen. Adult workers perform all the labour in the colony except for egg laying. Worker bees seem to go through something of an "apprenticeship" in that their duties tend to change as the bees grow older and their ability to do certain tasks improves with practice. There is much variation, but usually during the first few days as an adult the worker's only task is janitorial, cleaning cells so that they can be refused. At about three days of age she becomes a nurse bee, first feeding bee bread to older larvae and later, as her hypopharyngeal glands develop, feeding one-to-three-day-old larvae royal jelly. When the wax-producing glands on the underside of her abdomen develop, she becomes a comb builder. Later still she becomes a receiver bee, taking nectar from successful forager bees and transferring it to cells or performing any of a number of warehouse-type duties associated with food collection. Just before becoming field bees, some workers act as guards at the hive entrances. Bees become field foragers at around 10 to 34 days of age and normally continue in that role for the rest of their lives, possibly only three to four weeks. Usually the specialized food glands in the head and wax glands in the abdomen atrophy and are no longer productive by the time a bee becomes a forager. However, bees can adjust their activities to some extent to meet the needs' of the colony. If necessary, workers can continue to produce royal jelly for over 80 days when no young bees are available to take over this duty. Conversely, it is possible for hypopharyngeal glands of older workers to reenlarge after they have atrophied and for these bees to reassume nurse bee duties. Similarly the bees can redevelop wax glands and become comb builders to meet the needs of the colony, and bees as young as four days have been known to become field foragers. Apparently bees can change physiologically if necessary, although usually the physiology of the bee determines her role in the colony.

The *queen is* the largest bee in the colony and is responsible for all the egg laying. She can be distinguished from worker's by her size and the absence of pollen baskets on her hind legs. She cannot perform any of the worker bee takes and even must be fed by her workers, as she is unable to feed herself. The queen is genetically similar to the workers, and her different physical and behavioural characteristics are a result of her rearing environment and larval food. The queen is reared in a specially constructed queen cell, a long, tapered wax cylinder that usually hangs from the bottom of the comb. Queen larvae are fed royal jelly throughout their development and do not receive bee bread at all. A new queen leaves the hive a few days after emerging to mate high in the air with drones. She will often mate on several successive days, and perhaps with many drones, during this period but does not normally mate again after she begins egg laying. The sperm received from the drones are stored in her spermatcheca and are released as needed to fertilize the eggs. A good queen may lay as many as 2500 eggs per day during the summer and often lives several years. When her egg-laying ability begins to decline with age, the workers usually replace her by rearing a new queen.

A honey bee colony reproduces by swarming. Under conditions of crowding or fast population growth, a new queen is reared by the workers. After she has matured, about half of the bees and the old queen will leave the colony and fly en masse to a nearby site, frequently a tree limb. There the majority of bees will wait while scout bees seek an appropriate place for a new home. Eventually the scouts return, and the swarm flies off to establish a "new" colony. The "old" colony remains at the original site with the new queen and continues normal activities. During recruitment to a new nest site, worker bees employ much the same signals (*"dances"*) as they do in recruitment to food sources.

Bumble Bees

Bumble bees are generally considered to be efficient pollinators, but populations are normally too low to pollinate large areas of agricultural crops. Also, the number of bees fluctuates greatly from year to year and area to area, and consequently commercial growers find bumble bees undependable general pollinators. However, bumble bees are regarded as one of the most efficient individual pollinators of many crops, especially tree fruits, where their large size improves the chances of pollination during nectar collection visits. Some researchers also believe that bumble bees are better than honey bees as cross-pollinators because they tend to work only a few flowers on a plant before moving to another, rather than continuing to work blossoms of one plant for long periods. Bumble bees are generally less valuable as pollinators of early blooming plants, however, because their colonies are annual, and thus early spring populations are low when pollination requirements of most commercial food crops are high. The overwintering bumble bee queen emerges from hibernation in the spring and begins feeding on nectar and pollen. As a result, her ovaries develop and she begins to search for a nesting site. Some bumble bee species select sites below ground-an abandoned rodent nest, for example - while others choose concealed sites on the surface, such as under thick grass or in a shallow depression. After selecting the site, the queen digs a small cavity in the center, where she places a pollen mass. She constructs a wax cup on the *pollen,* in which she lays several eggs; then she seals the cup with more wax- The larvae feed on the pollen mass and on additional nectar and pollen introduced by the queen into the wax cup through temporary openings. The queen enlarges the cup as the larvae grow so that *they* remain enclosed. In about 10 days the larvae spin cocoons and pupate, and the queen removes and refuses the wax to build more egg cells on top of the pupae. New adults emerge after about 10 days. Total growth period from egg to adult requires about three *weeks,* although this is dependent on temperature and food availability. The old pupal cocoons become storage cells for pollen and nectar.

The first bees to emerge are all workers. At first they care for the larvae that are developing from a second egg group laid by the queen, but after a few days they begllz to forage for pollen and nectar. When the foraging workers are collecting sufficient food, the queen "retires" and stays in the nest where her only duties are to lay eggs and care for the developing larvae. As the population of the colony grows, the number of eggs laid by the queen also increases and in general is adjusted to the number of workers available to care for the larvae. Males and new queens are produced near the end of summer. These mate, and new queen develops large fat bodies that serve as her food reserve for the winter. In late summer she leaves the maternal nest, locates an over- wintering site in a protected place, and goes into hibernation. There are usually several new queens produced by an individual colony that will survive, but the old queen, the males, and all the workers die with the onset of winter.

Solitary Bees

Solitary bees are valuable pollinators of specific crops in many parts of the world, but like bumble bees their value is limited because of great fluctuations in population levels. However, certain species have proved valuable that great efforts have been made to increase populations artificially, and with some success. In studies on the relative efficiency of alfalfa pollinators, George Bohart found that honey bees visit an average of 7 to 17 flowers per minute, compared with 10 to 30 for bumble bees and 9 to 40 for the leafcutter bees (species of *Megachile*). Perhaps more important, researchers have found that honey bees generally visit alfalfa blossoms for nectar rather than for pollen and that they pollinate very few of the blossoms they visit. For example, leafcutter bees are reported to pollinate 95% to 100% of the flowers visited, compared with about 80% for certain bumble be species; but only 2% or fewer of the blossoms visited by nectar-gathering honey bees are pollinated.

The inefficiency of honey bees as pollinators of alfalfa seems to be in part a learned response. The alfalfa flower is constructed such that the stamina column is held under pressure within the keel. The keel makes a convenient landing pad, and when it is pressed down by the weight of a visiting bee, the stamens are released and snap forward, striking the bee on the under side of the head and depositing pollen there. This process, known as tripping the flower, ensures proper pollination and is generally necessary for seed set. After a nectar-gathering honey bee has been hit by the staminal column and/or trapped between the column and the flower petal several times, she learns to collect nectar from the side of the flower and thus to avoid triping it. Nectar-gathering honey bees that do not learn this avoidance technique within a few days usually desert the crop for a more hospitable food source. Solitary bees, especially leafcutter and alkali bees, primarily collect pollen rather than nectar. These bees cannot normally collect pollen from an alfalfa flower without tripping it and are therefore efficient pollinators of this crop.

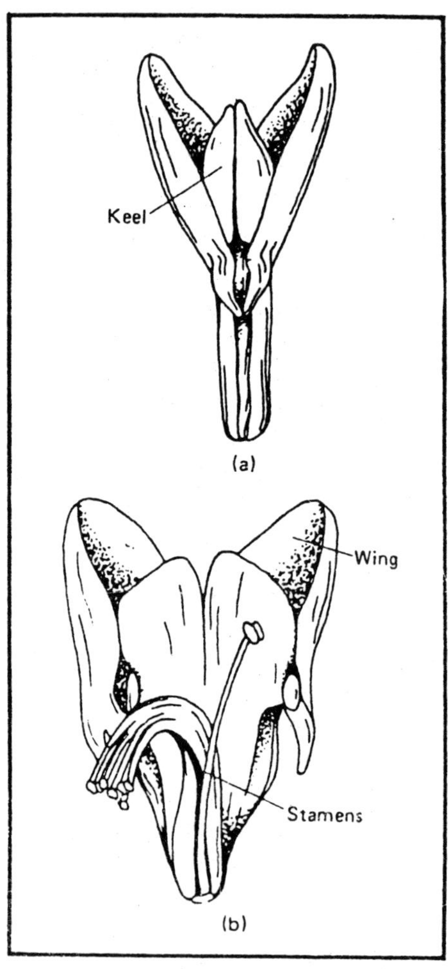

Fig. 9.3. An alfalfa flower untripped (a) and after having been tripped bye bee (b).

The life histories of solitary bees vary tremendously depending on the species involved. Here we shall present details on only two species important in alfalfa pollination; a cavity-nesting leafcutter bee *Megachile rotundata,* and the ground-nesting bee *Nomia melanderi. Megachile rotundata M. rotundata* occupies a variety of nesting sites but generally is found in hollow stems, beetle burows, nail holes, or similar tunnels in wood. *M. rotundata* adults emerge in late May when alfalfa is in bloom. After mating, the female selects a nesting site and makes a series of cells in it. She lines the walls of the cells with oblong leaf cuttings (hence the name) glued together with a salivary secretion. The cuttings are usually obtained from alfalfa, perhaps because it is often abundant, but other plants, including roses, are also used. Each cell is filled with a nectar-pollen mixture on which a single egg is laid. The cell is then capped with 3 to 10 circular leaf cuttings, and another cell is started. The line of cells is closed below the top of the cavity by another cap of circular leaf cuttings. The larvae feed on the nectar-pollen mass in their individual cells, reaching maturity in late summer and then changing into the overwintering prepupal stage. In the spring the bees pupate, the adults emerge through the tunnel entrance, and the cycle continues. Interestingly, the bee that develops from the last egg laid in the tunnel, and therefore the youngest by as many as several days, is the first to emerge as an adult. Emergence continues on down the series of cells, and thus bees do not destroy the cells of their not-yet- emerged siblings to get out the nest.

The alkali bee *Nomia melanderi* gets its common name from the fact that it nests in tunnels dug in alkali soil. Adults emerge from the overwintering state in the ground between late June and mid-July. The female mates and soon after begins digging a nesting tunnel in the soil, usually in the area where she originated. She completes the main burrow during the night and next day digs a cell, provisioning it with a ball of nectar-pollen mixture. The following day she lays an egg on the ball and seals the cell. A completed nest usually consists of a main vertical tunnel with 3 to 4 branches and 15 to 20 cells. The larvae mature as they feed on the nectar-pollen mixture and overwinter in the prepupal stage. In the spring the bees pupate, the adults emerge, and the cycle continues. Proper nesting sites of *N. melanderi* have narrow limits, especially regarding soil moisture. Under the right conditions nests may be highly concentrated, with over 500 entry tunnels per square meter in some natural areas. In order to be satisfactory, the nesting sites apparently require constant underground moisture extending up to the surface. It seems that alkali soil over an impermeable soil layer supplied with underground water provides the correct moisture levels, with the salt contained in the soil drawing moisture up at a relatively constant rate. These conditions occur infrequently and probably account for the heavy use of acceptable sites.

Artificially Increasing Bee Populations

The need for more efficient food production throughout the world has increased the need for pollinating insects. Also modern agricultural practices, especially the trend toward monoculture, have placed great demands on pollinator populations, and at the same time the use of pesticides has reduced the number of these valuable insects. In many areas researchers have attempted to protect existing pollinators and also to increase populations by artificially creating more favourable habitats and nesting sites. In the following section we present some of the approaches and methods used for a few pollinator species.

Increasing Honey Bee Populations

The methods used to increase honey bee populations are wellknown and have changed little for several hundred years. Essentially beekeepers provide a nesting cavity, or *hive,* consisting of a rectangular wooden box containing a series of removable wooden frames. These are often furnished with a wax foundation, to ensure that the bees will build their combs on them. The frames provide support for the fragile wax combs, allowing them to be removed without serious damage. The hive also has a removable top and bottom, providing easy access to the bees and honey. During the summer, as bees collect nectar and process it into honey, the beekeeper will add more boxes, or supers, to the top of the colony to provide additional storage space. Later the beekeeper will remove the "superfluous" honey for personal use, leaving enough for the bees to feed on over the winter. In addition to providing a nesting area, the beekeeper may also provide some protection from diseases and predators and, in more recent years, from pesticides. Generally honey bees survive well without assistance, however. One major reason that honey bees are such important pollinators is that populations can be quickly increased in an area where they are needed. This can be done msimply by moving hives of bees from one area to another or by buying "packages" of bees from southern bee producers to increase the number or strength of colonies.

Increasing Bumble Bees Populations

Bumble bee have been especially damaged by the destruction of nesting and overwintering sites caused by intensified land used and the use of insecticides. In addition herbicides have destroyed many of the wild flowering plants on which bumble bees depend, especially in early spring. Growers can encourage bumble bees by planting small plots of nectar-producing flowers to help colonies survive periods of low food levels and by leaving areas of uncultivated land for nesting and overwintering sites. Reducing the level of pesticide applications is also important for protection of all bees. The use of artificial nest sites to increase bumble bee populations has been investigated by several researchers. These workers placed cans or similar objects containing nesting material in the soil to attract ground-nesting species, and

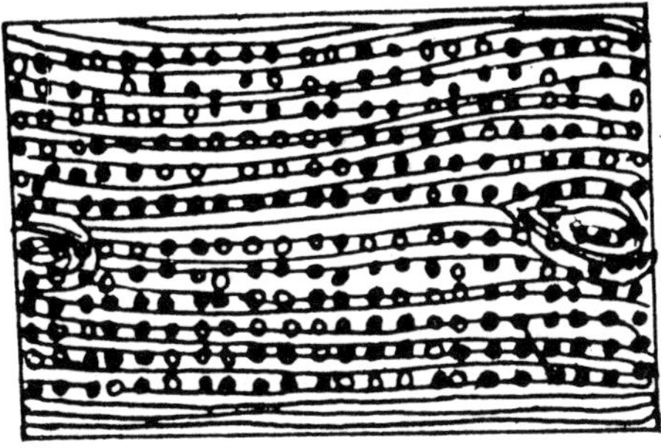

Fig. 9.4. An artificial nesting site for leafcutter bees. Many of the holes have been occupied by the bees, which have closed them off with plugs of leaf fragments.

wooden boxes, also containing nesting material, on the surface for above ground nesters. A number of variations on both themes have been tested and some researches have had as many as 50% of aboveground and 72% of below-ground sites accepted. Other approaches include the establishment of laboratory colonies for movement into the field and artificial hibernation of queens to increase overwinter survival. Although these efforts have been reasonably successful, the prospects of producing bumble bees for use as pollinators on a commercial scale are not yet feasible. At the present time even the most successful methods involve too much effort relative to the number of bees produced to justify the cost.

Artificial Nests for Solitary Bees

The use of artificial nesting, sites to encourage populations of solitary bee species has been successful in some areas. This is particularly true for *Magachile rotundata* and *Nomia melanderi.* Artificial nests for *M. rotundata* are most often made drilling holes of the proper diameter in large block of wood. The bees occupy the tunnels as though they were hollow stems, and in areas where nesting sites area limiting factor such nests have been used to increase populations substantially. Generally the nesting boards are mounted on posts provided with an overhanging "porch" for protection from the sun, wind and rain and screened to prevent bird prediction. Most boards are painted in a checkerboard pattern or otherwise marked to help the bees orient toward their individual tunnels. A great advantage of the nesting boards is that they can be moved to new locations where the bees are needed, as is done with hives of honey bees. The cost of increasing populations of *M. rotundata is* high, but the value of the bees for pollination is such that many alfalfa seed producers in the west have made use of the unusual approach to be management.

Construction of artificial nesting sites for *Nomia melanderi is* considerably more difficult than for *M. rotundata* because of its ground-nesting habits and specific site requirements. The recommendations are basically attempts to duplicate conditions found at natural nesting areas. Essentially a pit is dug and an impermeable layer created by covering the bottom with waterproof plastic. This is covered with a shallow layer of gravel, then one of sand, and the remainder of the pit is filled with soil. Water pipes run down to the plastic from the surface to provide the necessary underground moisture. Salt is mixed with the top 5 cm of soil to draw water upward at the proper rate to meet the moisture requirements of the bees. Such beds have been quite successful. For example, an artificial site created by William Stephen, and the ample food supplied by an adjacent alfalfa field, resulted in more than 2600 nests per square meter. Stephen estimated that a well-populated artificial site 8 by 15 meters would provide sufficient bees to pollinate 16 hectares of alfalfa. Such a field would require from 100 to 200 hives of honey bees at present recommended levels.

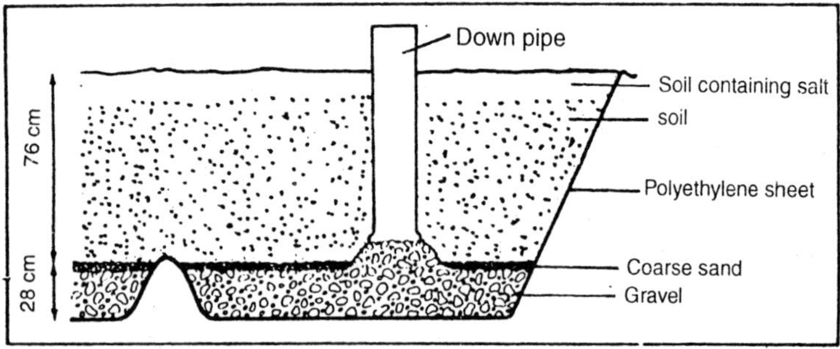

Fig. 9.5. Diagrammatic cross section of an artificial bed for colonizing alkali bees.

Other Hymenoptera

Hymenoptera other than bees are less intimately associated with flowers, but many wasps and ants feed on floral products during a part of their lives. Social and solitary wasps, for example, utilize insects or other meat for a protein source but usually visit flowers for nectar. Most wasp are smooth bodied and therefore are less efficient pollen collectors from a structural stand-point than are the hairy bees. In general wasps are not dependent on floral products for survival. An exception is an unusual wasp group, the Masarine, most of which, like bees, provision their nests exclusively with pollen and nectar. Unlike bees, however, masarine wasps are not very hairy and have no pollen-collecting structures on the body. Instead the female carries the pollen-nectar mixture in her crop, regurgitating it at the nest. Many masarines forage on only one or a few plant genera, and many species have specialized mouthparts with which they extract nectar from these plants. Most members of this group are not common insects, however, and it is apparent that the group has been less successful than bees at exploiting flowering plants as food sources. Regardless, these and other wasps are frequent nectar-directed floral visitors and undoubtedly account for a certain amount of pollination of native and commercial plants.

Flowers Pollinated by Hymenoptera

A number of plant groups have developed specialized flowers and associated structures that tend to favour pollination by Hymenoptera, especially bees. Most of these "bee flowers" produce nectar, and all advertise themselves with brightly coloured, showy flowers, usually with a sweet odour. Most bee flowers are blue, yellow, or some related colour, as one would expect from the range of colours bees perceive. Most bee flowers open during the day, closing, if they do, at night when bees are inactive. They often have'a distinct floral pattern that may include nectar guides. Nectar guides are especially valuable to bees since the nectar of bee flowers is frequently located at the base of a long floral tube and is not readily apparent. The deep floral tubes of many bee flowers and the long "tongues" of bees are another example of a coevolutionary development that favours a narrow group of pollinators. Many bee flowers have a protruding lip that serves as a landing platform for the visitors. Some bee flowers also have pollen-dispensing mechanisms, frequently activated or tripped by the bee's weight on the platform, as in the alfalfa flowers previously discussed.

Some of the evolutionary more advanced flowers have complex passageways or traps that force bees to follow a certain route to and/

or from the nectar source. These mechanisms ensure that the bees encounter the anthers or stigma at a particular point and thus acquire or deposit pollen. In the case of the orchid *Coryanthes speciosa,* a bücketliek lip of the flower is filled with a fluid that seems to be somewhat inebriating. Visiting bees land on the upper part of the flower, lose their footing, fall into the bucket, and can get out only by crawling through a narrow opening. As they do so, they must brush against the anthers, and thus they acquire pollen that they eventually transport to other flowers. Male bees of *Euglossa cordata* are attracted by the odour of another orchid, *Gongora maculata,* and land on its flowers in search of secretions. Having penetrated the inner floral parts in its search, a bee suddenly loses its footing on the slippery surface of the curved column and gets a tobogganlike ride to the bottom. As it slides past the anthers, pollinia (specialized pollen masses) become attached to a specific spot on the bee's abdomen. These are later carried to another flower, where a similar ride leaves the pollinia on the stigma. A number of flower species use this "give-and-take" approach to pollination. It is important in these cases that the pollinia be placed in specific location on the bee's body for it to be deposited on a stigma. Different flower species use different locations on the bee for depositing the pollen. The location is such that the normal activities of the bee, as influenced by the flower species, result in the proper part of the bee's body touching the reproductive structures of the flower and acquiring or leaving pollen.

A more elaborate adaptation is found in the orchids of the genus *Ophrys*. The labellum, or lip, of these flowers resembles female bees or wasps in both form and colour. Perhaps more important, the odour of the flower mimics the sexual attractant given off by females of particular be or wasp species. Male bees or wasps are attracted to these impostors and attempt to copulate with them, inadvertently pollinating the flowers at the same time. This phenomenon, called *pseudocopulation, is* responsible for the pollination of a number of orchid species and, of course, involves a very intimate floral-insect association.

Other Insect Pollinators

As noted previously, Hymenoptera, especially bees, are the most valuable general plant pollinators, although other insect groups also visit flowers and collect pollen and nectar. In general, non-bee pollinators lack sufficient body hairs and the necessary behaviour patterns to be important in plant fertilization. However, some groups may be important, or even essential, pollinators of certain plants. Ile orders Lepidoptera, Diptera, and Coleoptera contain members that are valuable pollinators.

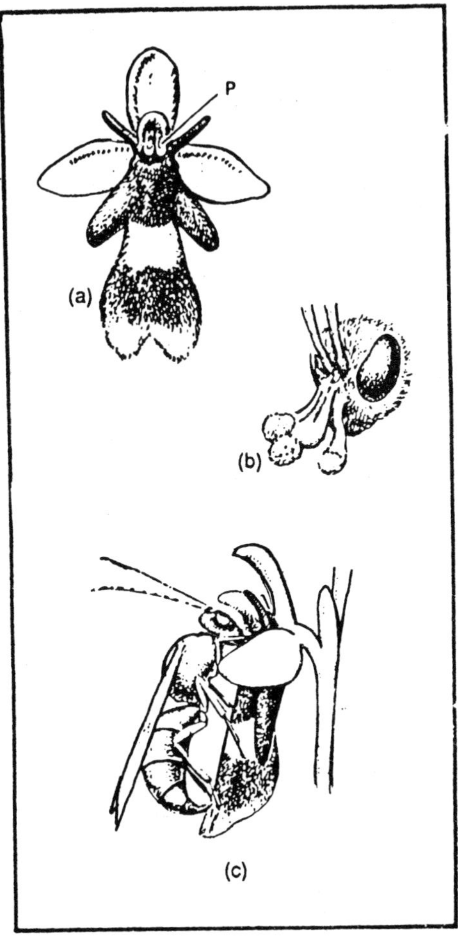

Fig. 9.6. (a) Blossom of an orchid of the, genus Ophrys, *the pollinia labelled P; (b) the pollinia attached to the head of a male bee that has attempted "pseudocopulation" with the flower. (c)* a *male bee at a blossom.*

Lepidoptera

Adults of most species of Lepidoptera feed on nectar, and nearly all larvae are plant feeders. Most Lepidoptera have permanent tubelike sucking mouthparts formed from the galeae, well-adapted for extracting nectar from plants. The proboscis tube is carried coiled beneath the head when not in use and is readily apparent only when the insect is actively collecting nectar. Tube length varies from 1 to 250 mm and in many groups apparently has coevolved with flowers having deep corollas. Butterflies generally frequent day-blooming flowers, and moths visit evening-or night-blooming varieties or those that remain constantly open. Since most past research on flower visitation has been done during the day, the value of moths as pollinators has likely been underestimated.

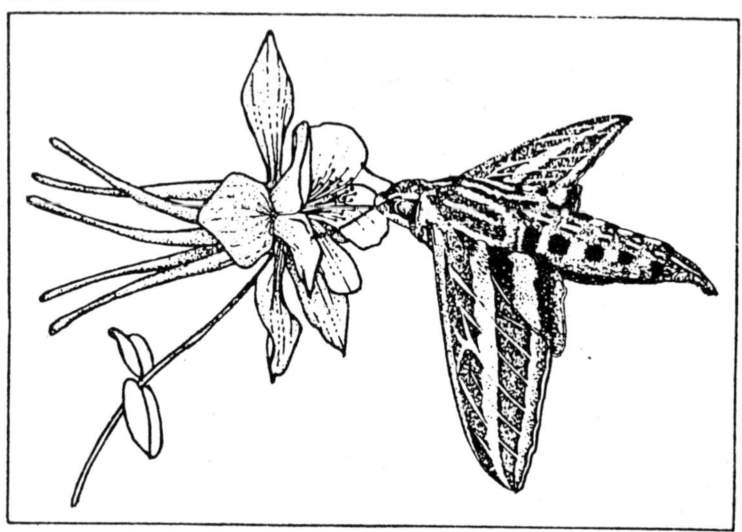

Fig. 9.7. A hawk moth, Hyles lineata, at a blossom of Colorado columbine, Aquilegia caerulea. These flowers are specialized for pollination by hawk moths, and bees are unable to reach the nectar in the long spurs. Variation in colour and spur length in columbines in various parts of the range is believed to be correlated with the presence of different species of hawk moths.

The most important groups of Lepidoptera from a pollination standpoint are probably the following; Papilionoidea, butterflies and skippers; Noctuidae, cutworm moths and owlet moths; Geometridae, loopers and inchworms; Pyralidae, snout moths; Archtiidae, tiger moths and woolly bears; Sphingidae, hawk moths. Flowers pollinated by butterflies frequently are bright red or. orange; at least some butterfly species can see red. Often they have long, narrow corollas with nectar at the bottom, accessible only to their specialized mouthparts. In most other respects flowers polli- nated by butterflies and diurnal moths are similar to bee-pollinated flowers, since these insects are also guided to the flowers by sight and odour. In contrast most moth flowers are white with a heavy fragrance usually emitted only after sunset. The non-white moth flowers -the yellow evening primrose, for example - display colours that stand out against a dark background. The hawk moths, perhaps the most interesting of the Lepidoptera pollinators, may be seen in the evening or at night darting rapidly from one blossom to another. Hawk moths often do not land on flowers but hover in the air while extending their long proboscises into the blossoms in search of nectar. Hence, the flowers they frequent do not normally have the landing platforms or the complex passageways of bee flowers. Adult hawk moths do not feed on anything but nectar, but recent research, on *Oenothera* flowers has demonstrated that they may get nutrients other than the normal carbohydrates from the nectar. Stockhouse and others have shown that when pollen grains fall into the nectar, amino acids are leeched out and may be taken up by nectar-feeding insects. Thus it appears that some non-pollen-feeding insects may be able to obtain additional nutrients via this pathway.

Diptera

The best-known fly pollinators include the families Syrphidae, Bombyliidae, Tephritidae, Tachinidae, Calliphoridae and Chironomidae.

Syrphidae

The syrphids, or hover flies, are common visitors to flowers, frequently hovering above the blossoms. Many resemble honey bees; other look like bumble bees; and others, like wasps. In some cases the mimicry is very striking. The syrphids may be the most important fly pollinators because, although they visit the same flower type as bees, they tend to continue their work under poor conditions when most bees are inactive. Also, like bees, they feed on pollen as well as nectar. Consequently these flies may be important pollinators in areas where plants frequently bloom during inclement weather. Syrphid larvae vary considerably in habits, but some species live in the nests of social Hymenoptera.

Bombyludae

The bee flies are common insects especially in the arid areas of the southwestern United States. Most are large, stout- bodied, hairy flies with a long, slender proboscis. As the common name implies, these flies greatly resemble bees in appearance and behaviour. Bombyliids are, considered important pollinators but seem to be less active under poor weather conditions than syrphids. The bombylid larvae are all parasitic, as far as is known, attacking Lepidoptera, Coleoptera, and Hymenoptera larvae and the eggs of grasshoppers.

Calliphoridae

Blow flies are about the size of a house fly, and many species, are metallic green or blue. Most blow flies are scavengers, with the larvae feeding in carrion, excrement, and similar materials, and have no specialized structure for collecting pollen or nectar. Even so blow flies of various species have been used for years in pollinating specific onion crops, especially for seed production, because they are attracted to the flowers and their activities result in high levels of fertilization.

Tephritidae, Tachinidae, Chironomidae and Tabanidae

Adults of these families are frequently seen on flowers, but detailed studies on their value as pollinators are generally lacking. It is assumed that they play only a supplemental role in pollination. Flowers visited by flies in the families Syrphidae and Bombyliidae tend to be similar to those normally visited by bees. This is not unexpected, since both fly groups contain visual and behavioural mimics of bees and thus are presumed to have evolved in close association with those insects. The really distinctive "fly flowers" are visited by a diverse group of about 30 families of flies that have no particular specialization for feeding on flowers. Most, like blow flies, probably get the majority of their nourishment from other sources, such as carrion, excrement, plant sap and blood. Unlike bees, butterflies, and the beelike flies, this group of diverse flies is attracted primarily by odour to the flowers they visit. Fly flowers, consequently, are usually dull coloured and odorous, frequently having an objectionable smell that mimics the oviposition sites of the flies. The odour of some fly flowers resembles decaying flesh; another group smells like human excrement; and still another group, like fish oil. These are "deceit flowers", providing no actual reward for the flies.

Coleoptera

Coleoptera are not as important as Diptera or Lepidoptera as pollinators, but there are numerous flower-visiting forms that may be of occasional significance. A few plant species are pollinated solely, or chiefly, by beetles. For example, flowers of magnolia, California poppy, and wild rose are generally pollinated by beetles. Deceit flowers often attract beetles as well as flies.

Some 16 beetle families are commonly seen in flowers, but the most commonly seen include the following:

Cantharidae: Most species of soldier beetles are predaceious as larvae and some also as adults, but many adults also feed on pollen and thus are frequent flower visitors.

Meloidae: Larvae of some species of blister beetles are parasitic in bee nests, others on grasshopper eggs, but most feed on nectar and pollen as adults.

Cleridae: Larvae of the flower-visiting species of checkered beetles are mostly parasitic in the nests of bees and wasps. The adults, while sometimes predaceous, all feed on pollen.

Bustidae: Larvae of the flat-headed borers eat wood. The m allic adults are pollen feeders and are frequently seen on flowers.

Cerambycidae: Like the Buprestidae, these long-homed beetles are wood borers as larvae but feed on pollen as adults.

An interesting beetle-flower association is found in the pollination of the giant water lily of the Amazon, Victoria *regina*. The flowers open in the evening and attract scarab beetles, which alight and begin to feed. The flowers soon close, and the beetles are trapped inside until the next evening, when the blossoms reopen. During the period they are trapped, the beetles feed on the interior parts of the flower and at the same time pollinate it. A number of species of angiosperms are pollinated mainly by beetles. Beetle flowers attract their pollinators primarily by odour rather than by sight and commonly have a sweet, spicy, or fruity smell. Like many flies, most beetles that pollinate flowers are general feeders and are not specially adapted for a floral diet. Most of their nourishment is probably obtained from other sources, such as fruit, leaves, excrement and carrion. Many beetles are quite destructive of the flowers they visit, and some devour the entire floral contents. Thus, although they probably pollinate the flower, their contribution is often of little consequence. As a result most flowers commonly pollinated by beetles have ovules well buried beneath the floral chamber, where they are safer from destruction by the feeding beetles. Beetles (and perhaps flies) have been suggested as the original insect pollinator of angiosperms, before bees and Lepidoptera evolved.

Other Animals as Pollinators

Some birds are regular visitors of flowers, where they feed on nectar, floral parts, or flower- visiting insects. During these visits many birds also serve as pollinators. As noted previously, pure red flowers are not perceived by most insects unless they also reflect ultraviolet, and they are usually pollinated by birds. Birds have keen vision and see a range of colours similar to that of humans. Most bird-pollinated flowers are colourful, with reds and yellows predominating. On the other hand, birds have little sense of smell, and the flowers they pollinate are usually odourless, or nearly so. Batpollinated flowers are found in the tropics of Africa and South America. Since bats are noctural, the flowers they visit are often dull and open only at night. Bats locate flowers largely through their sense of smell, and consequently bat-pollinated flowers are characterized by a strong odour. Bats that are close associates of flowers usually have slender, elongated faces and long, extensible tongues, sometimes with a brushlike tip. The front teeth of such bats may be reduced or completely missing. These bats will fly from tree to tree, often in groups, lapping nectar and eating pollen and other flower parts. Batpollinated flowers include the down-dowa tree (*Parika clappertioniana*), agave (*Agave schottii*), and saguaro and organ pipe cactus, as well as others.

Wind Pollination

Wind is the most important pollination agent for the gymnosperms, grasses, and some dicotyledonous plants. Successful wind pollination is purely a chance occurrence, but the chance is greatly increased by several floral characters. These plants usually produce enormous quantities of dry, lightweight pollen that is easily transported by the wind. Some plants have a mechanism for rapid, sometimes forceful dehiscence (release) of pollen, and most have anthers' that are exposed to the wind. Wind pollination is highly evolved mecha- nism, with complex plant structures developed that act to ensure successful pollen transport. Wind-pollinated plants frequently have a feathery stigma that acts to trap wind-blown pollen. In some cases the flowers will appear before the leaves, reducing the possibility of the leaves interfering with pollen transport. Clouds of yellow pollen from pine trees and com plants may be frequently seen in the spring and summer as they are carried by the wind. Wheat, barley, oats, and many graminaceous weeds are wind pollinated, as are walnut and oak trees.

The Pest Control

In science, the usefulness of a concept is measured ultimately by its contribution towards solving actual problems. The most pressing problem in entomology is that of pest control. Despite notable . successes, man's performance in this field has not been nearly as impressive as his achievements in other fields of applied science. One reason for the slow progress of pest control is that the issues involved do not appear to have been grasped fully. A discussion of the subject based on the concept of life system may help to clarify ideas, while putting the usefulness of our approach to a practical test. Pests are species whose existence conflicts with people's profit, convenience, or welfare. The injuriousness of pests varies according to the nature of their damage, to the degree of man's sensitiveness to their depredations, and to the number in which they occur. Because of man's characteristics as a species, the diversity of the requirements, and the extent of his enterprises, he competes necessarily with a great array of life forms for the resources which he draws from nature. Most of the organisms which are capable of interfering adversely with man are not serious pests. The damage caused by them remains 'negligible', meaning that it would be uneconomic under the prevailing conditions to prevent or reduce that damage. Such species are `potential' pests. Our main concern, however, is with the fewer, more serious, or `actual pests, i.e., with the species whose injuriousness is established and whose control is either a social or an economic necessity.

In most cases, development results in a drastic disturbance of the environment of the local insect fauna and in consequent changes in its composition. The essential practical feature these changes is a radical reconstruction of the injurious fauna of useful plants. The results of neglecting entonological aspects of development are clear in the older countries, where permanent problems of defensive pest control have been created and perentically require an expenditure on a vast and ever increasing scale. Clearly such statements imply, firstly, that pest problems are more often man-made, and result from artificially-induced upsets in *'natural balances'*, secondly, that the disadvantageous effects of man's activities on insect populations could be recognized in advance if enough attention were paid to 'entomological aspects of developments'; and thirdly, that pest problems could be avoided by devising suitable preventive measures. These inferences need to be examined carefully for their relevance to pest control. If they are both correct and relevant, the most effective approach to pest control should be not only to avoid creation of new pest situations, but also to try to remedy those situations from which present-day pest problems have arisen. However, consideration shows that, although they contain factual elements, the premisses of Uvarov and Elton are too limited to serve as a basis for discussion in the present context.

Actually, pest status appears to originate in four ways: by the entry of species into previously uncolonized regions; by changes in the characteristics of species that did not previously compete or otherwise interact directly with man; by changes in man's activities or habits, which make him sensitive to the existence of species to which he was previously in different; and by increases in the abundance of species whose interactions with man were previously negligible because of the low numbers in which they occurred. Such increases happen for one of three reasons, i.e., a lasting increase in the supply of a limiting resource, a lasting decrease in the frequency or severity of repressive interactions that previously prevented the species from exploiting fully the resources of their environments, and the simultaneous occurrence of both of these changes. In the third case, species can become pests without undergoing any change in their characteristics and usual abundance. Increased injuriousness follows man's need for greater returns or for new resources. New problems arise constantly in this way because higher- demands are placed on the quality of natural products, because technological progress creates new possibilities of conflict with previously negligible species, or because changing social and economic outlooks make even relatively harmless insects increasingly objectionable.

For example, some municipal authorities find it necessary to undertake the spraying of shade trees to avoid the soiling of cars by the excreta of aphids and other honeydew-producing insects.

The fourth way pertains to species gaining pest status after great and lasting increases in abundance due to favourable environmental changes, Thus, the recent development of continuous intensive crop production on the lower reaches of the Ord River of north-western Australia in the early 1960's entailed very severe attacks on cotton by *Prodenia litura,* because populations of the cutworm were able to increase, without seasonal checks, on the greatly increased supplies of food available at all times in and around the irrigated areas. Similar situations result from the disappearance or diminution of environmental influences that normally contain potential pests at commercially tolerable levels of abundance. For instance, Collyer has shown that the rise of phytophagous mites to the status of major pests of orchards in Britain during the 1940's and early 1950's wad caused primarily by the decrease in predator numbers which followed the extensive use of certain broad- spectrum insecticides. Fmally, the Australian leafroller *Epiphyas postvittana* provides an example of an insect acquiring pest status under the combined influence of an increased food supply and of a decrease in the effectiveness of its natural enemies. The increase in food supply occurred with the introduction of various deciduous plants, notably fruit trees, into the environment of the moth. These provide an abundance of young, favourable foliage in summer, i.e., at a time when populations formerly reached minimum numbers on the ageing foliage of their native hosts. Now, heavy infestations of the leafroller tend to build up on fruit trees throughout the summer months. Although commercial damage to crops sometimes ensues, severe injury is usually prevented by an effective array of natural enemies. When predators and parasites are destroyed by insecticides which fail to suppress the moth *E. postvittana* can cause losses so severe as to be one of the most harmful pests of apple orchards inn south-eastern Australia. The examples cited were chosen for their simplicity and most of them probably represent exceptional instances rather-than norms. Many pest situations eventuate under more complex conditions, involving influences of many kinds, e.g., as shown by the events surrounding the appearance and development of the pathological condition which causes the early degeneration and death of cacao trees in West Africa.

The cacao plants, *Theobnoma cacao* (Sterculaceae), is an understorey tree the American rainforest, which is grown for bean crops in areas with a mean rainfall exceeding forty-five inches, and mean annual temperatures of 70-75°F (21-24°C) or higher. Until about 1920, all cacao was produced under conditions closely resembling those of natural forest. Later attempts it more intensive cropping remained largely unsuccessful until the 1950's when means became available to overcome the consequences of pest attacks resulting from the removal of natural shade. Although'yields could be increased substantially in open plantations, this was found to impose conditions of management which, as a rule, could not be met on peasant farms. Agronomic experimentation has served to demonstrate the delicate balance between the performance of the cacao plant and environmental variables such as soil type and plant association, which ultimately governs the productivity of extensive plantations.

Cacao was introduced to the West African mainland in 1879 and, in the short period of thirty-five years, production there caught up with that of Trinidad, one of tlhe principal exporting areas at the time. This development, which is illustrated in figure 38 for Ghana, was attended by an increasing incidence of pests and diseases which became critical in the 1930's and strongly depressed production during the following decades. Two agents were held primarily responsible for the crisis: a virus causing the disease known as 'swollen shoot' (SSVD); and mind bugs (capsids) causing defoliation and loss of tree condition, often aggravated by fungus infection. Although both agents could act independently, it was found that their effects usually combined to produce compound and far-reaching sequels, and, therefore, that they were best regarded as co-acting elements in a single complex process which determined the premature degeneration of cacao plants. In 1936-37, 81,000 trees were destroyed deliberately in Ghana in an attempt to stamp out the disease. This method was revived in 1945, resulting in the destruction of sixty-three million cacao plants during the next ten years.

The degenerative situation is believed to have evolved in three successive, overlapping stages:

(i) *A preliminary stage* from the time of introduction of cacao through to the 1930's, characterized by a growing sensitiveness of the industry to loss of yield and an increasing susceptibility of the trees due to the extension and ageing of cacao plantings, a cryptic spread of SSVD, and progressive incidence of attacks by minds.

(ii) *A primary crisis,* extending from the 1930's into the 1940's in Ghana, which was precipitated by an acute incidence of SSVD, aggravated by further consequences of prolonged extensive farming. This phase was marked 'by rapid and widespread destruction attributed to the unchecked dissemination of virulent strains SSV. From 1939 to 1944, 74% of trees planted between 1904 and 1914, and 43% of trees planted between 1915 and 1922, were destroyed by virus *in* Eastern Province.

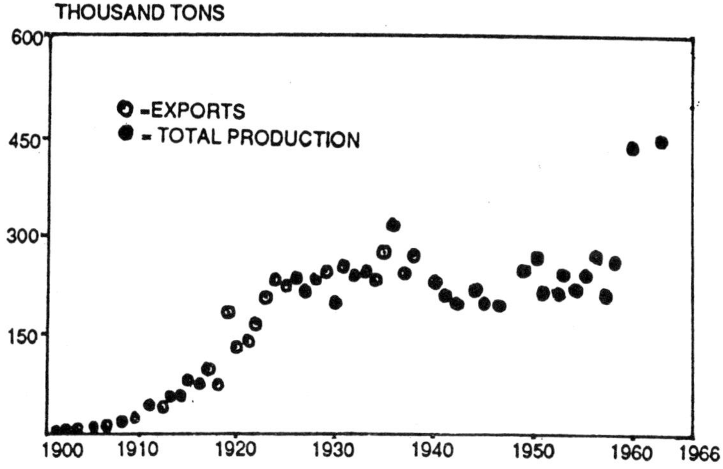

Fig. 10.1. Yearly output of cacao in Ghana.

(iii) An *endemic stage,* originating in the late 1940's and continuing in the 1960's, which was characterized by a trend towards stabilization of the degenerative situation following: the abandonment of devastated plantations, and ensuing changes in vegetation; a reduced'incidence of virulent strains of SSV due to a variety of causes; and finally increasingly effective measures of sanitation and control. Under those conditions, minds emerged as a disturbing agent of primary importance, whose action could upset the precarious balance established between cacao and SSVD.

The viruses affecting cacao fall into three distinct groups, each comprising a number of related strains. All appear to have existed in West African plants before the introduction of cacao. Of them, the SSV complex is by far the most damaging. This virus complex has produced numerous isolates of varying intrinsic virulence, whose effects on cacao can vary according to the age, vigour, etc., of infected trees. On the whole, infections of SSVD are most serious in old trees because those are least capable of regeneration. Infected cacao is the most efficient source of virus in the cacao-forest association. Several mealybugs can transmit SSV, the most important being *Planacoccoides njalensis,* a polyphagous native species whose pre- ponderant effectiveness as vector is determined by its feeding habits and its abundance on cacao. *P. njalensis is* attended by ants and, according to Strickland's findings, its abundance is dependent mainly upon that of the attendant ants. Populations of *P. njalensis* tend to be stabilized at densities which maximize disease transmission. The rate at which SSV can spread is limited by the ability of its vectors to transfer no new plants in the short time that they remain viruliferent. Experience has shown that SSV spreads slowly under natural conditions, and can readily be made to spread even more slowly if the dissemination of infective material by people is controlled.

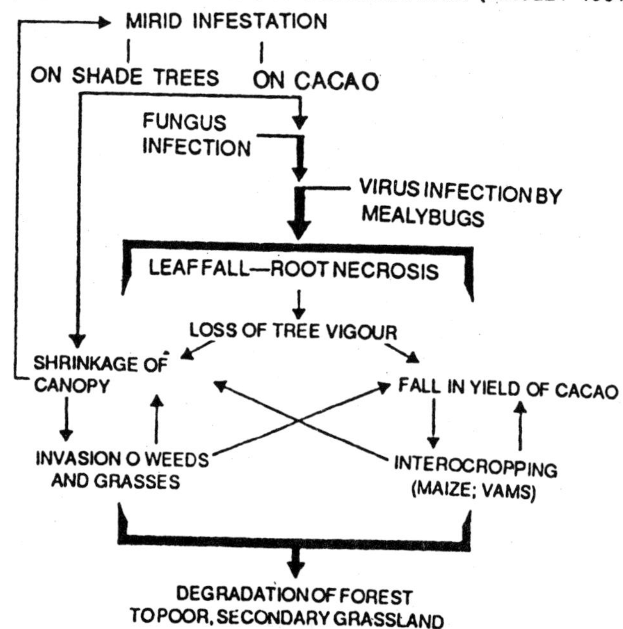

Fig. 10.2. Development of cacao degeneration, Nigeria.

African minds were recognized as potential pests of cacao at the turn of the century, and their incidence caused increasing concern during the development of the degenerative situation. The most injurious species are *Sahlbergella singularis* and *Distantiella theobroma* whose attacks were limited originally mature trees and to young seedlings, respectively. According to Taylor (*loc. cit,* a change occurred in their feeding habits during the 1940's, resulting in the indiscriminate infestation of cacao of all ages by both species. The minds feed on the vegetative parts of exposed, or inadequately shaded cacao trees which they can damage in two ways. Their primary effect results from feeding punctures and, more importantly, from the injection of histolytic saliva into injured tissue. Whereas this is of en enough to kill green shoots, hardened stems usually recover unless the wounds are invaded by the fungus *Calonectria >igidiusculus.* On unthrifty cacao, the fungus can spread from the site of invasion and destroy branches. Thus, the consequences of mind attacks on cacao can very from a 'slight temporary setback to death of the trees affected.

Each year, mind numbers increase to a seasonal peak, following the growth pattern of the host plants. The processes which stabilize population numbers are insufficiently known, but the indications are that mind densities might be limited both by competition for food and, more importantly, by competition for preferred oviposition sites in cacao pods and in the bark of sucker shoots. Considering the West African cacao problem in its broadest terms, one observes that it becomes serious when and where the impact of degenerative agents exceeds the capacity of cacao for natural regeneration. The degenerative situation has its origin in the temporal and spatial coincidence of six independent elements: man's use of cacao; polyphagous minds; a ubiquitous fungus; polyphagous mealybugs; plant viruses capable of infecting cacao; and the susceptibility of cacao under cropping conditions. The degenerative situation was made conspicuous by its sociological repercussions. Because man is dependent for existence on a complex system of goods production, such repercussions can be so farreaching as to be ultimately imponderable. They must therefore be considered in their more immediate aspects, such as changes induced in the economy of cacao farming or, more simply, in terms of crop yields. Using the latter criterion, the *seriousness* of the degenerative situation was found to vary between broad limits. In certain circumstances, the problem was negligible inasmuch as crops could be grown profitably despite its existence. In other instances, the situation could become so serious as to cause the loss of entire plantations. Investigations showed that the seriousness of the economic repercussions resulting from the existence of the degenerative situation was dependent upon a series of topical conditions.

Certain general conclusions regarding the origin and nature of the degenerative situation can be drawn from these facts. Firstly, the situation is seen to be the outcome of a network of natural events which man could not:

Anticipate, because 'what might appear in hindsight to be a consistent causal chain is actually no more than the highly improbable, cumulative result of an infinite succession of random steps; *recognize,* before the situation had developed enough to reveal its full economic implications and biological complexity; or *avoid,* because complete prevention could have been ensured only by keeping cacao out of West Africa.

Secondly, of the conditions that contribute towards establishing the degenerative situation as an economic problem, some pertain to the specific characteristics of the six life forms involved. Those conditions are *absolute* and provide the 'constants' of the problem. Their economic significance as such is qualified, however, by conditions of another kind, whose nature is *circumstantial.* The latter act to determine the seriousness of the problem in "space and in time. Their effects in maximizing or minimising the economic consequences of the degenerative situation result from the functioning of the life systems where by cacao and its pests co-exist under man's influence. The qualifying conditions of this pest situation, and of pest problems in general, are therefore naturally variable and recurrent in their effects. To sum up, pest problems can be said to originate from situations created by the coincidence of absolute conditions entailed in the general evolutionary process of nature. The significance of pest situations for man, however, is qualified by circumstantial conditions, amongst which ecological processes assume a predominant role. In the present state of knowledge, man cannot steer evolutionary processes at will, and must largely accept evolutionary facts as they come. On the other hand, he can modify ecological events.

It follows that the scope of pest control is limited essentially by man's ability to exploit potentially favourable ecological relationship. He cannot hope to avoid pest situations, but he can strive to minimize their repercussions on his economy by manipulating the life systems of the species concerned. For purposes of control, pest situations are therefore best conceived as problems whose solutions should, ideally, stabilize the numbers of the life forms involved-at levels entailing the least possible disadvantages under the prevailing economic conditions.

The Appreciation of Pest Situations

Action to control pests is, of course, motivated by the will to improve an unsatisfactory situation. This motivation implies that, firstly, a situations is found to compare unfavourably with an ideal or factual standard; secondly, the elements which contribute towards making situation unsatisfactory are known; thirdly, the changes needed for improvement are defined; and, finally, means are available to effect those changes. The appreciation of a pest situation can be regarded as a dynamic process operating in a recurrent sequence of three phases within which information is acquired, integrated, utilized and fed back:

(1) Recognition of a pest situation; identification of participating organisms; definition of the relevant characteristics and attributes of the species involved.

(2) Practical assessment and functional analysis of the pest situation.

(3) Definition of aims; choice of control strategy.

Phase 1-As a rule, problems involving insect pests cannot be recognized unless their manifestations are conspicuous to the layman. They, represent essentially an interaction between man and other organisms - at least one of which is a pest. Pest problems can involve man in two ways, i.e., as a target organism exposed to direct attack, or, less directly, as a competitor for space, food, shelter, and other resources.

Phase 1 is concerned with the facts determined by evolution that underlie a pest problem. The first aim is to relate recorded injury to causative organism (s), as illustrated by Kho and Braak's (1956) work in which serious reduction in the yield and viability of carrot seed in the Netherlands was traced back to early infestation by relatively low numbers of *Lygus* bugs. The second aim is to ascertain the range of effects which an identified pest can exert on the target organism or product.

Ideally, *phase* 1 is intended to produce a comprehensive picture of the injurious organisms participating in the pest situation and of their interactions. Although the defining of complex situations may require much time and effort, difficulties do not usually arise in pest control for lack of the information which phase 1 should provide.

Phase 2- The object of the second phase is twofold. It consists firstly of appraising a pest situation with a view to deciding how much effort the problem warrants. The second purpose is to distinguish between those features of the problem that pertain to the evolutionary development of the pest situation, i.e., its 'constants', and ecological events which pertain to the functioning of the life systems involved. The latter determine, in the immediate sense, the actual seriousness of the situation, and entail relationships more readily amenable to manipulation by man. In order to decide on appropriate control action, it is necessary to understand the ecological processes which keep pests operative, and to evaluate the respective function of those processes according to their influence on injuriousness.

It is extremely difficult to make accurate estimates of the damage caused by insect pests, the major problem in assessment work being that of method. Ideally, investigations should proceed at two levels. The first concerns the overall injury which man's interests are actually suffering, or are liable to suffer, under the prevailing conditions. The second consists of evaluating the contribution of single pest species to the overall injury. The two levels of study are complementary. Without the results of the first, interpretations of specific findings remain arbitrary, whereas overall measurements provide no guidance for remedial action. The difficulties encountered in damage assessment are typical of ecological studies embracing functional communities of species, as distinct form studies which deal with the life systems of single species. Of necessity, workers so far have reduced the 'community-centered' problem of pest appreciation to the conceptual level of single-species populations. A good example of this is seen in the studies by American authors of the injury which an array of pests could cause singly to cotton, e.g., spider mites *Heliothis bollworm, and pink bollworm.*

For the present, the difficulty created by the need to appraise the injuriousness of pests within the context of co-acting groups of species cannot be resolved, but only reduced. The difficulty is least in situations where one species predominates. It is partly overcome in other, more complex instances by the assumptions which experienced workers can make as to the dominant or 'key' species in a complex of pests, e.g., cotton boll-weevil.

The most comprehensive attempts made so far at evaluating the injuriousness of pests were carried out during the 1940's and 1950's in parts of the United Kingdom, and were conceived as an experiment to test the following three hypotheses: that relevant information which was lacking on the relation of pest numbers to injury, and on the conditions which determined changes in past numbers, could, if available, be used with great profit; that the required information could accrue from the judicious interpretation of results obtained in simply-designed surveys, supported by detailed complementary studies under controlled conditions; and that certain common pest situations would provide particularly suitable objects for such tests, e.g., the cabbage aphid on brussel sprouts.

The results of this pioneer work reflect the ad hoc nature of the enterprise, and have not fulfilled the authors' expectations. The factual information produced is technical and economic rather than ecological. One cannot emphasize too strongly that the information contains many valuable findings too seldom produced by economic entomologists. The criticism is rather that the project did not yield the ecological information which it was meant to supply. In particular, the work has suggested no explanation of changes in peSt numbers and, consequently, has provided no information of predictive value which Could, lead to significant improvements in control. The large-scale experiment attempted by Strickland ansl his associates demonstrates the need for a more effective approach to the appreciation of pest problems than is allowed by the views on popu- lation ecology that inspired Strickland's work (essentially those of Andrewartha-Birch):

Predicting the future injuriousness of pests is customarily discussed together with the assessment of damage. Forecasts can be required for a variety of purposes, such as: *evaluating* the variability of a pest's injuriousness in time; *preparing* for possible increases in the injuriousness of a pest; and *timing* the application of recurrent control measures. So far, forecasting has been successful only in particular instances involving, for example:

(i) species with long life cycles, like the *Melolontha* cockchafers in Europe, or slowly displacing infestations, like those of locusts;

(ii) pests whose seasonal power of increase increase is narrowly limited, and whose abundance in one year is therefore closely associated with numbers previously achieved, or with conditions prevailing at the outset of the season, like the cornborer in the American Mid-West;

(iii) species whose numbers and activity can be readily surveyed at a stage of development preceding that which causes damage, like codling moth; and

(iv) pests whose injurious outbreaks may be predicted on the basis of reliable (if unexplained) correlation with conspicuous precursory events, e.g., the spruce budworm, and *Melanoplus* grasshoppers in Canada.

This forecasting serves and relies on *ad hoc* methods implicit in the empirical approach to pest control. It represents a temporary expedient rather than an object worthy of lasting ecological attention. As progress is made in analyzing pest problems ecologically, the role that prediction plays as an aid to empirical control will gradually be replaced by the more fundamental purpose of testing the goodnessof-fit of life system models in the process of elaboration. In the form of verifiable hypotheses, prediction and the search for predictability constitute an integral part of any ecological study.

In *phase* 2, the relationship between pest and target species or product must be ! considered with a view to allowing an adequate evaluation of two critical variables, i.e., the levels of pest density which must be attained before the target is affected significantly, and the minimum amount of injury to which the target must be exposed in order to make control measures worthwhile. Tammes has discussed the principles and difficulties of such studies, pointing out that relation between injuriousness and pest density is in the nature of a logistic function characterized by a 'threshold' of pest abundance below which the target species can nullify the effects of infestation, and a level of maximum injury beyond which further increases in the density of the pest can have no more effect on the target. Information of the kind required is primarily 'target-based', and is not available unless the ecology of target organisms is studied as carefully as that of pests, a point that has often been overlooked. To conclude, *phase* 2 *is* by far the weakest link in the appreciation of pest situations. Frequently, it is either ignored in the elaboration of control measures, or else dealt with by assumptions extrapolated from phase 1 findings. The information which phase 2 must provide is the key to pest management. It cannot be gained for a pest situation unless some kind of a model has been produced of the life systems of the species involved.

Phase 3-The appreciation of a pest situation is completed by reviewing the information available from phases 1 and 2 to decide upon a course of action. This implies determining in turn: the maximum injuriousness of the pest, or group of pests, which can be tolerated; the consequent efficacy required of control measures; the conditions influencing injuriousness which couldusefully be modified or changed in order to achieve the degree of control needed; and the strategy, i.e., the approach and scheme of operation, most likely to be effective. The extent to which man is prepared to tolerate the existence of a pest has never been evaluated in.a strictly objective way. As a rule, the tendency is to exaggerate the danger of unfamiliar pests and, consequently, to set unrealistically low levels of tolerance for them. This is particularly obvious in the case of noxious species recently discovered in a new ares, e.g., the San Jose scale in western Europe 'during the late 1940's and 1950's. As, informations and experience accumulate, a more balanced view can be taken both of a pest's true status and of man's ability to cope with problem. On the other hand, practical workers would often regard as acceptable the damage which theycannot avoid by current procedures, and lift their standards only in consequence of progress in their competence to deal with pests in routine fashion. The definition of working levels at which the injuriousness of, pests should be contained is bound to require some compromise between the desirable and the possible.

From the kind of operational analysis, those determinants of injuriousness which are amenable to change by man can be inferred. Which of them require changing in order to accomplish a stated intention, and the extent of change needed, are questions that have to be answered by trial and error until the variance of injuriousness can be apportioned adequately amongst the causative influences and their interactions. A predictive identification of the required changes would accrue only from a comprehensive mathematical model of the pest situation of the type already discussed for single - species populations. This applies generally for pest situations, but, as yet, there is no realistic procedure for selecting deductively the optimum pathways to efficient pest control. The pathways leading to reduction in the injuriousness of insect pests can be defined as 'strategies'. Most of the examples given below to illustrate and support the views discussed are cases in which successful control was accomplished either intuitively or by good fortune. As a rule, such strokes of luck have resulted in uncritical attempts to emulate them-without regard to the prevailing circumstances, and without sufficient understanding of the principles involved. Successes of this sort can be made to serve a more useful purpose by helping to outline the pattern into which actions and reactions can be related predictably in a general theory of pest control.

Four basic strategies can be recognized in pest control. They are:

(1) *To evade* the consequences of pest activity by withdrawing the target organism or product from the range of attack by a pest, or by changing the use made of the target in such a way as to nullify the effects of the pests. For instance, seed potatoes are produced systematically today in districts specially selected for low incidences of virus-transmitting aphids, and characterized by geographic isolation and favourable wind regimes. During. the mid-1960's in some fruitgrowing areas, e.g., in Nova Scotia, increasing proportions of the local crop are being processed in factories-with the effect of lowering the economic value of much of the injury caused by pests.

(2) To *eliminate* those characteristics and attributes of the target

that make it susceptible to attack. For example, the practice developed during the last century of grafting susceptible grapevines on rootstocks unsuitable to the subterranean forms of the *Phylloxera* aphid has made vineyards practically immune to serious injury by the pest.

(3) To *suppress* those characteristics and attributes of a pest that make it injurious to the target. For example, the infectiveness of insect vectors of diseases can be suppressed either by reducing the number of infective sources, orr by minimizing their intrinsic infectivity.

(4) To reduce the numbers of a pest to levels at which the species ceases to be injurious. Examples of this strategy are the most common.

Although the possibilities of strategies 1, 2 and 3 deserve more systematic attention than they have received from economic entomologists, there are relatively few instances in which one of them has provided the complete answer to a pest problem. Quite generally, there seems to be little justification at present to hope for panaceas in pest control, or even for simple solutions. Instead, effective solutions appear more likely to accrue from flexible approaches with a shifting emphasis on particular strategies as needs and convenience dictate. This applies as much to strategy 4 as to the others. However, because it is the most widely-adopted and successful of the four, and because it lends itself most to the application of ecological principles, this strategy will be our main concern in the next part of this discussion.

Reducing Pest Numbers

Pest control is commonly envisaged as an operation, or series of operations, whereby one restraining agent is opposed to the normal multiplication of a noxious population. This is most often accomplished by means of an insecticide. In essence, control by insecticides is usually a kind of containment in which numbers are reduced whenever they reach critical levels of population density. Experience . shows that populations treated in this manner tend to respond in one of three ways to the restraint imposed upon them:

(i) they die out immediately if the mortality suffered exceeds a critical limit;

(ii) their numbers begin to fluctuate in phase with the treatments, more or less violently according to treatment frequency, the extent of the mortality inflicted, the power of increase of the subject species, and the side effects exerted on associated organisms; or

(iii) they reveal under pressure unsuspected qualities, e.g., the development of resistance to toxicants,, which enable them to overcome the imposed restraint.

The second of the three responses is the most frequent. It typifies situations in which the stabilization of population density is no longer implemented by the natural mechanisms which operated originally. In such instances, the stabilizing role is assumed by the imposed restraining agent whose action determines the phase in which pest numbers fluctuate henceforward. Whenever numerical stabilization is brought about in this way, the operative negative feedback mechanisms of the system must be supplied by man. Consequently, such control procedures tend to become onerous routines which, sooner or later, assume some or all of the disadvantageous features entailed by the continuing use of insecticides.

Clearly then, methods of protective management for reducing pest numbers must aim to create, within life systems, conditions under which naturally-existing agencies and processes are so reinforced and/or supplemented in their 'subtractive' function that endogenous stabilizing mechanisms, operating spontaneously, can hold numbers within tolerable limits.

The means whereby desirable changes can be effected in the life systems of pests have been classified by Geier, and discussed according to their immediate influence on the co-determinants of abundance. Each means, whether it affects the properties of a subject species or modifies a population's environment, can contribute to pest management in a variety of ways which differ both in the influences which they exert within life systems and inn their intrinsic effectiveness. The latter is measured on the one hand by *long-term reliability* of the protection offered, and on the other by the *frequency and intensity of human intervention* required. Using these criteria, all empirically-devised methods for reducing pest numbers can be classified conveniently into nine categories, each representing a particular *procedure of pest management* — characterized by the sort of numerical stabilization which it tends to produce. It must be noted, however, the procedures of pest management cannot be identified *a priori* by the nature of the means employed, but solely by the ultimate ecological situation that results form their use. Further, the distinctions proposed do not concern the immediate efficiency and convenience of the procedures, as distinct from their intrinsic, long-term value.

Procedure 1, as illustrated by the current method used to control the light-brown apple moth *Epiphyas postvittana* in Australian orchards, relies on the violent effect of a single, synthetic mortality agent on a pest population, e.g., a broad-spectrum insecticide, and therefore entails potentially all of the disadvantages mentioned already in this connexion. Procedure 1 should be regarded as a palliative, capable of. providing temporary relief from injury but basically inadequate to serve as a definitive method of management.

Procedure 2, represents essentially an improvement in which the most unsatisfactory eatures of procedure I have been minimized deliberately by research and development. This is achieved by closely adapting the use of synthetic killing agents to biology of the pest, and by exploiting to fullest advantage the complementary action of other possible limiting influences (synthetic or naturally-induced) in so-called 'integrated control.' As a simple case in point, Harley and Wilkinson have shown that cattle dipping in acaricide against the cattle tick *Boophilus microplus is* most efficient when repeated at intervals short enough to prevent the surviving ticks from reproducing between dippings.

Procedure 3, involves continually preventing a pest from gaining access to the full supply of material resources available naturally in the environment. Whenever economically feasible, procedure 3 has proved to be highly effective and dependable, as Wilkinson demonstrated in 'pasture spelling', a methodical rotation of cattle in grazing areas, designed to prevent the build-up of tick populations in northern Australia.

Procedure 4, applies to populations stabilized alternatively by containing and by adjusting mechanisms according to the prevailing weather conditions, etc., and whose numbers reach damaging proportions when released from containment, e.g. *Cardiaspina albitextura.* In such instances, it appears that containment is re-established after appropriate reductions induced either naturally or artificially in the densities of the subject species. A case in point is the lasting control of spruce budworm *Choristoneura fitmiferana* by infrequent, often single, applications of insecticide.

Procedure 5, involves the use of agencies whose containing action, under temporarily permissive environmental conditions, is sufficient to hold pest populations at commercially tolerable densities. The seasonal re-introduction of the parasite *Encarsia formosa* into greenhouses for the control of white fly *Trialeurodes vaporadorum is* a good example.

Procedure 6, differs from procedure 3 only in the lesser frequency and intensity of interventions required to maintain its effective operation.

It has been implemented successfully in a variety of instances, notably for the control of tsetse fly *Glossina spp.* To make places unfavourable for adult flies, part of the foliage of shelter plants was removed periodically in critical areas.

Procedure 7, results inn a form of containment which is induced by an agent whose action is not always closely related to the densities of the subject species, and which therefore cannot be depended upon to keep pest numbers constantly within tolerable limits. For instance, Huffaker *et al.* have indicated that the imported *Aphytis maculicomis* which is normally an effective parasite of olive scale *Parlatoria oleae* in California, could, in certain circumstances, be so reduced in numbers by extreme weather that damaging increases ensued in scale numbers.

Procedure 8, represents ultimate success in biological control, as exemplified by the case of the European spruce sawfly *Diprion hercyniae* in Canada.

Procedure 9, refers to the definitive elimination of a resource whose presence enables a pest to maintain injurious densities. This has been achieved, for instance, by Brimblecombe for the control of the pine bark weevil *Aesiotes notabilis* which seriously damaged hoop pine plantations in Queensland. Pruning operations were limited to dry periods inn winter, thus avoiding the presence of fresh wounds a times when the availability of access into the host plant determines the extent of larval survival.

As each successful method for solving pest problems by strategy 4 must correspond to one of the nine procedures listed, the improvement of any method will proceed ultimately according to steps indicated in the lay-out of the chart. However, the improvement of control can be sought at two levels. The first concerns immediate efficacy. Obviously, this must be pursued as a primary goal regardless of ecological niceties, even though the gain may necessitate discarding a previous procedure whose long- term value was inherently greater. Thus, the progression in desirability indicated by rank in the chart can apply solely to methods whose immediate efficacy is equivalent. With this proviso, procedures of pest management become more desirable from bottom to top, and from left to right, in the chart. The up-ward progression in straightf-orward, because it reflects increased economy of maintenance, following generally greater capital outlay in research and development. The horizontal trend requires some comment. Basically, procedures in Column A are the least reliable because they allow subject populations the most chances of escaping containment. Procedures in Column B each represent, in the ecological sequence, the most immediate improvement on their opposite number in Column A. For instance, a readily-conceived advance on procedure 4 would be to acquire the means to re-activate immediately those agencies which variable environmental influences render temporarily ineffective.

Procedures in Column B are rated 'satisfactory' in long-term reliability. By and large, they are less liable to breakdown following ecological or evolutionary changes in the co-determinants of abundance than are the procedures in Column A. They are less secure in this respect than the procedures in column C, because of the probabilistic nature of containment. But, whereas mechanisms which induce adjustment may prove to be more dependable in the long run, satisfactory containment is usually realized sooner in practice than effective adjustment. So far, the successful achievement of any procedure of pest management has been brought about more by good fortune than by design. Progress in these matters will remain empirical, or at least dependent on the quasintuitive insight of particular workers, for as long as adequate models of the life systems of pests are not available to predict the most feasible pathways to optimal procedures.

PROTECTION

Insects form the biggest group in animal kingdom. Despite the great numbers of phytophagous insect species and the destruction they sometimes cause, green plants continue to dominate the landscape. True, insects are to some extent kept in check by their own natural enemies; but the fact that most plants escape or survive the attacks of insects is often the result of defenses the plants themselves have evolved. Plants and plant-feeding insects have evolved together for many millions of years. Many features of plants, such as particular life histories, leaf forms, and secondary plant substances, have evolved (at least in part) in response to attacks by insects. Certain insects have, in turn, developed mechanisms for overcoming these defenses, even to the point of using "repellent" substances characteristic of certain plants (such as mustard oil) as oviposition cues or phagostimulants, as we saw in the preceding chapter. Plants have also acquired toxins that deter feeding by herbivorous mammals, such as hydrogen cyanide in cherry leaves and cardiac glycosides in milkweeds; but these too may serve as phagostimulants or sometimes may even be used by insects in their own defense, as we saw in the case of monarch butterfly. When an insect species breaches the defenses of a plant, natural selection may then result in a strengthening of those defenses. The coevolution of plants and animals is a subject of much current interest. Coevolution has been defined by Daniel Janzen, of the University of Pennsylvania, as "an evolutionary change in a trait of the individuals in one population in response to a trait of the individuals of a second population, followed by an evolūtionary response by the second population to the change in the first." Paul Feeny, of Cornell University, describes this aspect of plant-insect relationships as "an evolutionary arms race in which the plants, for survival, must deploy a fraction of their metabolic budgets on defense (physical as well as chemical) and the insects must devote a portion of their assimilated energy and nutrients on various devices for host location and attack." This chapter considers first some of the physical features of plants that deter insect feeding. Then it reviews the role of plant-produced chemical substances in repelling insects, deterring their feeding, or poisoning them. The effect of nutritional factors on insect feeding will also be considered, as well as the recruitment of natural enemies to assist in the plant's defense. Finally, this chapter discusses bricfly a rather special group of plants; those that include insects in their diet-the insectivorous plants.

MORPHOLOGICAL RESISTANCE

Morphological, or physical, resistance against insects involves plant structures that interfere physically with the insect's locomotive, feeding, or reproductive functions. These functions may include host selection, feeding, ingestion, digestion, mating, or oviposition. The plant morphological features that act to disrupt these functions may involve plant colour and shape or more specialized defensive adaptations such as trichomes, tough tissues, surface waxes, or cell silication. As with chemical factors, physical defenses may act at *close range,* as when plant trichomes prevent feeding or oviposition. They may also act at greater distances, as when host colour determines whether or not an insect alights on a plant; in these cases we refer to them as *remote factors*.

Remote Factors

A number of host cues are apparently used by insects in determining whether or not they will visit a plant. These include colour, plant size, shape and density.

Colour

The use of ,plant colour as a cue in insect visitation has been studied in aphids and their relatives. These insects seem to be most attracted to leaves that are yellow-green-that is, those that reflect light with wavelengths within the 500-to-60O-nm range. Alate aphids are attracted to leaves reflecting about 500 *rum* regardless of the plant species. Thus in many cases healthy, dark green plants are less attractive to these insects than yellowing plants under stress.

It seems difficult to alter the natural colour of a plant as a means of increasing resistance to insect attack. Specific colour-related resistance does, however, exist. For example, S. G. Stephens, at North Carolina State University, suggested some years ago that red cotton plants were less attractive to the cotton boll weevil than green plants when both types were grown together. It has clearly demonstrated that the red cabbage varieties were less susceptible to oviposition of the imported cabbageworm, *Pieris rapae,* than any of the green varieties. Their work also showed that these preferences were not related to the value of the plant as an insect food source, since larval survival was favoured on the red varieties. Other workers have reported similar findings. For example, oat cultivars with red tiller bases were less susceptible than others to attack bythe fruit fly, *Oscinella fruit.* This resistance in oats is likely the combined effect of colour and pubescence, since the latter has also been reported to inhibit oviposition.

Ronald Prokopy has demonstrated that apple maggot flies, *Rhagoletis pomonella,* respond visually to colours, shapes, and sizes. The response evoked by various stimuli varies with age and reproductive condition. His studies revealed that early in life adult flies are attracted to large yellow objects, probably because they are seeking feeding sites (usually honeydew on foliage). Yellow and green may in fact be indistinguishable to the flies, built yellow is more intensely reflective. When the females are sexually mature, they are attracted to dark, apple-sized objects where they normally find mates and oviposition sites. *Prokopy* has demonstrated that this information can be used in conjunction with sticky traps to monitor the number of flies in an orchard and to reduce populations.

Shape

The tropical *Heliconius* butterflies locate their passion vine hosts (*Passiflora* species) at least in part buy visual cues relating to leaf shape. Passion vines have a range of defensive chemicals and also have extrafloral nectaries that attract ants and parasitoid wasps, which add to the defense of the plants. *Heliconius* butterflies are among the few insects that exploit *Passiflora* species successfully. Passion vines show unusual variation in leaf shape, both within and between species. Lawrence E. Gilbert, of the University of Texas, believes that diversity in leaf shape has evolved so as to render the vines more difficult for *Heliconius* butterflies to locate. Furthermore, the leaves of some

Passiflora species closely resemble those of other tropical plants that *Heliconius* caterpillars find inedible, an example of plant mimicry similar to that employed by many insect.

Close-range Factors

Most of the known plant physical-defense factors function only at close range. In most cases these factors make it difficult for the attacking insect to feed or oviposit on the plant. These include such characteristics as thickened cell walls, increased toughness of tissues, proliferation of wounded tissues, solid stems, trichomes, surface waxes, silica in the cell wall, and other protective mechanisms.

Thickened cell walls

In plants the cells walls that are thicker than normal, usually owing to deposition of additional cellulose and lignin, are more resistant to the tearing action of insect mandibles or penetration of the stylets or ovipositor. M. T. Tanton, of the Imperial College Field Station, England, working with mustard beetle, *Phaedon cochleariae,* found that leaf toughness affected the amount of food eaten in a given time. He also demonstrated that there was increased larval and pupal mortality on leaves of greater toughness and that growth rates were reduced, especially for the early instars, when insects were reared on leaves with higher toughness ratings. Tanton speculated that growth rates of later instars were not affected as much because of the increased power of their mandibles. Researchers have also observed that the cowpea curculio, *Chalcodennus aeneus,* has difficulty penetrating cowpea pods that are thicker than normal, and thus these suffer less damage than pods with thinner walls. Thick hypodermal layers have also been considered a factor in resistance in rice to the rice stem borer.

In some cases it has been observed that the thick cell walls inhibit not only feeding but also digestion. For example, found that the grasshopper *Melanoplus confuses is* not capable of breaking down the cells of three grass species that are characterized by thick-walled bundle sheath cells. The cells of these plants pass through the insect's digestive tract largely unbroken and with the cellular contents intact. These workers suggest that the inability of the insects to digest these grasses properly accounts for the lower survival rates on those plants reported by other investigators.

Wound response

It has been observed that in some plants the response to wounding by insect feeding results in a proliferation of cells, or other products, that may act as a defense mechanism. For example, larvae of the pink bollworm, *Pectinophora gossypiella,* may be crushed or drowned by proliferating cells of injured tissues in certain varieties of cotton. Another example is evident in trees of the family Pinaceae, which are characterized by the presence of oleoresin systems. However, individual trees within and among species differ in their ability to "pitch out" bark beetles. Healthy, vigorous trees are apparently able to withstand repeated attacks, while unhealthy or injured trees quickly succumb. It is believed that 20% to 30% of the ponderosa pines are highly susceptible to attacks of bark beetles, such as the mountain, pine beetle, because of a lack of a sufficient resin flow system or oleoresin pressure to counter the attacks.

Stem Characteristics

Sometimes the stem inhabiting insects are seriously affected by differences in stem characteristics, and in many cases resistances to stem borers is related to the nature of the stem tissues. For example, solid stems are much more resistant to wheat stem sawfly, *Cephus cinctus,* than are hollow stems varieties. Also, the hard, woody stems of some species of *Cucurbita* with closely packed, tough vascular bundles are reported to be the main resistance factors against the squash vine borer, *Melittia satyriniformis.* Apparently, penetration of the stems and subsequent feeding by larvae are inhibited by the structural characteristics of the plant. This seems to be the case, too, with the wild tomato *Lycopersicon hirsutum,* where the thick cortex in the stem prevents the potato aphid, *Macrosiphum euphorbiae,* from reaching the vascular tissue.

Trichomes

The cellular, hairlike outgrowths of the plant, epidermis are called the *trichomes,* which may occur on leaves, shoots, or roots. Trichomes are important for various physiological reasons but are of particular value in water conservation and are probably the plant's most important morphological defense against insect attack. Insect species vary greatly in their response to the presence of plant trichomes. These structures may interfere with insect oviposition, attachment of the insect to the plant, feeding, or ingestion. It is generally believed that the mechanical effects of trichomes depend on four main characteristics; density, erectness, length and shape. Some trichomes possess glands that exude secondary plant products. If these are defensive chemicals, the plant may combine physical and chemical defense in one structure. In other cases, the exudate is a sticky material that acts physically to glue the insect's legs or other body parts together and thus reduce locomotion. Small insects or other arthropods with piercing-sucking mouthparts are generally though to be unable to feed on plants that are pubescent (those with high ' densities of trichomes) because the "hairs" prevent them from reaching the conductive tissues with their stylets. However, the effect of such plant "hairs" is determined in part by the tissues that the insects feed on. For example, phloem or xylem feeders must insert ' their stylets deeper into plant tissue to reach their food source than mesophyll feeders. Thus short trichomes may be an effective barrier against the former but not the latter. Obviously the length of the trichome in comparison with that of the proboscis of insect pests is important in determining the effect of this defense mechanism. For example, the trichomes on soybean are commonly about' 1 mm long and cover the plant at a density of about 8 trichomes per mm. Because the proboscis of the potato leaf hopper, *Empoasca fabae,* a common pest, varies from 0.2 to 0.4 mm in length, it is possible that the trichomes present a barrier to feeding by this insect. However, insects with longer stylets might be less deterred by this defense mechanism.

The presence of trichomes may alsobe detrimental to insects with chewing mouthparts. It has been observed that leaf pubescence in certain wheat varieties adversely affected oviposition behaviour of adults of the cereal leaf beetle *Oulema melanopus*. Egg viability and survival. and growth rates of young larvae were also reduced on varieties having densely pubsescent leaves. Females laid fewer eggs on such leaves, and less than 10% of those laid hatched, apparently owing to desiccation. Young larvae restricted to densely pubescent leaves died quickly, and those that did survive grew more slowly than their counterparts on less pubescent leaves. Schillinger and Gallun explained the high mortality by noting that the young larvae had to eat trichomes to reach the epidermis, where they would normally feed. In doing so, they ingested large amounts of cellulose and lignin, the basic constituents of the trichomes, and death resulted from this inadequate diet. Later on demonstrated that cereal leaf beetle larvae that fed on densely pubescent wheat leaves were filled with undigested trichomes and that some of these sharp "hairs" pierced the gut wall. It appears, then, that the trichomes of wheat leaves may act as defense mechanisms in several ways. First, they deter the females from ovipositing on the leaf surface. Second, the eggs that are deposited tend to desiccate, perhaps because they are raised above the leaf epidermis where air currents circulate more freely. Finally, many of the surviving larvae starve because of the nutritive-inadequacy diet of trichomes, and some of those that might survive such a' diet may have their gut walls pierced by the spike-like trichomes. The presence of trichomes is not always detrimental to oviposition. For example, glabrous (smooth) leafed cotton strains are less favoured sites for oviposition by *Heliothis zea* and *H. virescens* than are pubescent strains. It has been suggested that the pubescent leaves provide a better foothold for the females and thus facilitate oviposition.

It has been reported that the trichomes may also act as purely mechanical barriers to insect activity. In some instances insects and other arthropods are trapped or impaled by glandular or nonglandular trichomes. Certain varieties of bean plants possess hooked trichomes, and entomologists observed long ago that soft- bodied insects such as aphids or leafhoppers are sometimes implied on these hooks. It has been demonstrated that the efficiency of this defense through their studies on potato leafhoppers, *Empoasca fabae,* attacking field beans. These workers noticed leafhopper nymphs "clinging" to the leaves of the plants of some of the varieties. Scanning electron microscope examination revealed that some of the leafhoppers were impaled through the intersegmental membranes of the abdomen; others were captured by trichomes impaled in the tarsal segments of the leg or entangled in the tarsal claws. These workers demonstrated that the frequency or capture and mortality were highly correlated with trichome density of the leaves. They noted that the lower leaf surfaces had higher densities of trichomes than the upper surfaces. Since the leafhoppers feed almost exclusively on the underside of the leaves, the trichomes are ideally suited for defensive purposes.

It has been seen that the glandular trichomes may produce exudates that act as mechanical traps for small arthropods. For example, trichomes on wild potato, *Solanum polyademium,* produce an oozing liquid when contacted by aphids, leafhoppers, or other small arthropods. Upon contact with the air, the liquid hardens around the legs of aphids, and the immobilized insects quickly die. In other cases the glandular materials produced by trichomes cause toxic effects on the insect that encounters them. The trichomes of several species of *Nicotiana* (tobacco), for example, exude materials that produce symptoms in aphids similar to those caused by nicotine poisoning, that is, leg paralysis, loss of equilibrium, and death.

Silica

In a number of plant species silica incorporated into the epidermal walls, and this seems to be an effective defense mechanism against attack by some insects. Rice plants, in particular, seem able to incorporate silica from the soil into the epidermal walls. It has been noted that mandibles of rice stem borers feeding on varities with high levels of silica were markedly worn. Given a choice between rice varieties with high and low levels of silica, the stem borers select the latter. Agricultural workers have demonstrated that borer infestations can be reduced by adding silicon to low-silicon soils.

Surface waxes

In most vascular plants the cuticle is covered by a thin layer of *"waxy"* material, mostly of hydrophobic consituents. This layer functions primarily in maintaining the water balance of plants, but it also contains substances that reduce attacks by pathogens and some insects. For example, the normal waxy leaves of broccoli, *Brassica oleracea,* are more resistant to attack by the cabbage flea beetle, *Phyllotreta albionica,* than a glossy-leafed strain. In some cases, however, the waxy surface seems to promote success of insect infestation. The cabbage aphid, *Brevicoryne brassicae* and the whitefly, *Aleyrodes brassicae,* developed large colonies on the waxy leaves of brocoli but tended not to colonize the nonwaxy strain. It appears, however, that the wax affected only the initial infestation level. Once infestation was established on either plant type, the aphids did not differ significantly in their reproductive success.

CHEMICAL DEFENSES

It has been reported that the plant chemical systems may be important in the defense of plants against insects. We now recognize that they are indeed the most important deterrents to insect predation. Chemicals that benefit the producing plant may be called *allomones,* in much the same way that the term is used with respect to insects. Allomones may act as repellents, feeding deterrents, toxins, or growth regulators and may also affect the ability of insects to extract nutrition from ingested plant tissue. While there are thousands of chemical compounds that act in one or more of these ways, most can be grouped into five major categories: nitrogen compounds (primarily alkaloids), terpenoids, phenolics, proteinase inhibitors, and growth regulators related to insect hormones.

Nitrogen Compounds

There are certain nitrogen compounds, such as nonprotein amino acids, act as *antimetabolites*. The insect may mistakenly incorporate a non-protein amino acid and produce an unnatural protein. More

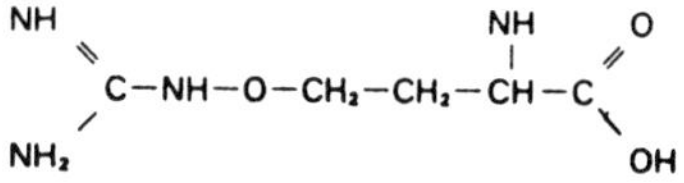

Canavanine: a toxic nonprotein amino acid

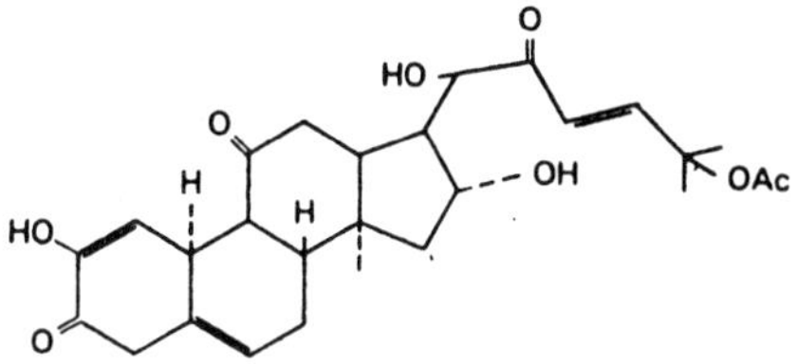

Cucurbitacin E: a bitter, toxic triterpenoid

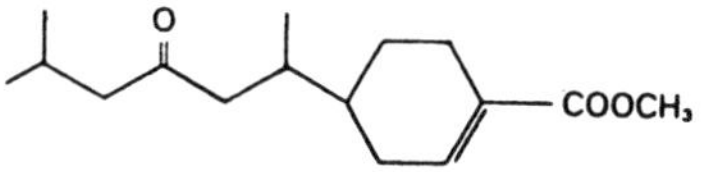

Juvabione: a juvenile hormone mimic

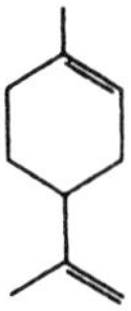

Limonene: a toxic monoterpene

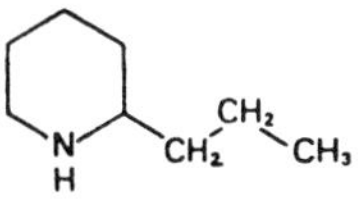

Coniine: a toxic alkaloid

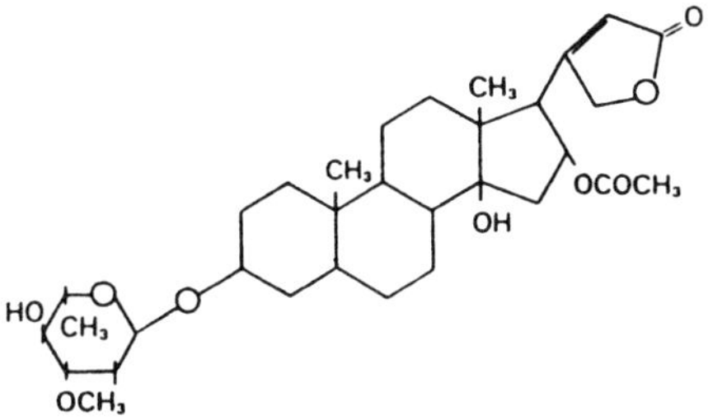

Oleadrin: a toxic ardeiac glycoside

Fig. 11.1. Some of the diversity in molecular structure among plant of defensive chemicals.

commonly, however, nonprotein amino acids act as feeding deterrents. They are especially common in seeds, which are normally rich sources of nutrients for herbivres. *Alkaloids* are complex nitrogenous bases of diverse molecular structure occurring in many plants. Their toxic properties have long been appreciated; Socrates was put to death with an alkaloid from hemlock. Alkaloids are among the best known of the toxins that serve as defenses against insects. One of them, nicotine, has a long history of use as an insecticide. Another, tomatine, is a major alkaloid in tomato and many other *Solanum* species. Colorado potato beetles, *Leptinoarsa decemlineata,* are deterred from feeding on tomatine-containing tissue, and if feeding does ensue, beetle mortality may result. Hence, potato beetles are not normally damaging to tomato, while potato (which is closely related but lacks tomatine) is very susceptible to injury. When tomatine solution is infiltrated into potato leaves, resistance results, suggesting that breeding programmes to transfer tomatine to potato might be productive in reducing insect damage.

In the ragwort, *Senecio jacobae,* the plant contains toxic pyrrolizidine alkaloids that provide protection from a wide variety of herbivores. Cattle poisoning is commonly associated with *Senecio.* However, some insects such as the cinnabar moth, *Tyria jacobaeae,* are not affected by the alkaloid and feed with impunity on *Senecio.* Moth larve sequester the toxic principles in their bodies, imparting protection against birds and other predators.

Terpenoids

Among the largest and biologically most important classes of natural plant products are the *terpenoids.* They are widely distributed and extremely diverse, both structurally and functionally. They are nonnitrogenous and use a 5-carbon, branch-chained hydrocarbon as a building unit. Terpenoids function as attractants for pollinators, as feeding deterrents, and as toxins. *Pyrethroids* are toxic monoterpenes from *Chrysanthemum.* Dried flowers and various extracts of *Chrysanthemum* have been used for centuries because they possess in secticidal properties. Synthetic formulations are widely used in agriculture and have largely replaced natural extracts. Pyrethroids exhibit low mammalian toxicity but rapid knockdown of insects. Other monoterpenes provide the major defense of some conifers against attacking bark beetles. When trees are attacked, the concentration of toxic or repellent monoterpenes found in resin increases.

The *Sequiterpenoid gossypol* provides a major defense of cotton against herbivory. Resistance against *Heliothis* species (bollworm and tobacco budworm) is directly correlated with gossypol content. Cotton leafhoppers show more than 50% higher survival on susceptible varieties of cotton than on resistant varieties, and development is more rapid on susceptible varieties. Although low-gossypol varieties have been developed to obtain cottonseed that is suitable as food, where insect damage is a problem high gossypol varieties are recommended. Cucurbitacins are triterpenoids that impart a bitter taste to plant materials; they are found throughout the Cucurbitaceae (squash family). Cucurbitacins are potent feeding deterrents for a wide variety of herbivores. However, they serve as attractants to cucumber beetles.

Azadirachtin is one of the most promising natural feeding deterrents to insects *Azadirachtin.* It is a triterpenoid and isolated from the neem tree, *Azadirachta indica.* It has long been known that migratory locusts avoid feeding on these trees but consume almost *all* other foliage. Azadirachtin is effective against many species and may be an effective deterrent at concentrations as low as 0.04 ppm.

Phenolics

These are nonnitrogenous compounds that contain one or more hydroxyl groups attached to benzene rings. Among the more important phenolics are the *flavonoids.* One isoflavonoid, rotenone, is used commercially as an insecticide. Others are effective feeding deterrents because of their bitter taste. *Tannins* are polymeric phenolic compounds that have strong protein-adsorbing properties. *Proanthocyanidins* (condensed tannins) are feeding inhibi ors and also reduce the digestibility of ingested foliage. *Hydrolyzabll tannins* elicit variable responses from herbivores, depending on concentration and herbivore. *Anthocyanin* provides colour to flowers, promoting attraction of pollinators, and is also important in fruit colouration, thus aiding in attraction of fruit and seed dispersers. The effects of condensed tannins in oak leaves on feeding behaviour of winter moth larve, *Operophtera brumata* dramatically illustrate the importance of phenolics. Moth larvae feed readily on oak foliage during the spring months, but switch abruptly to other species in mid-June. The switch is correlated with a sharp increase in condensed tannin levels of leaves. Oak trees that are defoliated also produce new foliage containing increased tannin levels. This presumably helps prevent additional defoliation.

Proteinase Inhibitors

Proteinase inhibitors are proteins or polypeptides that bind to the enzymes that split peptide bonds of proteins. This inhibits the proteolytic activity of the enzymes. Proteinase inhibitors in plants are found in large quantities indently in 1976 in two different laboratories that were involved in various aspects of research in the area of plant-herbivore interactions. Both of these groups converged on the ideas that (1) the defenses of plants are primarily a result of life history characteristics of the plants along with their predictability and availability as food resources to herbivores, and (2) based on the mode of action of natural plant products, there are two major types of chemical defenses that have been evolved by plants. *Predictable* resources are those that are abundant and persistent so they are subject to attack over longer periods of time, such as the stems and mature leaves of trees and other woody plants. In contrast, *unpredictable* resources are more ephemeral, such as plants and plant tissues that grow and disappear rapidly, including annual plants, flowers, buds, and new foliage of trees. One should note that woody plants will contain both ephemeral, unpredictable tissues (buds, new foliage) and predictable tissues (branches, mature leaves).

There are two major types of chemical defenses associated with these are spoken of as *quantitative* and *qualitative defenses,* respectively. Predictable resources that are exposed to phytophagous insects for long periods of time are chiefly characterized by proteincomplexing and digestibility-reducing substances (resins, tannins and the like). These are usually produced in high concentrations, hence the term*quantitative defenses*. Mature leaves, for example, remain on the plant for some time and may encounter high levels of herbivory. Consequently selection may favour a larve commitment to defense. Autotoxicity problems are reduced in these tissues by storing these compounds in vacuoles or specialized structures, but at considerable energy expense. In contrast, in ephemeral tissues most of the energy produced is devoted to rapid growth, flowering, and the production of large numbers of seeds that are readily dispersed. Thus natural selection has favoured a lower commitment to defense, chiefly to low-molecular-weight toxins. Toxins are active at low concentrations, often no more than 1% or 2% of the dry weight of the plant tissue; hence it is the quality of the defense and not its quantity that is critical. Toxins include alkaloids, mustard oils, hydrogen cyanide, and others.

It has been seen that the rapidly growing tissues need a defense system that will not require large amounts of energy for synthesis or storage. Under these constraints, qualitative systems are likely to evolve, since in general toxins are physiologically cheaper to synthesize in the amounts required for defense. These substances are either not toxic to the plants or they can be rendered innocuous to the plants with little energetic effort.

Host Specificity and Plant Defensive Systems

It has been reported that monophagous and oligophagous herbivores often show strong preferences for the more nutritioysm, younger leaf tissues that are high in toxins, whereas polyphagous herbivores demonstrate a strong preference for the less nutritious, mature leaf tissues. Investigation seeds and tubers but also occur in foliage. The inhibitory activity of proteinase inhibitors is rather specific for digestive proteinase and thus differs considerably from the generalized protein

TABLE 11.1

ESSENTIAL COMPONENTS IN THE THEORY OF THE EVOLUTION OF PLANT DEFENSES

I. Predictability of Resources	
Unpredictable	*Predictable resources*
1. Annuals, biennials, herbaceous perennials, deciduous trees and shrubs (ephemeral leaf and other tissues)	vs. Evergreen, long- lived woody perennials, mature leaf tissues, heartwood
2. Short generation times, rapid growth rates, numerous seeds	vs. Long generation times, slow growth rates, fewer large seeds
3. Available as food resources for a short time period	vs. Reasonably stable food resource over longer period of time
4. Unpredictable in space and time	vs. Predictable in space and time
5. Lwer commitment to defensive chemistry (qualitative	vs. Complicated, well-developed defensive chemistry (quantitative)
II. Expected Defensive Chemical Types Based on Function	
Toxins	*Digestibility-reducing substances*
1. Alkaloids, hydrogen cyanide, cardiac glycosides, mustard oils, phytoecdysones,-etc.	vs. Tannins, envvme inhibitors, resin, silica
2. Highly active in low concentrations against physiological systems of animals	vs. Form complexes with nutrients needed by herbivores
3. Low concentrations (1%-3%)	vs. Much higher concentrations (5%-50%)
4. Stored in "bound" form in plant tissues or in an inactive form	vs. Usually compartmentalized in cells or in specialized structures to reduce autotoxicity problems

complexing compounds, such as condensed tannins. Presumably they provide protection against insects, other animals and microorganisms. The level of proteinase inhibitors in potato plants increases when the plants are attacked by insects; even leaves distant from the site of attack respond. Foliage or other plant parts with elevated *proteinase* inhibitor levels should be less digestible to herbivores. Some plant species produce a variety of proteinase inhibitors, each having different specificities. Thus there plants possess defenses against a wide variety of herbivores.

Insect Growth Regulators

In plants the *phytoecdysones* close relative of ecdysone have been isolated. Phytoecdysones were discovered in primitive gymnosperms by K. Nakanishi and his co-workers while they were searching for anticancer drugs. The phytoecdysone content in some plants is astonishingly high. One gram of the rhizomes of an oriental fern contain ecdysone activity equivalent to 200,000 grams of silkworm pupae! Several dozen phytoecdysones have been isolated and identified from over 80 plant families.

It was later found that juvabionelike compounds are produced by relatives of balsam fir when those trees are infested by aphids. It may be that some of the compounds are produced only in response to herbivore attack.

In a systematic search for insect growth regulators from plants, Bowers later isolated two interesting substances, which he called *precocenes,* from the common bedding plant *Ageratum houstonianum.* When precocenes are applied to the cuticle of some insect species, the cells of the corpora allata are killed. Be destroying the source of juvenile hormone, precocenes accelerate metamorphosis to yield a precocious (and sterile) adult. But many species are insensitive to precocenes. Resistant insects can degrade precocenes and thus nullify the effect of the poison.

THE EVOLUTION OF CHEMICAL DEFENSES

From a wide variety of plants, many thousands of defensive substances have been isolated. These are highly diverse in their molecular structure, in their mode of action, and in their effects on specific insect predators. Fortunately a general theory of the evolution of plant defenses has been recently proposed, permitting us to see important patterns in this diversity. This theory was proposed simultaneously and indepentions suggest that specialized herbivores become well adapted to their hosts and are able to detoxify the chemicals, thereby being able to utilize a much more nutritious tissue. Polyphagous herbivores, however, feed on several plant species, all of which may contain several different toxin systems. It is thought that these herbivres cannot detoxify all of the numerous toxins in their various host plant tissues and therefore are forced to use a less nutritious tissue. The less toxic tissues may be heavily defended by quantitative defenses, but are usually much lower in lethal or growth-retarding chemicals. There are exceptions to these generalizations, but strong evidence does suggest that toxins are most effective against generalized herbivores.

The intricate detoxification systems have been evolved in some insects, which are chiefly specialized feeders. Degradation of toxins is accomplished by a variety of enzymes known as Mixed Function Oxidases (MFOs) located in the fat body and the midgut, which is the major area for nutrient and toxin uptake of insects. Mixed function oxidases catalyze numerous oxidative reactions. They are remarkably nonspecific in many cases and are often rapidly induced. Numerous other enzymes are capable of transforming extremely toxic compounds into innocuous chemicals that can be rapidly excreted by insects before poisoning occurs. It has been suggested that the MFO activity in the fat body may act as a secondary system for the detoxification of toxins that have survived the MFO activity in the midgut.

Chemical Defenses in Relation to Stress

Concentration and composition of defensive natural plant products are greatly modified by abnormal stresses that a plant may encounter during its lifetime. Changes in natural product chemistry due to drought, nutrients, shade, pollution, and other stresses may contribute significantly to population fluctuations of herbivorous animals. For example, changes in monoterpene, tannin, polyphenol, and nitrogen chemistry of Douglas fir foliage result in a 35% increase in the dry weight of female western spruce budworms. This increase is directly correlated with a highly significant increase in fecundity and larval survival.

Geographic Variation in Plant Chemistry

The plant species often show variation in the chemistry of their tissues. Ponderosa pines, for example, range throughout most of the western United States and have been shown to be highly polymorphic with respect to monoterpenes. Bark beetles of the genus *Dendroctonus* are serious pests of these pines. Certain of these monoterpenses, such as myrcene, play roles in aggregation and attack by the beetles (see

"Aggregation Pheromones,"), while another, limonene, is inhibitory or toxic. It has shown that population of trees having a past history of attack by bark beetles have a high frequency of trees with high concentrations of limonene, evidently as a result of natural selection for resistance.

NUTRITIONAL EFFECTS

There are natural and induced changes in nutrient availability that affect herbivores. In addition to variation in concentrations of defensive substances. The mineral elements nitrogen, potassium, and phosphorus are among those that have long been recognized as important. Nitrogen is a key component of protein, and when plant protein is made unavailable to insects because of proteinase inhibitors or condensed tannin, insects do not have access to the nitrogen necessary to create body protein. Potassium and phosphorus are also important for production of organic molecules. Natural variation in nitrogen, phosphorus, and potassium levels in plants is commonplace. New, rapidly growing plant tissue often has higher concentrations of minerals, and reproductive tissue, such as seeds, is a rich source of nutrients. The attractiveness of these tissues may be reduced, however, by plant defensive chemistry.

In general, herbivores tend to select the more nutritious tissues, and thus natural selection favours lowered nutritional quality in plants. Tissues of poor nutritive quality will tend to lower the growth rate of insects feeding on that tissue, increasing their likelihood of succumbing to predators or disease. However, insects feeding on leaves of low nutritional quality may consume many more leaves. Thus in some cases there may be counterselection for the production of increased palatability and nutritional value. When plants experience stresses, nutrient availability is sometimes enhanced. T. C. R. White, an Australian entomologist, has done much to increase our appreciation of weather-related change in plant nutrient concentration and its effect on insect population ecology. White argues that water stress increases the availability of nitrogen in plants, which results in a more nutrious food and enchanced survival of herbivorous: insects. Outbreaks of a variety of insects are correlated with abnormal weather patterns, presumably resulting in plant stress that increases nutrient availability.

Application of nitrogen frequently increases host plant suitability, and herbivores such as aphids, scales, mites, leafhoppers, and caterpillars exhibit significant population increases following heavy nitrogen applications. On the other hand, chinch bugs, *Blissue leucopterus* (Lygaeidae), are usually associated with nutrient-poor crops. This may be due to microclimate effects as well as nutrient effects. Fungal epizootics are more likely to occur in dense, well-fertilized crops, as the humidity is maintained at a higher level. Potassium applications often are deleterious to insect populations, while phosphorus applications produce variable result.

ESCAPE IN TIME AND SPACE

Plants or plant tissues that are short lived escape from insect attack in time or space. New, succulent tissue, which is highly favoured by aphids, is an example of plant material that occurs for a relatively brief time. Aphid populations often dissipate as plant tissue senesces. Genetic variability in plant development may be a for of "bet hedging," whereby at least some susceptible plants or plant products occur outside the range of normal temporal occurrence of the herbivore.

It is seen that the annual plants produce seeds and die after a single season. If the seeds do not germinate in the following season, any herbivores that had fed on the plants in the previous season would be forced to find 'a new food supply. This could pose a significant problem for specialist herbivores, as there often are dramatic differences in abundance of annuals from season to season. Plant seeds frequently can retain their germination ability for many years, while insects usually cannot persist for more than a few months without food. Agriculturalists assist this "natural" process by rotating among susceptible and nonsusceptible crops and by timing planting and harvesting procedures to minimize exposure of susceptible stages to insect pests. Early-successional plant species usually are short lived, and their distribution is often patchy. Insect herbivores therefore must be very mobile if they are to locate their specific host plant in a mosaic of vegetation types. Late-successional plants, however, tend to be long lived, and many generations of insects could develop on the same plant. Although a late-successional plant, such as a tree, cannot escape readily either in space or time, it nevertheless can reduce its susceptibility. A tree can escape by having susceptible or nutritious tissues available for only a brief period or by presenting a variety of defenses.

ATTRACTION OF NATURAL ENEMIES

Sometimes the plants are attractive to the natural enemies of insects. The presence of natural enemies reduces the susceptibility of the plant to herbivory. The most common method of attracting beneficial insects is to provide them with food, such as nectar from extrafloral nectaries. Extrafloral nectaries are glands located outside the flower that produce water and sugar secretions. Wasps, ants, flies, and moths are attracted to this food. While moths are generally considered to be pests, the presence of predators and parasites may offset an increase in caterpillars. However, in predator or parasitedeficient systems, nectaries could definitely be detrimental. Nectariless cotton varieties, for example, tend to have fewer pink bollworms than do cotton varieties with nectaries. Certain species of *Acacia* not only have extrafloral nectaries but also proteinaceous bodies that ants use as food; in addition the hollow thorns of these *Acacias* provide nesting sites for the ants. The ants aggressively attack other insects, and when these are removed experimentally the plants suffer increased herbivory. Species *of Acacia* that do not harbour ants are commonly defended by cyanogenic glycosides, but these substances are lacking *in Acacias* defended by ants a complementarity that serves to support the defensive tole of both the ants and the glycosides. It is possible to apply nectar or nectar equivalents to crops that lack nectaries. Honey, molasses, and yeast products have been applied experimentally to potatoes to increase the supply of food available to beneficial insects, with observed reductions in pest numbers.

ENTOMOPHAGOUS PLANTS

There are more than 500 species of photosynthetic plants that make use of organic compounds from insects they trap and digest. These plants can survive without their prey, but when they are successful "hunters," the nutrients they obtain stimulate more rapid growth. Apparently it is nitrogenous compounds that are of most benefit to the plant. Entomorphagous plants are usually found in nitrogen-poor soils, particularly in acid bogs and heavy volcanic clays, and their root systems are not extensive. *Entomophagous plants* trap insects using one, or a combination, of three basic mechanisms. First, a number of relatively normal-looking plants are covered with a sticky exudate that entangles the insects. Second, some plants have developed structural modifications that entrap insects, but the plants do not move. Third, a group of plants has developed mechanisms that move modified leaves to entrap insects. Regardless of the trapping mechanism used, the entomophagous plant must have three essential parts. First, it must have an attractant to entice the insects close enough to capture; second, a system to entrap or entangle the insect; and third, a mechanism to digest the prey.

The fly catcher, *Drosophyllum,* is an example of the plant group that entraps insects with sticky exudates. The stems of this plant is covered with special glands that secrete drops of a very sticky, nectarlike liquid that attracts insects. When an insect lands on the stem, it becomes entangled in the sticky fluid and cannot escape. After an insect has been trapped, a second type of gland, also on the stem, secretes a fluid rich in enzymes that dissolves and digests the insect, except for the exoskeleton. The digestive fluid, along with the dissolved insect material, is then reabsorbed, and the exoskeletal remains drop from the plant. The pitcher plants, *Sarracenia, Darlingtonia* and *Nepenthes,* capture insects by special structural modifications similar to a pitfall trap. The pitcher consists of the petiole of a leaf modified into a vaselike structure partially filled with water. The leaf itself is usually small, sometimes existing as a caplike structure that prevents excess rain from entering the pitcher. In pitcher plants the attractant is usually a bright spot of colour, often purple, yellow, or white, near the opening. This seems to attract insects much as coloured flowers attract pollinators. Drops of an attractant nectarlike fluid are sometimes secreted along the rim of the pitcher. Insects that enter the pitcher are prevented from climbing out by numerous stiff, downward-pointing hairs on the inside rim. The proteins of the trapped insect are digested by enzymes secreted into the water, and the products of digestion are absorbed by the inner surface of the pitcher.

In the another insect eating plants like sundew of the genus*Drosera* combine a sticky exudate trap with plant movement into a very effective insect-trapping mechanism. The plant grows in a rosette pattern close to the ground. Each leaf of the rosette is broad and spatulate at the tip. The upper surface is covered with many tentaclelike filaments, each tipped with a drop of glistening, sticky liquid. Insects are attracted to the glistening droplets, land on the leaf, and become entangled in the fluid. When an insect is caught, the other tentacles bend inward, and within minutes all the sticky tips touch the insect. The tentacles then secreted digestive enzymes that break down the insect body parts, and the amino acids are eventually absorbed. The sundew plant responds only to nitrogenous substances and not to objects such as sand, rain, or other non-nitrogenous materials. When digestion has been completed, the tentacles reassume their original position.

Among the most striking entomophagous plants the Venus flytrap, *Dionaea muscipula, is* very remarkable. Like the sundew, the flytrap grows in the form of a rosette on the ground of bogs in the eastern part of the United States. The leaf of the flytrap has an expanded blade with a hinge down the middle. There is a row of long, stiff spines along the margin of each half of the blade. The leaves have a purple area on the upper surface and also secrete a nectarlike substance. Apparently both act as attractants to insects. In the center of the upper surface of each leaf are three short hairs that act as a triggering mechanism. When an insect touches these sensitive hairs, the leaf quickly folds at the huge and the two bodies come together with the long marginal spines interlocked. The trapped insect is then digested by enzymes secreted from glands on the leaf surface, and the resulting amino acids are absorbed by the plant. For many years the rapid movement of the leaves of the flytrap was thought to involve changes in turgor pressure of the cells near the hinge in the center of the leaf. Very recently it is demonstrated that this is not the case. Rather the rapid closure movement involves irreversible acidstimulated cell enlargement in the midportion of the leaf blade. These workers suggest that such enlargement results from pH changes inside the cells caused by a rapid hydrogen ion pump. When leaves are infiltrated with neutral buffers that keep the pH above 4.5, the leaves do not close in response to stimulation of the trigger hairs.

INSECTS AND VERTEBRATES

Insects have coexisted with freshwater and terrestrial vertebrates throughout most of their evolutionary history. In the course of this long association, trophic relationships have evolved such that certain insects are parasitic on vertebrates and certain vertebrates are predatory on insects. The orders Phthiraptera and Siphonaptera, and various families and species of Dermaptera. Hemipt'era (Suborder Heteroptera Lepidoptera. Coleoptera and Diptera are dependent on the tissues or blood of vertebrates as food during part or all of their lives. The parasitic behaviour also has made possible the transmission of certain microbes and helminths among vertebrate hosts, including some of the most important diseases of human beings. In the geological past, the abundance of insects as food for vertebrates played a key role in, the early evolution of reptiles, birds, mammals, and the primates. Judging by the structure of fossils the early forms of each group appear to have been mainly insectivores. Today insects continue to be an important source of food for verte- brates. Many familiar birds in urban and rural areas feed almost exclusively on insects and in some instances significantly reduce pest populations. Likewise some freshwater fish include insects as a regular part of their diet. The mosquito fish, *Gambusia affinis, is* an ideal agent for biological control of mosquitoes in ponds and irrigated rice fields. By at least 200 A. D., human anglers had learned to imitate insects by making *'Flies"* of feathers of hair. Thus the popular recreation of fly-fishing takes advantage of the predatory behaviour of fish on insects.

INSECT PREDATORS OF VERTEBRATES

The difference in size between vertebrates and insects protects most vertebrates from insect predators. Some large insect predators, however, are able to catch and kill small vertebrates. Large dragonfly naiads, dytiscid larvae, and belostomatids capture small fish or tadpoles. These aquatic predators are unwelcome in home aquaria or in fish hatcheries. Large praying mantises may kill young birds. Chicks and young birds are also killed by ants as small as Argentine ants. Ants probably initially seek moisture, but soon also take blood. Poultry farms have reported losses of chicks killed by ants.

INSECT PARASITES OF VERTEBRATES

The vertebrates are larger than the insects as far as their size is concerned. Their larger size prevents predation on them by most insects, but does not prevent parasitism. All terrestrial vertebrates are subject to attack. Only vertebrates that remain partly or completely submerged in water throughout their lives-fish, whales, and seacows are exempt. Other marine vertebrates, such as seals and marine birds, including penguins, periodically leave the water and are hosts to lice and occasionally other kinds of parasites. For example, mosquitoes transmit filarial worms to sea lions and have even been seen fish at low tide.

In the parasitic forms blood is the usual food and often is ingested with the aid of anticoagulants in the saliva. Other parasites subsist on sebaceous (oil) secretions, mucus, pus, lachrymal (tear) secretions, epidermis, skin debris, hair or feathers, or internal tissues. In some instances, the eating of foreign matter, fungi, or microbes on the host's skin is probably beneficial, but most parasites are detrimental to their hosts in some degree. Nevertheless, the health and survival of the host are essential to the parasite. As a rule, the host's reaction to a new parasite is severe, while long-established parasites have evolved in such a way as to minimize irritation. On its normal host the bite of a bloodsucking insect is often apparently painless, but on other hosts the reaction may be swift. Occasionally hosts die as a direct result of parasitism. Excessive numbers of bloodsucking insects may kill a host by exsanguination or toxic effects, or internal parasites may destroy vital organs. Debilitating or fatal pathogens may be transmitted, or secondary infections may develop in wounds.

Parasites located on the outside of the host's body are *ectoparasites,* those inside the body are *endoparasites*. *Continuous* parasites remain on the host's body throughout the parasite's life. *Transitory* parasites spend a part of their life on the host and part elsewhere as a free-living insect, *intermittent,* or *temporary,* parasites visit the host only to feed. *Facultative* parasites are insects which normally complete their life without parasitism, but are able to survive as parasites under certain circumstances. *Obligatory* parasites require a host to complete their life. Parasites have evolved repeatedly from different lineages during the long association of insects and vertebrates as the codominant terrestrial animals. For our purposes, we divide parasites into three broad categories based on their general adaptation to parasitism:

(1) *crawling ectoparasites* are apterous or sometimes winged and cling to their host or crawl on their hosts at least during feeding;

(2) *flying ectoparasites* are winged, active fliers and alight at or near the site of feeding; and

(3) *myiasis producing Diptera* are tissue- or blood-feeding larvae.

PARASITES AND THEIR CHARACTERISTICS

Crawling, Ectoparasites

Names of taxonomic groups of *continuous or apparently continuous ectoparasites* follow

(1) Suborder Hemimerina (Dermaptera), 10 species, eat epidermis and skin debris of southern African rats of the genus Cricetomys.

(2) Polyctenidae (Hemiptera), or bat bugs, 6 species in the Old World and 12 in the New World, suck blood of bats.

(3) Phthiraptera, or lice are divided into four suborders: Amblycera and Ischnocera, the biting lice, include 2800 species, most of which feed on feathers, skin debris, and sometimes blood of birds, but some species in each suborder parasites mammals. Rhynchophthirina, or elephant lice, include only *Haematomyzus elephant is* on African and Asian elephants, and *H. hopkinsi* on African warthogs, Anoplura, or sucking lice, include over 400 species which suck blood of many mammals. Species attacking humans are the human body louse, *Pediculus humanus,* and the pubic louse *Pthirius pubis.*

(4) Hippoboscidae (Diptera), or louse flies, include about 100 species which suck blood from birds and large mammals.

(5) Streblidae (Diptera), or bat flies, suck blood of bats in both the New and Old Worlds.

(6) Mycteribiidae (Diptera), or spiderlike bat flies, 195 species, suck blood of bats, mostly in the Malaysian region.

(7) *Platypsylla castoris* (Platpsyllidae), or beaver beetles feed on skin debris of beavers in Europe and North America, and the relict *rodent, Aplodontia nafa,* of coastal Northwestern United States.

(8) Beetles of the tribe Amblyopinini (Staphylinidae, Coleoptera), 41 species feed mostly on rodents and also on marsupials in Central and South America; one species feeds on a rat from Tasmania. Parasites become embedded in skin where they may suck blood, but specimens have also been found in bat guano.

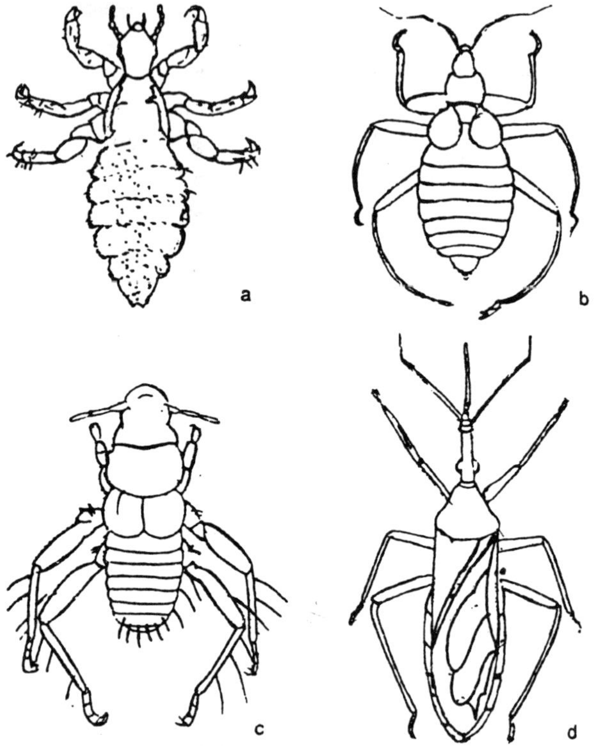

Fig. 12.1. Parasitic hemipteroids: a, human body louse, Pedicuius humanus (Pediculidae); b, primitive cimicid bat bug from Texas cave. Primcimer cavernis; c, polyetenid bat bug, Hesperoctenes fumarius, d, blood-sucking reduviid, Rhoodnus prolixus.

(9) Sloth moths are three species in the large family Pyralidae (Lepidoptera): *Bradypodicola hahneli* on the there-toed sloth, *Bradypus spp.; Cryptoses choloepi* on the two-toed sloth, *Choloepus hoffmanni* and *Bradypophila garbei* on *Bradypus marmoratus.* Adults are phoretic on sloths. It is not known whether they feed on sebaceous secretions or on the algae that grow in the grooves of the sloth's hair. When the sloth descends to the forest floor to defecate, the female moth leaves the host and oviposits in the feces. The larvae develop in the feces and later, as adults, find their way to a sloth.

Transitory ectoparasites are as follows :

(1) Siphonoaptera or fleas, including nearly 1800 species, are ectoparasitic bloodsuckers in the adult stage only. The larvae live as scavengers in the host's nest or in ground little of the host's habitat. Hosts are mostly mammals that nest in dens, holes, or caves. Fleas are not known to parasitize flying lemurs, primates (the so-called human flea, *Puler irritans,* normally attacks pigs; the burrowing flea, *Tunga penetrans,* burrows under toenails of humans; the oriental rat flea. *Xenopsylla cheopis,* and others also bite humans among other hosts), aardvarks, elephants, or most horses and their allies. Birds are also hosts, mostly seabirds and perchingbirds, especially swallows.

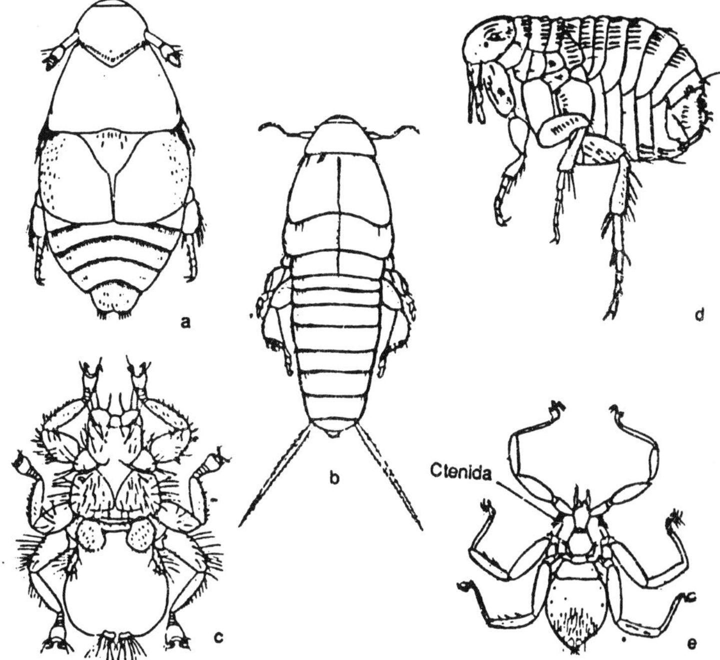

Fig. 12.2. Vark us parasites of vertebrates: a, beaver beetle, Platypsylia cactoris; b, parasitic dermapteran, Henunfmerus talpoidies; c, streblid bat fly, 4 oriental rat flies, Xnopsyllia cheopis, a vector of plague, e, nycterbiid bat fly.

(2) Ectoparasitic beetles of the Scarabaeidae include three genera; adults of *Uroxys gorgon* and *Trichillum barchyporum* live in the hair of the South American sloth, *Bradypus* and the larvae live in dung. Adults of species of *Onthophagus* (= *Macropocopris*) cling to hairs near the anus of kangaroos and wallabies, feeding on secretions and

'awaiting the host's reces, which are buried by the adult beetle as food for the larvae.

Intermittent, or temporary, ectoparasites are as follows :

(1) Cimicidae (Hemiptera) or bedbugs, including 74 species, suck blood from hosts in all stages but visit the host only to feed. Twelve genera feed only on bats, nine genera feed only on birds, and only *Cimex* has some species feeding on bats and others or birds. *Cimex hemipteras* and C. *lectularius* are human bedbugs which also feed on chicken and bats.

(2) Triatominae or conenose bugs, including about 80 species in the New World and 7 in the Old World, feed on blood in all stages and parasites lizards, birds, and mammals, including humans. The Arixeniina (Dermaptera) are sometimes regarded as ectoparasites because of their association with bat caves and bats, but actual parasitism has not been demonstrated.

Crawling ectoparasites exhibit a number of convergent adaptations associated with life in the hair or feathers of their hosts. In most species both sexes are parasitic an adults are more or less flattened. Siphonaptera are laterally compressed for movement through hair, the others are dorsoventrally flattened and manage equally well in hair or feathers. The adults of continuous parasites and Siphonaptera have generally reduced sensory and locomotory apparatus

(1) short antennae;

(2) compound eyes small in some absent in Hemimerina, Polyctenidae, some Anoplura, and Siphonaptera;

(3) ocelli absent in endopterygote parasites, except some Hippoboscidae;

(4) wings absent except in some Hippoboscidae and Streblidae, in which the wings may be well-developed, vestigal, or absents;

(5) legs usually short (Nycteribiidae have log legs), more or less stout, and with well-developed tarsal claws which may be single on mammalian hosts;

(6) stiff, posteriroly directed hairs or scales, or a comblike ctenidium in Polyctenidae, Siphonaptera. Nycteribiidae and *Platypsylla;* and

(7) where the life history is known, mating and oviposition usually takes place on or near the host. The temporary parasites Cimicidae and Triatominae move to and from their hosts. Consequently they retain long antennae, compound eyes, an waling legs. The Cimicidae are

otherwise apterous, and have small eyes and no ocelli. The Triatominae are winged and have well-developed eyes and ocelli.

Flying Ectoparasites

All flying ectoparasites are intermittent parasites in the adult stage. Three groups are

(1) *Mandibulate biting flies,* which include species of Psychodidae (or sand flies). Ceratopogonidae (or biting midges). Simuliidae (or blackflies), Culicidae (or mosquitoes), Tabanidae (or horse- and deerflies), and Rhagionidae (or snipe flies). The parasites are females with bloodsucking mouthparts which include functional mandibles. A wide range of vertebrate hosts, both warm- and cold-blooded, are attacked. Humans are attacked by species in all families. Blood meals are usually required for egg maturation and production. Some species are able to produce the first clutch of eggs without a blood meal and are termed *autogenous*. The immature stages are free-living and usually aquatic or associated with damp soil. Larvae of tabanids and snipe flies are also found in dry litter or soil.

(2) *Bloodsucking muscoid flies* include about 20 species of *Glossina,* or tsetse flies; *Stomoxys calcitrans,* or stable flies and their allies; *Haematobia irritans,* or hornfly; *H. exigua,* the buffalo fly of Australia; and *H. stimulans* the cattle fly of Europe. Both sexes suck blood. Most feed on mammals, but *Glossina palpalis* prefers crocodiles and monitor lizards. Humans are bitten by various species of *Glossina* and *Stomoxys*. Larvae of *Stomoxys* and *Haematobia* live in manure, but *Glossina is* viviparous, producing a mature larva which soon pupates.

(3) *Eye gnats* include species of *Hippelates* and certain muscids throughout the world.

(4) *Eye moths* include 23 species of Noctuidae. Pyralidae, and Geometridae in Africa and Southeast Asia. These insects are attracted to the eyes of mammals and humans, where they feed on lachrymal andd sebaceous secretions, pus, and sometimes blood. The fruit-puncturing noctuid moth, *Calpe eustrigata,* is able to puncture mammalian skin and take blood.

Myiasis-producing Diptera

Larvae of certain flies infest the bodies of animals, including humans, and produce a disease called myiasis. Pupation is usually in the soil, and adults of the flies are free-living. Four groups of myiasis flies have been recognized;

(1) *Enteric myiasis and pseudomyiasis.* producing larvae of many

species, mostly in Muscidae, Calliphoridae, Sarcophagidae, and Gasterophilidae, have been reported in ali- mentary canals of vertebrates. Pseudomyasis involves fly larvae which are ingested accidentally or enter through the anus and are able to survive for varying periods in the intestine. The larvae may eat the ingested food of the host or less frequently, tissues of the intestine. True enteric myiasis is created by the larvae of horse bot flies *Gasterophilus,* which live attached to the stomach wall while feeding on the wall and absorbing the host's food.

(2) *Facultative myiasis*—producing larvae of many species, mostly in Muscidae, Calliphoridae, and Sarcophagidae, normally live as scavengers in dead animals. Adult females, attracted by odours of decompositions, lay eggs on the carcass. Wounds or deep, soiled wool of sheep also attract ovipositing females. The resulting larvae become parasites in such places on living animals.

(3) *Obligatory myiasis*—producing larvae regularly infest living hosts. The primary screwworm. *Cochliomyia hominivorax* (Calliphoridae), of the New World; Old World screwworm, *Chrysomyia bezziana* and *Wohlfahrtia magnifica,* also of the Old World, enter the body at wounds or through mucous membranes and create local infestations. Larvae of the cattle grubs, *Hypoderma lineatum* and *H bovis* penetrate unbroken skin, migrate extensively in the host's body, and return to complete their development in tumours beneath the skin before dropping from the host to pupate. The female of the human bot, *Dennatobia hominis,* attaches her eggs to another fly, such as a blowfly, tabanid, or mosquito. While the carrier insect is feeding, the bot larva hatches and drops to the host's skin, burrows into the subcutaneous tissues, an remains in the same place until fully fed. Mature larvae drop from the host to pupate. These flies occur in Latin America.

(4) *Blood-sucking larvae* that are temporary feeders include the Congo floor maggot, *Auchmeromyia luteola,* which lives in huts and feeds on sleeping persons; and various species of *Protocalliphora* (Calliphoridae) in the Old and New Worlds which feed on nestling. birds.

EVOLUTION OF INSECT PARASITES

When insects first appeared abundantly as fossils in the Carboniferous Period, cold-blooded vertebrates were already present. Amphibians appeared earlier near the end of the Devonian Period, but the first reptiles coincide with the sudden appearance of insects.

In the Upper Carboniferous and Permian Periods, reptiles diversified and replaced amphibians as the mcst abundant land vertebrates. By the close of the Paleozoic Era, insects and vertebrates had coexisted for more than 80 million years, or nearly, the first quarter of their association. Did parasites evolve during the first radiation of insects?

Recalling that piercing-sucking mouthparts were well-developed at this time in both the Paleoptera and Neoptera, it would be surprising if some insects so equipped did not occasionally suck vertebrate blood or become regular parasites. Yet not Paleozoic insects are believed to be parasites, and parasites are almost entirely lacking among the more primitive insects which survive today; Apterygota, Paleoptera, and Orthopteroidea (except the Suborder Hemimerina, which probably evolved much later). Furthermore, no major groups of modern. insect parasites, are exclusively adapted to cold-blooded vertebrates, but some, such as sand flies, do attack lizards, snakes and toads. To answer our question, we must conclude that no positive evidence exists of early insect parasitism. The possibility remains, of course, that parasites of the first vertebrates perished with the progressive extinction of their hosts and left no record. In contrast, other arthropods, such as mites and ticks, did evolve specialized parasites of cold-blooded vertebrates. The Phylum Pentastomida or Linguatulida are sometimes considered arthropods. These are internal parasites of snakes, crocodiles, birds and mammals.

In the Mesozoic Era the reptiles deminated the land by virtue of their numbers and variety, plus the immense size of some species. The separate reptilian lineages leading to the mammals and to the birds are now thought to have been warm-blooded as early as the Permian and to have evoked insulating coats of hair or feathers during the Mesozoic. True mammals are recorded from the Triassic Period. If the Jurassic *Archaeopteryx* is considered really a dinosaur, then the first birds are known in the Cretaceous Period. Insects of the Mesozoic, therefore, had cold and warm-blooded reptiles, mammals, and birds and potential hosts. In this era we would expect definite evidence or inferences of parasitism, and we are not disappointed.

The earliest parasites were probably the mandibulate biting flies. The reasoning behind this inference is as follows; Four major subgroups of Diptera are recorded in the Triassic, indicating that considerable evolution had already occurred before the fossils were preserved. Among the modem flies in these groups, only the bloodsucking parasites and closely allied predators retain functional mandibles. Piercing mouthparts, with only slight modifications, serve either parasitic or predatory functions. Sucking blood, whether of insects or vertebrates, must have been the original habit or was developed early in the history of the Diptera before mandibles were lost in the main lineages. Flying ectoparasites are not dependent on the host's body covering for shelter. Biting flies today are noted for their broad spectrum of hosts, including cold-blooded vertebrates. Thus, the Diptera could have arisen in the Permian as the first parasites of vertebrates and could later have expanded their choice of hosts to include warm-blooded vertebrates. The latter offer additional cues for host finding, such as warmth, water vapor, and increased carbon dioxide from the higher metabolism. Carbon dioxide is a common attractant for parasites of mammals.

Some of the major groups of crawling ectoparasites also could have evolved at this time after some vertebrates acquired a coat of hair , or feathers. In contrast to the skin of cold-blooded vertebrates, this covering provides a uniformly warm, humid environment with something to clasp while the host is in motion, an protection against the host's efforts to rid itself of small passengers. When coupled with the nest-making habit of terrestrial vertebrates, the stage was set for repeated, independent evolution of crawling ectoparasites. Most of these probably evolved from insects that lived in the host's nest or den as scavengers or as predators on other insects. The scavengers probably crawled on the host and fed on hair, feathers, skin debris, or secretions. Later they could take blood from wounds made by their biting. This is probably the origin for most of the continuous and transitory crawling ectoparasites listed above. Bedbugs and conenose bugs probably arose from a predatory ancestor because the closest relatives of each are predators. The Siphonaptera are believed to have evolved first on hairy hosts, because the laterally compressed body seems suited for passage through a pelt. The ancestor was probably a mecopteran which lived in nests of vertebrates as a scavenger and became parasitic in the adult stage. Fleas retain the scavenging habit in the larval stage. Fossil Mecoptera are well represented in the Permian, and what may be fossil fleas have been described from the Lower Cretaceous.

The origins of the Phthiraptera are most difficult to unravel. The ancestor was doubtless a scavenging insect related to the Psocoptera. These insects commonly occur in or near the nests of vertebrates and freely crawl on the bodies of captive reptiles. Once the insects became flightless, continuous parasites, and dependent on their hosts, their evolution was strongly influenced by the evolution and habits of their hosts. Transfer among host individuals of the same species can occur when the hosts accidentally contact each other, copulate, or care for their young. Rare instances of phoresy are known, in which lice attach to flying insects and are possibly transported to other hosts. Opportunities to transfer to new species of hosts are presented when the normal host is killed and the lice seek the warmth of the vertebrate predator -or when cuckoo birds lay their eggs in the nests of other species. Host specificity, however, is highly developed in the lice. In fact, only rarely are lice species on two or more hosts that are not closely related phylogenctically. Yet the evolution of the higher categories of lice remains clouded. Both suborders of biting lice, Amblycera and Ischnocera, have bird and mammalian hosts, indicating that host transfer did occur at times in the past. Possibly the first hosts were warm-blooded reptiles whose extinction leaves the early history of lice unknown. The Rhyncho- phthirina and Anoplura, both exclusively on mammals, are though to have evolved from the Ischnocera.

Other parasites that are closely associated with certain birds or mammals probably evolved in the Tertiary Period, when these vertebrates became dominant. Bats, for example, are exclusive hosts for Nycteribiidae, Streblidae, Polyctenidae, and many Cimicidae, including the most primitive species *Primcimex cavemis*. The first bat fossils are from the Lower Eocene Epoch, and this would seem to be the earliest origin for this peculiar assemblage of parasites. Several circumstances favour bats as hosts, including the resting of bats in sheltered caves, the accumulations of guano that attract insect scavengers and their predators, and the inability of bats to groom themselves. Bats are oddly not now hosts for Phthiraptera, but possibly lice were displaced by other parasites at an earlier geologic time. Competition is apparently keen among individuals of several parasitic species on a single host. The nature of the competition is not well studied, but ordinarily one species predominates or excludes others from certain areas on the host or excludes them entirely from the host's body. this may provide an explanation for the curious absences of certain parasites from major vertebrate groups which are suitable hosts for other parasites.

Many insects seek moisture and proteinaceous substances such as mucus from the skin surfaces of vertebrates. The eye gnats and eye moths undoubtedly evolved their association with vertebrates in this manner. The sponging labella of muscoid flies is constructed for ingesting superficial fluids. One can easily imagine that the bloodsucking muscoids evolved from sweat- and mucus-seeking flies. As the labella was progressively sharpened and a rasping device developed at the tip, the flies were able to create wounds while taking moisture. Thus the bloodsucking habit was required independently by a second group of flies, probably long after the evolution of mandibulate biting flies. Their later appearance is inferred not only because the muscoids are advanced phylogenetically, but. also because the hosts are mainly perrisodactyls and artiodactyls which date from the Lower Eocene.

Even within the bloodsucking muscoids, there is evidence that the evolution of a piercing labella occurred more than once. The tsetse flies, *Glossina,* resemble the stable flies, *Stomoxys,* but Pollock has shown that tsetse flies actually are closer to Gasterophilidae and Hippoboscidae.. The mouthparts of the tsetse must have evolved convergently to resemble those of *Stomoxys. Glossina* is found as a fossil in the Florrisant shales of Colorado, which date back to the Oligocene Epoch. Apparently the flies became extinct in North America with the extinction of their hosts, and survive now only in Africa.

A recent event gives insight into the evolution of myiasisproducing Diptera. Blowflies are normally scavengers as larvae on dead animals and animal wastes. Several circumstances in Australia led to the rapid evolution of parasitic behaviour by the sheep blowfly,*Lucilia cuprina.* As a part of a range management plan, rabbits were killed in massive quantities. Large populations of flies were produced from the dead rabbits. Poisons used to kill rabbits and and dingos also killed carrion birds, which ordinarily reduce maggot populations by tearing open the carcasses. At the same time, sheep breeders developed animals with thick wool on wrinkled skin and with increased oily content. Bacteria thrive in deep folds where the oily wool is soiled and moist with seat. The increasingly abundant blowflies began to lay their eggs in such areas. When the larvae bore into the sheep's flesh, a myiasis is created which may lead to death of the host.

PREDATION BY INSECTIVOROUS VERTEBRATES

Insects are a regular part of the diet of many vertebrates; freshwater fish, amphibians, reptiles, birds, and small mammals, including bats. Even humans are known to vary their diet with insects. The predatory effectiveness of these insectivores is enhanced by one of the following or a combination of (1) physical agility; (2) keen senses of hararing, smell, taste, and/or vision (including colour perception by some fish, some reptiles, most birds, and primates); (3) hunting strategies; and

(4) the capacity to learn from experience. Insects are subject to predation in aquatic, terrestrial, and aerial habitats, during both day and night. To survive, exposed insects have evolved special patterns of colouration, behaviour, and defensive properties to take advantage of what the predator cannot detect, cannot capture, or will not eat.

The protective strategies in each case have evolved and are maintained by selection pressures from one or more kinds of insectivores in a given area. It follows that a widespread insect species may be attacked by different combinations of predators at different stages of its life, in different seasons, at different times of day, and accordingly may vary in response over its geographic range. In spite of the unique circumstances surrounding each instance of protective colouration and behaviour, certain strategies recur again and again in different insect taxa. This is because within each dominant group of predators (e.g., birds) the habits, learning ability, and senses are so much alike that closely similar strategies to escape capture are evolved convergently *by* insects. These convergences provide some of the best opportunities to study natural selection in action. Much speculation has been made, but too few instances of the protective strategies have been analyzed with critical experiments.

For our discussion, we first divide insect prey into those that are *palatable* (edible or acceptable) to a given kind of predator and those that are *unpalatable* (inedible or rejected). This distinction must be made with qualifications. Some individual insects will be relatively more or less palatable than others, and individual predators will vary in accepting prey depending on hunger and previous experience. Hard or spiny bodies, sticky secretions, stings, stinging hairs, and distasteful or toxic chemicals are defenses that tend to render an insect unpalatable. Even a low frequency of unpalatable individuals however, will be an advantage favoured by selection in the prey population. Unfortunately we do not know the palatability of most insects relative to their main predators, but observations indicate that most species of insects are edible be a wide variety of insectivores.

Palatable Insects

It is assumed that relatively palatable species evolve either an effective means of *escape,* or a disguise, or both. Two kinds of disguises are common: (1) *camouflage,* or *concealing colouration,* to avoid detection, and (2) *Batesian mimicry* or an unpalatable species to avoid attack. Batesian mimicry will be discussed later.

Escape by jumping or flying is often aided by colouration that diverts the predator's strike or attention. *Eyespots* may be of two main types: (1) small, dark spots, with or without a light mark simulating a reflection from the "eye"; and (2) large sports with concentric rings depicting a coloured iris and dark pupil marked with a reflected highlight. The first are thought to imitate an insect's eye, and the second are unmistakable representations of a terrestrial vertebrate's eye. The small eyespots may be situated at the posterior end of the insect in conjunction with antennalike processes, to imitate a head. Examples are hairstreak butterflies, which have tails that resemble antennae on the caudal part of their wings, and, at the bases of the tails, spots that resemble eyes. When perched, the butterfly moves its wings to wiggle the false antennae. The presumably directs a predator's attention to the wrong end of the body and permits the insect to escape in the opposite direction. Small spots near the outer wing margin of other butterflies, such as the satyrs, presumably attract the bird's peck away from the vital body and give the insect a chance to free itself. Evidence that such butterflies do escape is provided by collected specimens that have notched margins or V-shaped bill marks on their wings.

Larger eyespots have been shown to frighten vertebrate predators. Cryptically coloured insects may hide eyespots and suddenly display them when contacted by a predator. The nymhphalid butterfly *Caligo* and the lo moth, *Automeris,* have conspicuous eyspots. Unexpected displays of bright *flash colours* are similarly designed to startle enemies at the moment of escape. Underwing moths, *Catocala,* have conspicuous red or yellow bands on the hind wings. The colours are suddenly revealed and visible during the moth's erratic flight, but abruptly disappear when the moth alights and resumes a cryptic posture.

Insects with concealing colouration are overlooked by predators unless the predator learns to seek them. A low density of the insect or insects with similar protective strategies therefore prevents accidental detection and reinforcement of the predator's search image. The colouration may be one or a combination of the following; (1) *colour and pattern resemblance or cryptic colouration* such that the insect either closely matches the background against which it is seen, or resembles an inanimate object; (2) *obliterative shading* in which the rounded shape of the insect, such as a caterpillar, is obscured by having the illuminated surface of the body more darkly pigmented and the shaded surface lighter in colour; (3) *shadow elimination* by checkered borders or marginal fringes of hairs which reduce the contrast along shaded edges next to the substrate, and (4) *disruptive colouration of* contrasting patterns and colours to alter the perception *of* the true body outline or contour. These patterns are usually accompanied by one or a combination of special behavioural traits in which the insect — (1) selects an appropriate background and orients its body in a definite position relative to the background; (2) adopts a special posture to eliminate shadows or more closely resemble the object imitated; (3) rests motionless even when closely approached; and (4) escapes quickly, silently and erratically.

Concealing colouration is the rule among palatable insects exposed to diurnal, visually hunting predators. Aquatic nymphs and larvae may be complexly patterned to resemble aquatic vegetation, detritus, or the variegated gravels or other substrates of the bottom of the body of water. Immature and adult insects that inhabit plants, whether as predators or herbivores, are often green or coloured or scuptured to resemble leaves, stems, or bark. The larger insects of litter, soil, sand, or gravel may closely match their surroundings. The colour patterns are usually characteristic of the instar, not changing rapidly or in the manner of chameleons by physiological processes. The walkingstick, *Carausius* (Phasmatidae), however, does become darker or paler depending on various stimuli.

Industrial Melanism

The best-documented study of the evolution of concealing colouration concerns *industrial melanism, i.e.,* the evolution of dark or melanic populations of insects in industrially polluted areas. Prior to the Industrial Revolution in England, trunks of trees such as oak were naturally light in colour and often encrusted with light-coloured lichens. Resting against this background, the pepper moth. *Biston betularia, is* virtually invisible. With the development of smokeproducing industries in the latter half of the eighteenth century, soot accumulated on vegetation in the areas surrounding and downwind from the factories. Lichens were killed and the bark of trees was stained black. The light, or *typical,* form of the pepper moth was conspicuous against this darkened background. In 1848 a dark, or melanic, form of the moth, called *carbon aria,* was first recorded at Manchester in the polluted district. At that time the melanic form probably was not more than 1 per cent of the population, but 1898 it was estimated to be 95 per cent.

Melanic forms of over a 100 of the 780 species of larger moths in England have also increased in frequency during the last 130 years.

Such dark forms of moths are becoming evident elsewhere in industrial areas throughout the world's Temperate Zone, including North America. Industrial melanics are not known in tropical regions, possibly because the heat-absorbing dark colour is a disadvantage in warmer regions. The melanics are always members of species that are concealing coloured. They rest during the day on such objects as lichen-encrusted bark, rocks, or fallen logs. In the majority of species, the switch from predominantly light forms to dark forms does not involve intermediate shades and is usually controlled genetically by a single dominant gene.

Kettlewell carefully investigated various explanations for the rapid spread of the *carbonaria* form of the pepper moth. Mutagenic effects of the pollutants were discounted by experiments; the melanic forms must arise in population by normal, low rates of mutation. Except where the melancis are favoured by selection, the frequency remains quite low. In certain unpolluted environments such as heavily shaded forests, melanic forms of moths may increase in frequency because they are less visible when flying. In industrially blackened areas, the resting melanic forms are less visible to insectivorous birds. Observations in the field and experiments verified that birds of several species selectively eat the conspicuous form (*typica* against, dark trunks in polluted districts and *carbonaria* against light trunks-in unpolluted districts) and overlook the concealed forms. The rate of spread of melanics in polluted areas can be accounted for by predation alone. Analysis of other possible advantages, such as superior larval vigour in polluted areas, remains inconclusive. Thus in a relatively brief period, the cryptic patterns of many species of moths over wide areas shifted to a dark, patternless design as a result of bird predation in polluted areas. It now seems that this dynamic relationship is a sensitive monitor of pollution. With improved pollution controls now in England, nonmelanic moths are reappearing in districts where only melanic forms occur.

Unpalatable Insects

The colouration and behaviour of unpalatable species contrast strikingly with those of cryptic palatable species. The strategy there is twofold: (1) to create an unpleasant, but not lethal, ordeal for the vertebrate predator by means of poisonous or nauseous secretions, repulsive odours, effective stings or bites, or spiny surfaces; and (2) to be easily recognizable so that an experienced predator probably will not attack again. Unpalatable species usually have *aposematic*, or *warning*, colouration and behaviour, including one or more of the following; (a) bold, simple patterns of contrasting black and red, orange or yellow which are highly visible to vertebrates with colour vision and which also contrast against the predominantly green colour of the landscape (green is the complementary colour of red); (b) gregarious behaviour that leads to local, dense aggregations; (c) free exposure when walking or resting, and slow, conspicuous flight in full view of predators; (d) characteristic movements, sounds, or smells that warn against attack; and when attacked, (e) only sluggish efforts to escape, repulsive taste and a durable body permitting survival without fatal injury. For example when disturbed, caterpillars of Papilionidae release defensive odours from brightly coloured osmeteria.

A naive predator has ample opportunity to sample an aposematic species and, even without colour vision, has a number of cues by which to remember the experience. Bird predators are also known to learn vicariously by witnessing another predator's response. Learning can be reinforced by merely seeing an aposematic insect again without touching it. Not all the cues may be necessary to elicit an avoidance reaction. It is not known to what extent a predator's response includes some innate avoidance of aposematic colours or behaviour. In any event, the sensory and learning abilities or relatively long-lived vertebrate predators have allowed aposematic species to evolve. Furthermore, evidence exists that experienced predators may generalize their learning to avoid similar species after experience with only one. Aposematic colouration is oddly missing among most insects the alive in water, even though some fish are known to have colour vision and learning ability.

Mimicry

This last aspect of vertebrate psychology would give some advantage to insects that are in the process of evolving aposematic colouration and behaviour but have not acquired the full set of advertising characteristics. The predator's ability to generalize (or failure to discriminate) is also the basis for the evolution of two types of mimicry; (1) *Miillerian mimicry,* named for Fritz Miller involving two or more unpalatable and aposematic species; and (2) the previously mentioned *Batesian mimicry,* named for Henry W. Bates, involving one or more unpalatable species that serve as models and one or more palatable species that mimic the model's colouration and behaviour. The mutual resemblance of Mnllerian mimics confers protection on all members of the association in a given area. Because all are unpalatable, and predators can generalize, the resemblance among the species need not be exact, although it is often astonishingly precise. Naive predators presuamably attempt to eat mimics in proportion to the relative abundance of each species, and each species suffers fewer losses in the process of educating predators when several mimics are

Fig. 12.3. Multiple mimicry: a, monarch butterfly, Danaus plcx ppus; b, queen butterfly, Danaus gilippus; c, viceroy butterfly, L.imenitis archippus. See text for explanation.

together. Examples are found among the Neotropical butterflies, especially the genus *Heliconius* and the nymphalid Subfamily Ithomiinae;. the monarch and queen butterflies netwinged beetles and certain other insects and the convergent similarity of many ants, wasps and bees, the females of which are equipped with stings.

Batesian mimics are avoided by predators familiar with the unpalatable model. An argument can be made that the populations of mimics must remain less than the model's population. Otherwise a naive predator will be more likely to eat palatable mimics. Generally, Batesian mimics are rarer than their models (in some, only the female is the mimic), but recent studies show that unpalatable models may confer protection even when outnumbered. Apparently tasting a model is truly a memorable experience for the predator ! The resemblance of Batesian mimics to their models is often quite close. Examples include Neotropical moths and katydids that resemble wasps; the syrphid flies and other insects that resemble wasps and bees; and long-horned beetles (Cerambycidae) and moths that resemble lycid beetles. In some cases, however, the model and mimic share only a general resemblance, as in the viceroy butterfly mimic and monarch model.

Batesian mimicry may be though of as involving coevoutionary intractions similar to those occurring in host-parasite complexes. The mimic, of course, plays the role of the parasite. Its strategy is to take advantage of the model without destroying it. The model gains nothing -and faces the danger of a *"credibility gap"* developing in its potential predators. For at some point, if the mimics get too common, most predators will associate only pleasant experiences with the aposematic pattern of the model. Such a development, of course, ruins the game for both model and mimic, since a conspicuous pattern now means *"tastes good"* to the local insectivores. One would expect that the model should evolve a pattern different from that of the mimic at a maximum rate, everything else being equal. It is to the mimic's advantage to maintain a maximum of resemblance to the model, until that critical point mentioned above is reached. Then the advantage becomes a disadvantage–the mimic is conspicuously patterned, but predators now associate that pattern with tastefulness. As a result, selection would tend to move the mimic away from the model into a more cryptic pattern. It is not inconceivable that imperfect resemblances, such as that of the monarch and viceroy butterflies, often attributed to mimicry in the process of being perfected, are quite the opposite. They may represent mimics moving away from the model of mimics in an equilibrium situation between perfect mimicry and cryptic colouration.

In all cases it obviously is of advantage to the Batesian mimic to become distasteful if it can do so without sacrificing too much physiologically. In butterflies, at least, it appears that the usual source of noxious compounds is plant biochemicals, so that food-plant relationships must play a large role in the evolutionary dynamics of any given situation. A butterfly has several different routes to distastefulness open to it. If it eats a food plant which does not produce an appropriate compound, it may switch food plants. If it is feeding on a plant with an appropriate compound or its precursors, the butterfly may evolve the ability to use the compound or synthesize a noxious compound from precursors. Finally, the food plant of the butterfly may evolve and appropriate compound, which then may be picked up by the butterfly. In the latter case the mimetic butterfly would be involved in a complex of "selection races" involving the model, the food plant, and predators. As the food plant becomes more and more toxic, the butterfly must find ways' of "breaking even" by avoiding posioning or "winning" by turning the posion to its own advantage. Predators may simultaneously be undergoing selection for ability to discriminate between model and mimic, and for "resistance" to the noxious properties of the model. Of course, the presence or strength of such selection will depend on many variables. For instance, in some cases butterflies in a single population may make up such a small proportion of the targets of a single predator that selective influence on the predator will be negligible.

On careful analysis of mimetic associations, the distinction between lerian and Batesian becomes more difficult to make. Lincoln P. Brower and his associates have studied the mimetic relationships of the monarch butterfly, *Danaus plexippus* (Nymphalidae) and queen butterfly, *Danaus gilippus*. The larval food plants of both species are milkweeds, mostly in the genus *Asclepias*. Two species of milweeds in the Southeastern United States, *A. curassavica* and *A. humistrata,* contain cardiac glycosides. These chemical compounds cause vomiting or, in larger amounts, death to birds and cattle. In Costa Rica, cattle' learn to avoid eating *A. curassavica;* hence the plant is protected. Monarch larvae feed on these milkweeds and acquire various amounts of cardiac glycosides, which are retained in the body of the adult butterfly. Insectivorous birds vomit after eating a sufficiently toxic adult monarch and will avoid pursuing other monarchs when sighted. Thus, not only are emetic monarchs (those that cause vomiting) effectively unpalatable and aposematic, but also the larvae on the poisonous milkweed are undisturbed by grazing cattle. -

Not all milkweeds, however contain enough cardiac glycosides to cause emesis, and some lack the drugs altogether. Monarchs reared on these plants are palatable in laboratory tests with naive birds, but are rejected by birds previously fed emetic monarchs. The natural population of monarchs in an area may include both palatable and unpalatable individuals, yet the predators learn to avoid most of both types. Even as low as 25 per centt unpalatable monarchs theoretically will gain protection for 75 per cent of the population. Brower has called this kind of intraspecific *relationship automimicry*. The same concept would apply, for example, to aposematic male bees and wasp that lack the stings of the females.

The queen butterfly also feeds on toxic milkweeds and resembles the monarch. Where they occur together, they are usually considered Mulerian mimics. In Trinidad, however, Brower found both monarch and queen larvae feeding on both poisonous and nonpoisonous species of milkweed. Adult monarchs were 65 per cent emetic, but only 15 per cent of queen adults were emetic. The mimetic relationships here include automimicry between palatable and unpalatable members of each species, Batesian mimicry between palatable members of one species and unpalatable members of the other, and Mullerian mimicry between unpalatable members of both species.

In many ways mimetic assemblages make ideal subjects for the study of coevolution—as has been amply demonstrated by the Browers,

Phillip Sheppard, and others. A great deal is understood about them, and yet many questions remain to be answered. For instance, detailed studies of supposed Mullerian complexes are needed to solve a variety of problem. One would expect, for example, that the various members of the complex would have different effects on predators, since they presumably are , picking up poisons form different sources. As an example, one Mulerian butterfly complex consists of a *Lycorea* species (Danainae), presumably feeding on Asclepidadaceae or Apocynaceae, several ithomiines on Solanaceae, two *Heliconius* (Nymphalinae) on Passifloraceae, and *a Perrhybris* (Pieridae) with an unknown food plant. Ideally or course, each member of the complex would give strong and similar reinforcement to all local predators, so that multivalent noxiousness might evolve in varies members. It would be particularly interesting if, biochemical mimicry could be detected in some of these organisms, i.e., two quite different chemical compounds obviously selected to give similar effects in the same predator. Rothschild has suggested that this occurs with defensive odours.

Although it is clear that, in general, Batesian complexes should evolve toward Miillerian complexes, the fate of Miillerian complexes is less obvious. It would probably be unwise to think of them as stable "end points" of evolutionary sequences. If this were the case, one might picture all the diurnal Lepidoptera (and perhaps many other herbivores and small predators) in an area eventually being recruited into one large complex. It would really save the memories of the birds, but the birds would not have to remember for long because they would starve to death. Obviously, the larger a Mullerian complex gets, and the more similar the defenses of its members become, the more "profit" accrues to a predator which devises a way of consuming the Mill llerian mimics. Thus a large selective premium is placed on a strong stomach, and one would expect predators evolving rapidly to deal with the entire complex. If this happens, the advantages of belonging to the Mi llerian complex are reduced, and one might expect it to break up.

13

INSECTS AND MAN

In the present study we shall focus on those insects that Man describes, in his economically minded way, as beneficial or harmful, though it should be appreciated from the outset that these constitute only a very small fraction of the total number of species. Further, it must also be realized that the ecological principles that govern the interactions between insects and Man are no different from those between insects and any other living species, even though Man with his modern technology can modify considerably the nature of these interactions. Of an estimated 3 million species of insects, probably not more than about 15,000 (0.5%) interact, directly or indirectly, with Man. Perhaps some 30000 species constitute pests that, either alone or in conjunction with microorganisms, cause significant damage or death to Man, agricultural products, and manufactured goods. In the United States alone, for example, it is estimated that harmful insects annually do about 5 billion dollars' worth of damage. On the other hand, according to Horror *et al.*, the value of benefits derived from insects each year amounts to more than 7 billion dollars. That insects do more good than harm probably would some as a surprise to lay persons whose familiarity with insects is normally limited to mosquitoes, houseflies, cockroaches, various garden pests, etc., and to farmers who must protect their livestock and crops against a variety of pests. If asked to prepare a list of useful insects, many people most likely would not get farther than the honeybee and, perhaps, the silkmoth, and would entirely overlook the enormous number of species that act as pollinating agents or prey on harmful insects which might otherwise reach pest proportions.

Man has long recognized the importance of insects in his wellbeing. Insects and/or their products have been eaten by Man for thousands of years. Production of silk from silkworm pupae has been carried out for almost 5000 years. Locust swarms which originally may have been an important seasonal food for Man, took on new significance as he became a farmer rather than a hunter. However, except for the honeybee and silkworm, whose management is relatively simple and labour-intensive, until recently. Man neither desired nor was able, due to his lack of basic knowledge as well as of technology, to attempt large-scale modification of the environment of insects, either to increase the number of beneficial insects or to decrease the number of those designated as pests. Several features of Man's recent evolution have made such attempts imperative. These include a massive increase in human population, a trend toward urbanization, increased geographic move- ment of people and agricultural products, and associated with the need to feed more people, a trend toward monoculture as an agricultural practice.

The relatively crowded conditions of urban areas enable insects parasitic on humans both to locate a host (frequently a prerequisite to reproduction) and to transfer between host. individuals. Thus, urbanization facilitates the spread of insect-borne human diseases such as typhus, plague, and malaria whose spectacular effects on human population are well-documented. For example, in the sixth century A. D., plague was responsible for the death of about 50% of the population in the Roman Empire, and *"Black Death"* killed a similar proportion of England's population in the mid-1300s. An increasing need to produce more and cheaper food led, through agricultural mechanization, to the practice of monoculture, the growing of a crop over the same large area of land for many years consecutively. However, two faults of monoculture are (1) the ecosystem is simplified, and (2) as the crop plant is frequently graminaceous (a member of the grass family, including wheat, barley, oats, rice and corn), the ecosystem is artificially maintained at an early stage of ecological succession. By simplifying the ecosystem. Man encourages the buildup of populations of the insects that compete with him for the food being grown. Further, as the competing insects are primary consumers, that is, near the start of the food chain, they typically have a high reproductive rate and short generation time. In other words, populations of such species have the potential to increase at a rapid rate.

A massive increase in Man's geographic movements and a concomitant increase in trade, led to the transplantation of a number of species, both plant and animal, into areas previously unoccupied by them. Some of these were able to establish themselves and, in the absence of normal regulators of population (especially predators); increased rapidly in number and became important pests. Sometimes, as Man colonized new areas, some of the cultivated plants he introduced proved to be an excellent food for species of insects endemic to these areas. For example, the Colorado beetle', *Leptinotarsa decemlineata,* was originally restricted to the southern'Rockey Mountains and fed on wild Solanaceae. With the introduction of the potato by settlers, the beetle had an alternate, more easily accessible source of food, as a result of which both the abundance and distribution of the beetle increased and the species became an important pest. Likewise, , the apple maggot, *Regulates pomonella,* apparently fed on hawthorn until apples were introduced into the eastern United States.

BENEFICIAL INSECTS

Insects may benefit Man in various ways, both directly and indirectly. The most obvious of the beneficial species are those whose products are commercially valuable. Considerably more important, however, are the insects that pollinate crop plants. Other beneficial insects are those which are used as food, in biological control of pest insects and plants, and in research. For some of these useful species, Man modifies their environment in order to increase their distribution and abundance so that he may gain the benefits.

Insects of Commerciall Importance

The best-known insects that fall in this category are the honeybee (*Apis melifera*), silkworm (*Bombyx mori*), and lac insect (*Laccifer lacca*). The honeybee originally occupied the African continent, most of Europe (except the northern part), and western Asia, and within this area the usefulness of its products, honey and beeswax, has been known for many thousands of years. Though the discovery of sugar in Cane (in India, about 500 B. C.) and in beet led to a decline in the importance of honey, it is nevertheless still a very valuable product.

Bee management was probably first practiced by the ancient. Egyptians. Honeybees were brought to North America by colonists in the early 1600s, and today honey and beeswax production is a multimillion dollar industry. Good bee management aims to maintain a honeybee colony under optimum conditions for maximum honey and wax production. Management details vary according to the climate and customs of different geographical areas but may include (1) moving hives to locations where nectar-producing plants are plentiful; (2) artificial feeding of newly established, spring colonies with sugar - syrup in order to build up colony size in time for the summer nectar flow; (3) checking that the queen is laying well and, if not, replacing her; (4) checking and treating colonies for diseases such as foulbrood and nosema; and (5) increasing the size of a hive as the colony develops, in order to prevent swarming.

Silk production has been commercially important for about 4700 years. The industry originated in East Asia and spread into Europe after eggs were smuggled from China to Italy in the sixth century A. D. The development of cheap synthetic fibers has had a severely deleterious effect on the silk industry which is labour-intensive, making production costs high. Nevertheless, the annual world production is about 30-35 million kilograms.

The lac insect is a scale insect endemic to India and southeast Asia that secretes about itself a coating of lac, which may before than 1 cm thick. The twigs on which the insects rest are collected and either used to spread the insects to new areas or ground up and heated in order to separate the lac. The lac is a component of shellac, though its importance has declined considerably with the development of synthetic materials.

Insects as Pollinators

An intimate, mutualistic relationship has evolved between many species of insects and plants, in which plants produce nectar and pollen for use by insects, while the latter provide a transport system to ensure effective cross-pollination. Though some crop plants are wind-pollinated, for example, graminaceous species, a large number, including fruits, vegetables, and field crops such as clovers, rape, and sunflower, require the service of insects. In addition, ornamental flowers are almost all insect- pollinated. The best-known, though by no means the only, important insect pollinator is the honeybee, and it is standard practice in parts of the world for fruit and vegetables growers either to set up their own beehives in their orchards and fields or to contract this job out to beekeepers in the vicinity. Indeed, it is apparent that under such conditions the value of the bee as a pollinator may be 15 to 20 times its value as a honey producer. Certainly, the presence of bees in orchards, alfalfa fields, etc., may result in a three- or fourfold increase in the yield of fruit or seed. Borror et al. estimate the annual value of insect-pollinated crops to be about 6 billion dollars.

Insects of Biological Control

It is only relatively recently that Man has gained an appreciation of the importance of insects in the regulation of populations of potentially harmful insects and plants. In many instances, this appreciation was gained only when, as a result of Man's own activities, the natural regulators were absent, a situation which was rapidly exploited by these organisms whose status was soon elevated to that of pest. In the first three examples given below, none of the organisms is a pest in its country of origin due to the occurrence there of carious insect regulators. The discovery of these regulators, followed by their successful culture and release in the area where the pest occurs, constitutes biological control.

Probably the best-known examples of anintroduced plant pest are the prickly pear cacti (*Opuntia spp.*) taken into Australia as ornamental plants by early settlers. Once established, the plants spread rapidly so that by 1925 some 60 million acesof and were infested, mostly in Queensland and New South Wales. Surveys in both North and South America, where *Opuntia spp.* are endemic, revealed about 150 species of cactus-eating insects, of which about 50 were judged to have biological control potential and were subsequently sent to Australia for culture and trials. Larvae of one species, *Cactoblastis cactorum,* a moth, brought in from Argentina in January 1925, proved to have the required qualities and within 10 years had virtually destroyed the cacti. Perhaps the most remarkable feature of this success story is that only 2750 *Cactoblastis* larvae were brought to Australia, of which only 1070 became adults. From these, however, more than 100,000 eggs were produced, and in February- March of 4926 more than 2.2d million eggs were released in the field !

Additional releases, and redistribution of almost 400 million fieldproduced eggs until the end of 1929, ensured the project's success.

The classical example of an insect brought under biological control is the cottony-cushion scale, *Icerya purchasi,* which was introduced into California, probably from Australia, in the 1860s. within 20 years, the scale had virtually destroyed the recently established, citrusfruit industry in Southern California. As a result of correspondence between American and Australian entomologists and of a visit to Australia by and American entomologist, Albert Koebele, two insect species were introduced into the United States as biological control agents for the scale. The first, in 1887, *was Cryptochaetum iceryae, a* parasitic fly, about which little is heard, though DeBach considers that it had excellent potential for control of the scale had it alone been imported. However, the abilities of this species appear to have been largely ignored with the discovery by Koebele of the vedalia beetle. *Vedalia cardinalis,* feeding .on the scale. In total, only 514 vedalia were brought into the United States, between November 1888 and March 1889 to be cultured on caged trees infested with scale. By the end of July 1889, the vedalia had reproduced to such an extent that one orchardist, on whose trees about 150 of the imported beetles had been placed for culture, reported having distributed 63,000 of their descendants since June 1 ! By 1890, the scale was virtually wiped out. Similar successes in controlling scale by means of vedalia or Cryptochaetum have been reported from more than 50 countries.

As a third example *of* an introduced pest being brought under control by biological agents, we may cite the winter moth, *Operophtera brumata,* which, though endemic to Europe and parts *of* Asia, was accidentally introduced into Nova Scotia in the 1930s. Its initial colonization was slow, and it did not reach economically significant proportions until the early 1950s, and by 1962 it had spread to Prince Edwared Island and New Brunswick. The larvae of the winter moth feed on the foliage of hardwoods such as oak and apple. Though more than 60 parasites of the winter moth are known in western Europe, only six of these were considered to be potential control agents and introduced into eastern Canada between 1955 and 1960. Only two of these, *Cyzenis albicans,* a tachinid, and *Agrypon flaveolatum,* an *ichneumonid,* became established, but between them they brought the moth under control by 1963. Embree notes that the two parasites are both compatible and supplementary to each other. When the density of moth larvae, is high, *C. albicans,* which is attracted to feeding damage caused by the larvae, is a more efficient parasite than *A. flaveolatum.* However, once in the vicinity of damage, it does not specifically seek out winter moth larvae. Thus, at lower density, it wastes eggs on nonsusceptiable defoliators such as caterpillars of the fall cankerworm. *Alsophila pometaria.* Hence, at low host densities, *A. flaveolatum is* more effective because it oviposits specifically on winter moth larvae.

The three examples described above indicate one method whereby the importance of biological control can be demonstrated, namely, by introduction of potential pests into areas where natural regulators are absent. Another way of demonstrating the same phenomenon is to destroy the natural regulators in the original habitat, which enables potential pests to undergo a population explosion. This has been achieved frequently through the use of nonselective insecticides such as DDT. For example, the use of DDT against the codling moth, *Carposcpsa pomonella,* in the walnut orchards of California, led to outbreaks of native frosted scale, *Lecanium pruinosum,* which was unaffected by DDT, whereas its main predator, an encyrtid, *Metaphycus californicus,* suffered high mortality. Another *Lecanium* scale, *L. coryli,* introduced from Europe in the 1600s is a potentially serious pest of apple orchards in Nova Scotia but is normally regulated by various natural parasitoids (especially the chalcidoids *Blastothrix sericea* and *Coccophagus sp.*) and predators (especially mirid bugs). Experimentally it was clearly demonstrated in the 1960*s* that application of DDT destroyed a large proportion of the *Blastothrix* and mirid population, and this was followed in the next 2 years by medium to heavy scale infestations. Recovery of the parasite and predators was rapid, however, and by the third year after spraying the scale population density had been reduced to its original value.

Insects as Food

In addition to the many predaceous which feed on other insects, many vertebrates are insectivorous to a variable degree. Some *of* these vertebrates, especially some freshwater fish and game birds, in turn, may be eaten by humans. In some areas *of* the world, insects "in season" routinely form part of the human diet. Locusts, termites, caterpillars, and grubs of various kinds are eaten in Africa; edible caterpillars are sold fresh or in cans in Mexico; and Australian aborigines are reported to eat roasted bugong moths (*Agrotis infusa*) Most North Americans and Europeans have not yet been educated to the delights (and nutritional value) of insects, and despite the efforts of authors such as Taylor and Carter to increase the popularity of insects as food, at present cans of edible insects are restricted to the gourmet counter of food stores.

Scavenging Insects

By their very habit the majority of soil-dwelling insects aree ignored by Man. Only those which adversely affect his well-being, for example, termites, wireworms and cutworms, normally "merit" his attention. When placed in perspective, however, it seems probable that the damage done by such pests is greatly outweighed by thebenefits which soil-dwelling insects as a group confer. The benefits include aeration, drainage and turnover of soil as a result of burrowing activity. Many species carry animal and plant material underground for nesting, feeding, and/or reproduction, which Metcalf*et. al.* compare to ploughing in a cover crop.

Many insects, including a large number of soil-dwelling species, are scavenger; that is, they feed on decaying animal or plant: tissues, including dung, and thus accelerate the return of elements to food chains. In addition, through their activity they may prevent use of the decaying material by other, pest insects, for example, flies. Perhaps of special, interest are the dung beetles, most species of which bury pieces of fresh dung for use as egg-laying sites. Generally, the beetles are sufficiently abundant that a pat of fresh dung may completely disappear within a few hours, thus reducing the number of dungbreeding flies that can locate it. Furthermore, the chances of fly eggs or larvae surviving within the dung are very low because the dung is ground into a fine paste as the beetles or their larvae feed. Likewise, the survival of the eggs of tapeworms, roundwarms, etc., present in the dung producer, is severely reduced by this activity.

In Australia, which has a large population of cattle (derived largely from animals taken in by early settlers), cow dung presents a serious problem because, until recently, the beetle species that normally dispose of this kind of dung were absent. (Australia does have dung beetles but these are specialized for dealing with the dung of kangaroos and other marsupials.) In addition to providing food for a massive number of fly larvae when freshly deposited, the dung, because of the dry climate, soon dries and then may remain unchanged for a considerable time. Rank herbage grows around each pad of dung, but this is not normally eaten by cattle. Thus, at any time, a considerable proportion of all grazing land (estimated at 20% or 6 million acres total) is not usable. In 1963, it was decided to initiate a programme of biological control of dung using various South African species of dung beetles. After extensive research, in 1967 the first beetles were released in northern Australia. Several species have become established and are spreading rapidly down the eastern side of Australia. In general, the beetles are doing an excellent job of "cleaning up," except for the cooler months when they are inactive. Additional species, which are active at lower temperatures are being tested so as to obtain year round dung removal.

Other Benefits of Insects

Their relatively simple food and other requirements, short generation time, and high fecundity enable many insects to be reared cheaply and easily under laboratory conditions and, consequently, make them valuable in teaching and research. The fruit fly, *Drosophila melonogaster,* with its array of mutants, is familiar to all who take an elementary genetics class, though it must also be appreciated that the insect continues to have an important role in advanced genetic research. Studies on other insects have provided us with much of our basic knowledge of animal and cell physiology, particularly in the areas of nutrition, metabolism, endocrinology, and neuromuscular physiology. Grain beetles are good subjects for the study of population ecology.

Many insects give us pleasure through their aesthetic value. Because of their beauty, certain groups, especially butterflies, moths, and beetles, are sometimes collected as a hobby. Some are embedded in clear materials from which jewelry, paperweights, bookends, place mats, etc., are made. Others are simply as models on which paintings and jewellery are based.

PEST INSECTS

Since man evolved, insects have fed on him, competed with him for food and other resources, and acted as vectors of microorganism, that cause diseases in man or the organisms of value to him. However, as was noted in the Introduction, the impact, of such insects increased considerably as the human population grew and became more urbanized. Urbanization presented easy opportunities for the dissemination of Man's insect parasites and the diseases they carry. Large-scale and long-term cultivation of the same crop over an area facilitated rapid population increases in certain plant-feeding species and the spread of plant diseases. Modern transportation, too, encourages the spread of pest insects and insect-borne diseases. Further, as described already, some of man's attempts at pest eradication have backfired, resulting in even greater economic damage.

Insects Affecting Man Directly

A large number of insect species may be external, or temporary internal, parasites of Man. Some of these are specific to Man, for example, the body louse (*Pediculus humanus*) and pubic louse (*Phthinus pubis*), but most have a variable number of alternate hosts which compounds the problem of their eradication. With rare exceptions; for example, some myiasis-causing flies, insect parasites are not fatal to humans. In large numbers, insect parasites may generally weaken their host, making him more susceptible to the attacks of disease-causing organisms. Or the parasites, as a result of feeding, may cause irritation or sores which may then become infected. But by far the greatest importance of insect parasites of man is their role as vectors of pathogenic microorganisms (including various "worms"). The pathogen is picked up when a parasitic insect feeds and may or may not go through specific stages of its life cycle in the insect. Bacteria and viruses are directly transmitted to new hosts, an insect serving as a mechanical vector, whereas for protozoa and worms (tapeworms and nematodes), an insect serves as an intermediate host in which an essential part of the parasites' life cycle occurs. In the latter arrangement the insect is known as a biological vector. A pathogen may reside (and multiply) in alternate vertebrate hosts which are immune to or only mildly infected by it. For example, the bacterium *Pasteurella pestis,* which causes bubonic plague (Black Death), is endemic in wild rodent populations. However, in domestic rats and humans, to which it is transmitted by certain fleas, it is highly pathogenic. Similarly, in South America, yellow fever virus, transmitted by mosquitoes, is found in monkeys though these are immune to it. Such alternate hosts are thus an important reservoir of disease.

Tranmission of human disease-causing microorganisms is not, however, entirely the domain of parasitic insects. Many insects, especially flies, may act as mechanical vectors, contaminating human food as they rest or defecate on it, with pathogens picked up during contact with feces or other organic waste. A third category of insects that directly affect man includes those which may bite or sting when accidental contact is made with them, for example, bees, wasps, ants, some caterpillars (with poisonous hairs on their dorsal surface), and blister beetles. Normally, the effect of the bite or sting is temporary and nothing more than skin irritation, swelling, or blister formation. Bee stings, however, may cause anaphylaxis or death in some sensitive individuals.

Pests of Domesticated Animals

A range of insect parasites may cause economically important levels of damage to domestic animals. The majority of these parasites are external and include bloodsucking flies (for example, mosquitoes, horseflies, deerflies, blackflies, and stable flies), biting and sucking lice and fleas. Other parasites are internal for part of their history, for example, bot-, warble, and screw-worm flies, which as larvae live

TABLE 13.1

EXAMPLES OF INSECTS WHICH SERVE AS VECTORS FOR DISEASES OF MAN AND DOMESTIC ANIMALS

Insect vector	*Pathogen*	*Disease*	*Host*	*Distribution*
ANOPLURA				
Pediculus humanus (body louse)	*Rickettsia prowazekii* (rickettsiah)	Epidemic typhus (Brills disease)	Man, rodents	Worldwide
	Pasteurella tularensis (bacterium)	Tularemia	Man, rodents.	N. America, Europe, the Orient
HEMIPTERA				
Rhodnius spp. (assassin bugs)	Trypanosoma cruzi (protozoan)	Chagas disease	Man, rodents	S. America, Central America, Mexico, Texas
DIPTERA				
Phelbotomus spp. (sand flies)	*Leishmania donovani* (protozoan)	Kala-azar (Dumdum fever) -	Man	Mediterranan region, Asia, S. America
	L tropica	Oriental sore	Man	Africa, Asia S. America
	L bruziliensis	Espundia	Man	S. America, Central America, N. Africa southern Asia
	(virus) (Sand fly fever)	Pappataci fever	Man	Mediterranean region, India, Sri Lanka
Anopheles spp.	*Plasmodium* vivax (protozoan)	Malaria	Man	Worldwide in tropical, subtropical, and temperate regions
	P. malariae	Malaria	Man	
	P. folciparum	Malaria	Man	

Insect vector	*Pathogen*	*Disease*	*Host*	*Distribution*
Aedes spp. (mosquitoes)	*(virus)*	Yellow fever	Man, monkeys, rodents	American and African tropics and subtropics
	(virus)	Dengue	Man	Worldwide in tropics and subtropics
	(virus)	Encephalitis	Man, horses	N. America, S. America, Europe, Asia
	Wucheria bancrofti (nematode)	Filariasis (Elephantiasis)	Man and subtropics	Worldwide in tropics
Culex spp. (mosquitoes)	(virus)	Dengue	Man	Worldwide in tropics and subtropics
	(virus)	Encephalitis	Man, horses	N. America, S. America, Europe, Asia
	Wucheria bancrofti (nematode)	Filariasis (Elephantiasis)	Man and subtropics	Worldwide in tropics
Tabanus spp. (horse flies)	*Bacillus anthracis* (bacterium)	Anthrax	Man, other animals	Worldwide
Chrysops spp. (deer flies)	*Posteurella tularensis* (bacterium)	Tularemia	Man, rodents	N. America, Europe, the Orient
	Loa loa (nematode)	Loiasis (Calabar swelling)	Man	Africa
Glossina spp. (tsetse flies)	*Trypanosoma rhodesiense* (protozoan)	Sleeping sickness	Man, other animals	Equotorial Africa
	T. gombiense	Sleeping sickness	Man, other animals	Equatorial Africa
	T. bnwei	Nagana	Cattle, wild ungulates	Equatorial Africa

Insect vector	*Pathogen*	*Disease*	*Host*	*Distribution*
SIPHONAPTERA				
Xenopsylla cheopsis (oriental rat flea)	*Pasteurella pestis* (bacterium)	Bubonic plague (Black Death)	Man, rodents	Worldwide
Xenopsylla spp.	*Rickettsia typhi* (rickettsian)	Endemic (murine) typhus	Man, rodents	Worldwide
Xenopsylla cheopsis	*Hymenolepis nana* (cestode)	*Tapeworm*	*Man*	*Europe and N America*
H. diminuta	Tapeworm (cestode)	Man	Worldwide	
Nosopsyllus fasciatus (northern rat flea)	*Pasteurella pestis* (bacterium)	Bubonic plague (Black Death)	Man, rodents	Worldwide
	Rickettsia typhi (rickettsian)	Endemic (murine) - typhus	Man, rodents	Worldwide
	Hymenolepis diminuta (cestode)	Tapeworm	Man	Worldwide
Ctenocephalides canis (dog flea)	*Dipylidium caninum* (cestode)	Tapeworm	Man, dogs, cats	Worldwide
	Hymenolepis nana (cestode)	Tapeworm	Man	Europe, N. America
Pulex irritans (human flea)	*Hymenolepis nana* (cestode)	Tapeworm	Man	Europe, N. America

TABLE 13.2

EXAMPLES OF PLANT DISEASES TRANSMITTED BY INSECTS

Disease	*Important hosts*	*Vectors*	*Distribution*
Viruses	Alfalfa mosaic	Alfalfa, tobacco, potato, beans, peas, celery, zinnia, petunia	Aphids (at least 16 spp.) incl. *Acynhosiphon primulae, A. solani, Aphis craccivora, A. fabae, A. gossypii Macrosiphum cuphorbiae, M. pisi Myzus ornatus, M. persicae, M. vialae*
	Barley yellow dwarf	Barley, oat, wheat, rye, wild and tame grasses	Numerous aphids incl. *Macrosiphum ganariwn, M. miscanthi, Myzus circumflexes, Rhopalosiphum padi, R maidis*
	Bean common mosaic	Beans	Aphids (at least 11 spp.) esp. *Aphis nunicis. Macrosiphum pisi, M. gi*
	Beet yellows	Sugarbeet, spinach	Aphids esp. *Aphis fabae, Myzus persicae*
Cauliflower mosaic	Cauliflower, cabbage, Chinese cabbage		Aphids esp. *Brevicoryne brassicae, Rhaopalosiphum pseudobrassicae, Myzus Persicae*
	Dahlia mosaic	Dahlia, zinnia, calendula	Aphids esp. *Myzus persicae, Aphis fabae, A. gossypii, Macrosiphum gi, Myzus Convolvuli*
	Lettuce mosaic	Lettuce, sweet pea, garden pea, endive, aster, zinnia	Aphids esp. *Myzus persicae, Aphis gossypii. Mocrosiphum euphorbiae*

Disease	Important hosts	Vectors	Distribution
	Pea mosaic	Garden pea, sweet pea, broadbean, lupin, clovers	Aphids: Acyrthosiphon pisi, Myzus persicae, Aphis fabae, A. ru nicis
	Potato virus Y	Potato, tobacco, tomato, petunia, dahlia	Aphids esp. Myzus persicae, M certus, M. ornotus, Macrosiphum cuphorbiae
	Soyabean mosaic	Soybean	Aphids incl. Myzus persicae, Macrosiphum pisi
	sugarcane mosaic	Sugarcane, corn, sorghum, other tame and wild grasses	Numerous aphids incl. Rhopalosiphwn maidis, Aphis gosspii, Schizaphis raminum, Myzus pers g
	Tomato spotted wilt	Tomato, tobacco, dahlia, pineapple	Thrips : Thrips tabaci. Frankliniella schultzeri, F. fuscq F., occidentalis
	Turnip yellow mosaic	Turnip, cauliflower, Chinese cabbage, kohlrabi, cabbage broccoli	Flea beetles (Phyllotreta spp.); Mustard beetle Grasshopper (*Leptophyes punctatissima, Chorthippus bicolor*); Earwig (*Forficula auricularia*
Mycoplasmas	Aster llows	Aster, celery, carrot, squash, cucumber, wheat, barley	Numerous leafhoppers incl. *Gyponana hasta*, *Scaphytopius acutus*, *S. irroratus*, *Macrosteles fascifrons*, *Paraphiepsius apertinus*, *Texannanus* (several species)

Disease	*Important hosts*	*Vectors*	*Distribution*
	Clover phyllody	Most clovers	Leafhoppers incl. Aphrodes albifrons, Macrosteles cristata m. fascifrons; M. viridig'iseus, Euscelis lineolatus E. plebeja
	Corn stunt	Corn	Leafhoppers esp. *Dalbulus* elimatus, D. maidis, *Grominella nigifrons*
Bacteria	Stewarts bacterial wilt	Corn	Corn flea beetle *(Chaetocneme pulicara);* toothed flea beetle (C. denticulata)
	Cucurbit wilt	Cucumber, muskmelon	Cucumber beetles (Diabrotica vittata, D. duodecimpunctata)
	Potato blacking	Potato	Seedcorn maggot (Hylemya cilicrura), H. trichodactyla
	Fire blight	90 spp. of orchard trees and ornamentals, esp. apple, pear, quince	Wide range of insect vectors, esp. bees, wasps, flies, ants, aphids
Fungi	Dutch elm disease	Elm	Elm bark beetles, esp. *Scolytus multistriatus, S. scolyucg Hylurgeopinus rufpes*
	Ergot	Cereals and other grasses	About 40 spp. of insects esp. flies, beetles, aphids

in the gut (horse bot). Other examples are given in the chapters that deal with the orders of insects. In addition to insects, other arthropods are also important livestock pests, for example, various mites and ticks. Generally the effect of such parasites is to cause a reduction in the health of the infected animal. In turn, this results in a loss of quality and/or quantity of meat, wool, hide, milk, etc., produced. When severely infected by parasites, an animal may eventually die.

Pests of Cultivated Plants

Damage to crops and other cultivated plants by insects is enormous and is valued at about 3 billion dollars annually in the United States. Damage is caused either directly by insects as they feed (by chewing or sucking) or oviposit, or by viral, bacterial, or fungal diseases, for which insects serve as vectors. Especially important as "direct damagers" of plants are Orthoptera, Lepidoptera, Coleoptera, and Hemiptera, and the reader should consult the chapters that deal with these orders for specific examples of such pests. Several hundred diseases of plants are known to be transmitted by insects including about 300 which are caused by viruses. Especially important in disease transmission are Hemiptera, particularly leafhoppers and aphids. Three aspects of the behaviour of these insects facilitate their role as disease vectors: (1) they make brief but frequent probes with their mouthparts into host plants; (2) as the population density reaches a critical level, winged migratory individuals are produced; and (3) in many species, winged females deposit a few progeny on each of many plants, from which new colonies develop. On the basis of their method of transmission and viability (persistence in the vector), viruses may be arranged in three categories. The nonpersistent (stylet-borne) viruses are those believed to be transmitted as contaminants of the mouthparts. Such viruses remain infective in a vector for only a very short time, usually an hour or less. Semipersistent viruses are carried in the anterior regions of the gut of a vector, where they may multiply to a certain extent Vectors do not normally remain infective after a molt, presumably because the viruses are lost when the foregut intima is shed. Persistent (circulative or circulative-propagative) viruses are those which, when acquired by a vector, pass through the midgut wall to the salivary glands from where they can infect new hosts. Such viruses may multiply within tissues of a vector which retains the ability to transmit the virus for a considerable time, in some instances for the rest of its life. Persistent viruses, in contrast to those in the first two categories, may be quite specific with respect to the vectors capable of transmitting them.

Insect Pests of Stored Products

Almost any stored material, whether of plant or animal origin, may be subject to attack by insects, especially species of Coleoptera (larvae and adults) and Lepidoptera (larvae only). Among the products that are frequently damaged are grains and their derivatives, beans, peas, nuts, fruit, meat, dairy products, leather, and woolen goods. In addition, wood and its products may be spoiled by termites or ants. Again the reader is referred to the appropriate chapters describing these groups for specific examples. Borror *et. al.* cite a figure of about 1 billion dollars for the estimated value of losses caused by pests of stored products. The nature of the damage caused by these pests varies. Pests of household goods, including clothes, furniture, and various grain-based foods, cause damage as a result of spoilage, for example, by tunneling through or defecation on/in their food. Grain and other seed pests eat economically valuable quantities of food.

Pest Control

On the basis of what has been told above, pests are organisms which damage, to an economically significant extent, man or his possessions or which in some other way are a source of "annoyance" to Man. Implicit in the above description are value judgments which may vary according to who is making them, as well as where and when they are being made. Nevertheless, in a given set of circumstances, there will be an economic injury threshold, measured in terms of a species' population density, above which it is desirable to take control measures that will reduce the species density. As the margin between economic injury threshold and actual population density widens, the desirability of control increases. Pest control is, then, essentially a sociological problem -a matter of economics, politics and psychology. A range of methods is available for the control of insect pests. Each of these methods, has its advantages and disadvantages and these must be balanced against each other in determining which method(s) is most appropriate in a given instance. Some of these methods are spectacular but short-term and will be appropriate, for example, where massive outbreaks of pests are relatively sudden, yet unpredictable and temporary. Others are more slowly acting but relatively permanent in effect, and may be used for pests that are more or less permanent but whose populations are relatively stable. Conway and Southwood have proposed that pests can be arranged in a spectrum according to their "ecological strategies" and that the principle (best) method of control is based on their position in the spectrum. At

TABLE 13.3.
Principal Control Methods in Relation to Ecological Strategies of Pests[A]

	r Pests	*Intermediate pests*	*k Pests*
Control method	*Pesticides* →	*Biological control*	
		←	*Cultural control*
		←	*Genetic control*
Examples (with Important features):	*Schistocerca gregaria* (desert locust) Fecundity/= 400 eggs Generation time = 1-2 months Migratory, defoliates many crops *Aphis fabae* (black bean aphid) Fecundity/= 100 eggs Generation time = 1-2 weeks Feeds on wide range of plants *Musca domestica* (housefly) Fecundity/ = 500 eggs Generation time = 2-3 weeks Feeds on organic waste *Agrotis psilon* (black cutworm) Fecundity/ = 1500 eggs Generation time = $1-1-\frac{1}{2}$ months Feeds on seedlings of most crops	(Most deciduous forest pests, fruit pest, and some vegetables pests) Generation time = 1-2 months External parasite of sheep	*Oryctes rhinoceros* (rhinoceros beetle) Fecundity/ = 50 eggs Generation time = 3-4 months Feeds on apical growing points of coconuts Glossina spp. (tsetse fly) Fecundity/= 10 eggs Generation time = 2-3 months Feeds on narrow range of hosts Carpocapsa pomonella (codling moth) Fecundity/ = 40 eggs Generation time = 2-6 months Larvae feed on apple and some other fruits Melophagus ovinus (sheep ked) Fecundity/ = 15 eggs

either end of the spectrum are the so-called "r *pest*" and *"K pests,"* respectively, with in between, the intermediate pests.

The *r* pests are characterized by their potentially high rates of population increase (due to the high fecundity and short generation time), well-developed powers of dispersal (migration) and ability to locate new food sources, and rather general food preferences. These features enable *r* pests to colonize temporarily suitable habitats, in which there is typically little interspecific competition for the resources available. Because *r* pests may occur in such large but unpredictable numbers and rapidly change their location, predators (of which there may be many) have relatively little effect on their population. Further, although like other organisms r pests are subject to disease, the latter is slow to take effect, by which time significant damage may have been done. Finally, because of their high reproductive potential, *r* pests are able to tolerate mass mortality and rapidly regenerate their original density. Hence, biological control, which is a relatively slow but long term method, is of little use against *r* pests. For such pests specific insecticides, which can be stored for application at short notice, continue to be the most important tool in their control. Included in the *r*-pest group are the *"classic"* pests; locusts, aphids, mosquitoes and houseflies.

On the other hand, *K* pests, have lower fecundity and longer generation time, poor ability to disperse, relatively specialized food preferences, and are found in habitats threat remain stable over long periods of time. Under natural conditions, insects with the features of K strategists seldom become pests. If, however, probably as a result of Man's activity, their niche is expanded (e.g., their food plant becomes an important crop), or if they can occupy a new niche (e.g., feeding on domestic cattle rather than wild ungulates) they may become a pest. Once established, such pests are often difficult to eradicate over the sort term, for example, through the use of insecticides. Insecticides are frequently not feasible tools because the K pests attack the fruit rather than the foliage of crop plants, or because the cost is prohibitive in view of the low density of the pest population. (In some instances, however, where even at low population density a pest may cause considerable damage, for example, codling moth on apple, insecticidal control may be profitable). Nor is biological control an appropriate method because *K* pests have few natural enemies, a feature probably related to their low density under natural conditions. For K pests, the best methods of control are those which disturb a pest's habitat, for example, the breeding of resistant strains of plant(s) or animals(s) attacked by it, and cultural practices.

The majority of pests are classified as intermediate pests in the Conway scheme because they exhibit a mixture of the features of *r* and K, pests. For some of these, with a relatively high reproductive potential, insecticidal control may be necessary under certain conditions, and conversely, for pests approaching the K end of the spectrum, cultural control sometimes may be adequate. However, the most important feature of intermediate pests is the relatively large number of natural enemies that they have. These enemies, under normal circumstances, are important regulators, of the pest population. In addition, intermediate pests are frequently foliage- or root-damaging pests, for example, spruce budworm and some scale insects, and, therefore, the economic injury threshold is reasonably high; that is, a fair amount of damage can be tolerated without economic loss. Hence, for these pests, biological control would appear to be the single most appropriate method of control, which can be supplemented as necessary with insecticidal and other methods. The latter is, in other words, an integrated control programme. With these general considerations in mind, it is now appropriate to consider in more detail the methods available for pest control.

Legal Control or Regulatory Control

It is based primarily on the old adage "Prevention is better than cure." Legal control is the enactment of legislation to prevent or control damage by insects. It includes, therefore, establishment of quarrantine stations at major ports of entry into an area. Usually the stations are located at international borders, though in some instances domestic quarantines are necessary, for example, when certain parts of a country are widely separated from the rest. At quarantine stations people and goods are inspected to prevent the accidental introduction of potential insect pests and plant and animal diseases. Prior to the introduction of quarantine legislation in the United. States early this century a number of insect species had been accidentally introduced and become established as plant pests, for example, the cottony-cushion scale quarantine has severely reduced the number of pest introductions. The Mediteranean fruit fly was successfully exterminated using insecticides following each of its invasions, though at a cost of several million dollars. However, the cereal leaf beetle is now established in several midwestern states and efforts must now be directed toward restricting its dispersal. Thus, another aspect of legal-control is the setting up of surveilance systems for monitoring the insect population in a given area so that, should an outbreak occur, it can be dealt with before it has a chance to spread. Such surveillance is an important duty of state/provincial entomologists, in cooperation with local agriculture representatives and crop and livestock producers. As an adjunct to quarantine, many countries (or areas within countries) have legislation that requires international or interstate shipments of animals or plants, or their products, to be certified as disease- or insects free by qualified personnel prior to shipment.

Another aspect of legal control, and one which is becoming increasingly important, is the licensing of insecticides and the establishment of (1) regulations regarding their use, and (2) monitoring systems to assess their total impact on the environment. In the United States the Environmental Protection Agency is responsible for assessing the effectiveness of pesticides, as well as their possible hazardous effects on humans, wildlife, and other organisms, including bees, other pollinating species, and beneficial parasitoids. As noted earlier, indiscriminate use of insecticides can result in greatly increased rather than decreased pest damage.

Chemical Control

Pest control by the use of chemicals either to kill or to repel insect is the oldest method. Fronk notes that sulfur was used by the Greeks against pests almost 3000 years ago and the Romans used asphalt fumes to rid their vineyards of insects pests. The Chinese used arsenic compounds against garden pests before 900 A. D., though arsenic was not used in the Western world until the second half of the seventeenth century. Until about 1940, insecticides belonged to two major categories, the "inorganics" and the "botanicals."' Among the inorganic insecticides are arsenic and its derivatives (arsenicals), including Paris green (cooper acetoarsenite), which was the first insecticide to be used on a large scale in the. United States - against Colorado potato beetle in 1865. Other inorganics include fluoride salts (developed at about the end of the nineteenth century, following realization that toxic residues were left by arsenicals), sulfur, borax, phosphorus, mercury salts, and tartar. These inorganic insecticides were typically sprayed on the pest's food plant or mixed with a suitable bait. In other words, all are "stomach poisons" that require infusion and absorption to be effective. Thus, they were unsatisfactory pesticides for sucking insects for which "contact poisons," absorbed through the integument or tracheal system are necessary. The "botanicals" are organic contact poisons produced by certain plants in which they serve as protectants against insects. The group includes (1) nicotine alkaloids, derived from certain species of *Nicotiana,* including *N. tabaca* (tobacco); (2) rotenoids extracted from the roots of derris (*Dens spp.*) and cube (*Lonchocarpus spp.*); and (3) pyrethroids, produced by plants in the genus *Pyrethnim.* The pyrethroids. When first available commercially, were an important group of insecticides for use in the home, as livestock sprays, and against stored-product, vegetable, or fruit pests, primarily because of their low toxicity to mammals. The great disadvantage or pyrethroids has been their photolable nature (instability in light) and the need, therefore, to reapply them frequently made them expensive to use. Thus, they were largely replaced by cheaper, synthetic insecticides in the 1940s, an important consequence of which is that very few insects (6 of 364 species with insecticide resistance of some type) are presently resistant to them. This feature, in conjunction with the recent synthesis'of photostable pyrethroids may lead to renewed importance for this group of compounds.

Though two synthetic organic insecticides had been commercially available prior to 1939 (dinitrophenols in Germany, first used in 1892; organic thicocyanates in the United States from 1932 on) it is generally acknowledged that this is the date at which the synthetic organic insecticide industry took off.. After several years of research for a better mothproofing compound, Muller, who worked for the Geigy company in Switzerland, discovered the value of DDT as an insecticide. In the next few years, production of DDT began at the company's plants in the United Kingdom and United States, although because of the second world war, knowledge of DDT was kept a closely guarded secret. In early 1944, DDT, was first used on a large scale, in a delousing programme in Naples where typhus had recently broken out. Some 1.3 million civilians were treated with DDT, and within 3 weeks the epidemic was controlled. Later that year the identity of the 'miracle cure' was revealed, and the world soon became convinced that with DDT pest insects would become a thing of the past. In 1948 Muller was awarded a Nobel prize, though, interestingly, the first example of insect resistance to DDT had been reported two years earlier ! Through the 1940s and into the 1950s, much research was carried out in Western Europe and the United States for other insecticides as effective as DDT. Three major groups of compounds emerged : (1) chlorinated hydrocarbons, such as DDT, lindane, chlordane, aldrin, dieldrin, endrin, and heptachlor; (2) organophosphates, like TEPP diazinon, dichlorvos, parathion, and malathion; and (3) carbamates, for example, sevin isolan and furadan.

The search for suitable synthetic insecticides continues today, though at a somewhat reduced rate because the profitability of such ventures for industrial concerns has greatly diminished, for a variety of interrelated reasons. The primary reasons are (1) the time and cost of producing and testing an insecticide, estimated at an average of 7 years and nor than 10 million dollars, with no guaranree of its final approval for use; (2) a general unwillingness of government agencies to grant approval for use of new insecticides following public outcry against the environmental hazards of such compounds; if approval is granted, it may restrict the use of an insecticide; and (3) the relatively short "life" of an insecticide due to its being no longer effective and/ or becoming an environmental hazard. As a result, some of the largest companies in the chemical industry have either considerably reduced or abandoned research into the development of new insecticides.

TABLE 13.4

NUMBER OF SPECIES INSECTS AND MITES IN WHICH RESISTANCE TO ONE OR MORE CHEMICALS HAS BEEN DOCUMENTED

Year	*Species*
1908	1
1928	5
1938	7
1948	14
1954	25
1957	76
1960	137
1963	157
1965	185
1967	224
1975	364b

As a result of the massive use of insecticides over the past 70 years, three major problems have arisen first, many insects and mites have developed resistance to one or more of the chemicals. *Quadraspidiotus pemicisus* takes credit for being the first recorded species to develop resistance to an insecticide in 1908, less than 30 years after use of the insecticide began. The housefly was the first species resistant to a synthetic insecticide, and by the end of 1975 the total had reached 364, of which 139 species are of medical or veterinary importance and 225 are agricultural pests. Depending on the method of resistance developed by a species against an insecticide, the species may also have resistance to other chemicals of the same group (class resistance) or even to chemicals of other groups (cross resistance). The development of resistance necessitates the use of ever-increasing doses of insecticide to achieve the same benefits, with a concomitant enhancement of the second and third problems described below, as well as increased cost to the user. Alternatively, the user may turn to newly developed insecticides though again, the cost will be high.

The second problem associated with insecticide use is one already mentioned, namely, the nonspecificity of action of these chemicals, with the result that nonficial as well as pect species are destroyed. As pest species typically can recover from insecticide application more rapidly than their natuial enemies (because of their greater reproductive

TABLE 13.5

NUMBER OF SPECIES OF ARTHROPODA WITH REPORTED CASES OF RESISTANCE TO PESTICIDES

	Pesticide group					*Nature of pest*		
	DDT	*Cyrlo- dienes*	*Orgao- Phosphates*	*Carba- mates*	*Other*	*Medical veterinary*	*Agri cultural*	*Total*
Acarina	21	10	32	6	13	10	33	43
Anoplura	5	3	2			5		5
Coleoptera	26	48	18	7	8		56	56
Dermaptera	1						1	1
Diptera	91	100	40	6	4	110	23	133
Ephemeroptera	2						2	2
Hemipt./Het.	4	12	3			4	10	14
Hemipt./Hom.	10	11	28	4	4		52	52
Hymenoptera	1	2						
Lepidoptera	31	32	22	12	4			
Mallophaga		2				2		2
Orthoptera	3	1		1		3		3
Siphonaptera	5	3	1.		5			5
Thysanoptera	3	2				5		5
Total	203	225	147	36	35	139	225	364

potential), they rebound with even greater force, necessitating additional insecticidal treatment and increasing costs to the user. The third problem, the potential health hazard of many of the synthetic insecticides to humans and wildlife, is of especial interest because it is based on a feature of the synthetics that was once considered highly beneficial, namely, their highly persistent nature. To the user this means that one or a few insecticide treatments will suffice for the entire season. For example, DDT is highly stable and only slowly degraded in the presence of sunlight and oxygen. Thus, a single spraying in a house or barn may remain effective up to a year, and even outdoor applications (on foliage) may be stable through an entire growing season. Unfortunately, this stability is retained following ingestion or absorption of DDT by living organisms. Thus, DDT tends to be stored in fatty tissue, due to its lipid solubility, and is concentrated as it is transferred from organism to organism in food webs. Recognition of the phenomenon of bioconcentration via food webs and observation of harmful effects of insecticides in the terminal members of food chains (especially predatory birds but not, so far, humans) led to enormous public outcry against insecticides. As a result, governments have been forced to examine carefully the balance between the benefits gained and the risks entailed in the use of insecticides, and where necessary enact legislation to protect human interest. One result of this was the banning in 1972 of DDT use in the United States, in all except a very few situations where benefits clearly outweighed risks.

Despite this rather gloomy picture, it must be strongly emphasized that synthetic insecticided have saved and will continue to save millions of human lives and billions of dollars worth of food and organic manufactured goods. They are still by far the principal method for control of insect pest, though there is a slowly growing realization among users that insecticides are probably more valuable when used selectively, in conjunction with other methods such as biological control, rather than in a "blanket" manner as in the past. This is associated with an appreciation that actual extermination of a pest is almost never achievable, or is even necessary in most situations; that is, a certain amount of pest damage can be tolerated without suffering economic loss. The chemicals discussed above operate on the principal of control through rapid death of (most) members of a pest population. Recently, however, great interest has been shown in other chemicals which, though widely different in nature, are collectively known as, insectistatics because they suppress insects growth and reproduction. They include (1) substances that inhibit chitin synthesis or tanning, rendering an insect more susceptible to microbial (especially fungal) infection or preventing normal activity because the muscles do not have a firm structural base; (2) antagonists ; or analogues of essential metabolites (e.g., essential amino acids and vitamins) whose effect is to prolong larval life and or retard egg production, frequently resulting in death; (3) insect growth regulators, substances with juvenile-hormone or ecdysonelike activity; and (4) sex attractants.

Some 600 compounds are known to *mimic juvenile hormone* to various degrees and in different species. Work on the possible use of IGRs in pest control is still largely at the stage of laboratory experi ment or small-scale field trial, though early results indicate considerable promise for IGRs against pests of some orders. Among the effects noted are (1) interefence with embryogenesis, followed by death, at IGR doses about 1000th the value of con- ventional ovicides; (2) abnormal development of the integument in post embryonic stages, leading to inability to molt properly and impaired sensory function (hence inability to locate food, mates, oviposition sites, etc.); (3) improper metamorphosis of internal organs or external genitalia, causing sterility and/or inability to mate; (4) interference with diapause, so that an insect becomes seasonally maladjusted, and (5) abnormal polymorphism in aphids. Despite the seemingly bright picture for IGRs at the present time, 'they might, if used indiscriminately, soon become subject to the same criticisms that have been leveled at conventional insecticides.

Another area of chemical control that holds considerable promise is the use of sex attractants. Considerable progress has been made in the elucidation of their structure and artificial synthesis. Though the substances exert their effect at extremely low concentrations, the high cost of manufacture and technical problems associated with their application presently prohibit large-scale use. However, it may be anticipated that pheromones may find the following uses in pest control; (1) estimation of population density (followed by treatment, if necessary, with a suitable control method); (2) attraction of pests into traps in which they are then killed; and (3) permeation of an environment with sex attractant, so that individuals are unable to locate mates.

BIOLOGICAL CONTROL

It is the regulation of pest populations by, natural enemies (parasites, predators and pathogens). It includes both naturally occurring control and control achieved as a result of Maid's augmentation of the natural enemy component. As in the history of chemical control, several early successes with biological control led some scientists to believe that this method might be the one to solve the world's pest problems. However, with an increase in knowledge of ecology, specifically predator-prey and host-parasite relationships, and in the length of the list of "failures" in biological control projects, this view has been markedly tempered. It is now realized that for some pest species, biological control will not work, and that for some others, biological control has been or will be a highly effective method. Between these two extremes, and forming the majority of pests, are those for which biological control will be an effective tool when used in conjunction with other methods of pest control, that is, as a component of integrated pest control. For many years, biological control was a "poor relation" to chemical control, even though several outstanding successes of biological control were recorded before the advent of synthetic insecticides. However, with the increasing appreciation of the problems caused by synthetic insecticides, biological control began to receive a greater share of the attention of applied entomologists, industrial concerns and government agencies. The importance of naturally occurring biological control must be emphasized. DeBach suggests that "Upon it rests our entire ability to successfully grow crops because without it, the potential pests would overwhelm us." He estimates that "99 per cent or more of potential pests (are) under natural biological control." However, by its very effect, namely, the prevention of species from becoming sufficiently populous to be designated as pests, it is easily overlooked. Only by very careful study of ecosystems in equilibrium or by disturbance of ecosystems can its value be appreciated. Two common (man-made) methods of ecosystem distruption are (1) transfer of a species from its original habitat where it is not a pest to a new habitat where, in the absence of natural enemies, it flourishes and becomes a pest, and (2) indiscriminate use of broad-spectrum insecticides which decimate both pest and natural enemy populations. As noted above, the pest normally recovers more rapidly than its predators or parasitoids and becomes even more destructive than before.

Man's first recorded attempts at biological control were made by the ancient Chinese who used predatory ants in their citrus orchards against caterpillars and boring beetles. This practice is still used in parts of Burma and perhaps China. In the eighteenth century, mynah birds imported from India were successfully used in the control of red locusts (*Nomadacris septemfasciata*) in Mauritius. However, full appreciation of the potential that insect parasitoids and predators might have as control agents developed only in the middle of the nineteenth century, following careful studies of the biology of such insects in the early 1800s. During the latter half of the nineteenth century, many well-known entomologists, both in Europe and North Amrica, studied biological control and extolled its virtues, though these were largely unheeded until cottony-cushion scale was spectacularly controlled by the vedalia beetle in 1888-1889. More or less concurrently, based on studies of insect diseases (especially those of the silkworm), several authorities, most notably Pasteur and an Amreican entomologist Le Conte, suggested that microorganisms might be used in the control of pest species. However, for reasons outlined below, successful biological control through the use of microorganisms has been achieved relatively infrequently.

Biological control, when successful, has several advantages over control through the use of insecticides. First, it is persistent; that is, once a control agent is established, it will exert a continuing influence on the population density of the pest. In part related to this, biological control is cheap because one application of the control agent is sufficient. Furthermore, the control agent is "ready-made" it does not have to go through an extended and costly phase of research and development, though determination of the most suitable controls agent(s) may take some time. As an example of the cheapness of biological control. DeBach notes that the cottony-cushion scale project in 1888-1890 cost less than 5000 dollars, yet it has saved the California citrusfruit industry millions of dollars each year since. Because of escalating costs of insecticides, biological control may be the only (or principal) method of pest control in underdeveloped countries. A third advantage is that biological control does not stimulate "genetic counterattack" by the pests. Fourth, it does not result in the growth to pest status of species that are economically unimportant. And finally, it is a method that does not endanger humans or wildlife through pollution of the environment. If biological control offers so many advantages over insecticides, why has it, in most instances, come only a distant second to these compounds in terms of usage? What are its disadvantages? Perhaps the main one is psychological because users like to see immediate results for their efforts. In biological control it may take sometime for a control agent to subdue a pest, by which time a user's patience (and profit margin) have worn thin, especially under the considerable and continuous advertising pressure of insecticide producers. Further, the new equilibrium density that a pest attains when controlled biologically is almost certainly higher than the density immediately after insecticide treatment, which again may be unsatisfactory so far as a user is concerned, especially if the crop being grown is of high unit value, for example, fresh fruit. Consumers, too, are involved here, since they have become accustomed to "blemish-free" produce and may not buy even slightly damaged-material.

Biological control has not always been successful, and proponents of insecticidal control (which include a significant number of applied entomologists as well as industrial concerns) have been quick to point this out. As a result many governments and universities have been loath to invest money and manpower in research on biological control. According to DeBach, had such research been possible, a number of major pests could have been controlled long before they were. In the few countries or states (most notably, California) where significant research effort has been put into biological control, the success rate for this method is high. In other words, in many instances, failure to control a pest by biological measures has stemmed from incomplete or poorly performed study of the pest and its predators or parasites, not from the unsuitability of biological control per se. The greatest success has been achieved through the use of insects, especially parasitoids, as control agents. According to DeBach biological control using insects as control agents had been attempted against 223 pest species throughout the world. Forty-two of these species were completely controlled; that is, their population densities were reduced, then permanently maintained, below the economic threshold, making insecticide treatment only rarely or never necessary. Substantial control was achieved over 48 species. Substantial control includes instances where the pest or crop is not of major importance, where control is only partial in some areas of infestation, and where occasional insecticide treatment is required. Another 30 species fall into the "partial control" category, where pest density was reduced but not consistently below the economic threshold, making regular, though less frequent, insecticidal treatment necessary. In short, some degree of success was achieved against more than one half of the species against which the method was used. Indeed, the total number of successful projects up to 1970 was 253 on a world basis, since some of the pests were controlled in several different countries.

Not surprisingly, in view of the *"unprofitability"* of successful biological control using insect agentss, industry has shown little interest in the method. Research and development in this area have been the domains of government and university scientists. Biological control using microorganisms (microbial control), specifically viruses, bacteria, protozoa, fungi, and nematodes has not met with an equivalent degree of success. This stems largely from the nature of the control agents, many of which are obligate pathogens, relatively labile (short-lived) outside the host, have poor powers of dispersal, and are active only in certain environmental conditions. Added to these problems, are technical difficulties that have hampered research in this area, especially the inability to mass-produce microorganisms on a year-round basis for laboratory study as well as field trials. This is slowly being overcome through the use of artificial insect diets, enabling cultures of the host insect to be maintained year-round and tissue culture. However, these methods are not, by and large, satisfactory for large-scale commercial production because of their labour-intensive nature and high costs. Another major technical problem that requires solution is the development of suitable protectants against sunlight to which most microorganisms are especially sensitive. The poor viability of most microorganisms outside their host means that; to be effective, *they* must be reintroduced at least on an annual basis, if not more frequently. In this regard they are of course, comparable with chemical insecticides, though they do not pose the same environmental hazards. The continuing need for reapplication of microbial agents has not gone unnoticed by industrial concerns, and a number of commercial preparations are now available or under development.

Four examples are known of microorganisms that exert a permanent regulatory effect on pest insects. These are *Bacillus popullae* and *B. lentimorbus,* which cause milky disease in the Japanese beetle, *Popillia japonica,* an important pest of lawn and other grasses in the United States; a nuclear polyhedrosis virus, accidentally introduced into Canada. in the early 1940s, which has kept populations of the European spruce sawfly (*Tiprion heryniae*) below the economic injury threshold for more than 30 years since the initial epizootic: and a nuclear polyhedrosis virus which exerts good control over the European pine sawfly (*Neodiprion sertifer*) in Canada.

Bacillus thuringiensis, which is pathogenic to a large number of Lepidoptera. As of 1981 it was the only microbial agent registered for use against crop, as well as forest and shade-tree, pests. The great advantage of B. thuringiensis, is that it can be cultured outside its hosts by fermentation and is therefore cheap to produce. The bacterium is short-lived, however, and several applications may be necessary each season. A number of viruses (especially, nuclear polyhedrosis viruses) have been developed for use against insect, especially lepidopteran, pests, though only a few of these have been registered for commercial use. Two major problems beset the use of viruses as icrobial control agents, their low viability in sunlight and their culture. Although in soil viruses may survive from season to season, when exposed to ultraviolet light, their half-life is usually less than 1 day. Even when additives which screen out ultraviolet light are added to the preparation, the half-life is only extended to a few days. As of 1985 all viruses used in field trials or available commercially were produced in living insects, the mass-rearing of which may be time-consuming and expensive. This difficulty may eventually be overcome through the use of tissue culture, though at the moment this method is also relatively costly.

TABLE 13.6

EXAMPLES OF SUCCESSFUL BIOLOGICAL CONTROL PROJECTS USING INSECTS AS CONTROL AGENTS

Pest	*Primary control agent and source*
Kerya purchasi (cottony-cushion scale)	*Vedalia cardinalis* (vedalia beetle) (Australia)
Perkinsiella saccharicida (sugarcane leafhopper)	*Paranagrus optabilis* (mymarid) (Australia)
	Cytorhinus mundulus (mind) (Australia)
Levauana irridescens (coconut moth) (Malaysia)	*Prychomyia remota* (tachinid)
Aleurocanthus wogiwni (citrus blackfly)	*Erednocerus series* (aphelinid) (Malaysia)
	Amitus hespeiidum (platygasterid)
	Prospaltella opulenta (aphelinid)
	P. clypealis

	(aphelinid) (India and Pakistan)
Planococcus kenyae	*Anagyrus kivuensis* (coffee mealybug) (encyrtid) (Uganda)
Pseudococcus citriculus (citriculus mealybug)	*Clausenia purpurea* (encyrtid) (Japan)
Dacus dorsalis (oriental fruit fly)	*Opius oophilus* (braconid) (Phillipines and Malaysia)
Lepidosaphes beekii (purple scale)	*Aphytis lepidosaphes* (eulophid) (China)
Antonina graminis (rhodesgrass scale)	*Neodusmetia sangwani* (encyrtid) (India)
Operophtera bnanata (winter moth)	*Cyzenis albicans* (tachinid) (Europe) *Agrypon laveolatum* (ichneumon) (Europe)
Chrysomphalus aonidum (Florida redscale)	*Aphytis holoxanthus* (eulophid) (Hong Kong)
Chrysomphalus dictyospenni (dictyospermum scale)	*Aphyds melinus* (eulophid) (California)
Nezara viridula (green vegetable bug)	*Trissolcus basalis* (scelionid) (Egypt and Pakistan) *T. basalis* and *Trichopoda pennispes var. pibpes*

	(tachinid) (Antigua and Monserrat)
Opuntia spp. (prickly pear cactus)	*Cactoblastis cactorum* (moth) (Argentina)
Hypericum perforatum (Klamath weed)	*Chrysolina quadrigemina* (chrysomelid beetle) (Australia)

It was a fungus (*Metarrhizium anisopliae*) that was the control agent in the first attempt at microbial control. Generally speaking, however, the potential of fungi as pest control agents has not been widely stgdied. Roberts suggests three reasons why workers may have been unwilling to commit themselves to such a study. First,. fungi appear to be unpredictable; that is, in some tests high infectivity of hosts was achieved, whereas in others the opposite occurred. Roberts considers this inconsistency to stem from inadequate information on the fungal requirements for infectivity. Second, because fungal

TABLE 13.7

Examples of Insect Pathogens Developed by Industry and Various Agencies

Group	Pathogen	Product name
Bacteria	*Bacillus lentimorbus*	Japidemic
	B. populliae	Doom
	B. sphaericus	-
	B. thuringiensis	Agritroi Bakthane L69 Bactospeine Bathurin Biospor 2802 Biotrol BTB Dendrobacillin Lntobakterinz HD-1 (Experimental) Parasporin Sporeine
	Thuricide	
Fungi	*Beauveria bassiana*	—

		Biotrol FBB
	Metarrhizium anisopliae	
Polyhedrosis Viruses	Heliothis	Biotrol VHZ Viron/H
	Neodiprion	Polyvircocide
	Prodenia	Biotrol VPO Biotrol VSE
	Trichoplusia	
		Biotrol VTN
Nematodes	*Neoaplectana carpocapsae* (DD-136)	Biotrol NCS

infections depend heavily on weather conditions, which cannot be controlled, the use of fungi as control agents was though to be impractical. However, it is the microclimate which is important, and this is amenable to modification under certain circumstances. Third, because some fungi that are pathogenic in insects are also known to affect vertebrates, the tendency has been to ignore the group as a whole on the grounds of safety. Nonetheless, fungi have some qualities that indicate potential as control agents, for example, many (even some which were once thought to be obligate parasites) can be cultured on artificial media, they may be highly virulent, and among different species a range of host specificity can be found, so that a species appropriate for a given control problem may be selected.

Very little work has been done on the possibility of using pathogenic protozoa in the biological control of insect pest, though some, especially species of Microsporidia, are probably important natural control agents. As with other microorganisms, a serious deterrent has been, the inability to culture the protozoa outside the host. However, using spores produced in mass-reared hosts, a number of *Nosema* spp. have been field tested with good results. For example, an extensive study is being undertaken in the United States by Henry and colleagues on the potential use of *N. locustae. N. acridophaga,* and *N. euneatum* as control agents against grasshoppers. Using *NN locustae* spores mixed with bran bait. Henry and co-workers obtained significant reductions in the grasshopper populations of experunental plots. However, the timing of spore application was found to be critical. Application too early in the season, that is, when grasshoppers were in the early larval instars, caused rapid and high mortality, with the result that too few spores were produced for infection of other grasshoppers. Conversely, application to older (adult) grasshoppers, while resulting in a high incidence of infection (most individuals were infected), caused little mortality because the grasshoppers were able to tolerate the protozoa. The best time of application appeared to be when the dominant, early summer species were in the third instar. Such applications caused the greatest initial mortality and highest infection in later populations.

Like protozoa, pathogenic nematodes have been little studied with regard to their potential as control agents, largely because of the difficulty of culturing them on artificial media. As of 1974 only two species of nematodes pathogenic in insects [*Neoaplectana glaseri* and *N. carpocapsae* (=*dutkyi*)] could be cultured outside their hos *Neoaplectana carpocapsae* appears to be a good candidate for a biological control agent. Its advantages, apart from ease of culture, include a high reproductive capacity, a potentially long-lived infective stage, and resistance of the infective stage to many insecticides (making it possible to use the nematode in conjunction with conventional chemical methods of pest control). Another possible advantage is its wide host range, which includes many pests, though this must be weighed against its detrimental effects on some beneficial insects. Its disadvantages include the need for a moist surface in order to migrate in search of a host and its sensitivity to high temperatures and desiccation.

Genetic Control

Methods for genetic control fall into two distinct categories: (1) those by which pests are rendered less capable of reproduction, and (2) those in which resistance is increased in the organism attacked by the pest. A variety of genetic methods are potentially applicable for regulation of a pest's reproductive capability. To date, however, only one of these, the sterile insect release method (SIRM), has been used on a full scale; the rest are either under examination in laboratories or in field trials or still at the theoretical stage. Knipling first proposed the idea of releasing sterile insects into wild populations of the pest so as to reduce total fecundity. Successive releases of sterile insects over a number of generations would lead, comulatively, to eradication of the pest. SIRM has been used with striking success against the screwworm fly (*Cochliomyia hominivorax*). Flies are mass-cultured and sterlized by irradiation. SIRM has also been used successfully against small, isolated population of other pests, for example, melon fly (*Dacus cucurbitae*) and Oriental fruit fly (*D. dorsalis*) *in* the Marian Islands.

Field tests have indicated that the method holds promise for the control of codling moth (*Carpocapsa pomonelia*) Mediterranean fruit fly (*Ceratitis capitata*) and Queensland, fruit fly (*D. tryoni*). The advantages of SIRM are its specificity, the permanency of its effect (though it may take several years to achieve this), and the fact that it does not pollute the environment. An important disadvantage is its limited applicability. It is not a very suitable method for species that mate frequently as the chances of successful (fertile) mating are increased. In this regard, it is worth nothing that the pests controlled by this method are mostly Diptera or Lepidoptera, in many species of which females mate only once or a very few times. Nor is it feasible to use SIRM on pests that appear sporadically or in high density, the latter would make it very difficult to achieve the necessary high ratio of sterile; wild males in the field. In addition, there are several technical problems related to the mass production of individuals all of the same sex. Presently, both males and females reared in culture are irradiated and released. Thus, irradiated females will compete with wild females for the males' attention, reducing the efficacy of the method. Two solutions have been proposed for this dilemma: (1) Incorporation of lethal sex-linked mutants into laboratory cultures. Such mutants might be, for example, temperature-sensitive, so that exposure of the population to a certain temperature would kill one sex, or sensitive to a particular insecticide. Thus, treatment of juvenile stages with the insecticide would leave only the resistant sex alive. (2) Chemosterilization of wild populations. This probably would be cheaper than mass-rearing followed by irradiation, though this would have to be weighed against the potential nonspecificity and pollution of the environment by the sterilant. The use of irradiation or chemosteilants to achieve sterility may not always be feasible due to health hazards, costs, etc., and a number of workers are now examining various methods of causing inherited sterility. This is sterility which results either from matings between genetically or cytoplasmically incompatible partners, with production of inviable zygotes, or because gametogenesis is abnormal in one or both sexes. The development of plant varieties capable of resisting attack by pests is a well-known method of pest control. Probably the classic example . of plant resistance is the resistance of wheat varieties to attack by the Hessian fly (*Mayetiola destructor*).

Basically, increased resistance can be achieved by introducing either physical or biochemical changes in plants. For example, wheat resistant to attack by wheat stem sawfly (*Cephus cinctus*) has solid rather than hollow stems; wheat grown in Michigan and resistant to cereal leaf beetle (*Oulema melanopus*) has "hairier" leaves than other varieties; resistance to Hessian fly is due to the presence of antibiotics in the plant tissues which cause the death of the larvae. Other examples of plants having varities resistant to pests are corn to the corn borer (*Ostrinia nubilalis*), and corn earworm (*Heliothis zea*); alfalfa to the pea aphid (*Atyrthosiphon pisum*); cabbage to the potato leafhopper (*Empossca fabae*), and beans to the Mexican bean beetle (*Epilachna varivestis*). All told, plant varieties resistant to more than 100 pest species are known. The advantages of using resistant varities include greater crop yield, relatively low cost of development, and absence of side effects (environmental damage, etc.). In addition, pests that feed on these plants may be more susceptible to disease, adverse weather cond:tons, and insecticides which can therefore be used in lesser amounts. Disadvantages include the length of time required to develop a resistant variety, ordinarily 10 to 15 years with crop plants and even longer with trees. Related to this,' an extensive programme of screening must be carried out to ensure that the varities are totally satisfactory. Thus, resistance may vary according to the form of the insect, for example, between apterous and winged aphids. Or increased resistance to one pest may result in decreased resistance to another. Another problem may be psychological, that is, to persuade a grower that a new variety is superior to the one previously used.

Cultural Control

Cultural control, the use of various agricultural practices to make a habitat less suitable for reproduction and/or survival of pests, is a long-established method of pest control. Cultural control aims, therefore, to reduce rather than eradicate pest populations and is typically used in conjunction with other control methods. However, in some instances, cultural practices alone may effect almost complete control of pest, as occurs with the tobacco hornworm (*Manduca sexta*) and the Pink bollworm (*Pectinophora gosypiella*). The agricultural practices used either may have a direct effect on the pest or may act indirectly by stimulating population buildup of a pest's predators or parasites, or by making plants more tolerant of pest attack. An essential prerequisite for effective cultural control is detailed knowledge of a pest's life history so that its most susceptible stages can be determined. Important agricultural practices include (1) crop rotation to prevent buildup of pest populations: (2) planting or harvesting out of 'phase with a pest's injurious stage(s), which is especially important against species that have a limited period of infestation or for plants with a short period of susceptibility, (3) use of trap crops on which a pest will concentrate, making its subsequent destruction easy; (4) soil preparation, so as to bury or expose a pest, or increase the crop's strength so that it can more easily tolerate a pest: and (5) clean culture, the removal, destruction, or ploughing under of crop remains, in or under which pests may hibernate.

Integrated Control

It is "a pest population management system that utilizes all suitable techniques either to reduce pest populations and maintain them at levels below those causing economic injury, or to so manipulate the populations that they are prevented from causing such injury'. The techniques employed must be compatible and the system must be flexible to accommodate changes in an ecosystem. It is an approach to pest control that arose, of necessity, with the realization that, for almost all pests, existing methods either individually wee not capable of exerting permanent control gave rise to harmful side effects, or created, by their very use, new past problems. Integrated control is not a new concept. It was not in most instances given serious consideration until the use of insecticides alone had increased to the point at which an entire crop-growing operation became unprofitable. As has been noted on previous occasions, a major fault of pesticide use has been its indiscriminate nature. Insecticides were not used only as necessary (a decision based on pest population density) but on a regular basis as a form of *`preventive medicine"* or *"insurance."* This approach to the use of pesticides, referred to by Doutt and Smith as "the pesticide syndrome," led rapidly to the development of resistance in the pests against which it was aimed, to the use of larger dose or of different insecticides, to a rise to pest status of previously innocuous species, and ultimately to greatly elevated costs and decreased profits.

The primary step toward integrated control is collation of as much information as possible about the agroecosystem being studied, the more information that is available, the closer an integrated control programme will, come to providing maximum returns from the investment of time, effort, and money. In many early integrated control projects, relatively little information was available on which to base integrated control projects, relatively little information was available on which to base integrated control programmes, and these were developed largely by intuition, despite which they were remarkably successful. Nowadays the considerably greater body of information generally available is stored in computers for use in constructing and testing mathematical models of the agroecosystem. Once developed, such models can be used to examine the effects of varying one or more of the factors that influence the population density of a pest and, therefore, to determine the optimum method of reducing and maintaining this density below the economic injury threshold.

Some of the important questions to be answered in an integrated control programme might be as follows : (1) What is the economic injury threshold? It has been observed frequently that insecticide users were maintaining pest .population density at levels much below the economic injury threshold, increasing their operational costs in both the short and the long term. (2) What are the best parasitoids and predators to use and how might their abundance be increased? (3) What are the best insecticides to use, when should they be applied, and what are suitable doses? To answer this question requires consideration of the specificity of action, potential side effects, and stability of the insecticides. (4) Are suitable cultural procedures available? (5) Are resistant strains of the crop available? It will be apparent from these questions that pest management is interdisciplinary in nature and may require collaboration between experts in widely different areas, for example, economists, statisticians, meterorologists, plant breeders, entomologists, chemists and toxicologists. Many examples of pest management might be cited, that differ in complexity, geographic location, and crop pest being controlled. In its simplest form, pest management involves only one method of control and, strictly speaking, cannot be described as "integrated control." Thus, biological control is entirely satisfactory for control of sugarcane pests. More often, two or more control methods are employed. For example, at the height of the pesticide syndrome, apple growers in Nova Scotia used a battery of fungicides and insecticides against apple pests. Far from achieving the desired effects, this led to even greater problems. By about 1950 earlier pests such as codling moth (*Carpocapsa ponionella*), eye-spotted bud moth (*Spilonota ocellana*), and oyster-shell scale (*Lepidosaphes ulmi*) had become even more serious, and other species, for example, European red mite (*Panonychus ulmi*) and fruit-tree leafroller (*Archips argyrospilus*) had become pests due to destruction of their natural enemies. The need to reduce the escalating costs of this programme stimulated intensive study of apple orchard ecology, including the effects of pesticides on the natural enemy complex. The outcome of this work was the development of an integrated control programme which utilized fewer but more specific insecticides (as well as different fungicides, some of which had killed some natural enemies) and allowed for recovery of many of the natural enemies. By 1955 the mite and scale insect had practically disappeared, and the density of the eye-spotted bud moth had fallen significantly.

As a final example, the integrated control programme for cotton pests in the San Joaquin Valley. California will be outlined. The usual picture emerges. After extensive use of organochlorine insecticides, followed by organophosphates and carbamates, there was a population resurgence and an increase in resistance of the two major pests, the corn earworm (*Heliothis zea*) and a mirid bug (*Lygus hesperus*), as well as outbreaks of secondary pests such as cabbage looper (*Trichoplusia ni*), beet armyworm (*Spodoptera exigua*), salt-marsh caterpillar (*Estigmene acraea*), and spider mites (Tetranychidae). Early in the development of the integrated programme, it was realized that no reliably established economic injury thresholds existed for either of the major pests and that, for *Lygus*, time of insecticide application was critical. For *Lygus*, it was determined that the generally accepted injury threshold of 10 bugs 50 net sweeps was invalid; rather, the major period of importance was June 1 to July 20 and only if the density exceeded 10 bugs/50 net sweeps in this period should insecticides be applied. After July 20, *Lygus* densities of 20 or more bugs/50 net sweeps would not affect the quantity or quality of cotton produced, provided that the plants had flowered normally in June and early July.

It was noted that corn earworms seldom became pests except in fields treated for *Lygus* outbreaks where the corn earworms natural enemies (the bugs *Geocoris pallens* and *Nabis mericoferus* and the lacewing. *Ghrysopa camea*) were destroyed by insecticide. With the new threshold for economic injury due to *Lygus*, tied in with the plant's seasonal development, he use of insecticides was reduced, especially after late July, and the earworms' natural enemies survived. Further reduction in insecticide usage came about with the raising of the economic injury threshold for corn earworms from 4 earworms/plant to 15 *treatable earworms* (first and second instar larvae)/plant. This arose, in part, from realization that larvae often feed on surplus buds, flowers, and small bolls that are not picked.

Cultural control is also used to reduce the effects of *Lygus* on the cotton crop. *Lygus* prefers alfalfa (*Medicago sativa*) to cotton and will remain on the former plant when given a choice. Traditionally, however, alfalfa fields are solid cut provoking mass migration of *Lygus* into adjacent cotton fields. Alfalfa growers are now being persuaded to practice strip cutting to prevent such migration, though the method is not widely adopted. Probably a better technique is for cotton growers to plant strips of alfalfa through their cotton fields, on which *Lygus* will concentrate. Another cultural method that may become commercially feasible is the use of food sprays in attempts to prolong the seasonal effectiveness of natural enemies whose populations frequently decline after midseason. For example, in experimental plots adult *Chrysopa* were attracted to the food sprays and produced more eggs, resulting in significantly less injury to plants by corn earworms.

Finally, microbial control may become an important method for use against the corn eaıworm and other lepidopteran pests of cotton, Some growers use homeade sprays of cabbage looper nuclear polyheadrosis virus, prepared from infected larvae which they collect. *Heliothis* nuclear polyhedrosis virus is now registered for use on cotton. *Bacillus thuringiensis is* also registered for commercial use but is expensive and not sufficiently virulent against corn earworm to merit widespread application.

Integrated control results in substantial saving, both financial and in terms of pollution, through the greatly decreased use of insecticides. For example, the traditional control programme for cotton pests cost about twice as much per acre as the integrated programme, and even greater savings may be incurred as the integrated programme is improved. Indeed, a 50-80% reduction in the use of insecticides, after the initiation of an integrated control programme, has been observed in many other instances. Despite these remarkable savings, a great majority of crop growers and government officials remain convinced that the present method of pest control, the unilateral use of insecticides, is best. Persuading these individuals that to continue with this approach will lead not only to financial ruin but to long-term, perhaps irreversible, deterioration of environmental quality is perhaps the greatest challenge that scientists have ever faced.

Index

B

C

I

K

L

M

N

Q

R

S

T

U

V

W

X

Y